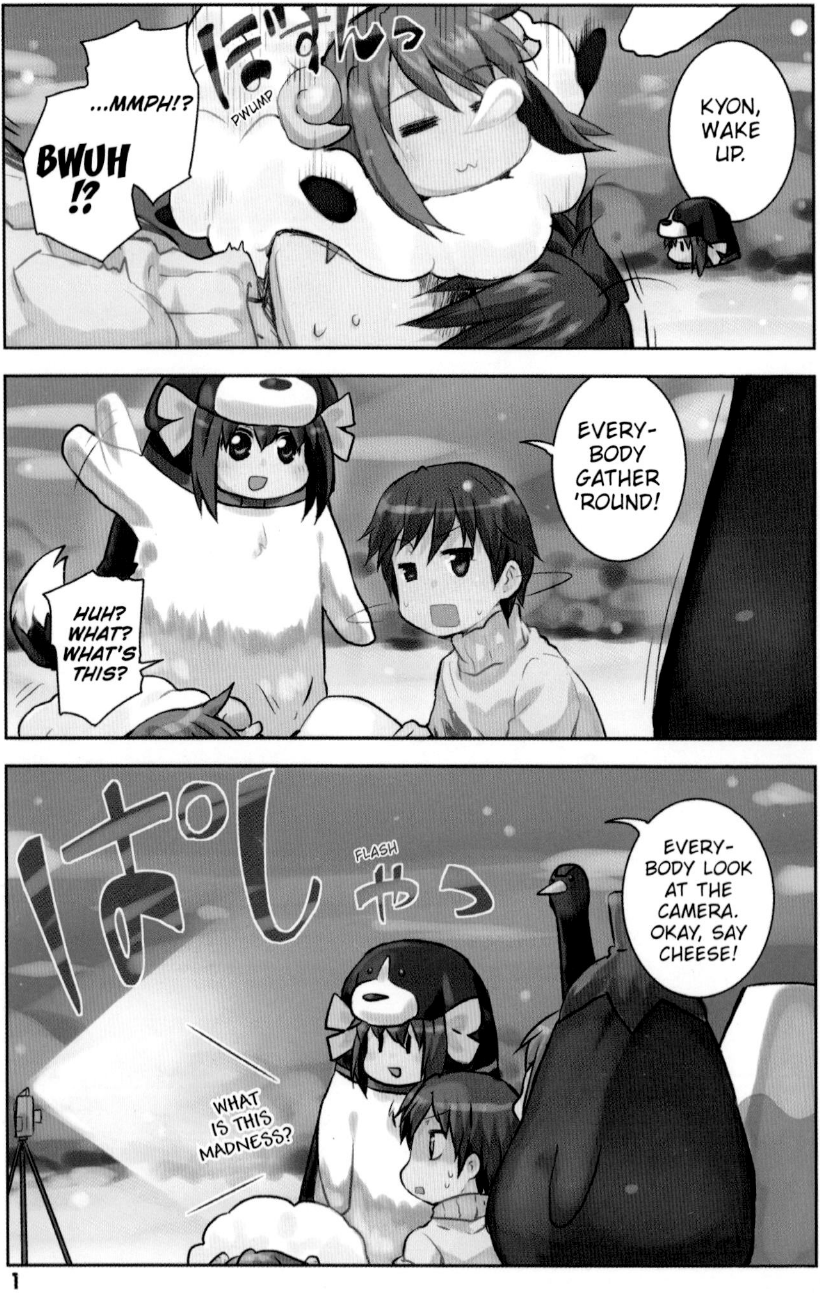
KYON, WAKE UP.
ぼすんっ
PWUMP
...MMPH!?
BWUH!?
EVERY-BODY GATHER 'ROUND!
HUH? WHAT? WHAT'S THIS?
EVERY-BODY LOOK AT THE CAMERA. OKAY, SAY CHEESE!
ぱしゃっ
FLASH
WHAT IS THIS MADNESS?

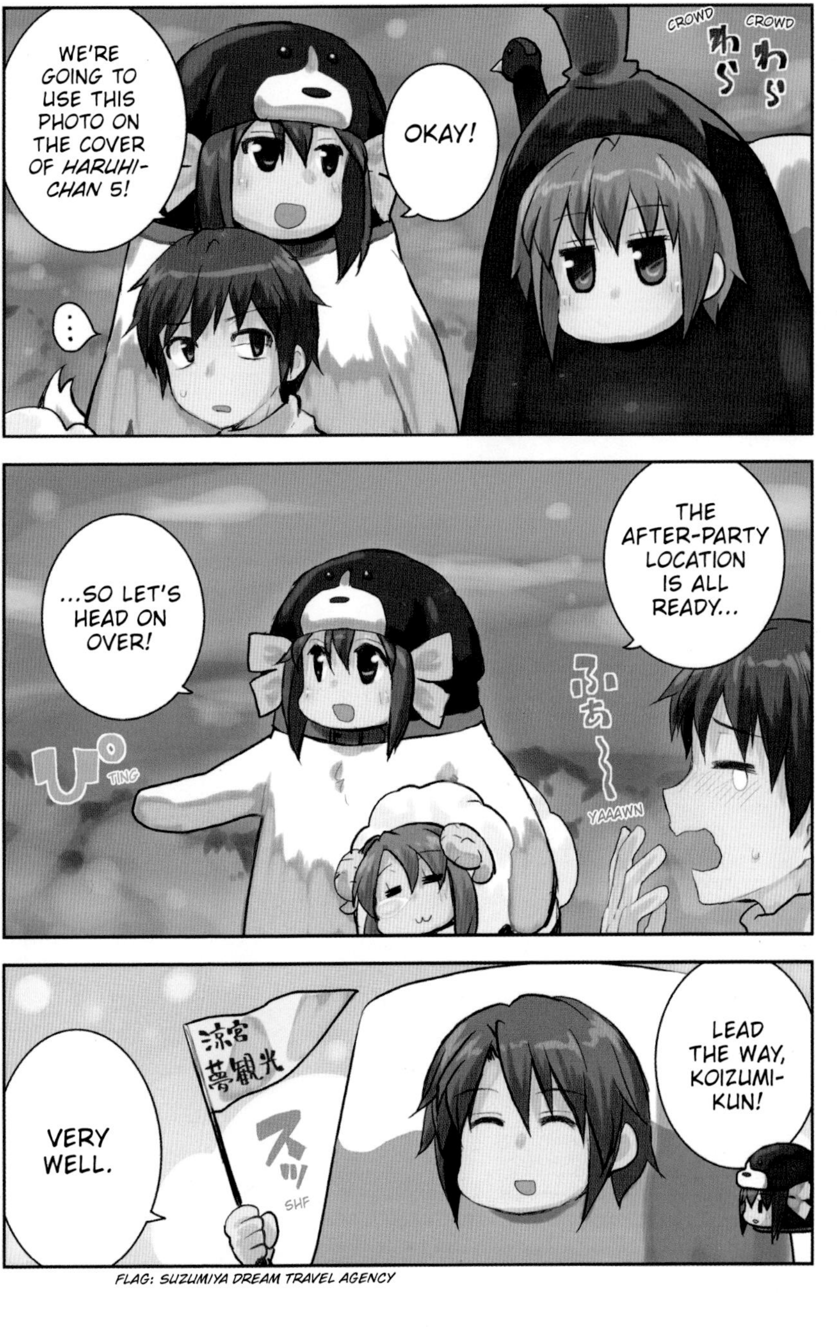

わら CROWD
わら CROWD
WE'RE GOING TO USE THIS PHOTO ON THE COVER OF *HARUHI-CHAN 5*!
OKAY!
...
THE AFTER-PARTY LOCATION IS ALL READY...
ふぁ〜〜 YAAAWN
...SO LET'S HEAD ON OVER!
ぴ TING
LEAD THE WAY, KOIZUMI-KUN!
VERY WELL.
涼宮夢観光
スッ SHF

FLAG: SUZUMIYA DREAM TRAVEL AGENCY

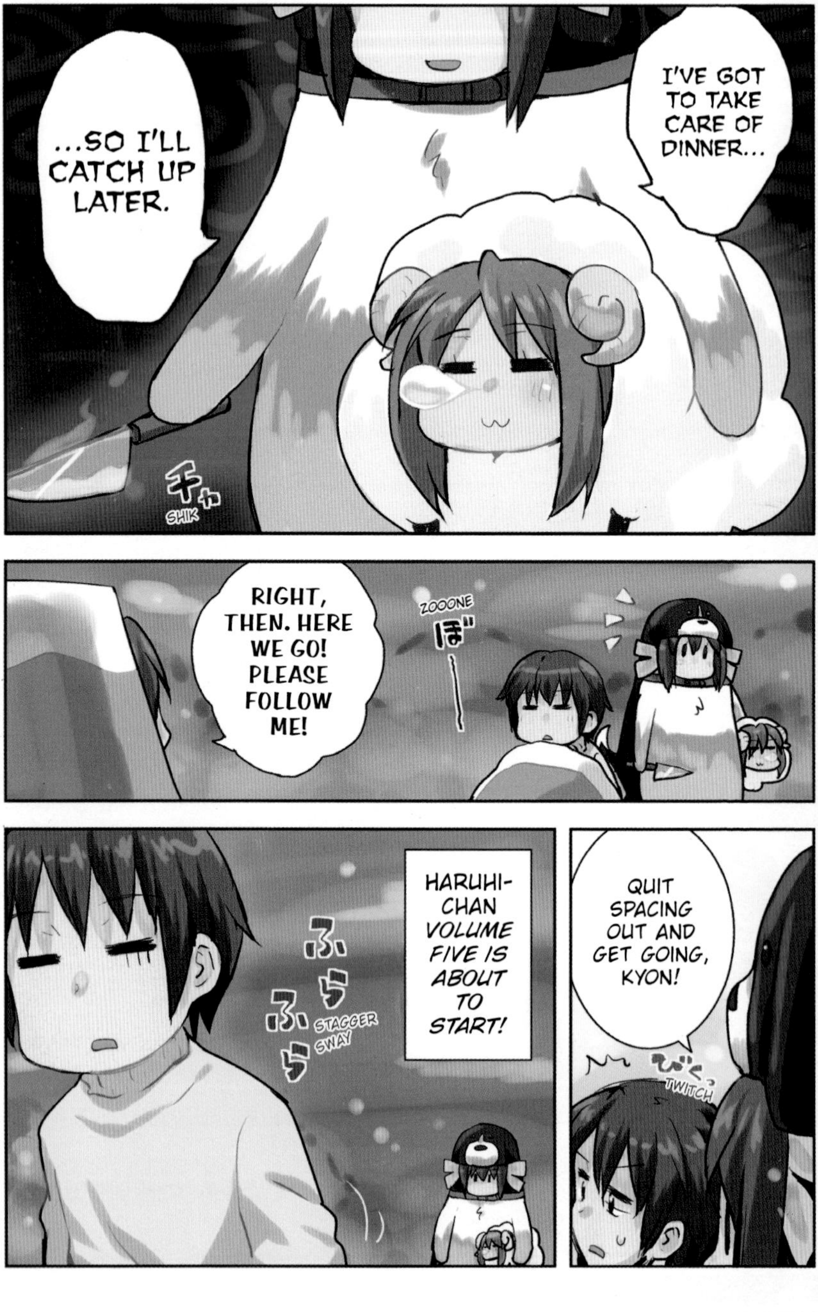
I'VE GOT TO TAKE CARE OF DINNER...
...SO I'LL CATCH UP LATER.
チャ
SHIK
ぼ~~
ZOOONE
RIGHT, THEN. HERE WE GO! PLEASE FOLLOW ME!
QUIT SPACING OUT AND GET GOING, KYON!
びくっ
TWITCH
HARUHI-CHAN VOLUME FIVE IS ABOUT TO START!
ふらふら
STAGGER SWAY

1
A CHAOTIC NEW YEAR'S DREAM

17
RYOUKO ASAKURA'S APPRENTICESHIP

27
IDENTITY LOSS

45
IT'S ALWAYS MY TURN

63
THE ACTIVITIES OF MIKURU ASAHINA

81
STARTING OVER WITH TINY-SIZED CHARACTERS

99
KOIZUMI, WITH ARAKAWA-SAN...

117
KYON NURSING BATTLE

127
BACK TO THAT WONDERFUL YOUTH

144
SWITCHING THE CHARACTERS' PERSONALITIES
AROUND

148
INFINITY LION RESCUE MISSION

152
BIG-TIME CLEANUP, THANKFULLY

156
GAG COMIC COMPETITION

160
PREVIEW OF THE NEXT VOLUME

The Melancholy of Suzumiya
Haruhi-chan
05

INDEX

THE MELANCHOLY of SUZUMIYA
HARUHI-CHAN
The Untold Adventures of the SOS Brigade

05

WHETHER IT BE FICTION OR NOT, SO LONG AS YOU BELIEVE IN ME, I WILL BE HERE.

SMILE

STORY: **NAGARU TANIGAWA** ART: **PUYO** CHARACTERS: NOIZI ITO

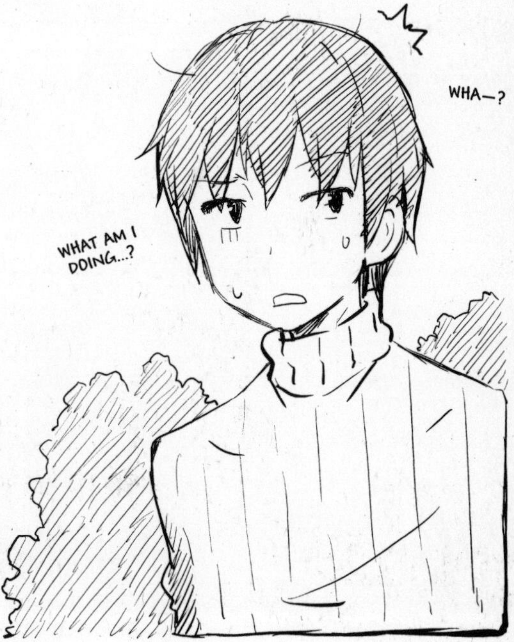
WHA—?
WHAT AM I DOING...?

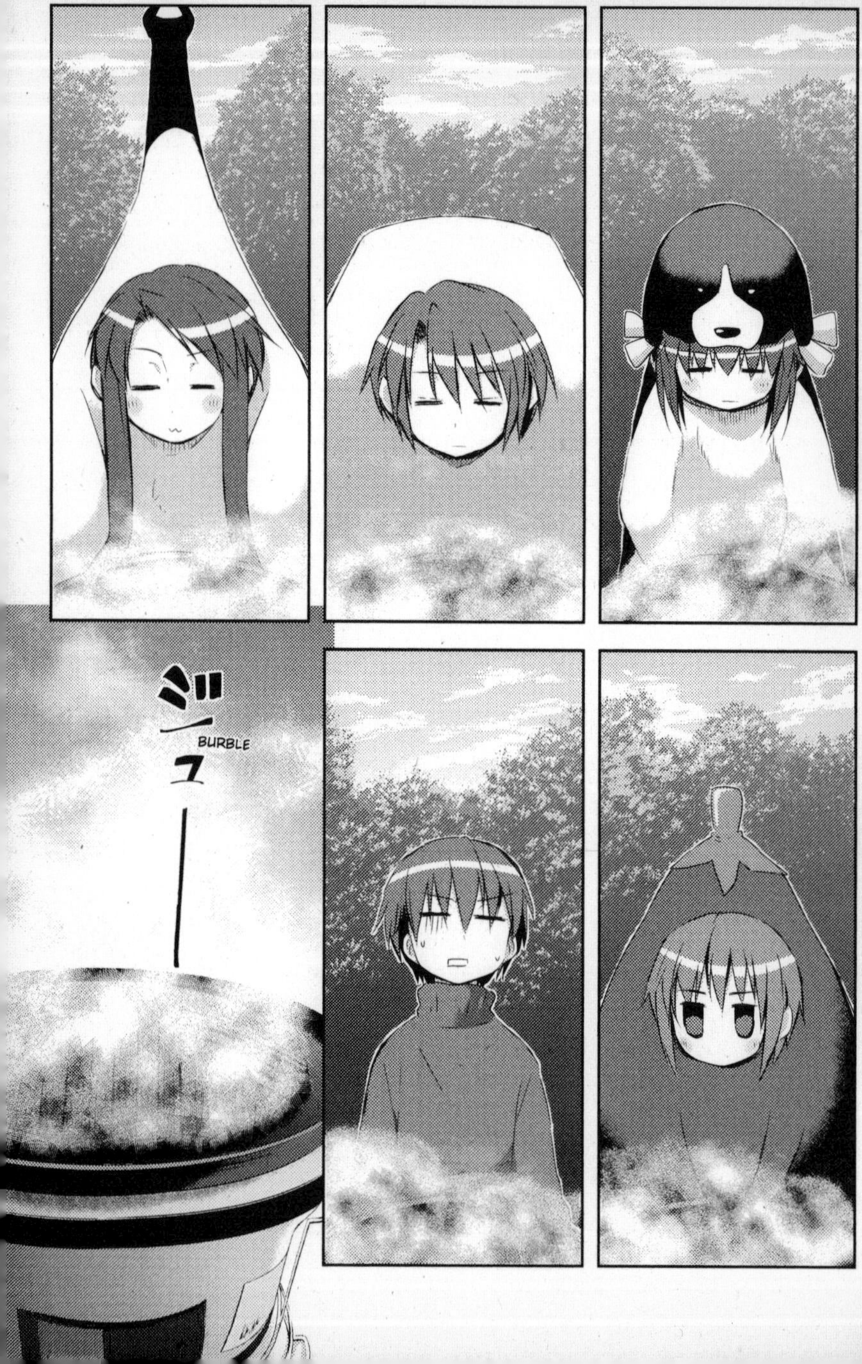
ジュー
BURBLE

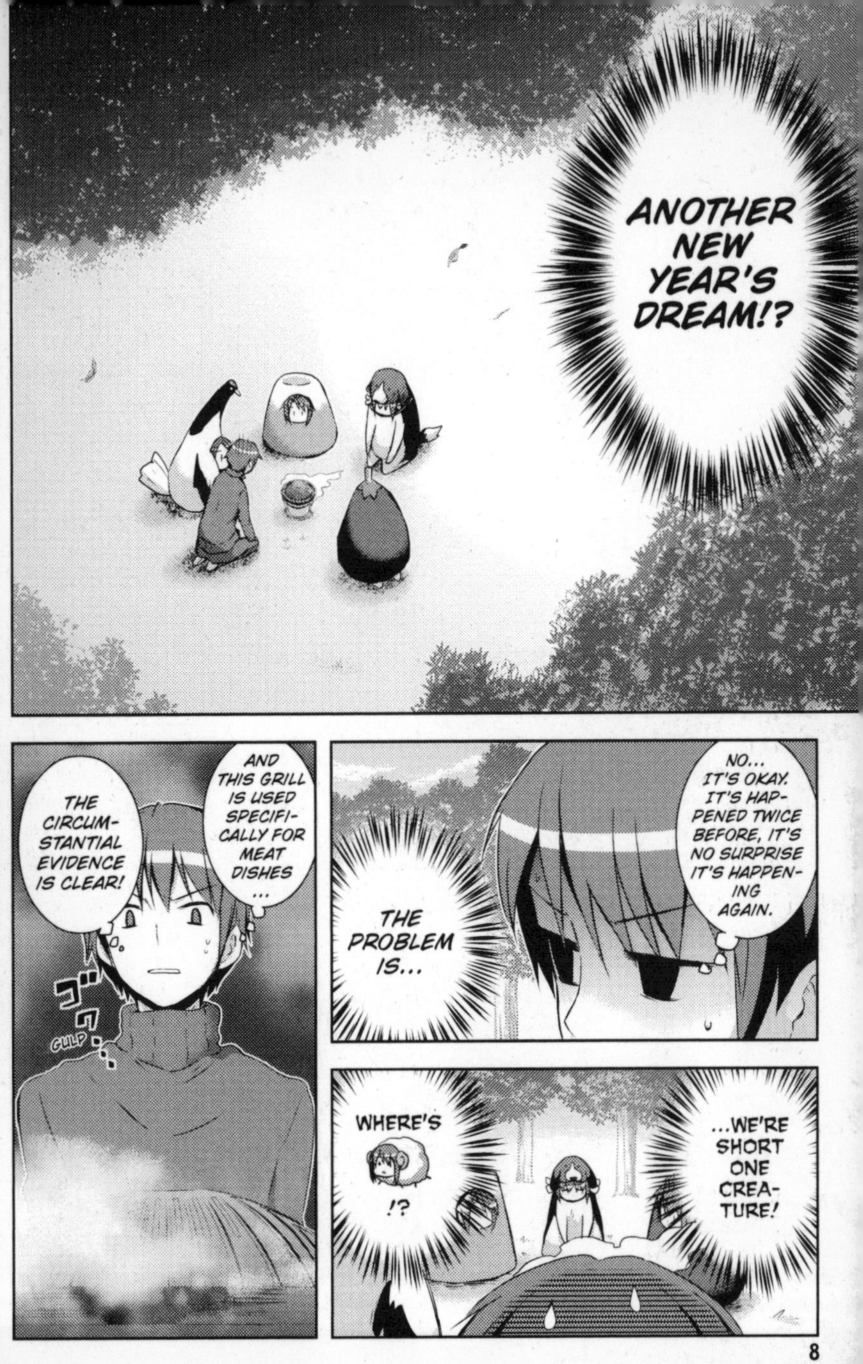
ANOTHER NEW YEAR'S DREAM!?
NO... IT'S OKAY. IT'S HAPPENED TWICE BEFORE, IT'S NO SURPRISE IT'S HAPPENING AGAIN.
THE PROBLEM IS...
...WE'RE SHORT ONE CREATURE!
WHERE'S !?
AND THIS GRILL IS USED SPECIFICALLY FOR MEAT DISHES ...
THE CIRCUMSTANTIAL EVIDENCE IS CLEAR!
GULP

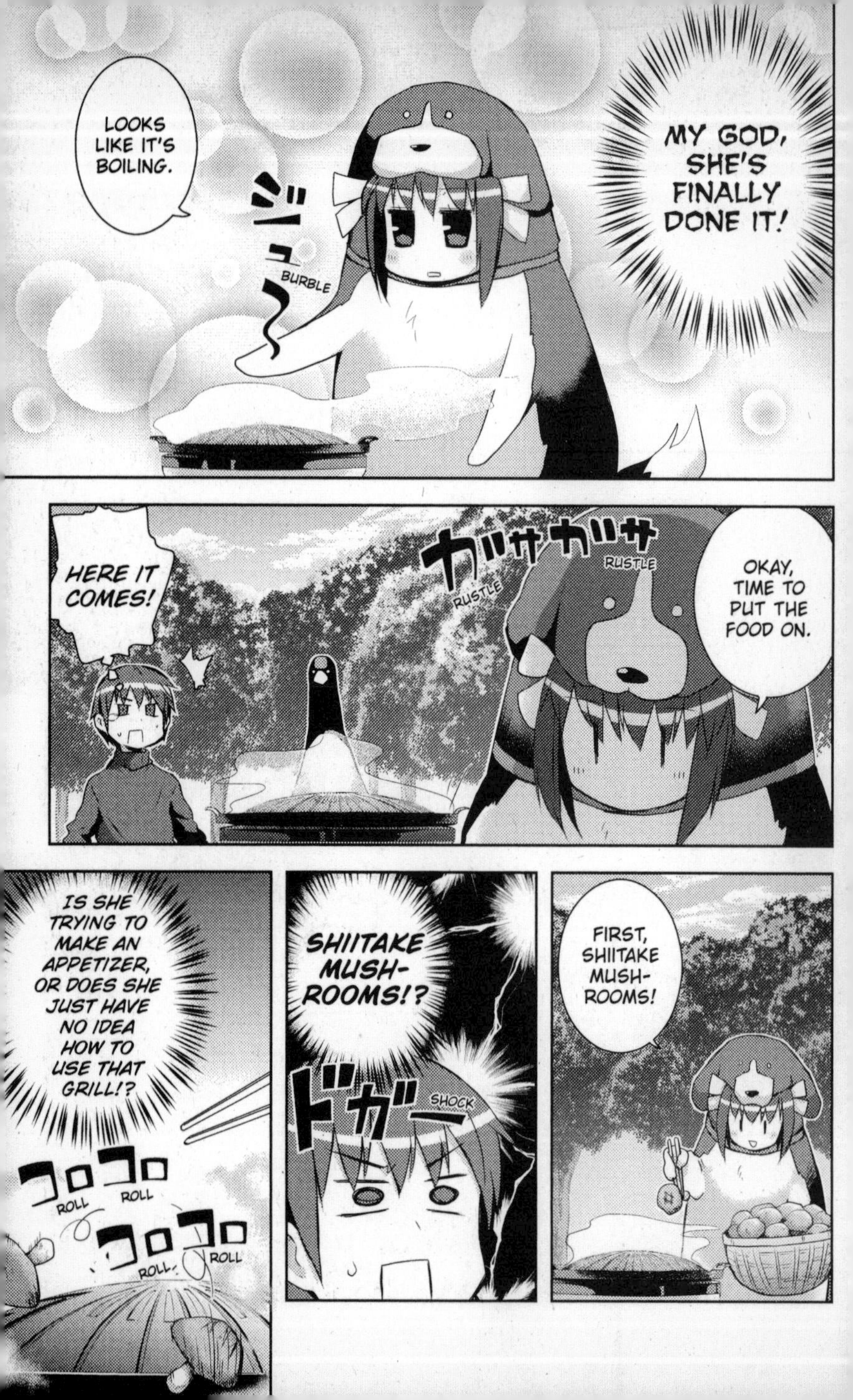
LOOKS LIKE IT'S BOILING.
ジュ
BURBLE
MY GOD, SHE'S FINALLY DONE IT!
OKAY, TIME TO PUT THE FOOD ON.
ガサガサ
RUSTLE
RUSTLE
HERE IT COMES!
FIRST, SHIITAKE MUSH-ROOMS!
SHIITAKE MUSH-ROOMS!?
ドガー
SHOCK
IS SHE TRYING TO MAKE AN APPETIZER, OR DOES SHE JUST HAVE NO IDEA HOW TO USE THAT GRILL!?
コロコロ
ROLL
ROLL
コロコロ
ROLL
ROLL

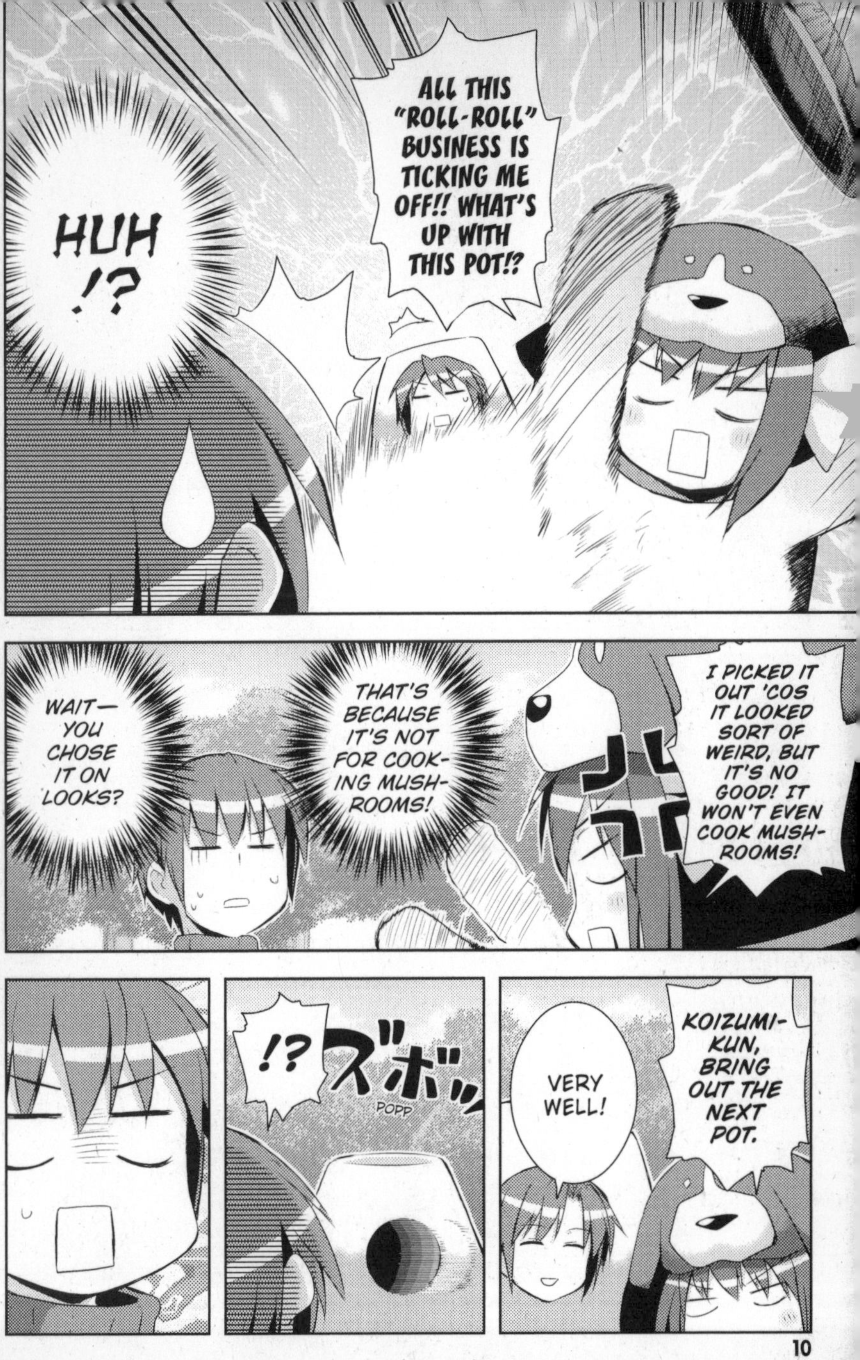
ALL THIS "ROLL-ROLL" BUSINESS IS TICKING ME OFF!! WHAT'S UP WITH THIS POT!?
HUH!?
I PICKED IT OUT 'COS IT LOOKED SORT OF WEIRD, BUT IT'S NO GOOD! IT WON'T EVEN COOK MUSH-ROOMS!
THAT'S BECAUSE IT'S NOT FOR COOK-ING MUSH-ROOMS!
WAIT— YOU CHOSE IT ON LOOKS?
KOIZUMI-KUN, BRING OUT THE NEXT POT.
VERY WELL!
ズボッ
POPP
!?

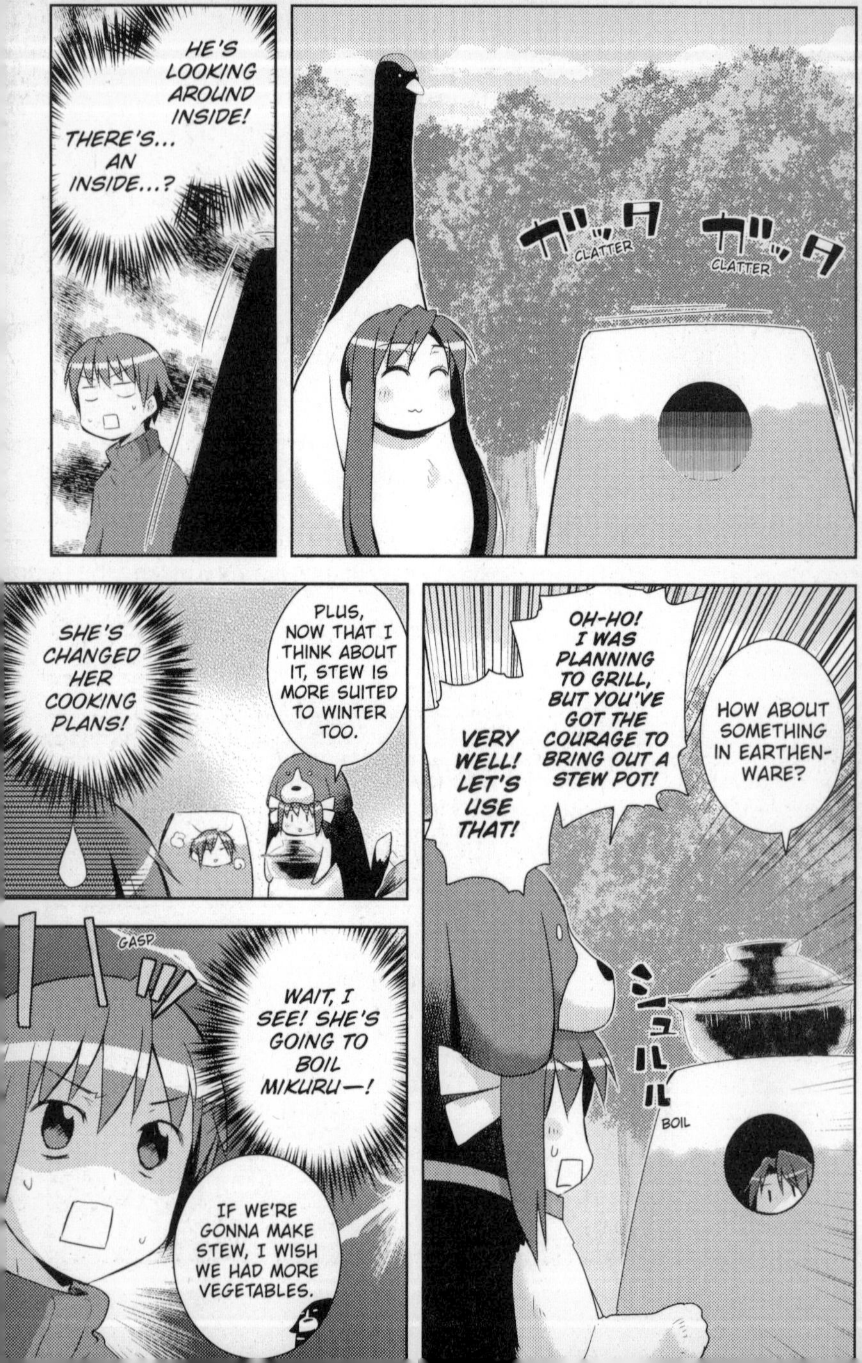
ガッタ
CLATTER
ガッタ
CLATTER
HE'S LOOKING AROUND INSIDE!
THERE'S... AN INSIDE...?
HOW ABOUT SOMETHING IN EARTHEN-WARE?
OH-HO! I WAS PLANNING TO GRILL, BUT YOU'VE GOT THE COURAGE TO BRING OUT A STEW POT!
VERY WELL! LET'S USE THAT!
シュルル
BOIL
PLUS, NOW THAT I THINK ABOUT IT, STEW IS MORE SUITED TO WINTER TOO.
SHE'S CHANGED HER COOKING PLANS!
GASP
WAIT, I SEE! SHE'S GOING TO BOIL MIKURU—!
IF WE'RE GONNA MAKE STEW, I WISH WE HAD MORE VEGETABLES.

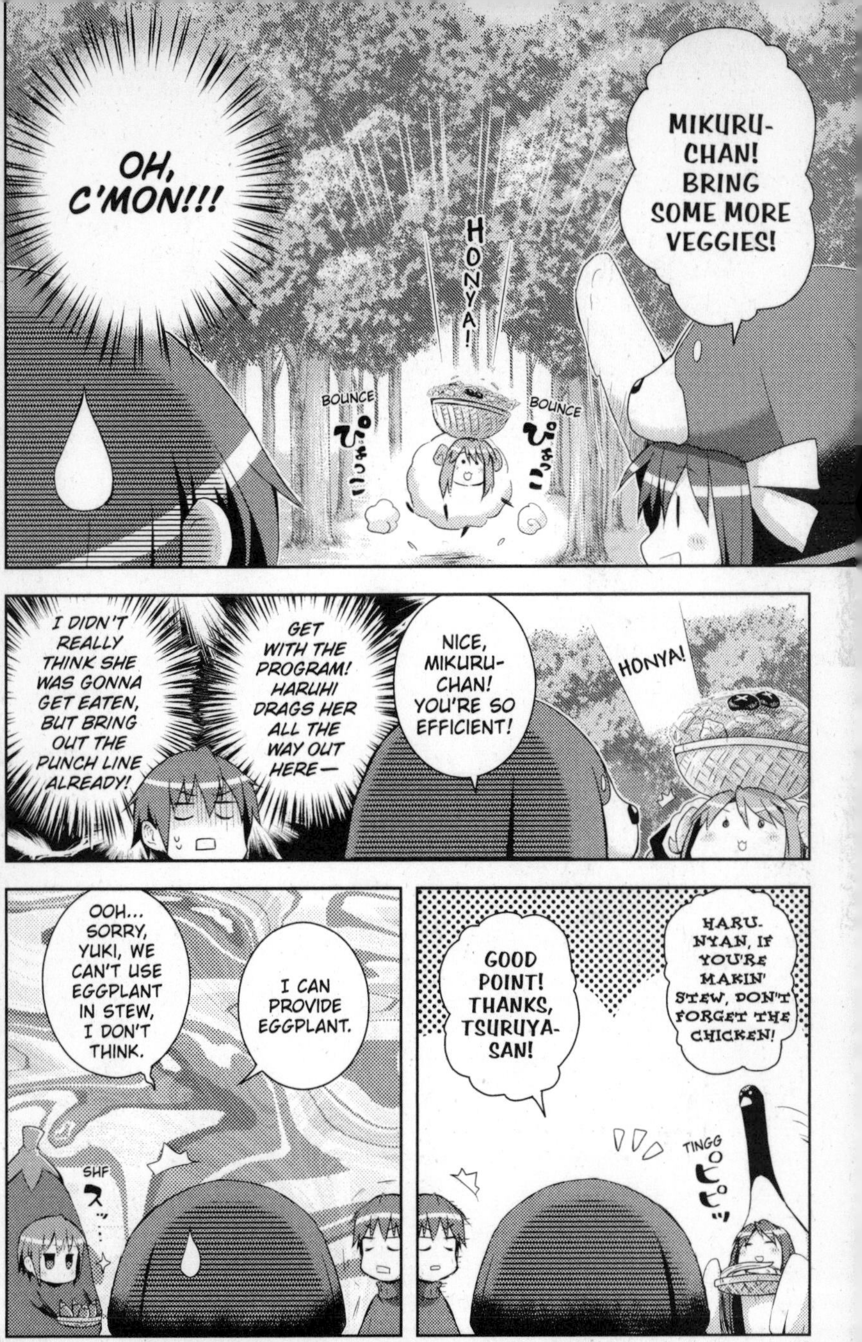
MIKURU-CHAN! BRING SOME MORE VEGGIES!
HONYA!
BOUNCE
BOUNCE
OH, C'MON!!!
HONYA!
NICE, MIKURU-CHAN! YOU'RE SO EFFICIENT!
GET WITH THE PROGRAM! HARUHI DRAGS HER ALL THE WAY OUT HERE—
I DIDN'T REALLY THINK SHE WAS GONNA GET EATEN, BUT BRING OUT THE PUNCH LINE ALREADY!
HARU-NYAN, IF YOU'RE MAKIN' STEW, DON'T FORGET THE CHICKEN!
GOOD POINT! THANKS, TSURUYA-SAN!
TINGG
I CAN PROVIDE EGGPLANT.
OOH... SORRY, YUKI, WE CAN'T USE EGGPLANT IN STEW, I DON'T THINK.
SHF

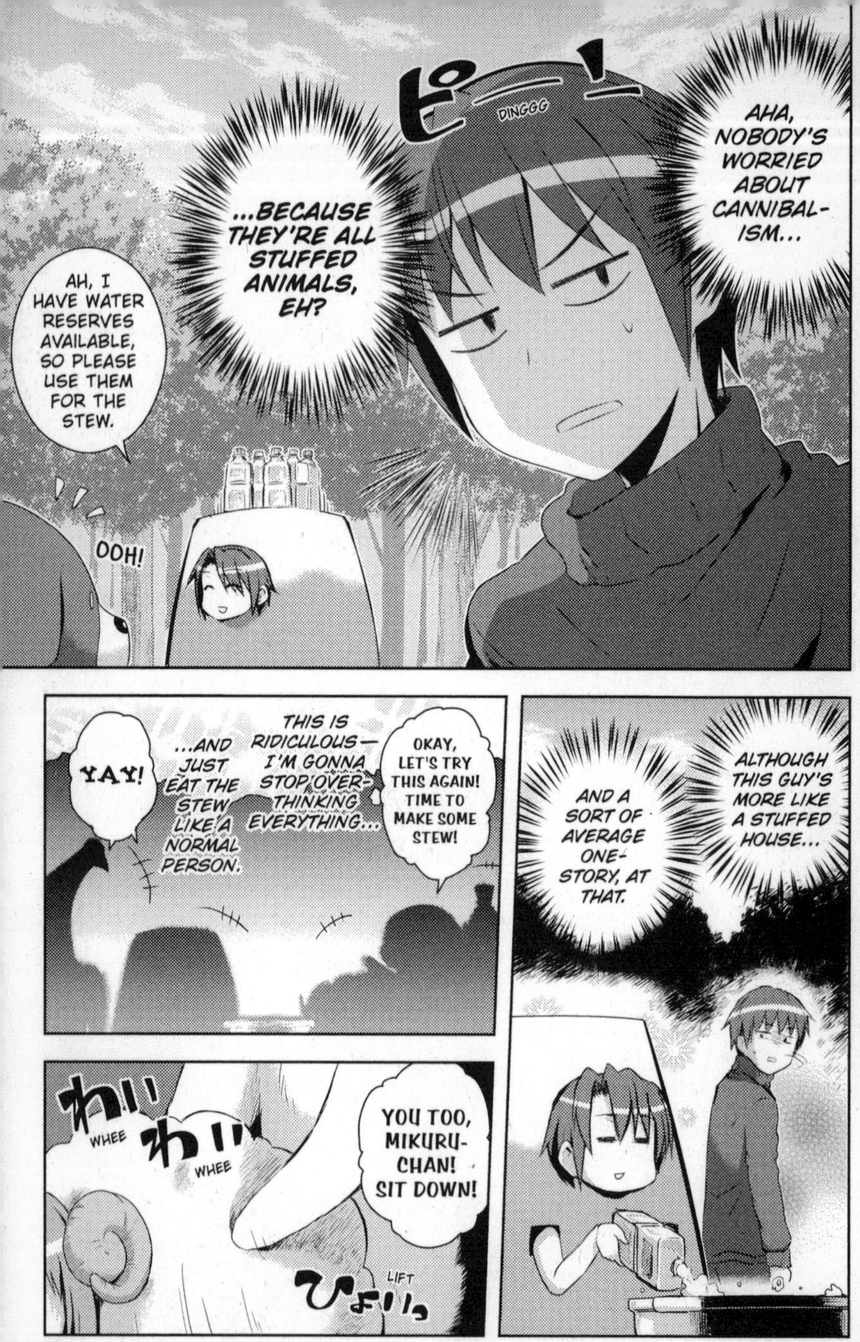
DINGGG
AHA, NOBODY'S WORRIED ABOUT CANNIBALISM...
...BECAUSE THEY'RE ALL STUFFED ANIMALS, EH?
AH, I HAVE WATER RESERVES AVAILABLE, SO PLEASE USE THEM FOR THE STEW.
OOH!
ALTHOUGH THIS GUY'S MORE LIKE A STUFFED HOUSE...
AND A SORT OF AVERAGE ONE-STORY, AT THAT.
OKAY, LET'S TRY THIS AGAIN! TIME TO MAKE SOME STEW!
THIS IS RIDICULOUS— I'M GONNA STOP OVERTHINKING EVERYTHING...
...AND JUST EAT THE STEW LIKE A NORMAL PERSON.
YAY!
YOU TOO, MIKURU-CHAN! SIT DOWN!
WHEE
WHEE
LIFT

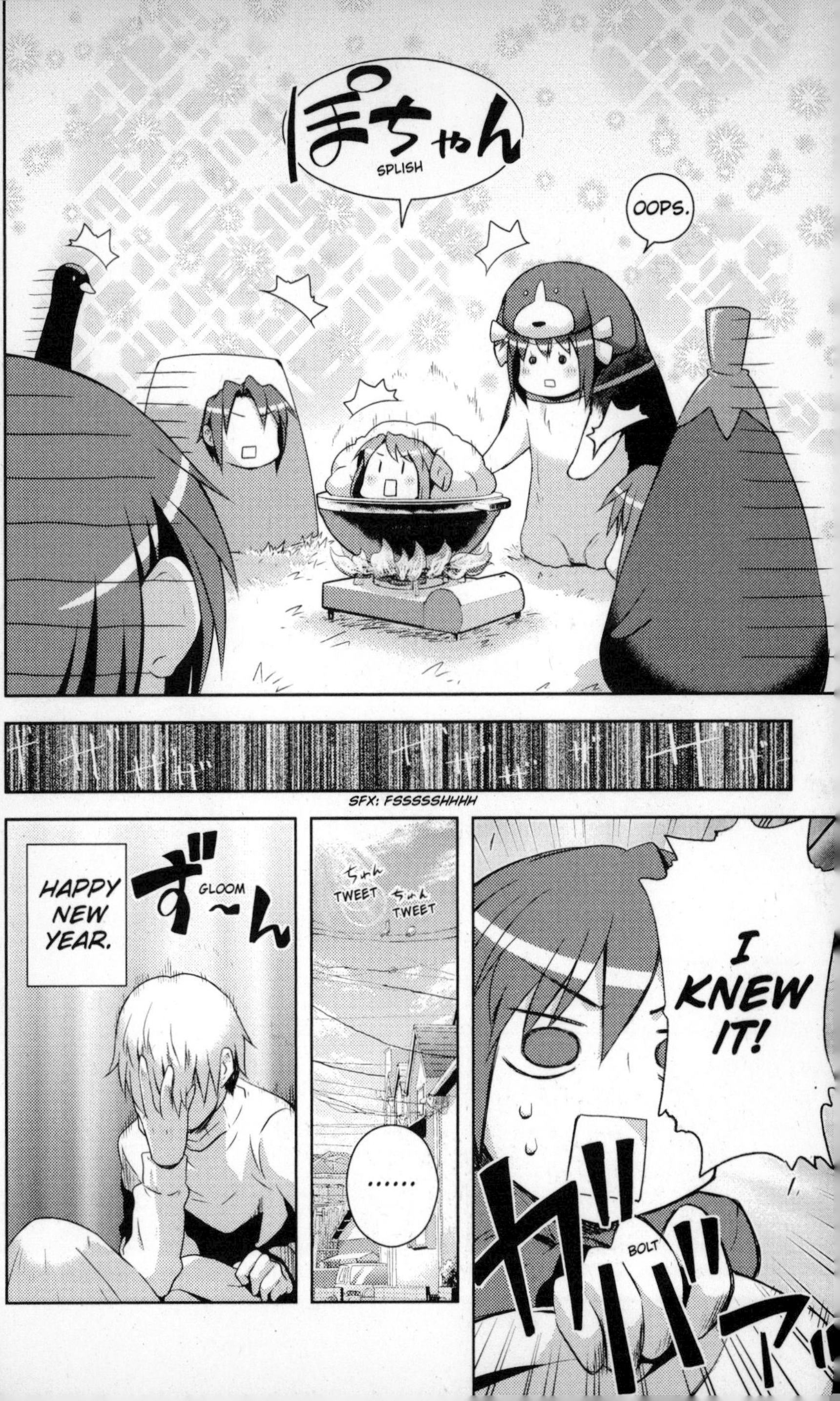
ぽちゃん
SPLISH
OOPS.
SFX: FSSSSSHHHH
I KNEW IT!
ガバッ
BOLT
ちゅん
TWEET
ちゅん
TWEET
......
HAPPY NEW YEAR.
ず〜ん
GLOOM

MAYBE SHE LIKES IT IN THERE...
PERHAPS IT'S RELAXING?

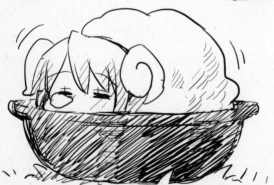

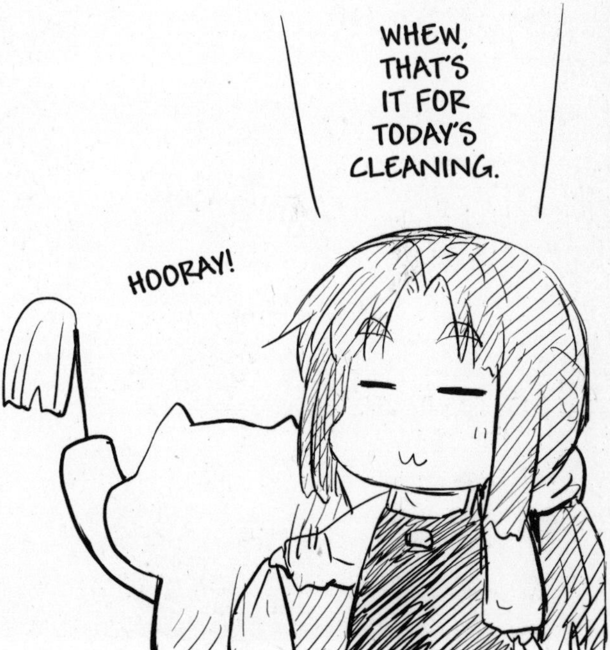
WHEW, THAT'S IT FOR TODAY'S CLEANING.
HOORAY!

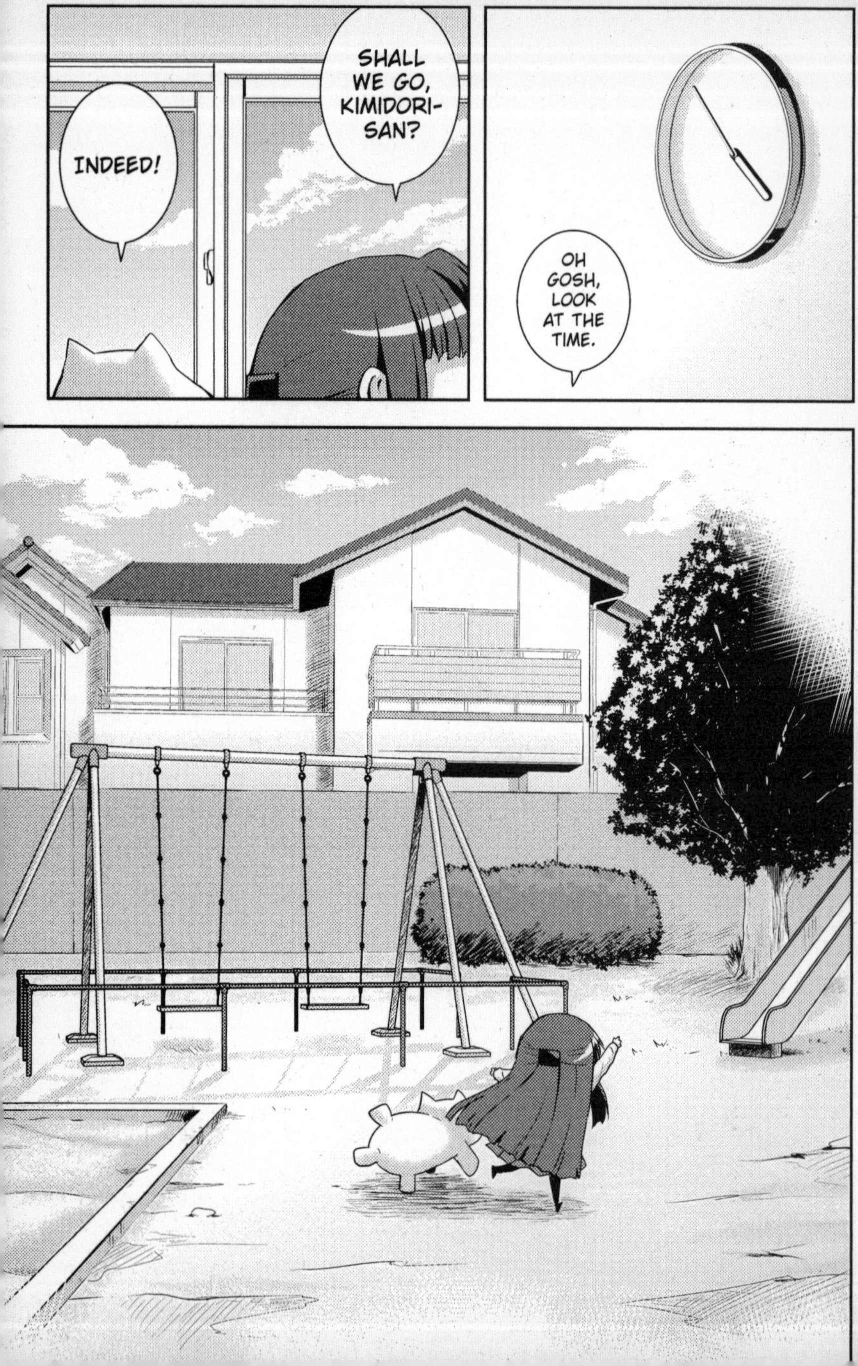
OH GOSH, LOOK AT THE TIME.
SHALL WE GO, KIMIDORI-SAN?
INDEED!

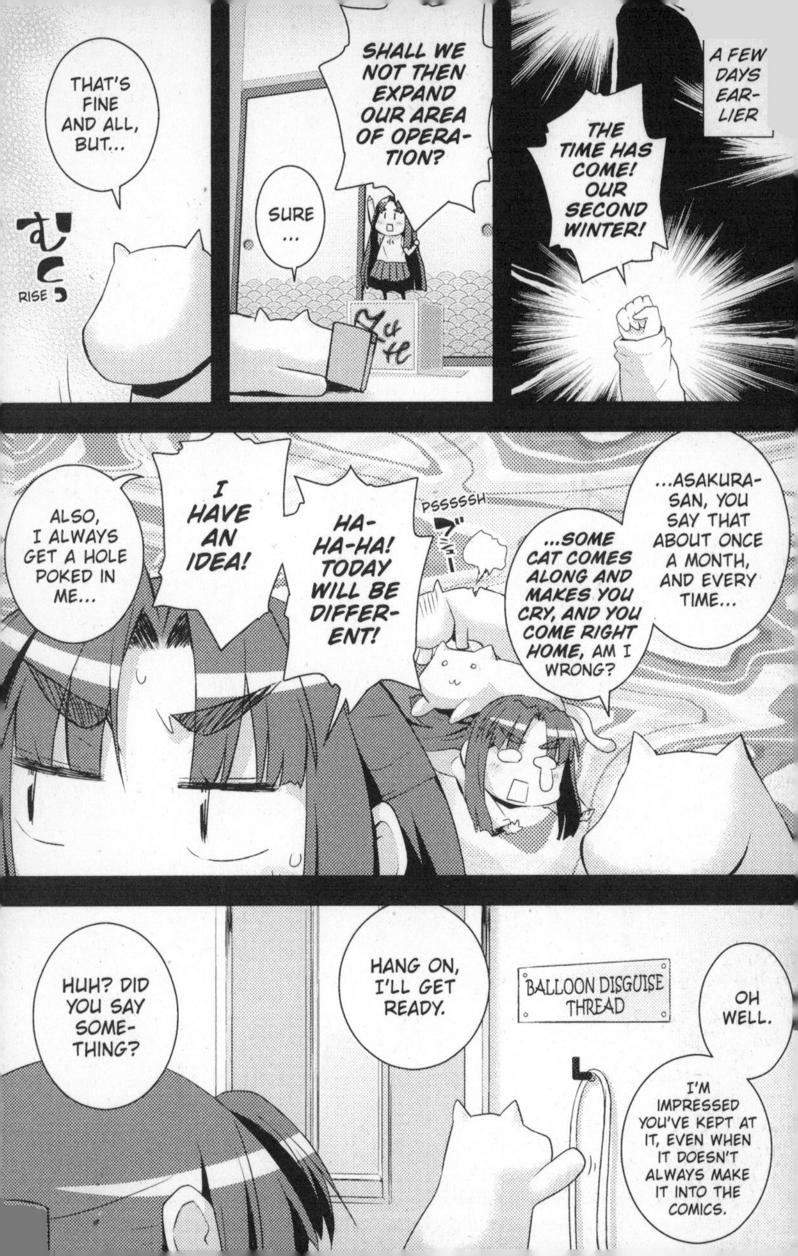
A FEW DAYS EARLIER
THE TIME HAS COME! OUR SECOND WINTER!
SHALL WE NOT THEN EXPAND OUR AREA OF OPERATION?
SURE...
THAT'S FINE AND ALL, BUT...
RISE
...ASAKURA-SAN, YOU SAY THAT ABOUT ONCE A MONTH, AND EVERY TIME...
...SOME CAT COMES ALONG AND MAKES YOU CRY, AND YOU COME RIGHT HOME, AM I WRONG?
PSSSSSH
HA-HA-HA! TODAY WILL BE DIFFERENT!
I HAVE AN IDEA!
ALSO, I ALWAYS GET A HOLE POKED IN ME...
OH WELL.
I'M IMPRESSED YOU'VE KEPT AT IT, EVEN WHEN IT DOESN'T ALWAYS MAKE IT INTO THE COMICS.
BALLOON DISGUISE THREAD
HANG ON, I'LL GET READY.
HUH? DID YOU SAY SOMETHING?

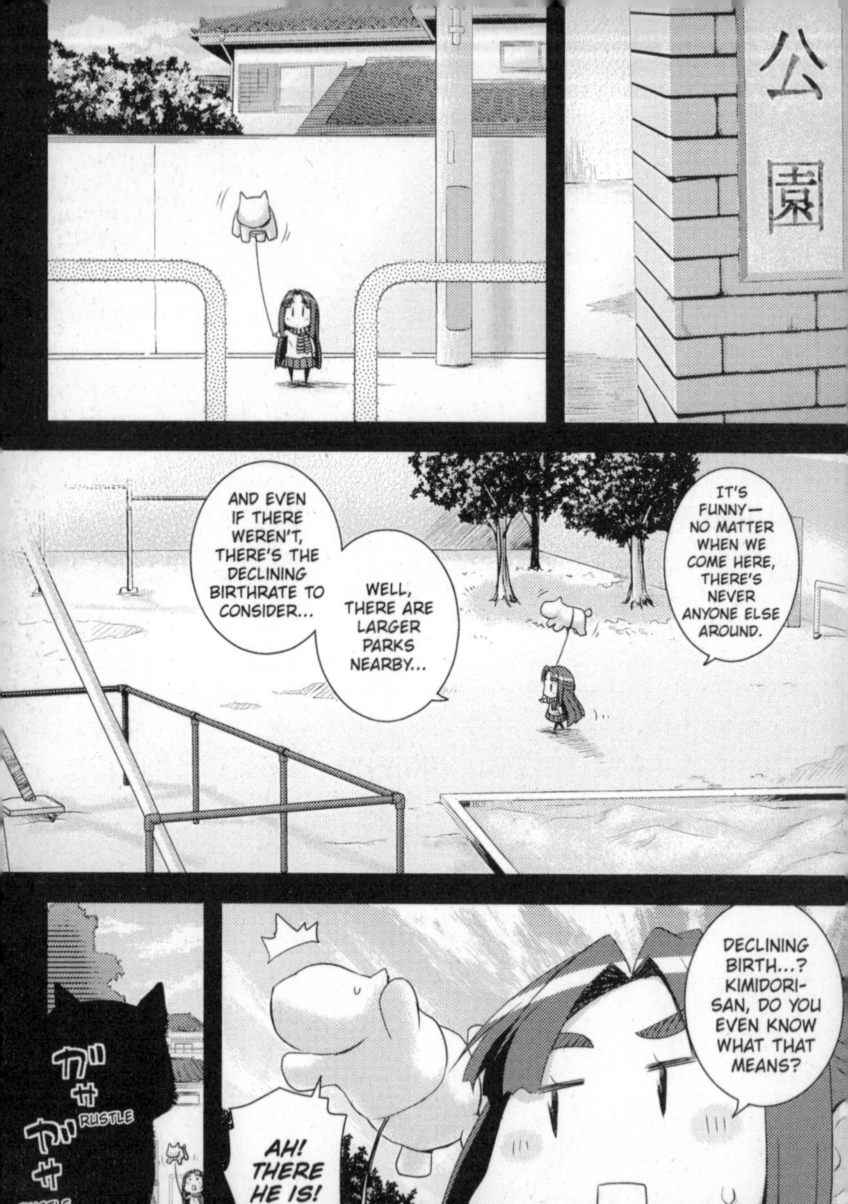

公園
IT'S FUNNY—NO MATTER WHEN WE COME HERE, THERE'S NEVER ANYONE ELSE AROUND.
WELL, THERE ARE LARGER PARKS NEARBY...
AND EVEN IF THERE WEREN'T, THERE'S THE DECLINING BIRTHRATE TO CONSIDER...
DECLINING BIRTH...? KIMIDORI-SAN, DO YOU EVEN KNOW WHAT THAT MEANS?
AH! THERE HE IS!
ガサ
RUSTLE
ガサ
RUSTLE

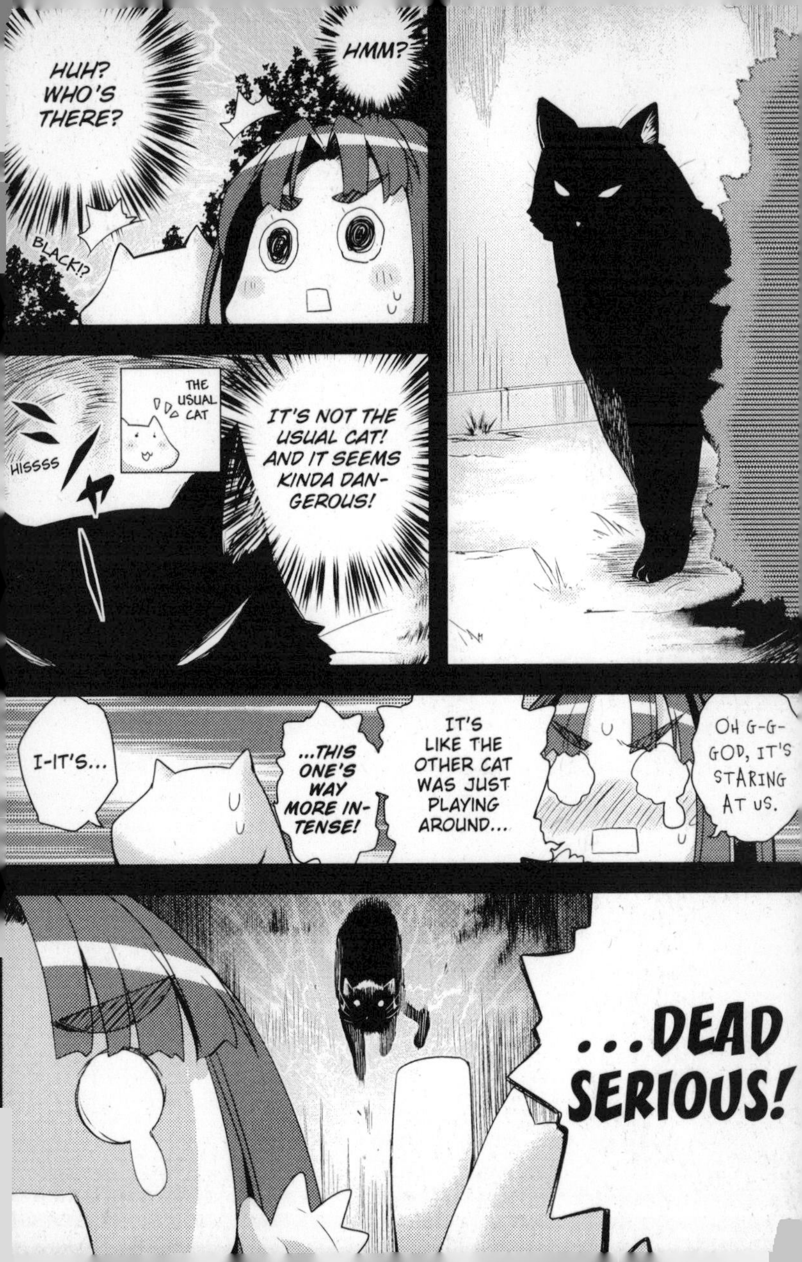
HMM?
HUH? WHO'S THERE?
BLACK!?
IT'S NOT THE USUAL CAT! AND IT SEEMS KINDA DAN-GEROUS!
THE USUAL CAT
HISSSS
OH G-G-GOD, IT'S STARING AT US.
IT'S LIKE THE OTHER CAT WAS JUST PLAYING AROUND...
...THIS ONE'S WAY MORE IN-TENSE!
I-IT'S...
...DEAD SERIOUS!

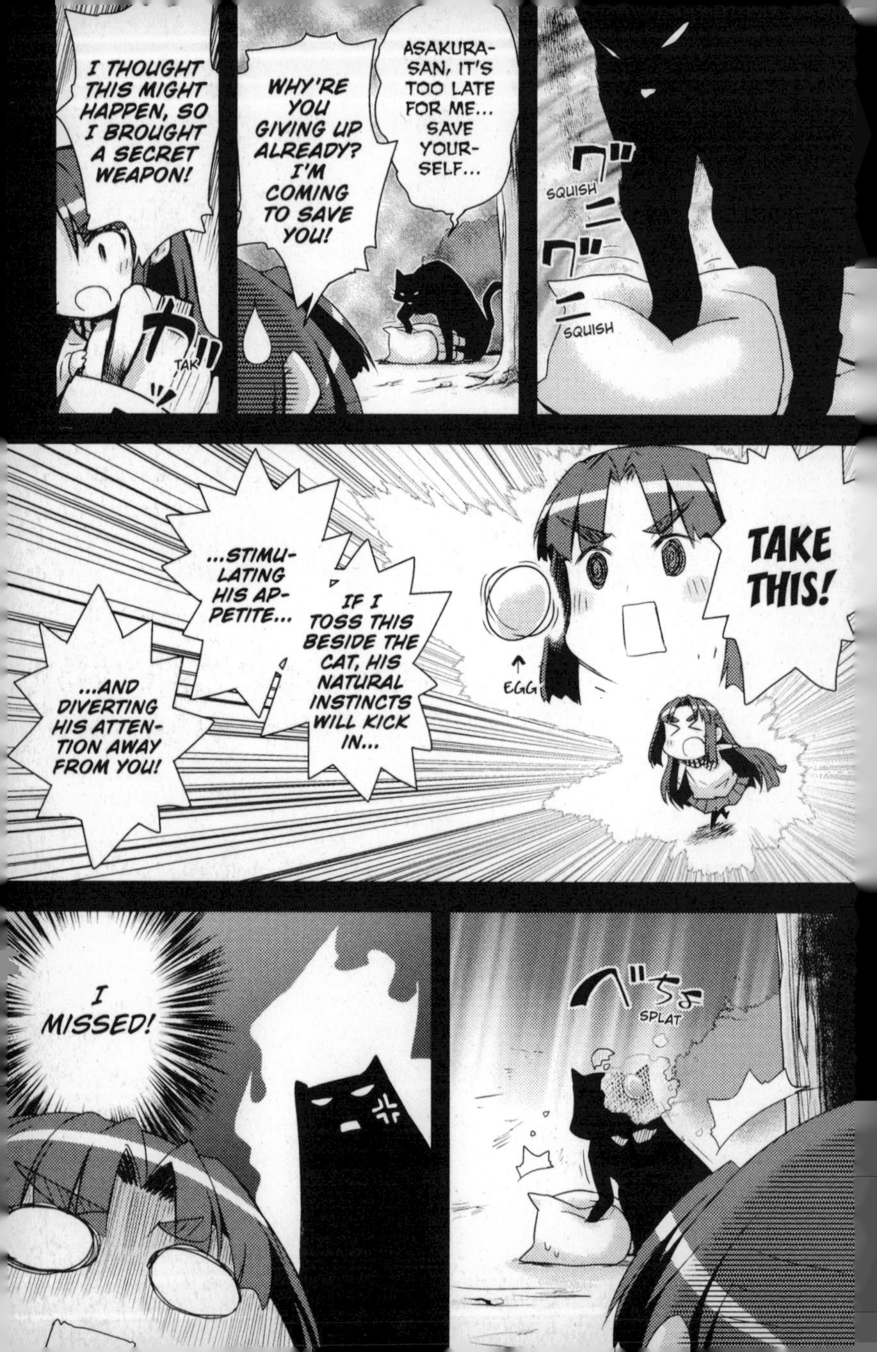
SQUISH
SQUISH
ASAKURA-SAN, IT'S TOO LATE FOR ME... SAVE YOURSELF...
WHY'RE YOU GIVING UP ALREADY? I'M COMING TO SAVE YOU!
I THOUGHT THIS MIGHT HAPPEN, SO I BROUGHT A SECRET WEAPON!
TAK
TAKE THIS!
EGG
IF I TOSS THIS BESIDE THE CAT, HIS NATURAL INSTINCTS WILL KICK IN...
...STIMULATING HIS APPETITE...
...AND DIVERTING HIS ATTENTION AWAY FROM YOU!
SPLAT
I MISSED!

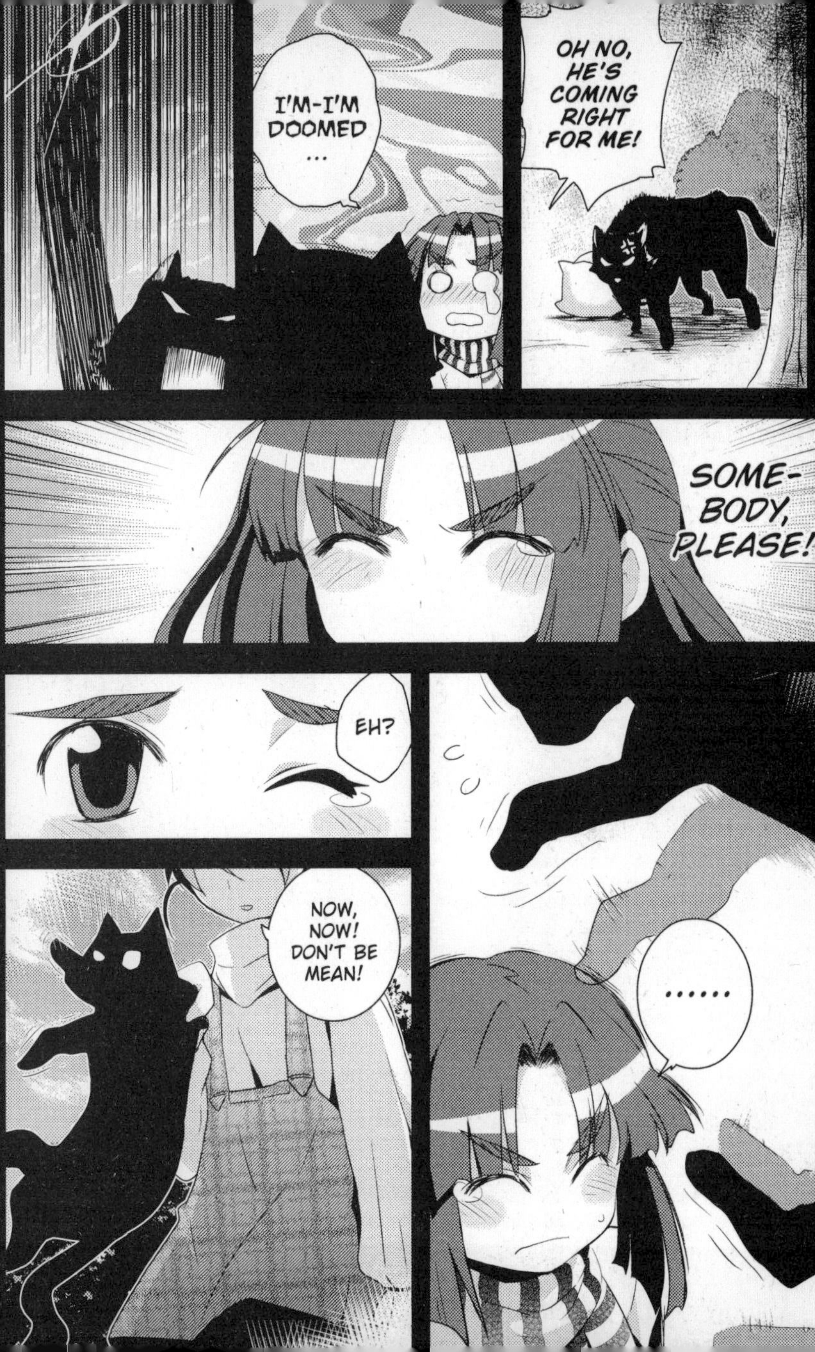
OH NO, HE'S COMING RIGHT FOR ME!
I'M-I'M DOOMED ...
SOME-BODY, PLEASE!
......
EH?
NOW, NOW! DON'T BE MEAN!

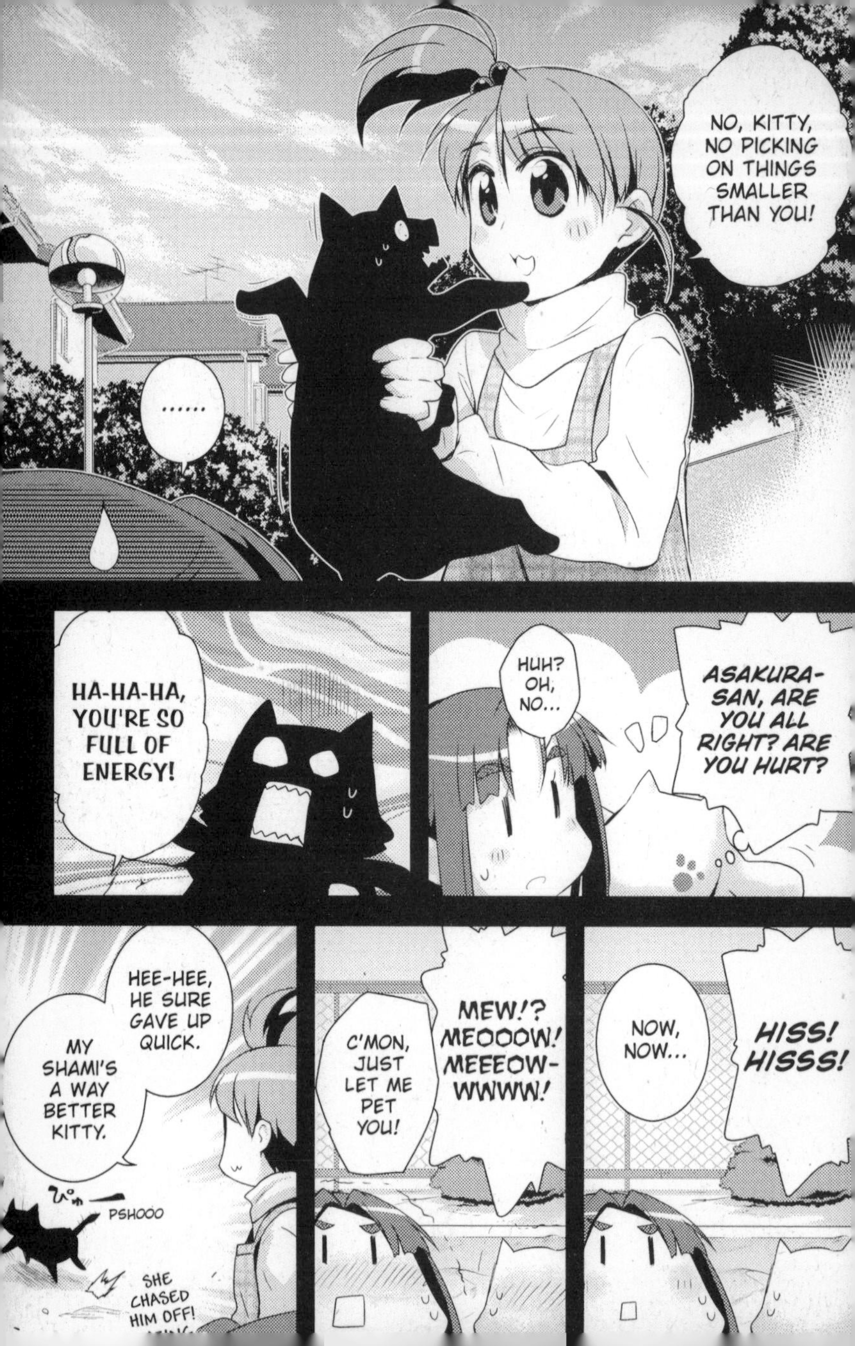
NO, KITTY, NO PICKING ON THINGS SMALLER THAN YOU!
......
ASAKURA-SAN, ARE YOU ALL RIGHT? ARE YOU HURT?
HUH? OH, NO...
HA-HA-HA, YOU'RE SO FULL OF ENERGY!
HISS! HISSS!
NOW, NOW...
MEW!? MEOOOW! MEEEOW-WWWW!
C'MON, JUST LET ME PET YOU!
HEE-HEE, HE SURE GAVE UP QUICK.
MY SHAMI'S A WAY BETTER KITTY.
PSHOOO
SHE CHASED HIM OFF!

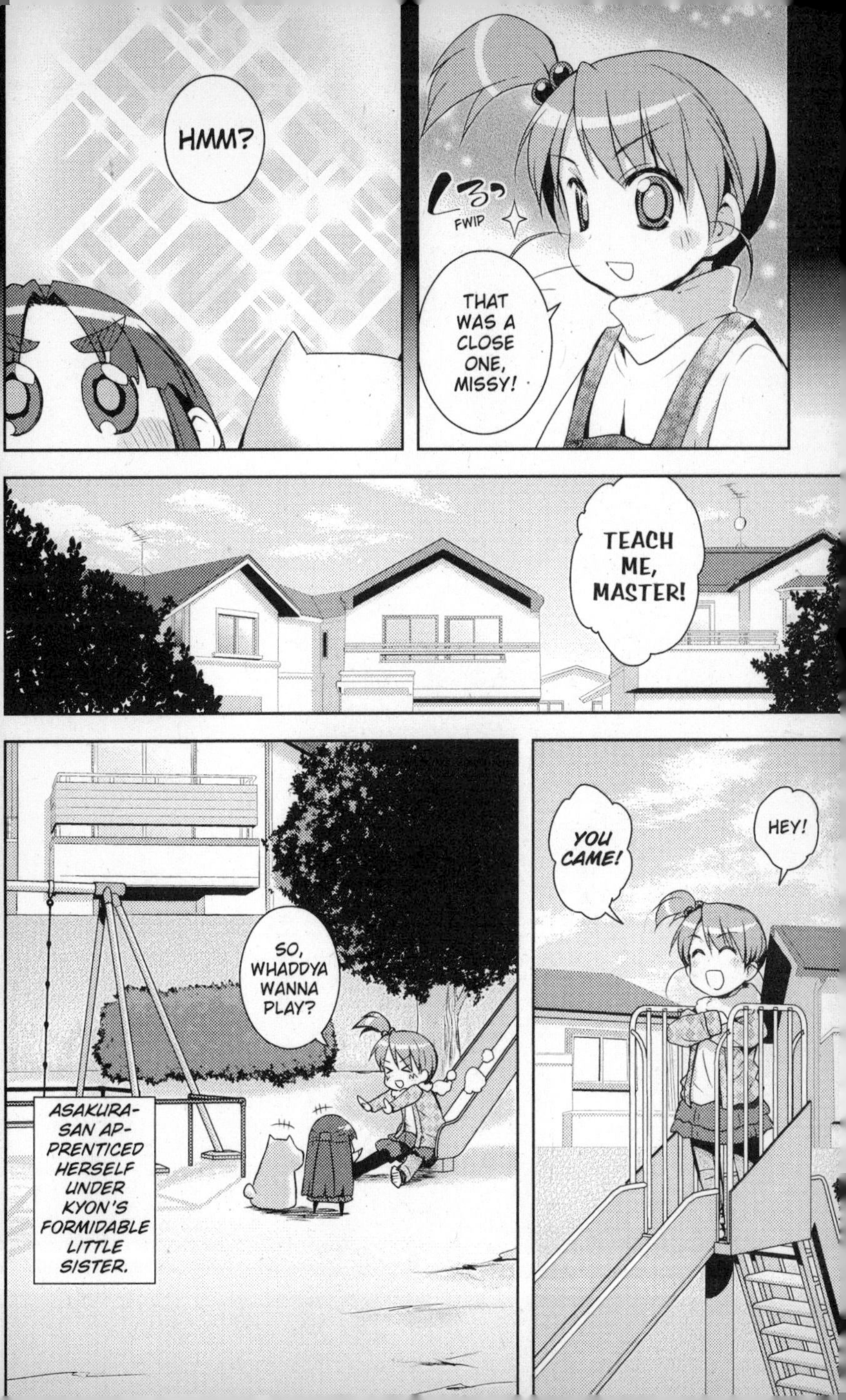
くるっ
FWIP
THAT WAS A CLOSE ONE, MISSY!
HMM?
TEACH ME, MASTER!
HEY!
YOU CAME!
SO, WHADDYA WANNA PLAY?
ASAKURA-SAN AP-PRENTICED HERSELF UNDER KYON'S FORMIDABLE LITTLE SISTER.

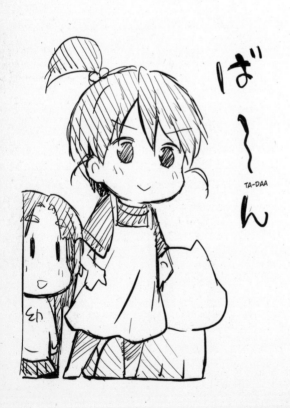

ば〜ん

TA-DAA

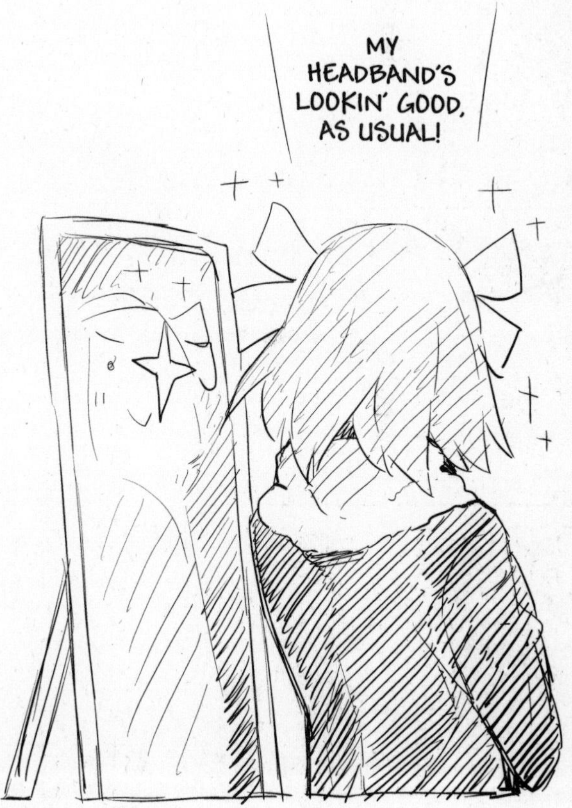
MY HEADBAND'S LOOKIN' GOOD, AS USUAL!

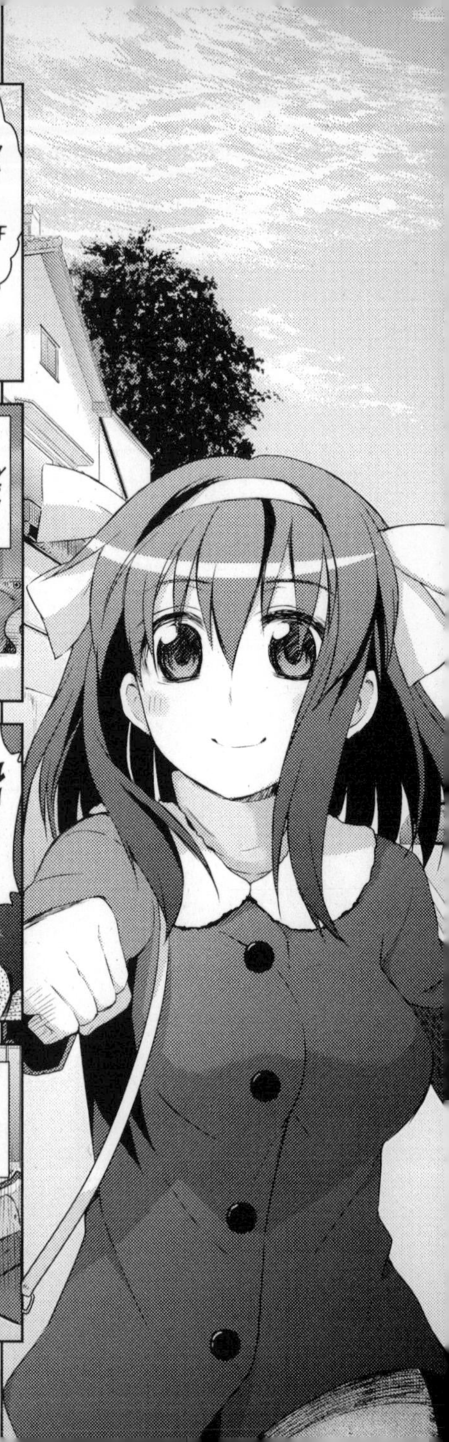

HARUHI-CHAN, JUMP!

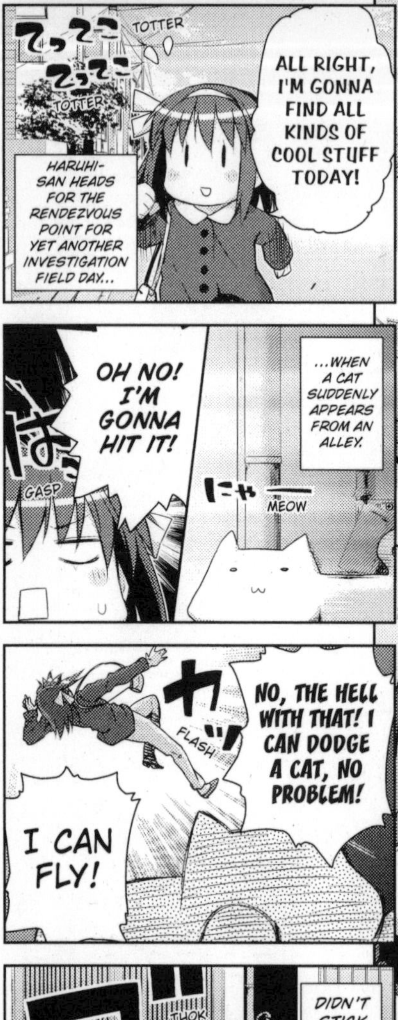
ALL RIGHT, I'M GONNA FIND ALL KINDS OF COOL STUFF TODAY!
TOTTER
TOTTER
HARUHI-SAN HEADS FOR THE RENDEZVOUS POINT FOR YET ANOTHER INVESTIGATION FIELD DAY...
...WHEN A CAT SUDDENLY APPEARS FROM AN ALLEY.
OH NO! I'M GONNA HIT IT!
MEOW
GASP
NO, THE HELL WITH THAT! I CAN DODGE A CAT, NO PROBLEM!
FLASH
I CAN FLY!
DIDN'T STICK THE LAND-ING.
THOK

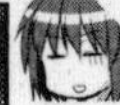

•Haruhi-chan •SOS Brigade brigade chief. Has her trademark ribbon stolen by a cat...!?

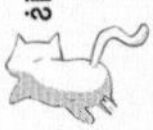

•Cat •Veteran of many duels with Achakura-chan. Now it's taking on Haruhi...?

MINE

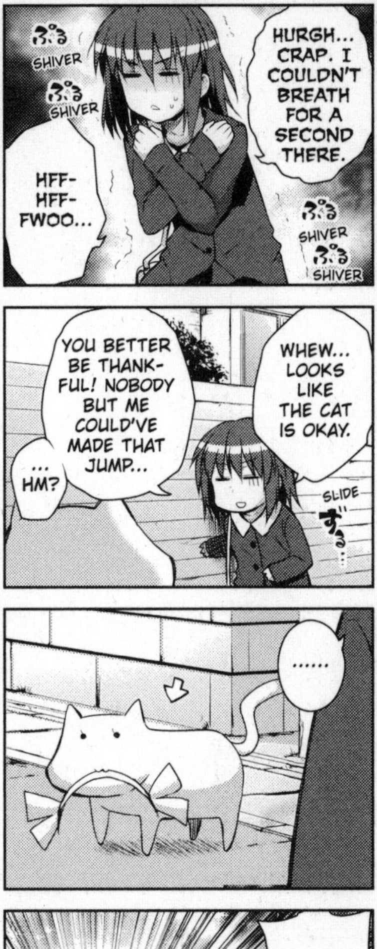
HURGH... CRAP. I COULDN'T BREATH FOR A SECOND THERE.
ぷる SHIVER
ぷる SHIVER
HFF-HFF-FWOO...
ぷる SHIVER
ぷる SHIVER
WHEW... LOOKS LIKE THE CAT IS OKAY.
YOU BETTER BE THANKFUL! NOBODY BUT ME COULD'VE MADE THAT JUMP...
...HM?
ずる... SLIDE
......
WAA-AAAH!
ダッ DASH

FLEEING THE SCENE

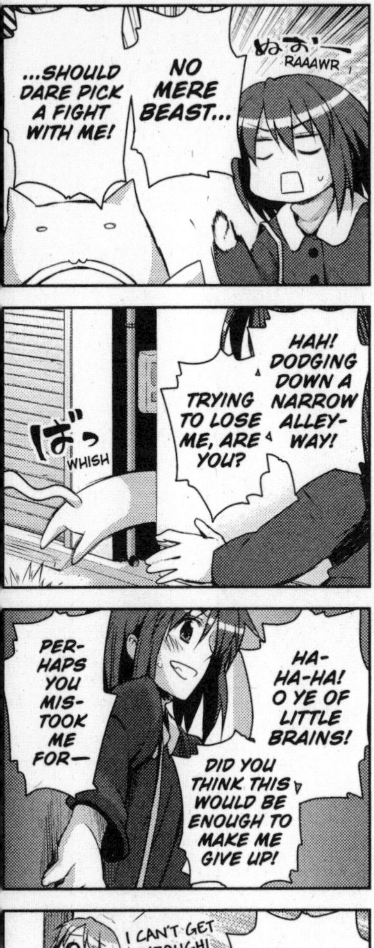
ぬおー RAAAWR
NO MERE BEAST...
...SHOULD DARE PICK A FIGHT WITH ME!
HAH! DODGING DOWN A NARROW ALLEY-WAY!
TRYING TO LOSE ME, ARE YOU?
ばっ WHISH
HA-HA-HA! O YE OF LITTLE BRAINS!
DID YOU THINK THIS WOULD BE ENOUGH TO MAKE ME GIVE UP!
PER-HAPS YOU MIS-TOOK ME FOR—
MIKURU-CHAN, EH!?
I CAN'T GET THROUGH!
HARUHI-SAN, CALM YOUR-SELF!

WONDERLAND

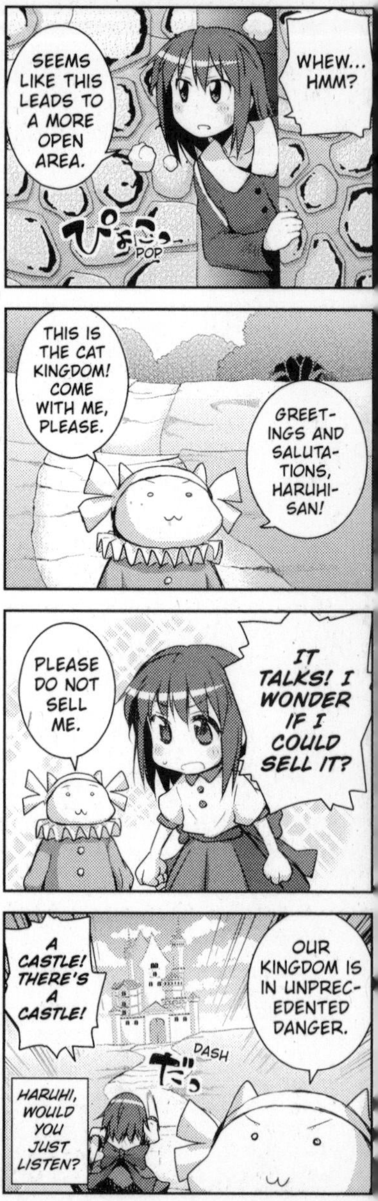
WHEW... HMM?
SEEMS LIKE THIS LEADS TO A MORE OPEN AREA.
POP
GREETINGS AND SALUTATIONS, HARUHI-SAN!
THIS IS THE CAT KINGDOM! COME WITH ME, PLEASE.
IT TALKS! I WONDER IF I COULD SELL IT?
PLEASE DO NOT SELL ME.
OUR KINGDOM IS IN UNPRECEDENTED DANGER.
A CASTLE! THERE'S A CASTLE!
DASH
HARUHI, WOULD YOU JUST LISTEN?

DIGEST

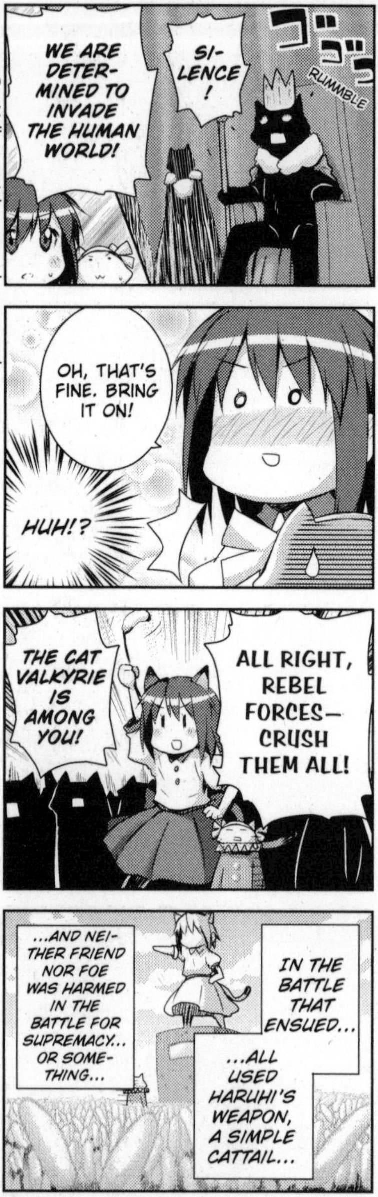
RUMMBLE
SILENCE!
WE ARE DETERMINED TO INVADE THE HUMAN WORLD!
OH, THAT'S FINE. BRING IT ON!
HUH!?
ALL RIGHT, REBEL FORCES—CRUSH THEM ALL!
THE CAT VALKYRIE IS AMONG YOU!
IN THE BATTLE THAT ENSUED...
...ALL USED HARUHI'S WEAPON, A SIMPLE CATTAIL...
...AND NEITHER FRIEND NOR FOE WAS HARMED IN THE BATTLE FOR SUPREMACY... OR SOMETHING...

•Cat Valkyrie •A human girl summoned to the cat kingdom. There, her destiny was changed forever...

BACK TO REALITY

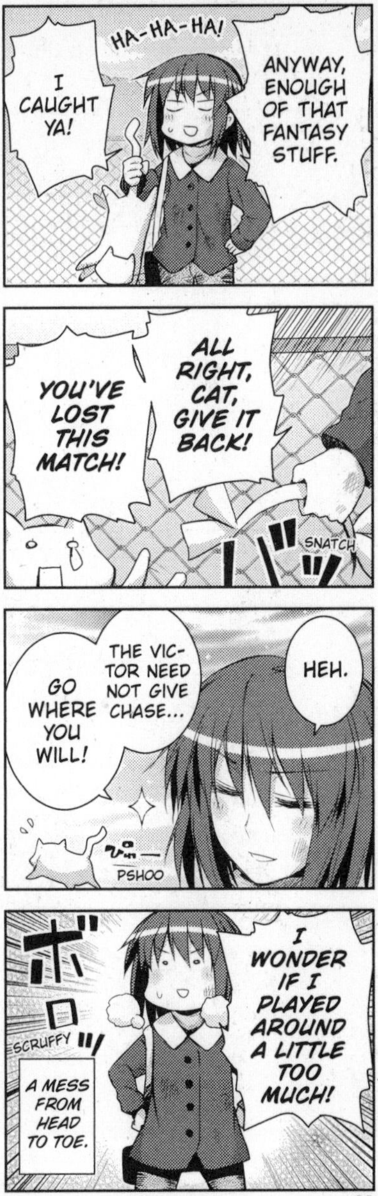
HA-HA-HA!
ANYWAY, ENOUGH OF THAT FANTASY STUFF.
I CAUGHT YA!
ALL RIGHT, CAT, GIVE IT BACK!
YOU'VE LOST THIS MATCH!
SNATCH
HEH.
THE VICTOR NEED NOT GIVE CHASE...
GO WHERE YOU WILL!
PSHOO
I WONDER IF I PLAYED AROUND A LITTLE TOO MUCH!
SCRUFFY
A MESS FROM HEAD TO TOE.

TRADEMARK

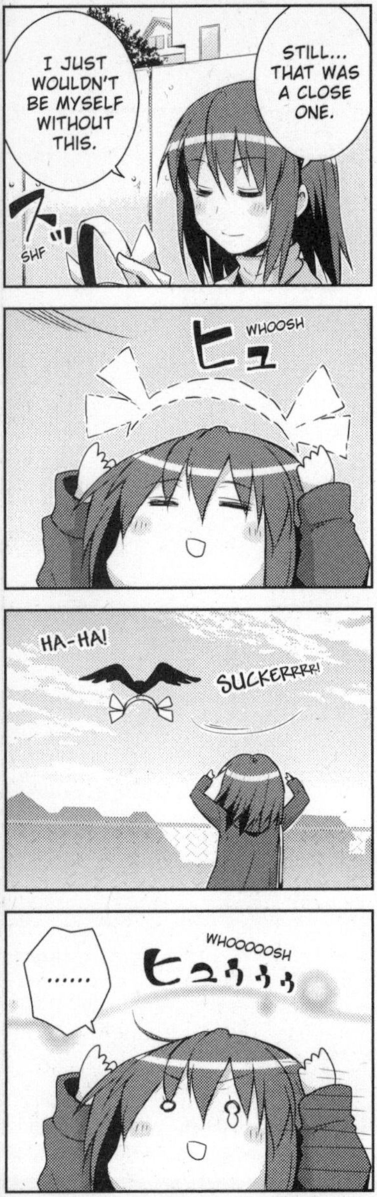
STILL... THAT WAS A CLOSE ONE.
I JUST WOULDN'T BE MYSELF WITHOUT THIS.
SHF
ヒュ
WHOOSH
SUCKERRRR!
HA-HA!
WHOOOOOSH
......

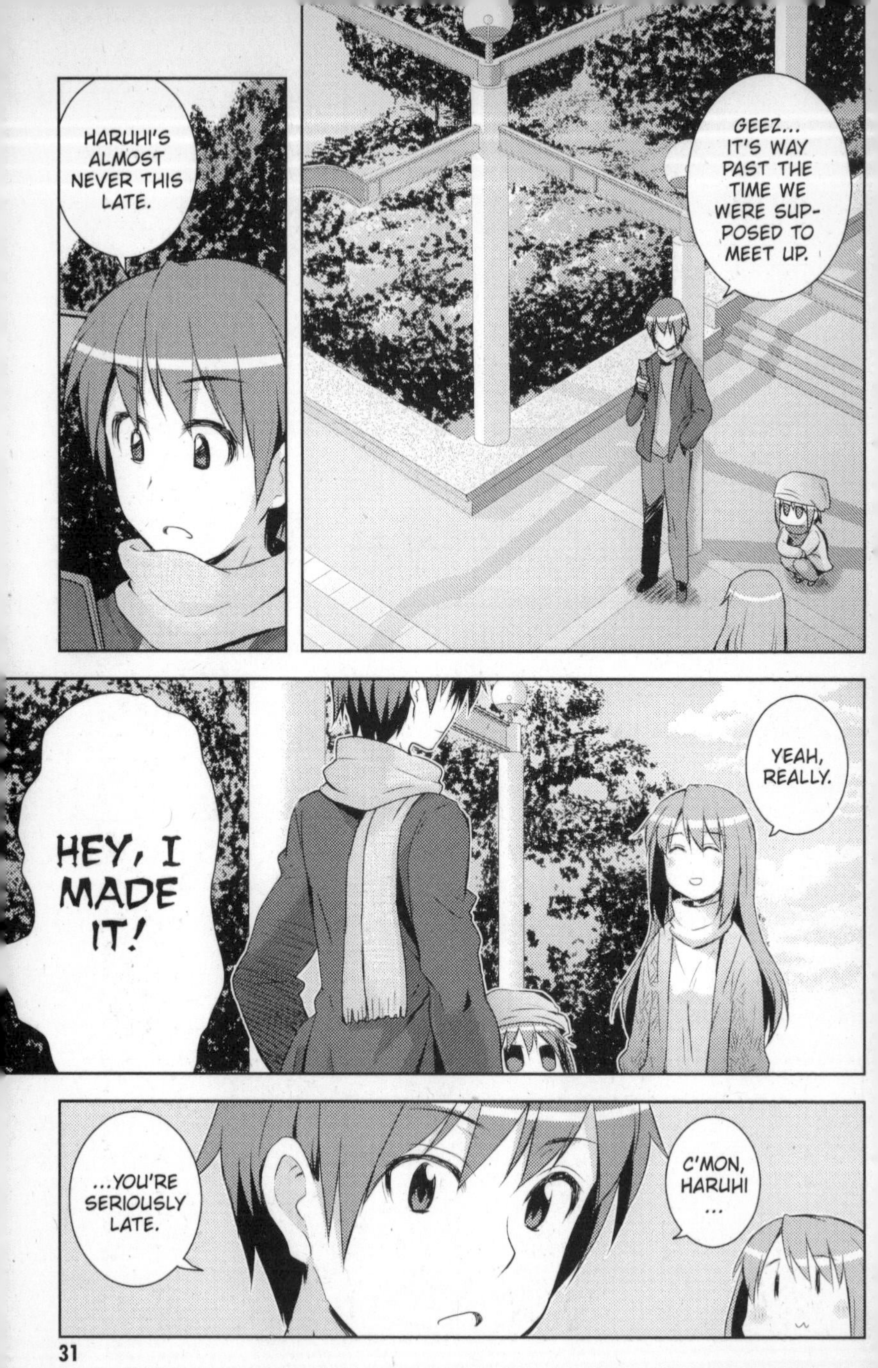
GEEZ... IT'S WAY PAST THE TIME WE WERE SUP-POSED TO MEET UP.
HARUHI'S ALMOST NEVER THIS LATE.
YEAH, REALLY.
HEY, I MADE IT!
C'MON, HARUHI ...
...YOU'RE SERIOUSLY LATE.

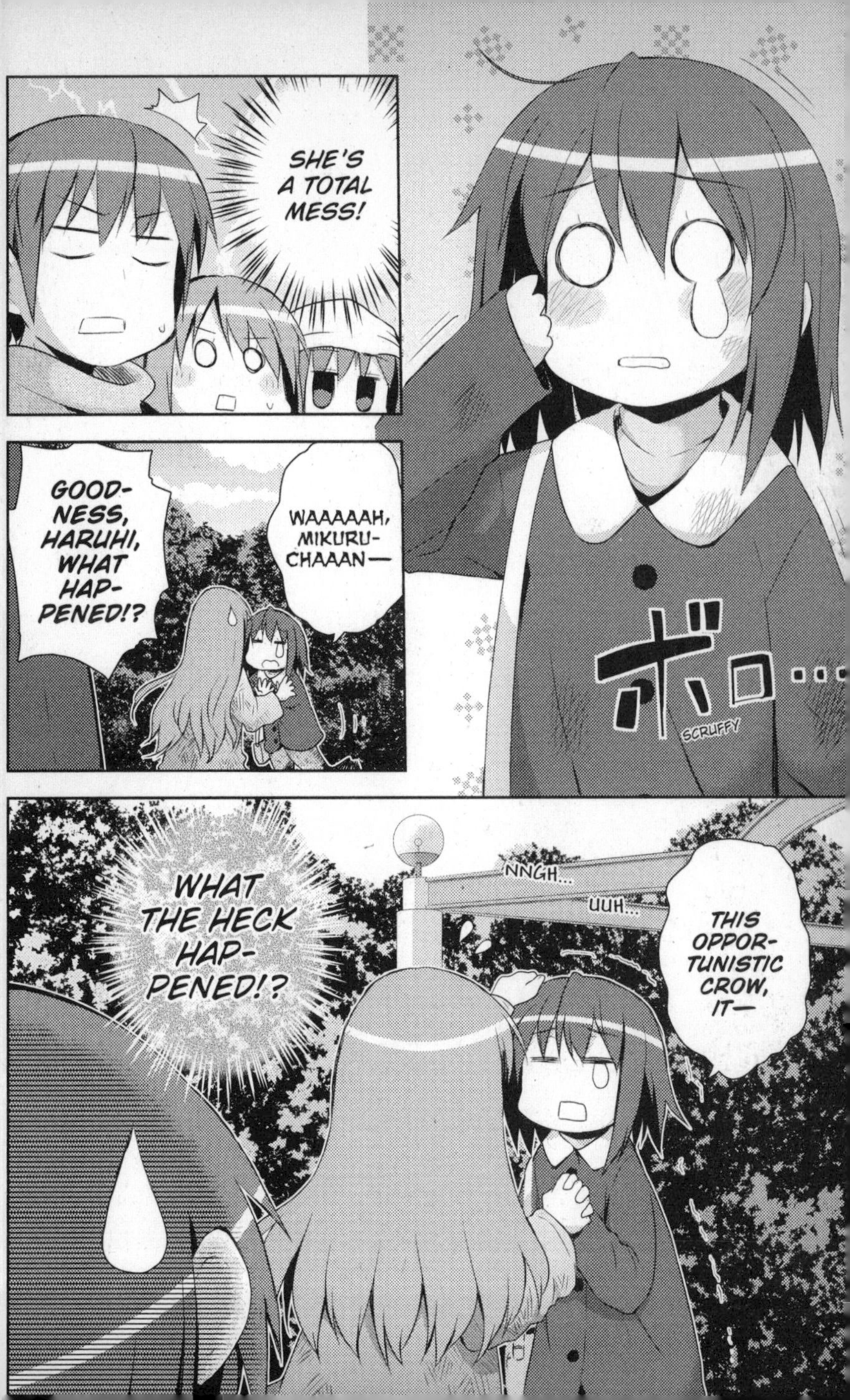
ボロ…
SCRUFFY
SHE'S A TOTAL MESS!
WAAAAAH, MIKURU-CHAAAN—
GOODNESS, HARUHI, WHAT HAPPENED!?
NNGH...
UUH...
THIS OPPORTUNISTIC CROW, IT—
WHAT THE HECK HAPPENED!?

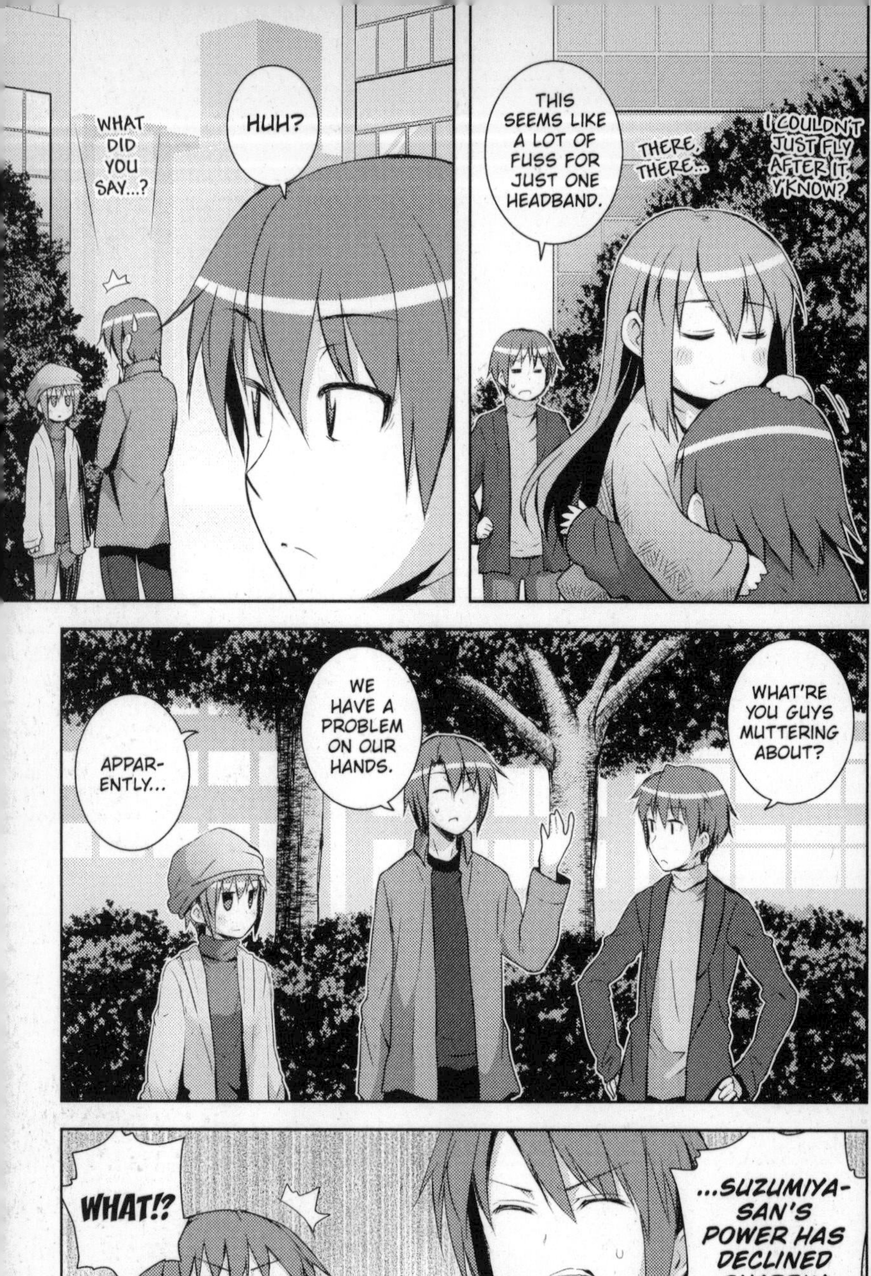
I COULDN'T JUST FLY AFTER IT, Y'KNOW?
THERE, THERE...
THIS SEEMS LIKE A LOT OF FUSS FOR JUST ONE HEADBAND.
HUH?
WHAT DID YOU SAY...?
WHAT'RE YOU GUYS MUTTERING ABOUT?
WE HAVE A PROBLEM ON OUR HANDS.
APPARENTLY...
...SUZUMIYA-SAN'S POWER HAS DECLINED SHARPLY.
WHAT!?

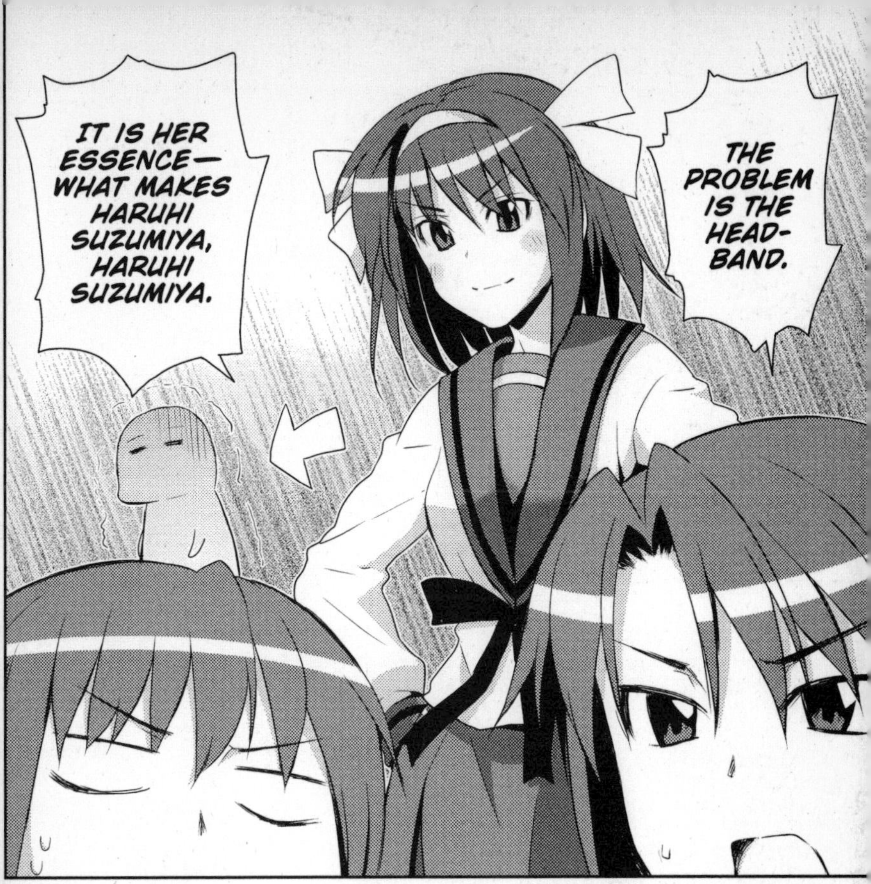
THE PROBLEM IS THE HEAD-BAND.
IT IS HER ESSENCE—WHAT MAKES HARUHI SUZUMIYA, HARUHI SUZUMIYA.

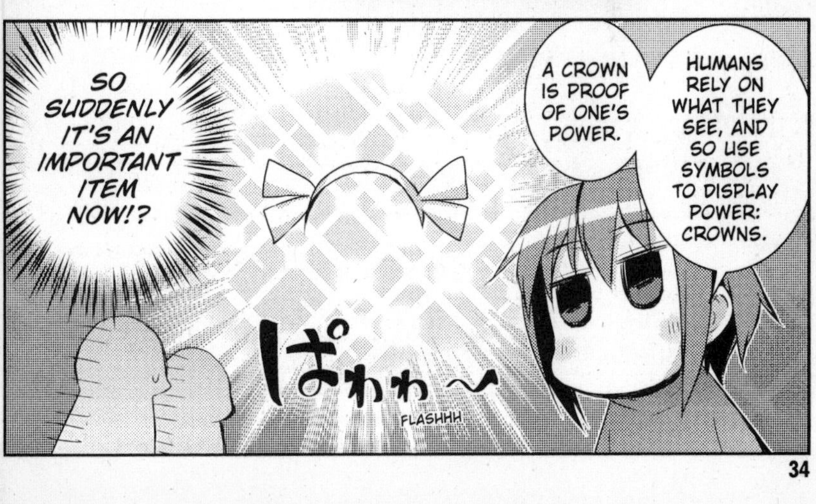
HUMANS RELY ON WHAT THEY SEE, AND SO USE SYMBOLS TO DISPLAY POWER: CROWNS.
A CROWN IS PROOF OF ONE'S POWER.
ぱわわ～
FLASHHH
SO SUDDENLY IT'S AN IMPORTANT ITEM NOW!?

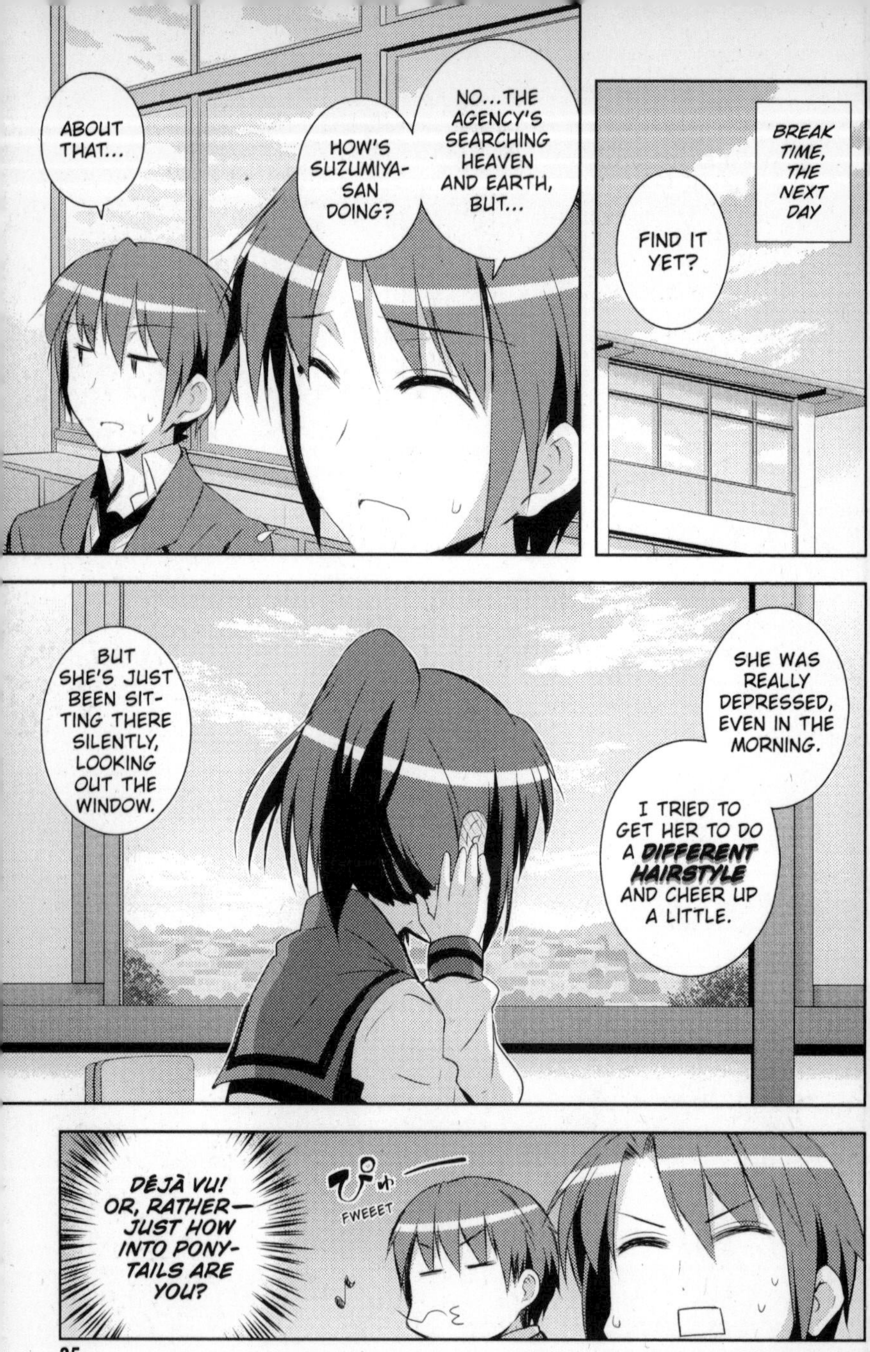
BREAK TIME, THE NEXT DAY
FIND IT YET?
NO...THE AGENCY'S SEARCHING HEAVEN AND EARTH, BUT...
HOW'S SUZUMIYA-SAN DOING?
ABOUT THAT...
SHE WAS REALLY DEPRESSED, EVEN IN THE MORNING.
I TRIED TO GET HER TO DO A ***DIFFERENT HAIRSTYLE*** AND CHEER UP A LITTLE.
BUT SHE'S JUST BEEN SITTING THERE SILENTLY, LOOKING OUT THE WINDOW.
ぴゅ——
FWEEET
DÉJÀ VU! OR, RATHER— JUST HOW INTO PONYTAILS ARE YOU?

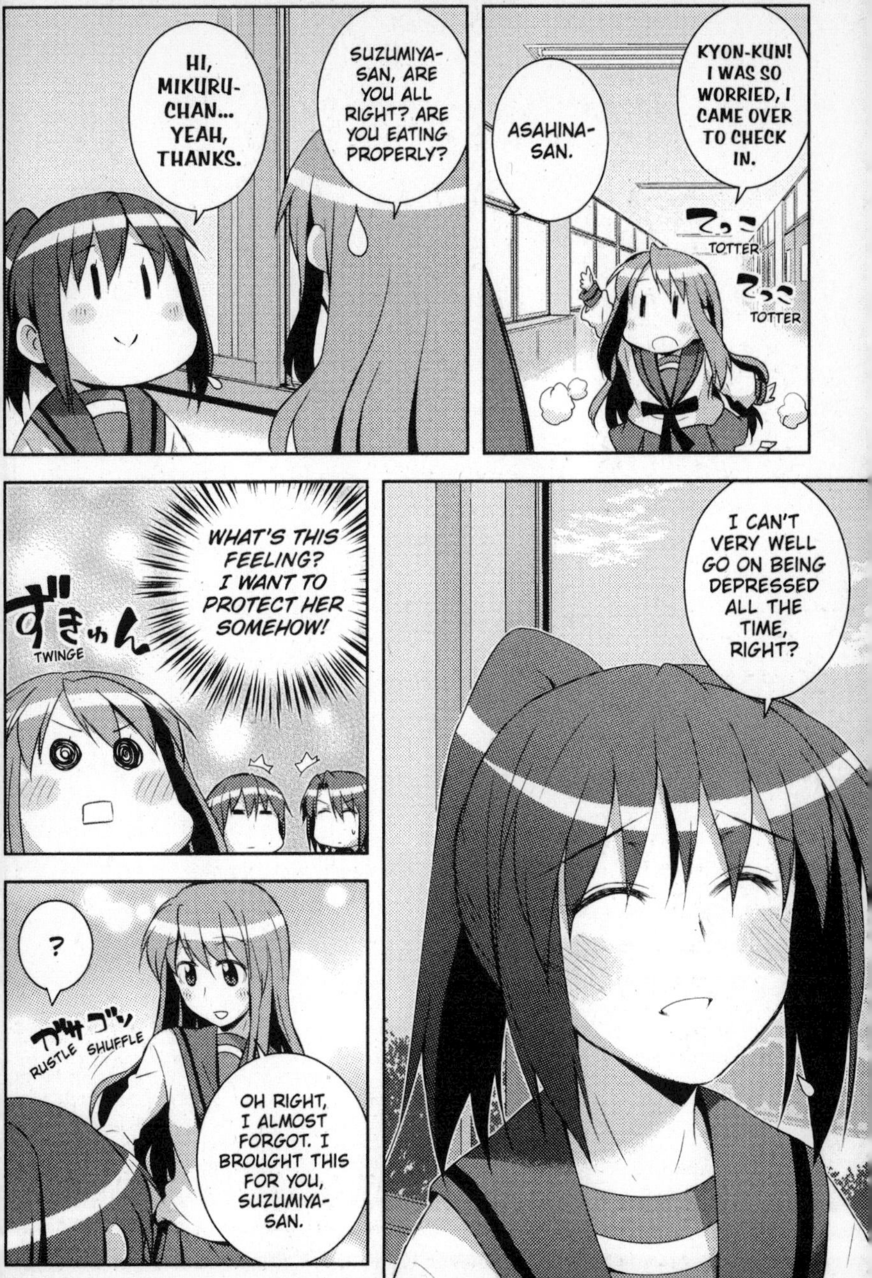
KYON-KUN! I WAS SO WORRIED, I CAME OVER TO CHECK IN.
ASAHINA-SAN.
てっこ
TOTTER
てっこ
TOTTER
SUZUMIYA-SAN, ARE YOU ALL RIGHT? ARE YOU EATING PROPERLY?
HI, MIKURU-CHAN... YEAH, THANKS.
I CAN'T VERY WELL GO ON BEING DEPRESSED ALL THE TIME, RIGHT?
WHAT'S THIS FEELING? I WANT TO PROTECT HER SOMEHOW!
ずきゅん
TWINGE
?
ガサゴソ
RUSTLE SHUFFLE
OH RIGHT, I ALMOST FORGOT. I BROUGHT THIS FOR YOU, SUZUMIYA-SAN.

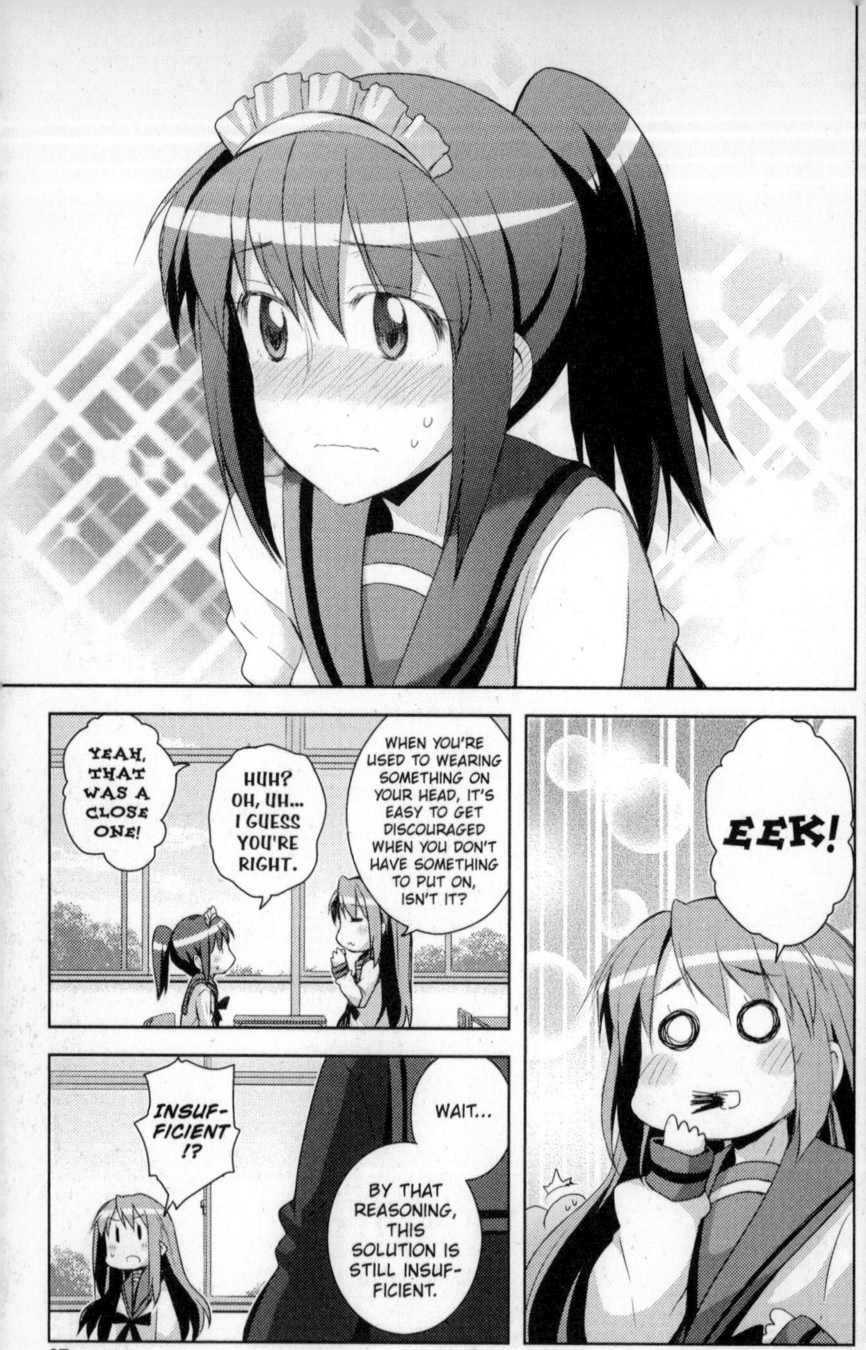
EEK!
WHEN YOU'RE USED TO WEARING SOMETHING ON YOUR HEAD, IT'S EASY TO GET DISCOURAGED WHEN YOU DON'T HAVE SOMETHING TO PUT ON, ISN'T IT?
HUH? OH, UH... I GUESS YOU'RE RIGHT.
YEAH, THAT WAS A CLOSE ONE!
WAIT...
BY THAT REASONING, THIS SOLUTION IS STILL INSUFFICIENT.
INSUFFICIENT!?

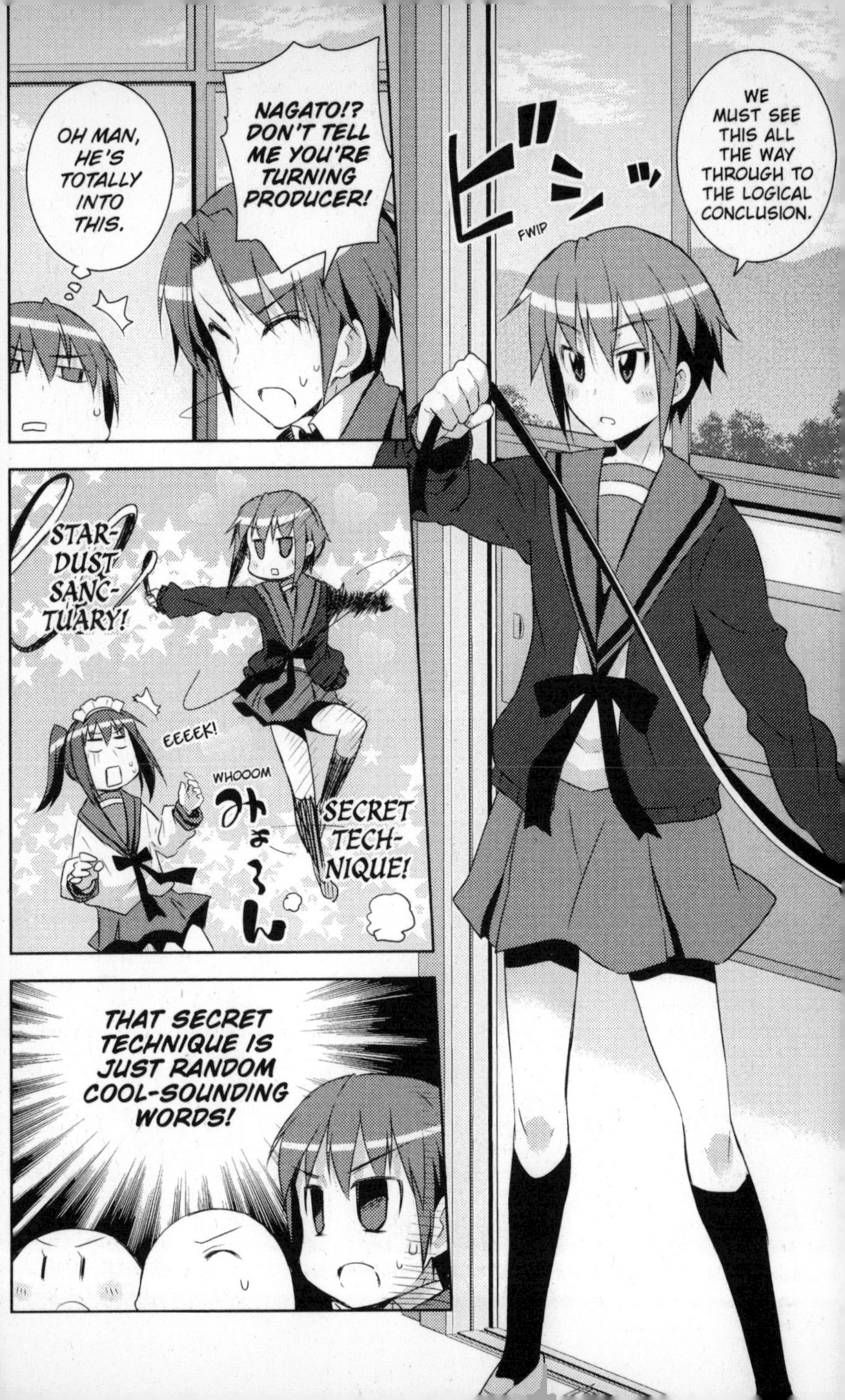
WE MUST SEE THIS ALL THE WAY THROUGH TO THE LOGICAL CONCLUSION.
FWIP
NAGATO!? DON'T TELL ME YOU'RE TURNING PRODUCER!
OH MAN, HE'S TOTALLY INTO THIS.
SECRET TECHNIQUE!
WHOOOM
EEEEK!
STARDUST SANCTUARY!
THAT SECRET TECHNIQUE IS JUST RANDOM COOL-SOUNDING WORDS!

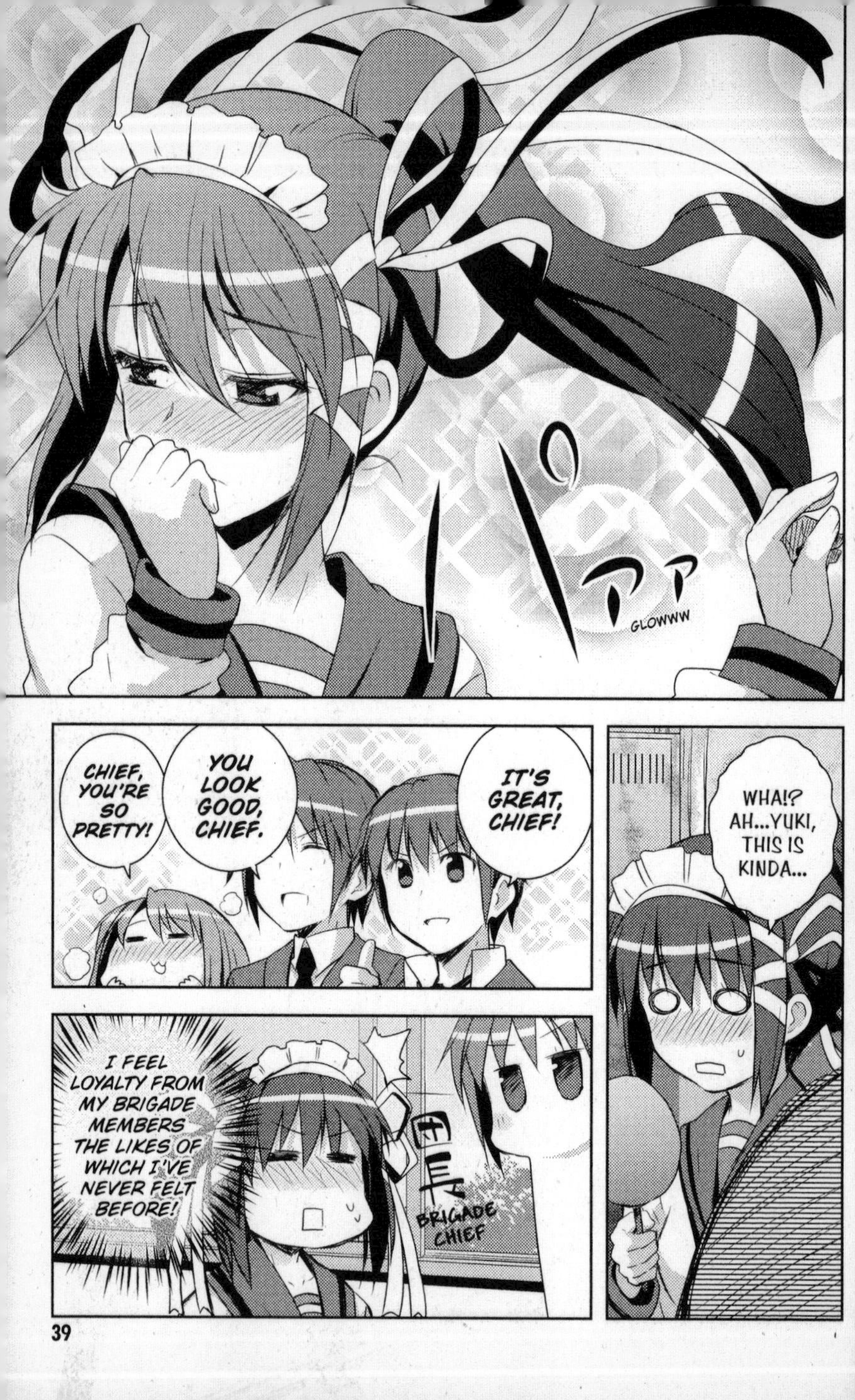
GLOWWW
WHA!? AH...YUKI, THIS IS KINDA...
IT'S GREAT, CHIEF!
YOU LOOK GOOD, CHIEF.
CHIEF, YOU'RE SO PRETTY!
BRIGADE CHIEF
I FEEL LOYALTY FROM MY BRIGADE MEMBERS THE LIKES OF WHICH I'VE NEVER FELT BEFORE!

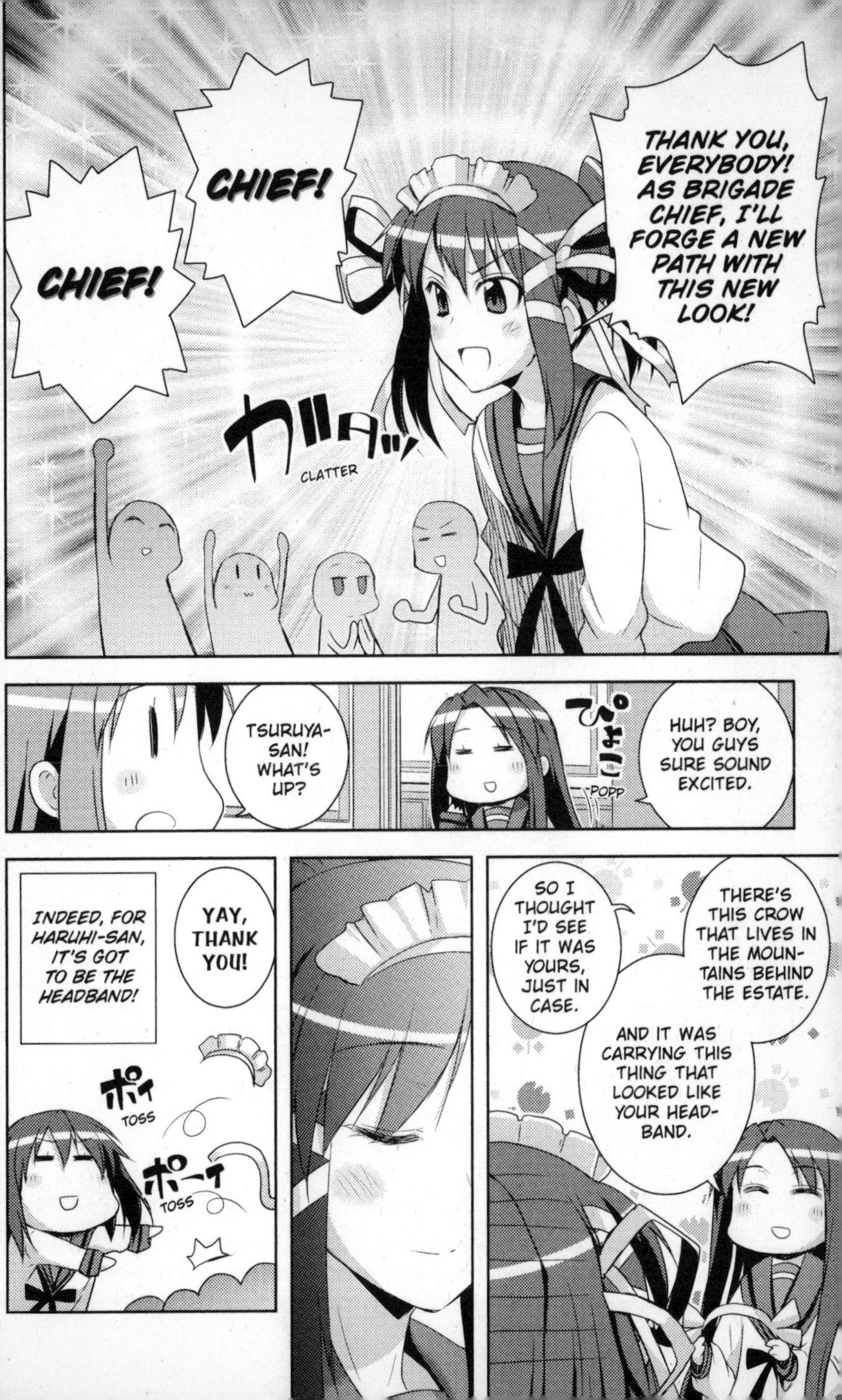
THANK YOU, EVERYBODY! AS BRIGADE CHIEF, I'LL FORGE A NEW PATH WITH THIS NEW LOOK!
CHIEF!
CHIEF!
ガタッ
CLATTER
HUH? BOY, YOU GUYS SURE SOUND EXCITED.
ぴょこ
-POPP
TSURUYA-SAN! WHAT'S UP?
THERE'S THIS CROW THAT LIVES IN THE MOUN-TAINS BEHIND THE ESTATE.
AND IT WAS CARRYING THIS THING THAT LOOKED LIKE YOUR HEAD-BAND.
SO I THOUGHT I'D SEE IF IT WAS YOURS, JUST IN CASE.
YAY, THANK YOU!
INDEED, FOR HARUHI-SAN, IT'S GOT TO BE THE HEADBAND!
ポイ
TOSS
ポーイ
TOSS

UNREASONABLE

EARLY AFTERNOON, AT THE PARK
ROCK, PAPER, SCISSORS ON THREE! ONE, TWO...
...THREE!
YOU LOSE, KIMIDORI-CHAN!
THAT MEANS YOU'RE IT, KIMIDORI-SAN!
......
OBJECTION!

EXCUSES

I CAN ONLY MAKE "ROCK!" THIS IS COMPLETELY UNFAIR!
UH... COME TO THINK OF IT...
I MEAN...
PLEASE EXPLAIN TO ME JUST HOW A BALLOON CAN TALK, EXACTLY!
AWKWARD!
IT'S ALL RIGHT, KIMIDORI-SAN.
WE'LL JUST DO WHAT NAGATO-SAN TOLD US TO!
RIGHT!
HE'S THE LATEST MODEL OF AIBO.
WHOAH! THE CUTTING EDGE OF TECHNOLOGY!

•Little Sister •Kyon's younger sister. Saved Achakura from an evil cat, then became her master.

•Achakura-san •Small version of Ryouko Asakura. Uses that excuse more than Kimidori-san...

•Kimidori-san •Not the latest AIBO model. Actually an artificial life-form created from a balloon.

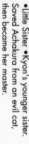

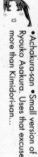

TRUE MOTIVES

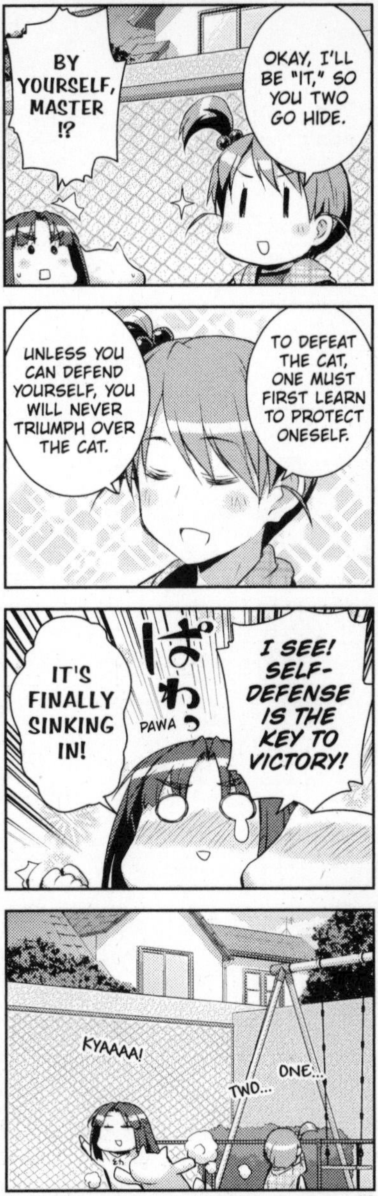

OKAY, I'LL BE "IT," SO YOU TWO GO HIDE.
BY YOURSELF, MASTER!?
TO DEFEAT THE CAT, ONE MUST FIRST LEARN TO PROTECT ONESELF.
UNLESS YOU CAN DEFEND YOURSELF, YOU WILL NEVER TRIUMPH OVER THE CAT.
I SEE! SELF-DEFENSE IS THE KEY TO VICTORY!
ぱわっ
PAWA
IT'S FINALLY SINKING IN!
ONE...
TWO...
KYAAAA!

COMING HOME

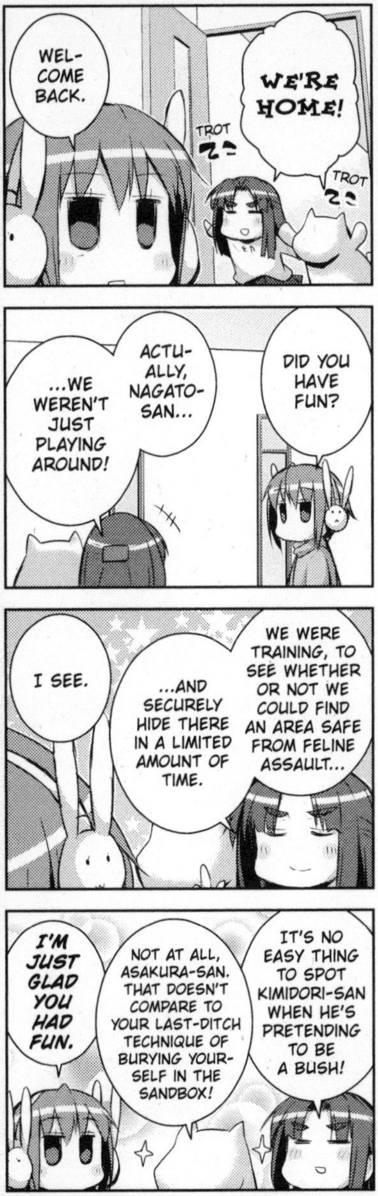

WE'RE HOME!
TROT
TROT
WEL-COME BACK.
DID YOU HAVE FUN?
ACTU-ALLY, NAGATO-SAN...
...WE WEREN'T JUST PLAYING AROUND!
WE WERE TRAINING, TO SEE WHETHER OR NOT WE COULD FIND AN AREA SAFE FROM FELINE ASSAULT...
...AND SECURELY HIDE THERE IN A LIMITED AMOUNT OF TIME.
I SEE.
IT'S NO EASY THING TO SPOT KIMIDORI-SAN WHEN HE'S PRETENDING TO BE A BUSH!
NOT AT ALL, ASAKURA-SAN. THAT DOESN'T COMPARE TO YOUR LAST-DITCH TECHNIQUE OF BURYING YOUR-SELF IN THE SANDBOX!
I'M JUST GLAD YOU HAD FUN.

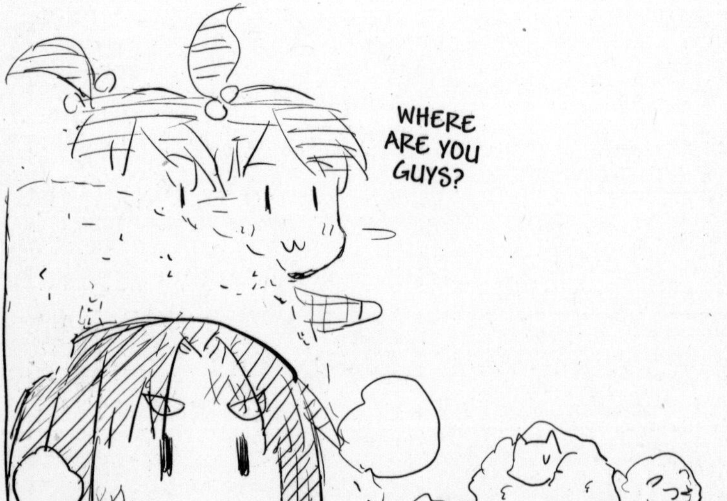
WHERE ARE YOU GUYS?

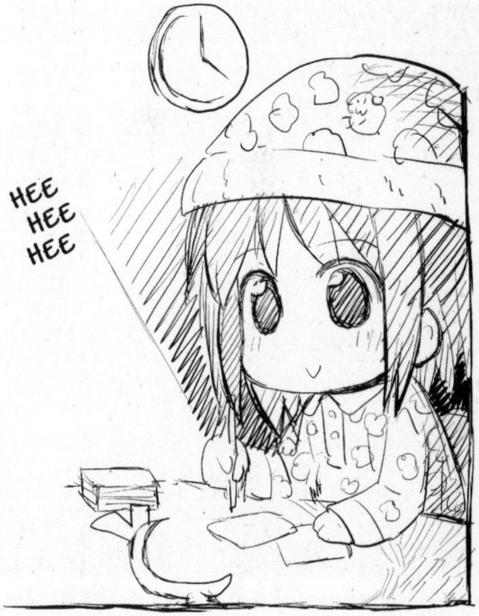
HEE
HEE
HEE

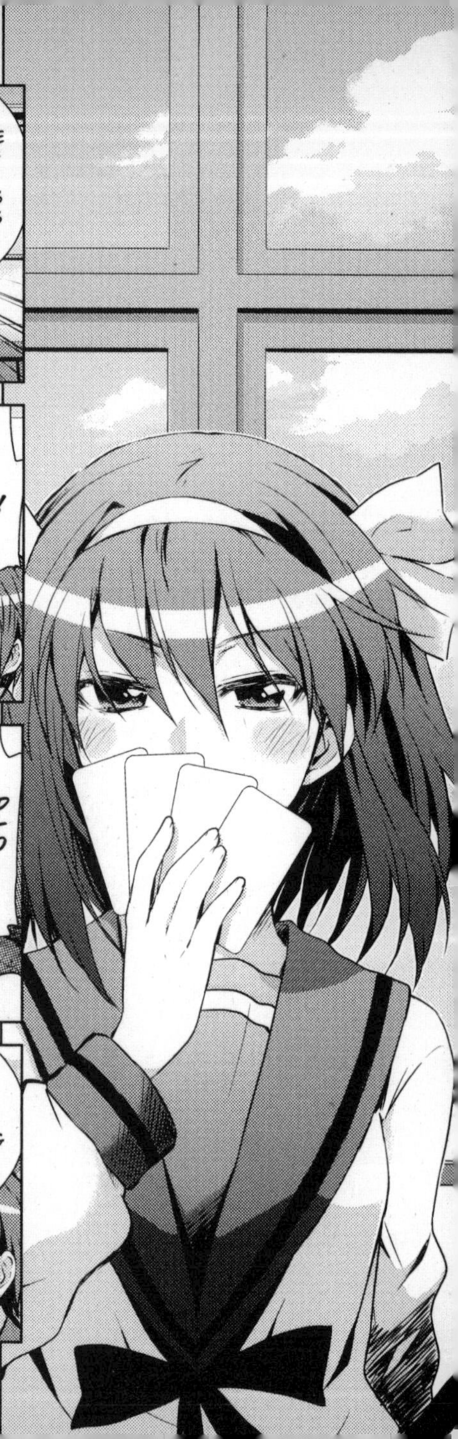

THEME

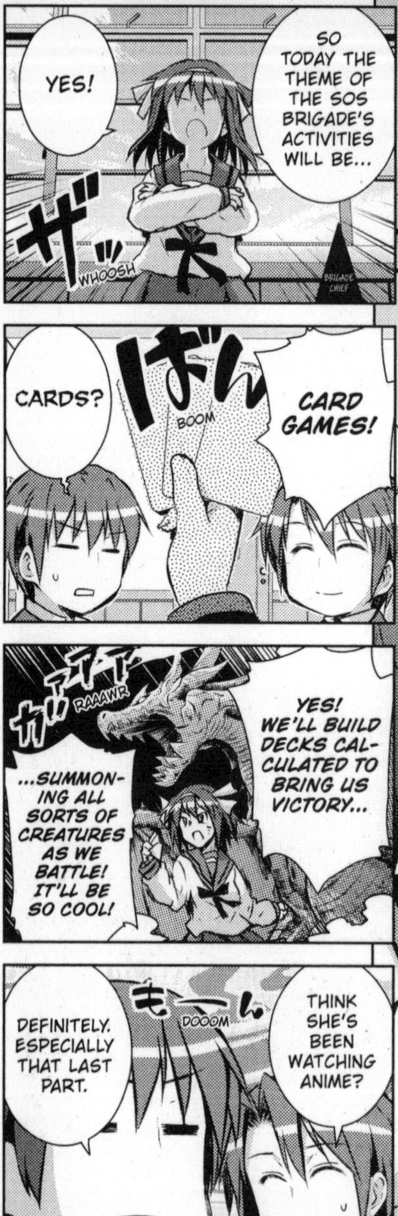
SO TODAY THE THEME OF THE SOS BRIGADE'S ACTIVITIES WILL BE...
BRIGADE CHIEF
YES!
WHOOSH
CARD GAMES!
BOOM
CARDS?
YES! WE'LL BUILD DECKS CAL-CULATED TO BRING US VICTORY...
RAAAWR
...SUMMON-ING ALL SORTS OF CREATURES AS WE BATTLE! IT'LL BE SO COOL!
THINK SHE'S BEEN WATCHING ANIME?
DOOOM
DEFINITELY. ESPECIALLY THAT LAST PART.

HOMEMADE

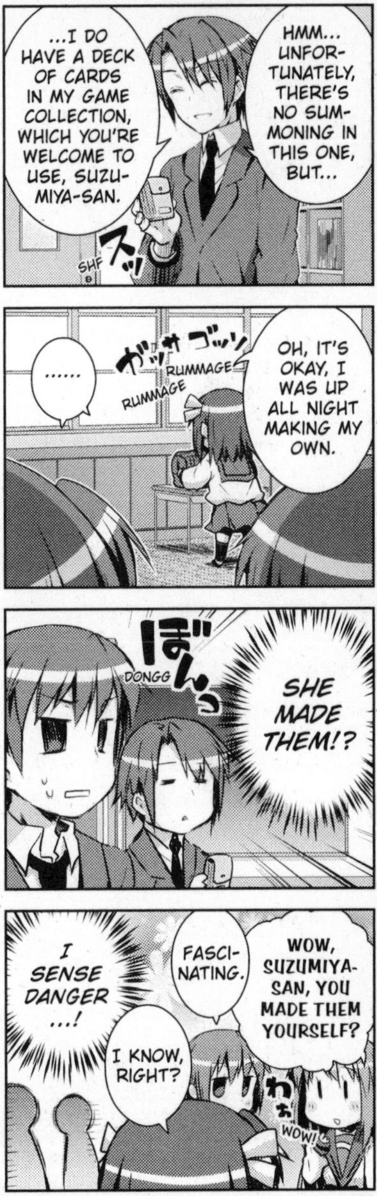
HMM... UNFORTUNATELY, THERE'S NO SUMMONING IN THIS ONE, BUT...
...I DO HAVE A DECK OF CARDS IN MY GAME COLLECTION, WHICH YOU'RE WELCOME TO USE, SUZUMIYA-SAN.
スッ
SHF
OH, IT'S OKAY, I WAS UP ALL NIGHT MAKING MY OWN.
RUMMAGE
RUMMAGE
......
ぼんっ
DONGG
SHE MADE THEM!?
WOW, SUZUMIYA-SAN, YOU MADE THEM YOURSELF?
FASCINATING.
I KNOW, RIGHT?
I SENSE DANGER...!
わぉ
WOW!

•Haruhi-chan •SOS Brigade brigade chief. A mysterious seeker who creates whatever she needs to have fun.

•Kyon •The protagonist of this story. Although in this chapter he winds up being a summoned creature.

•Koizumi •Enigmatic transfer student and esper. A summoned creature who's a bit on the pretty side.

SUZUMIYA SUMMONING SYSTEM

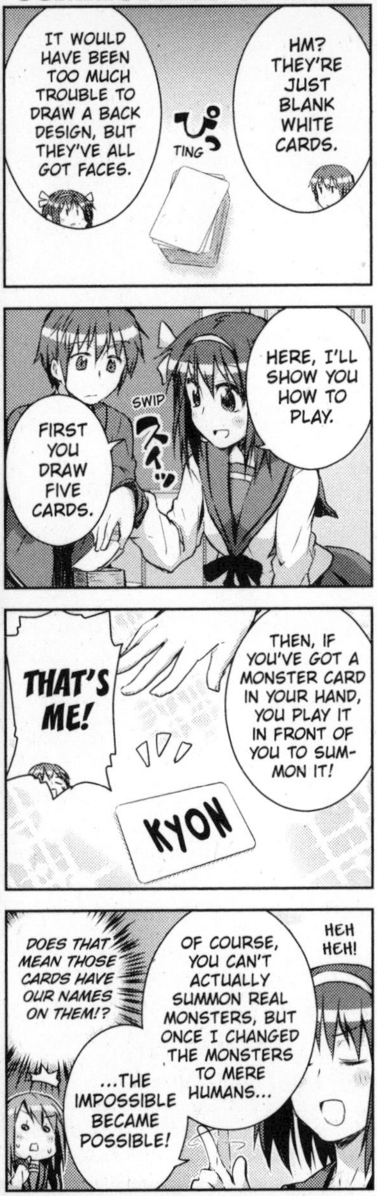
HM? THEY'RE JUST BLANK WHITE CARDS.
ぴっ
TING
IT WOULD HAVE BEEN TOO MUCH TROUBLE TO DRAW A BACK DESIGN, BUT THEY'VE ALL GOT FACES.
HERE, I'LL SHOW YOU HOW TO PLAY.
SWIP
FIRST YOU DRAW FIVE CARDS.
THEN, IF YOU'VE GOT A MONSTER CARD IN YOUR HAND, YOU PLAY IT IN FRONT OF YOU TO SUMMON IT!
KYON
THAT'S ME!
HEH HEH!
OF COURSE, YOU CAN'T ACTUALLY SUMMON REAL MONSTERS, BUT ONCE I CHANGED THE MONSTERS TO MERE HUMANS...
...THE IMPOSSIBLE BECAME POSSIBLE!
DOES THAT MEAN THOSE CARDS HAVE OUR NAMES ON THEM!?

EQUIPPED ITEM

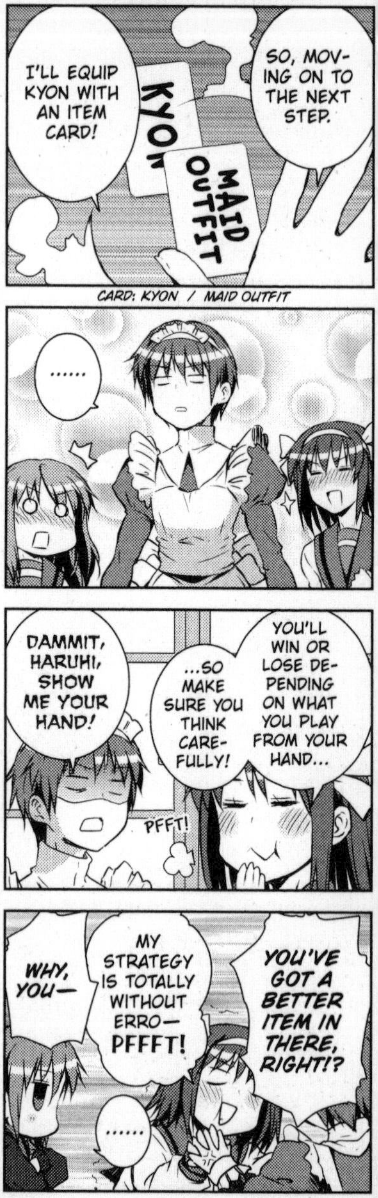
SO, MOVING ON TO THE NEXT STEP.
I'LL EQUIP KYON WITH AN ITEM CARD!
KYON
MAID OUTFIT
......
YOU'LL WIN OR LOSE DEPENDING ON WHAT YOU PLAY FROM YOUR HAND...
...SO MAKE SURE YOU THINK CAREFULLY!
PFFT!
DAMMIT, HARUHI, SHOW ME YOUR HAND!
YOU'VE GOT A BETTER ITEM IN THERE, RIGHT!?
MY STRATEGY IS TOTALLY WITHOUT ERRO—PFFFT!
WHY, YOU—
......

CARD: KYON / MAID OUTFIT

NAGATO'S TURN

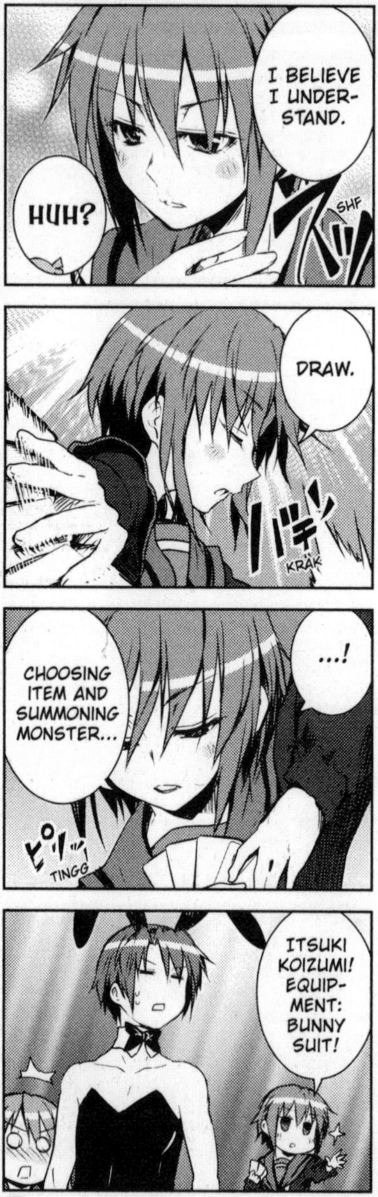
I BELIEVE I UNDERSTAND.
SHF
HUH?
DRAW.
KRAK
...!
CHOOSING ITEM AND SUMMONING MONSTER...
TINGG
ITSUKI KOIZUMI! EQUIPMENT: BUNNY SUIT!

•Nagato •Alien. Goes head-to-head with Haruhi in a card battle.

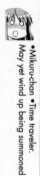

•Mikuru-chan •Time traveler. May yet wind up being summoned.

RIVALS

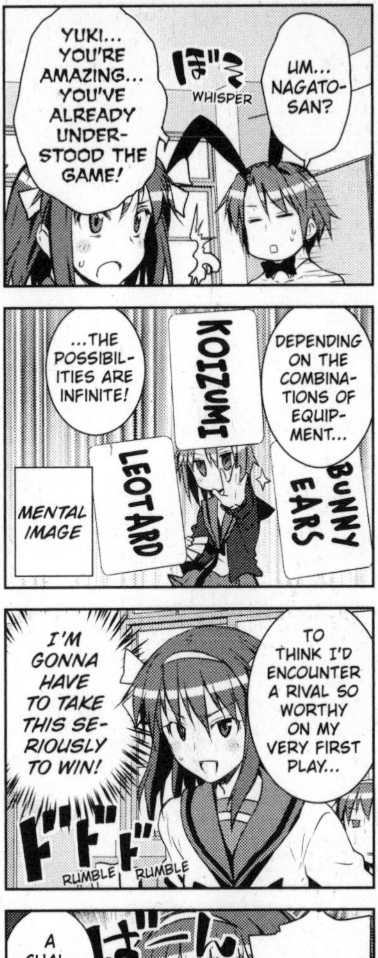
UM... NAGATO-SAN?
WHISPER
YUKI... YOU'RE AMAZING... YOU'VE ALREADY UNDERSTOOD THE GAME!
DEPENDING ON THE COMBINATIONS OF EQUIPMENT...
...THE POSSIBILITIES ARE INFINITE!
KOIZUMI
BUNNY EARS
LEOTARD
MENTAL IMAGE
TO THINK I'D ENCOUNTER A RIVAL SO WORTHY ON MY VERY FIRST PLAY...
I'M GONNA HAVE TO TAKE THIS SERIOUSLY TO WIN!
RUMBLE RUMBLE
YUKI! AGAIN!
WHOOSH
A CHALLENGE ...!

COME TO THINK OF IT

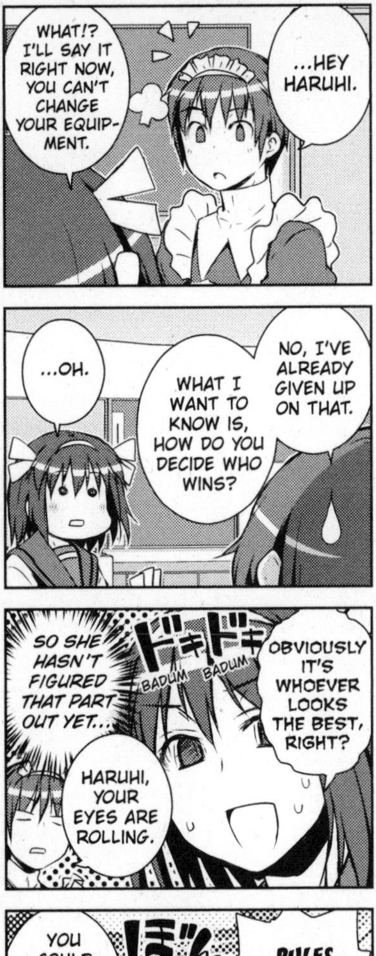
...HEY HARUHI.
WHAT!? I'LL SAY IT RIGHT NOW, YOU CAN'T CHANGE YOUR EQUIPMENT.
NO, I'VE ALREADY GIVEN UP ON THAT.
WHAT I WANT TO KNOW IS, HOW DO YOU DECIDE WHO WINS?
...OH.
OBVIOUSLY IT'S WHOEVER LOOKS THE BEST, RIGHT?
BADUM BADUM
SO SHE HASN'T FIGURED THAT PART OUT YET...
HARUHI, YOUR EYES ARE ROLLING.
RULES ARE SOMETHING YOU FIGURE OUT AS YOU GO!
BONK
YOU COULD AT LEAST FIGURE OUT THE BASICS!

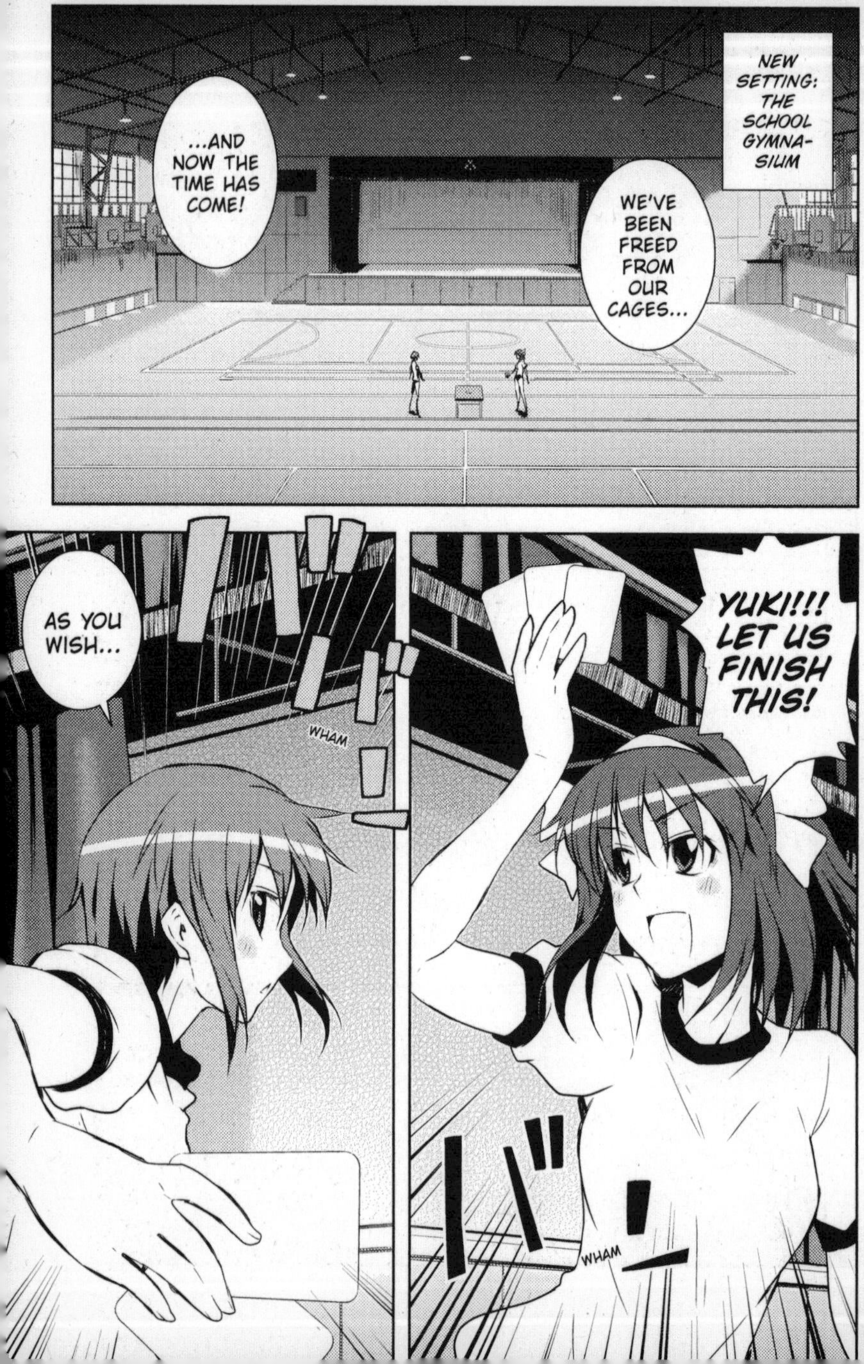
NEW SETTING: THE SCHOOL GYMNASIUM
WE'VE BEEN FREED FROM OUR CAGES...
...AND NOW THE TIME HAS COME!
YUKI!!! LET US FINISH THIS!
WHAM
AS YOU WISH...
WHAM

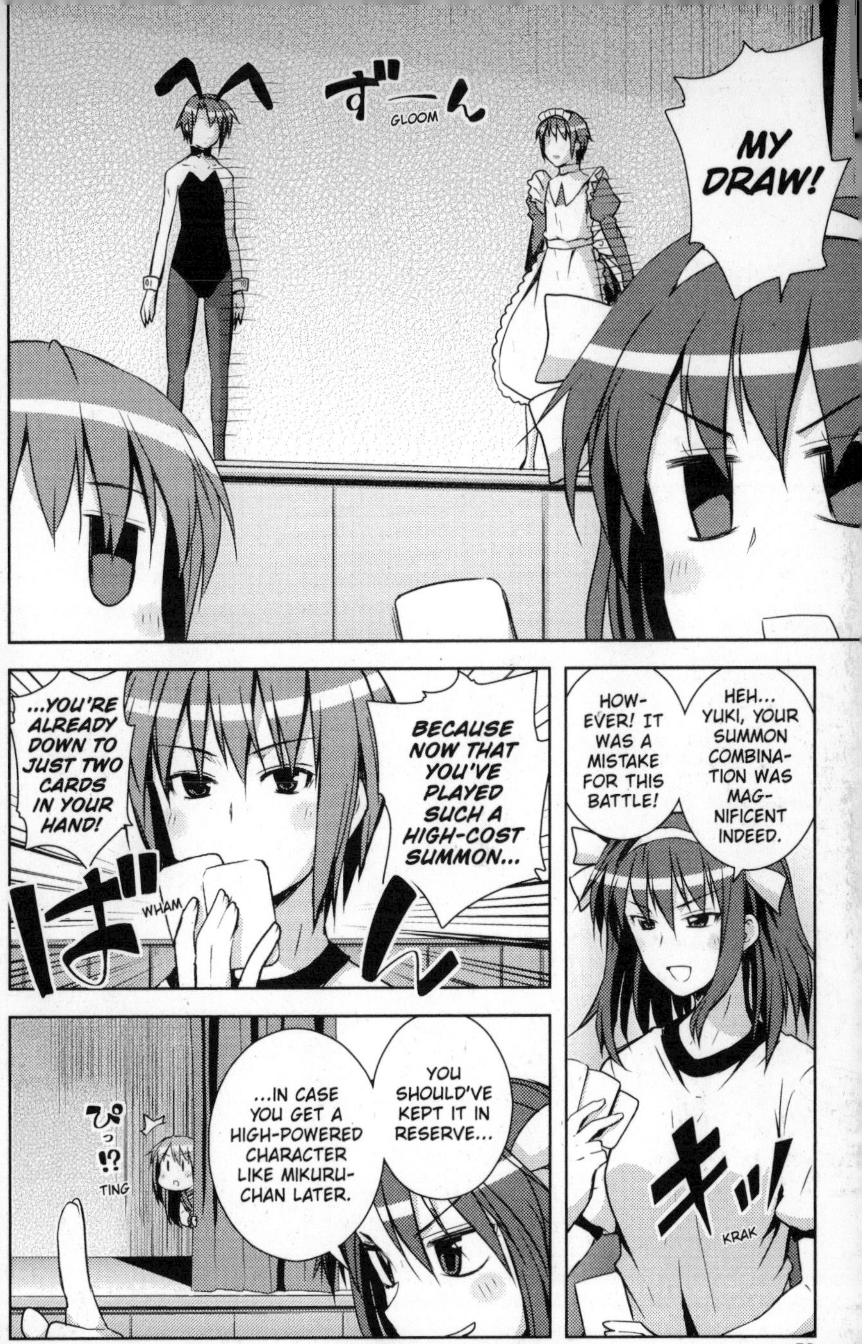
MY DRAW!
ずーん
GLOOM
HEH... YUKI, YOUR SUMMON COMBINATION WAS MAGNIFICENT INDEED.
HOW-EVER! IT WAS A MISTAKE FOR THIS BATTLE!
キッ
KRAK
BECAUSE NOW THAT YOU'VE PLAYED SUCH A HIGH-COST SUMMON...
...YOU'RE ALREADY DOWN TO JUST TWO CARDS IN YOUR HAND!
ばん
WHAM
YOU SHOULD'VE KEPT IT IN RESERVE...
...IN CASE YOU GET A HIGH-POWERED CHARACTER LIKE MIKURU-CHAN LATER.
ぴっ!?
TING

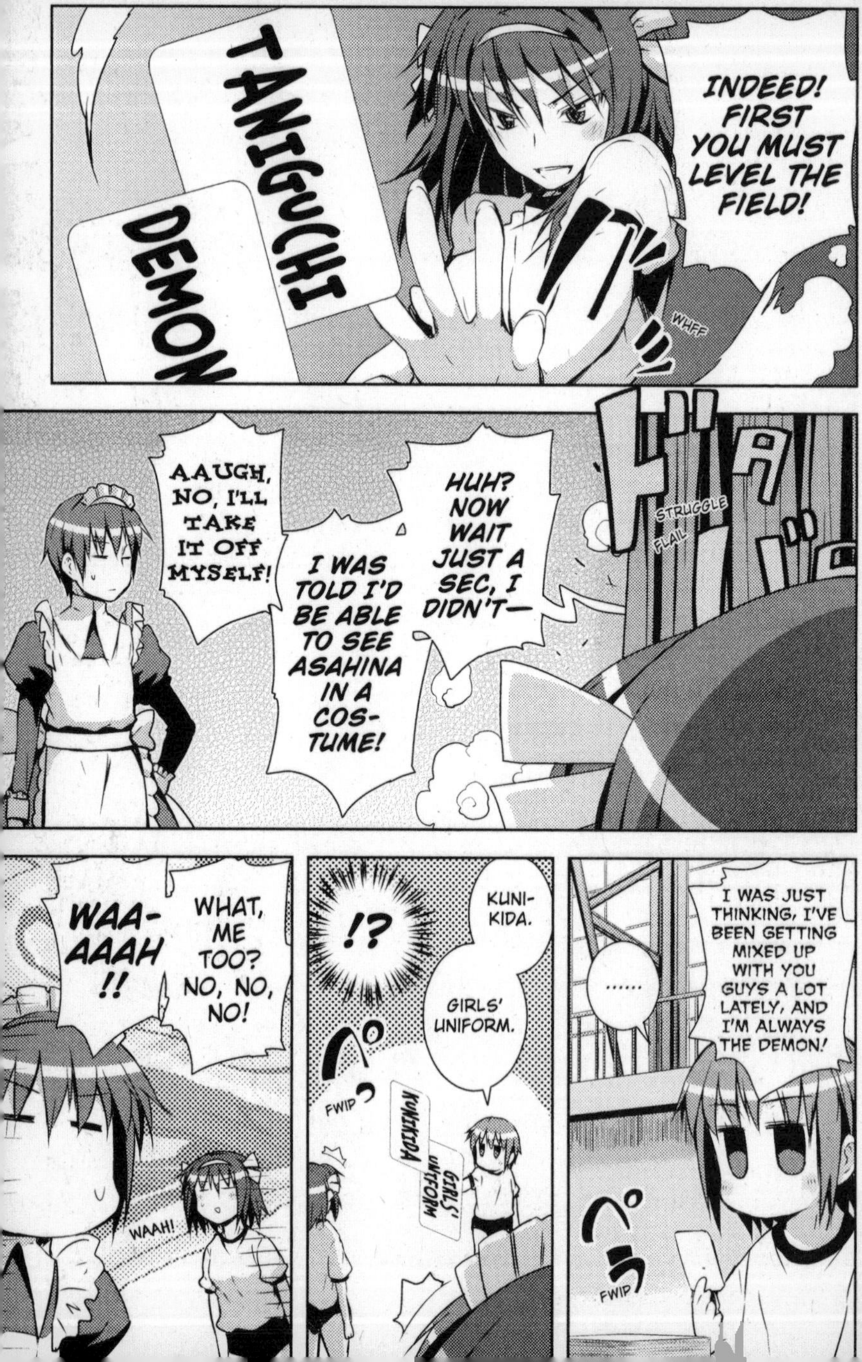
INDEED! FIRST YOU MUST LEVEL THE FIELD!
WHFF
TANIGUCHI
DEMON
STRUGGLE
FLAIL
HUH? NOW WAIT JUST A SEC, I DIDN'T—
I WAS TOLD I'D BE ABLE TO SEE ASAHINA IN A COS-TUME!
AAUGH, NO, I'LL TAKE IT OFF MYSELF!
I WAS JUST THINKING, I'VE BEEN GETTING MIXED UP WITH YOU GUYS A LOT LATELY, AND I'M ALWAYS THE DEMON!
......
FWIP
KUNI-KIDA.
GIRLS' UNIFORM.
!?
FWIP
GIRLS' UNIFORM
KUNIKIDA
WHAT, ME TOO? NO, NO, NO!
WAA-AAAH!!
WAAH!

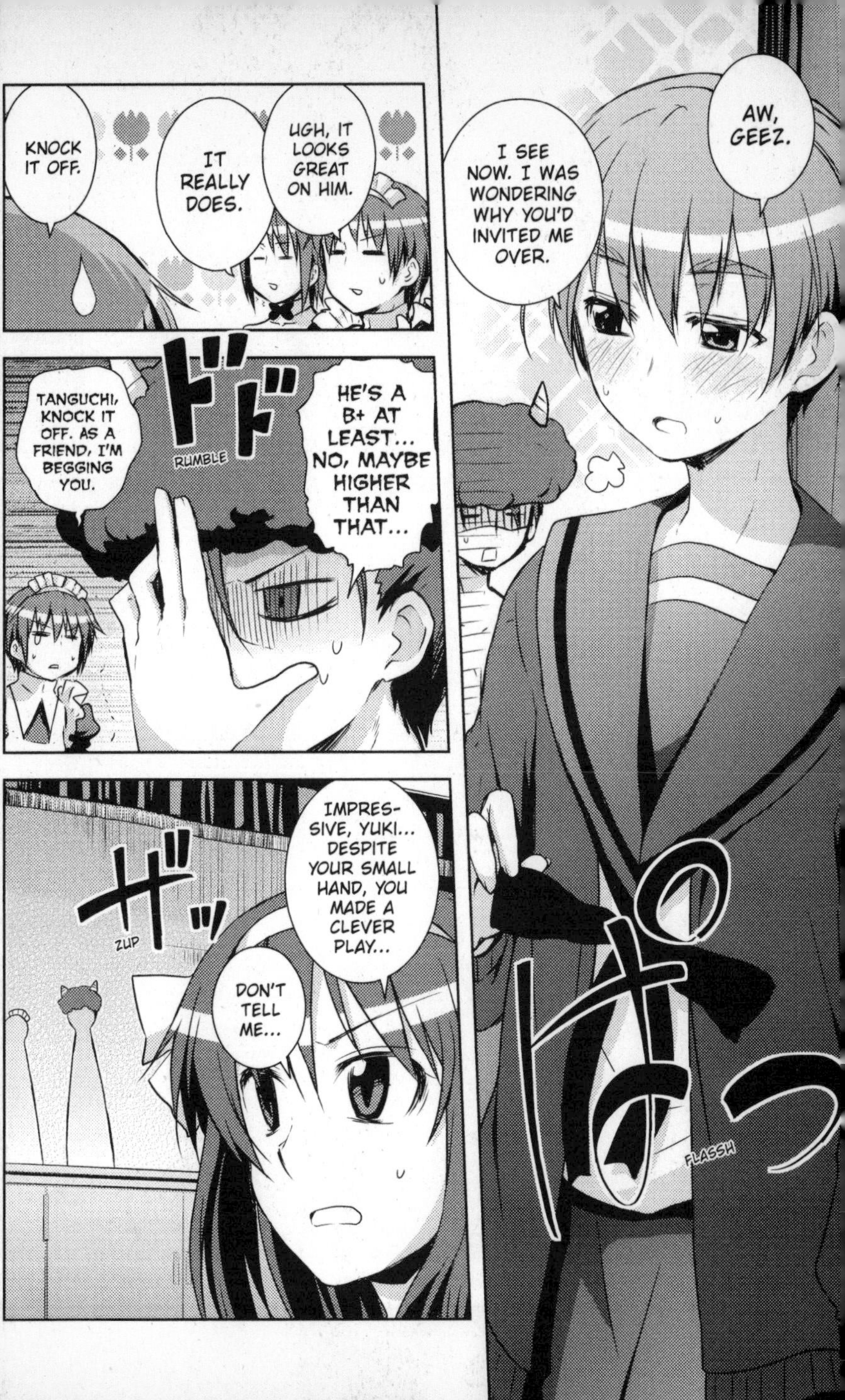
AW, GEEZ.
I SEE NOW. I WAS WONDERING WHY YOU'D INVITED ME OVER.
FLASSH
UGH, IT LOOKS GREAT ON HIM.
IT REALLY DOES.
KNOCK IT OFF.
HE'S A B+ AT LEAST... NO, MAYBE HIGHER THAN THAT...
RUMBLE
TANGUCHI, KNOCK IT OFF. AS A FRIEND, I'M BEGGING YOU.
IMPRES-SIVE, YUKI... DESPITE YOUR SMALL HAND, YOU MADE A CLEVER PLAY...
ZUP
DON'T TELL ME...

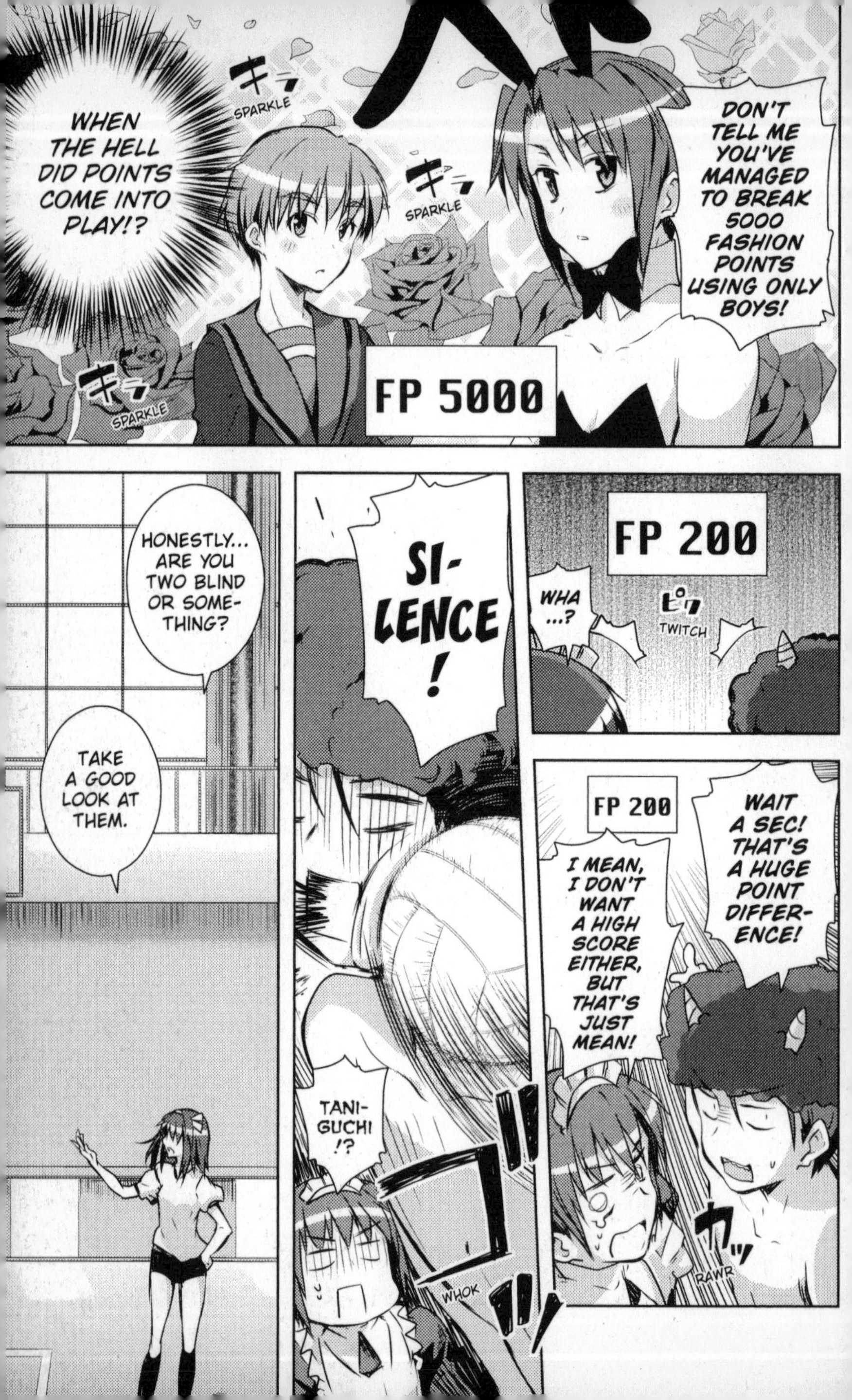
DON'T TELL ME YOU'VE MANAGED TO BREAK 5000 FASHION POINTS USING ONLY BOYS!
FP 5000
SPARKLE
SPARKLE
SPARKLE
WHEN THE HELL DID POINTS COME INTO PLAY!?
FP 200
WHA ...?
TWITCH
FP 200
WAIT A SEC! THAT'S A HUGE POINT DIFFERENCE!
I MEAN, I DON'T WANT A HIGH SCORE EITHER, BUT THAT'S JUST MEAN!
RAWR
SI-LENCE!
TANI-GUCHI!?
WHOK
HONESTLY... ARE YOU TWO BLIND OR SOME-THING?
TAKE A GOOD LOOK AT THEM.

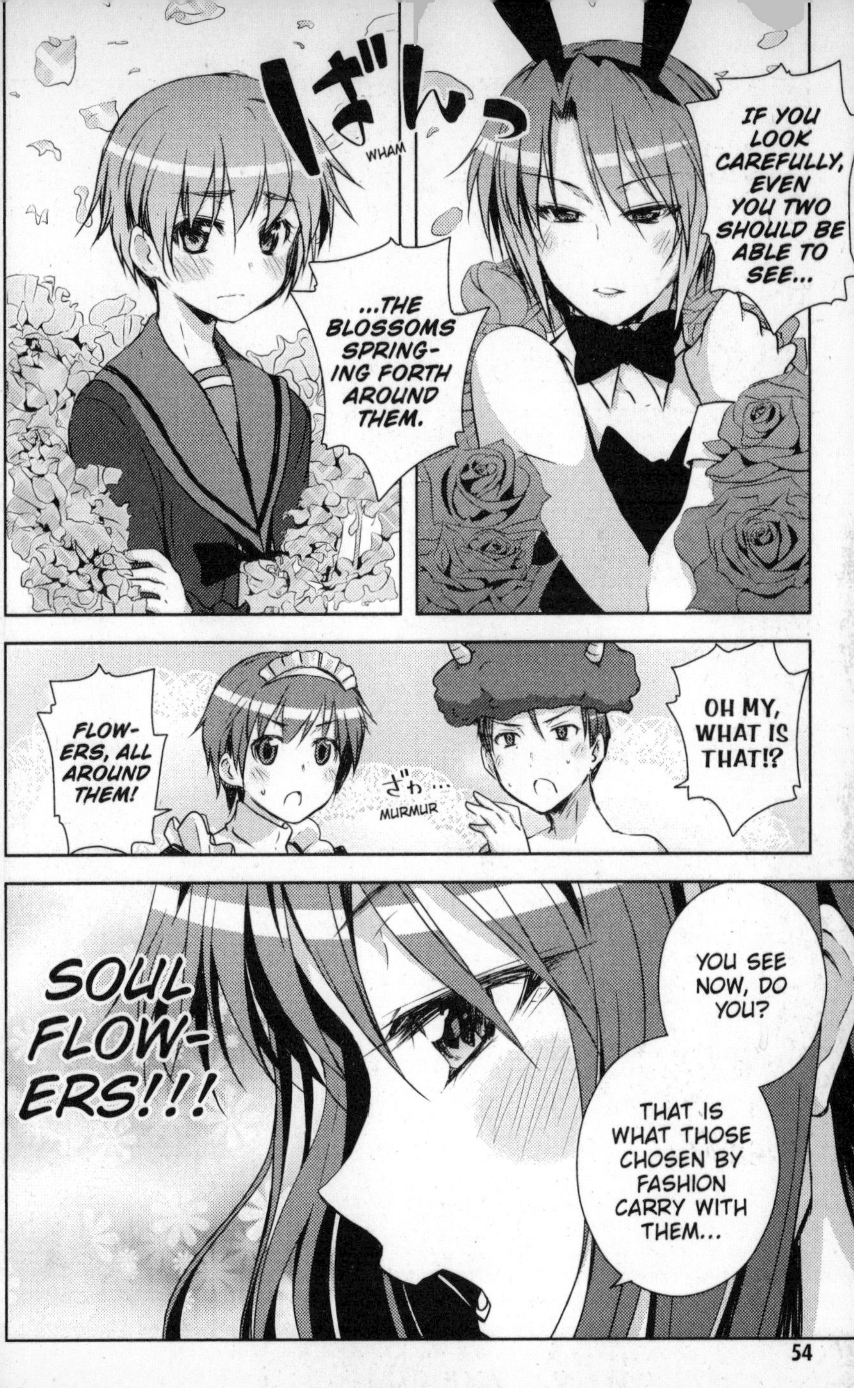
IF YOU LOOK CAREFULLY, EVEN YOU TWO SHOULD BE ABLE TO SEE...
ばんっ
WHAM
...THE BLOSSOMS SPRINGING FORTH AROUND THEM.
OH MY, WHAT IS THAT!?
ざわ…
MURMUR
FLOWERS, ALL AROUND THEM!
YOU SEE NOW, DO YOU?
THAT IS WHAT THOSE CHOSEN BY FASHION CARRY WITH THEM...
SOUL FLOWERS!!!

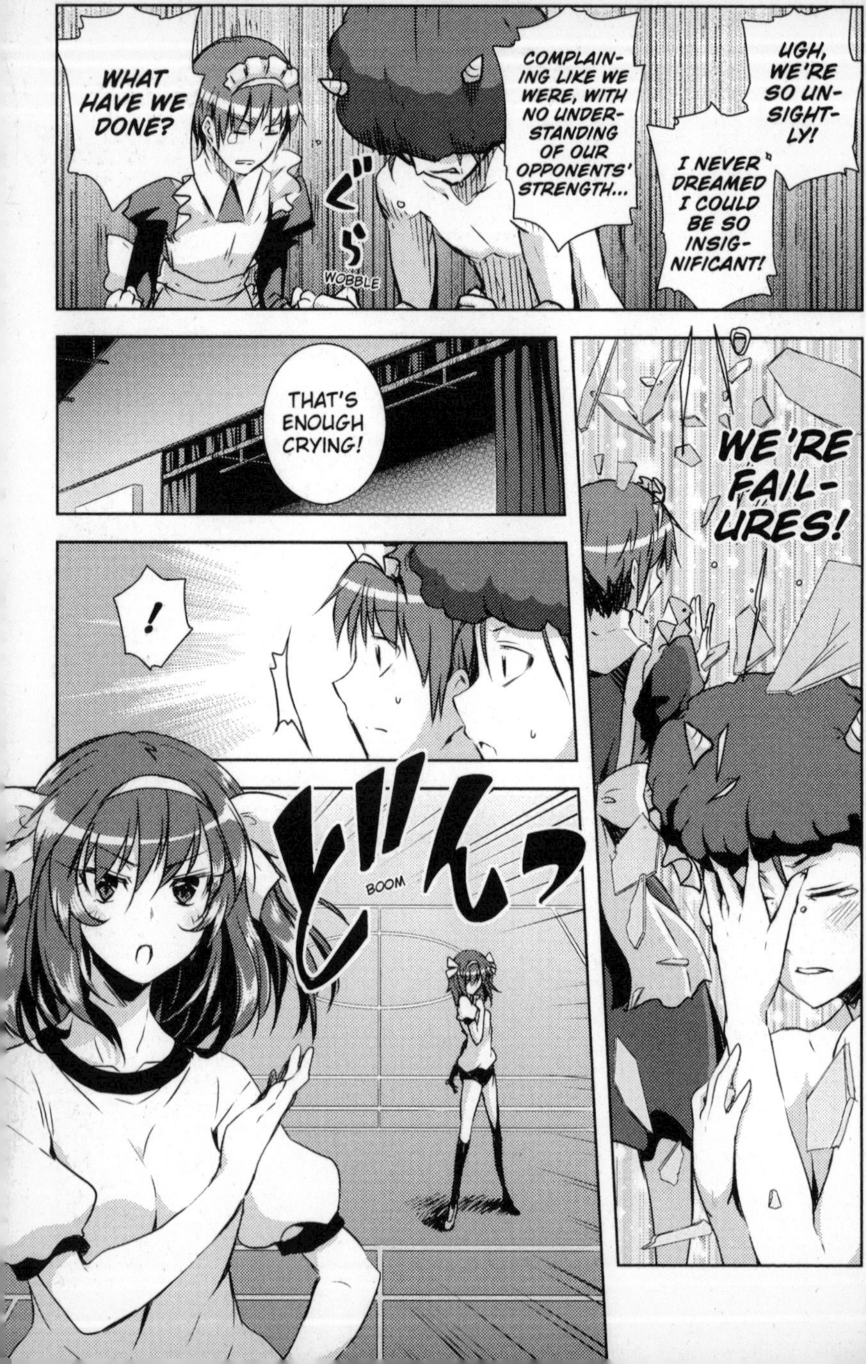
UGH, WE'RE SO UN-SIGHT-LY!
I NEVER DREAMED I COULD BE SO INSIG-NIFICANT!
COMPLAIN-ING LIKE WE WERE, WITH NO UNDER-STANDING OF OUR OPPONENTS' STRENGTH...
WOBBLE
WHAT HAVE WE DONE?
WE'RE FAIL-URES!
THAT'S ENOUGH CRYING!
!
BOOM

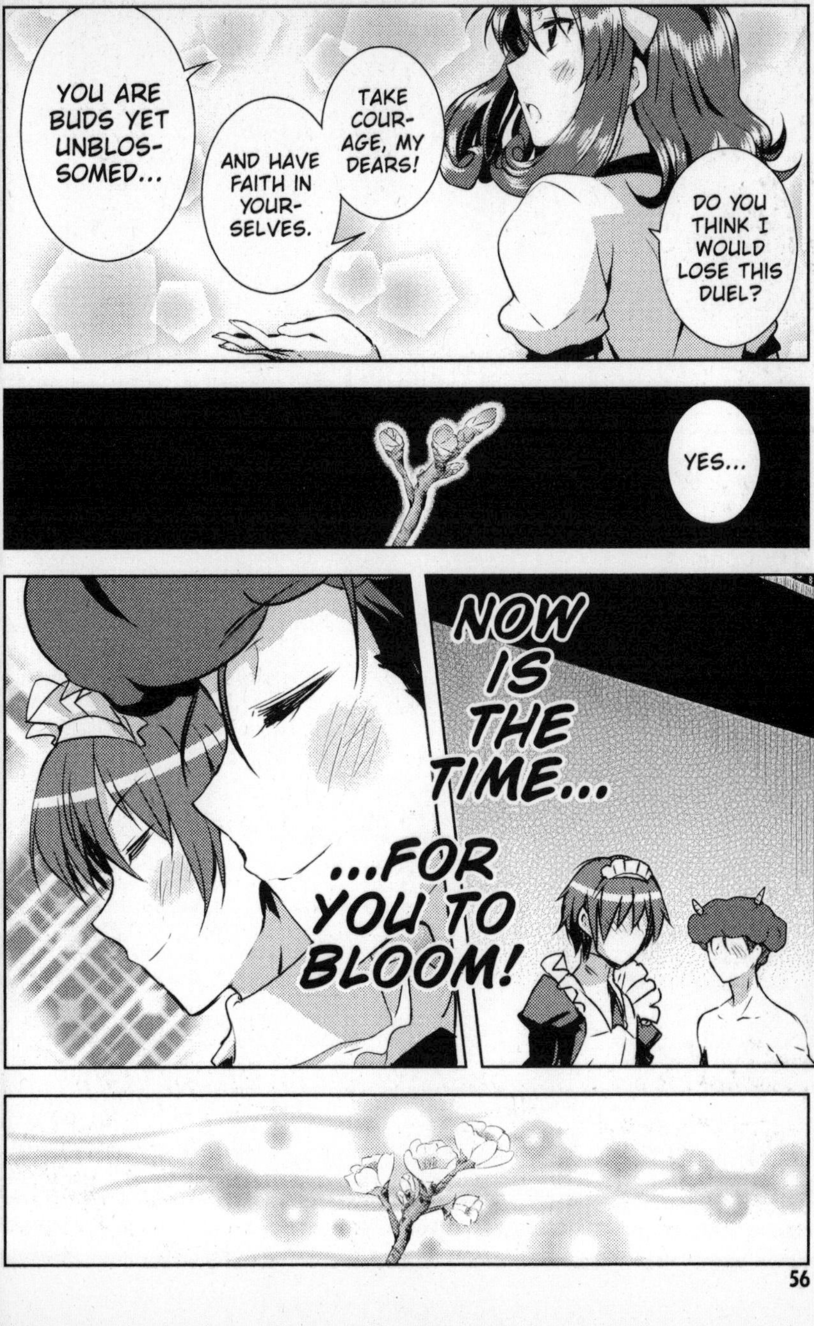
DO YOU THINK I WOULD LOSE THIS DUEL?
TAKE COURAGE, MY DEARS!
AND HAVE FAITH IN YOURSELVES.
YOU ARE BUDS YET UNBLOSSOMED...
YES...
NOW IS THE TIME...
...FOR YOU TO BLOOM!

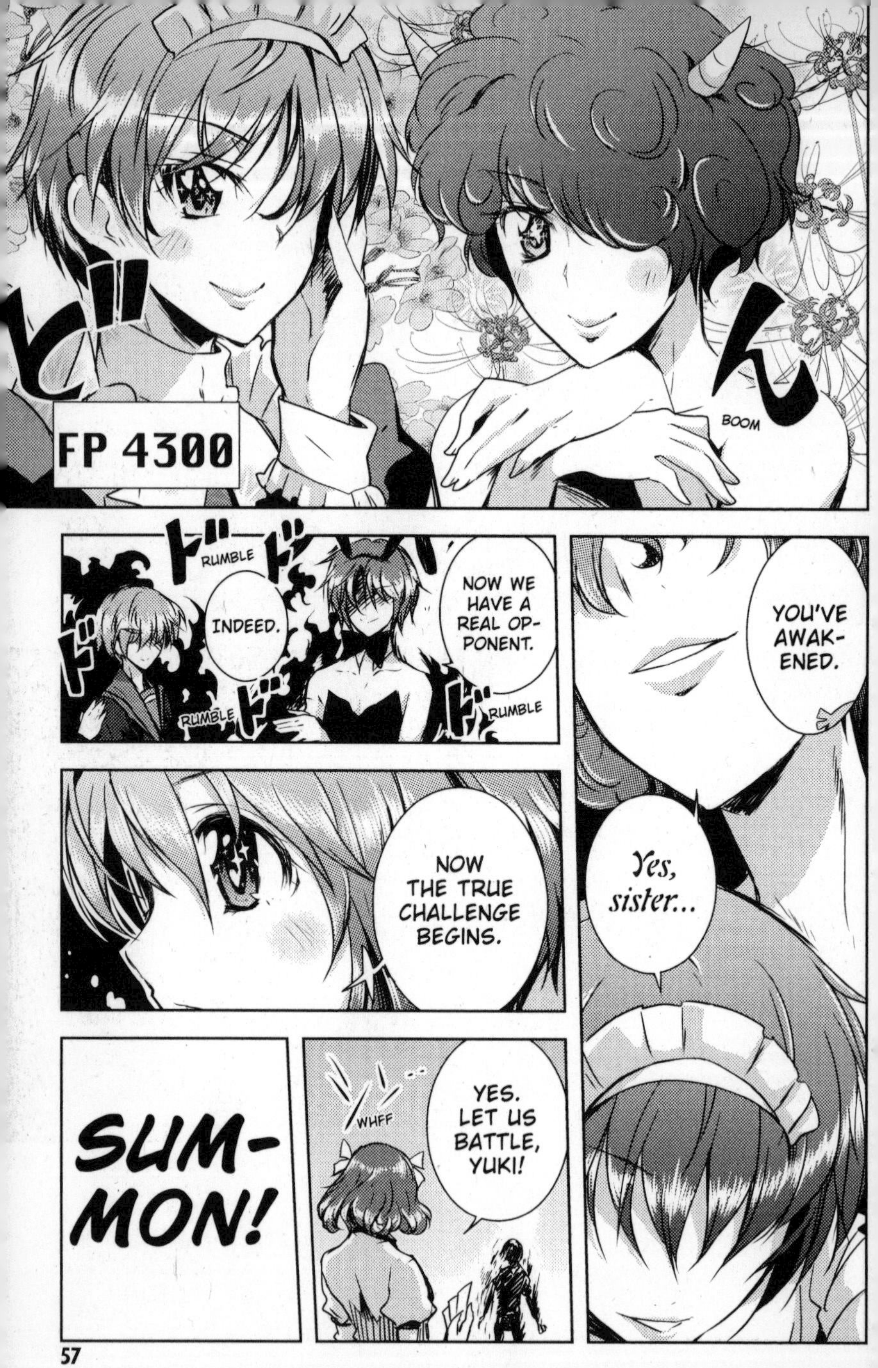
BOOM
FP 4300
YOU'VE AWAKENED.
Yes, sister...
RUMBLE
NOW WE HAVE A REAL OPPONENT.
INDEED.
RUMBLE
RUMBLE
NOW THE TRUE CHALLENGE BEGINS.
YES. LET US BATTLE, YUKI!
WHFF
SUMMON!

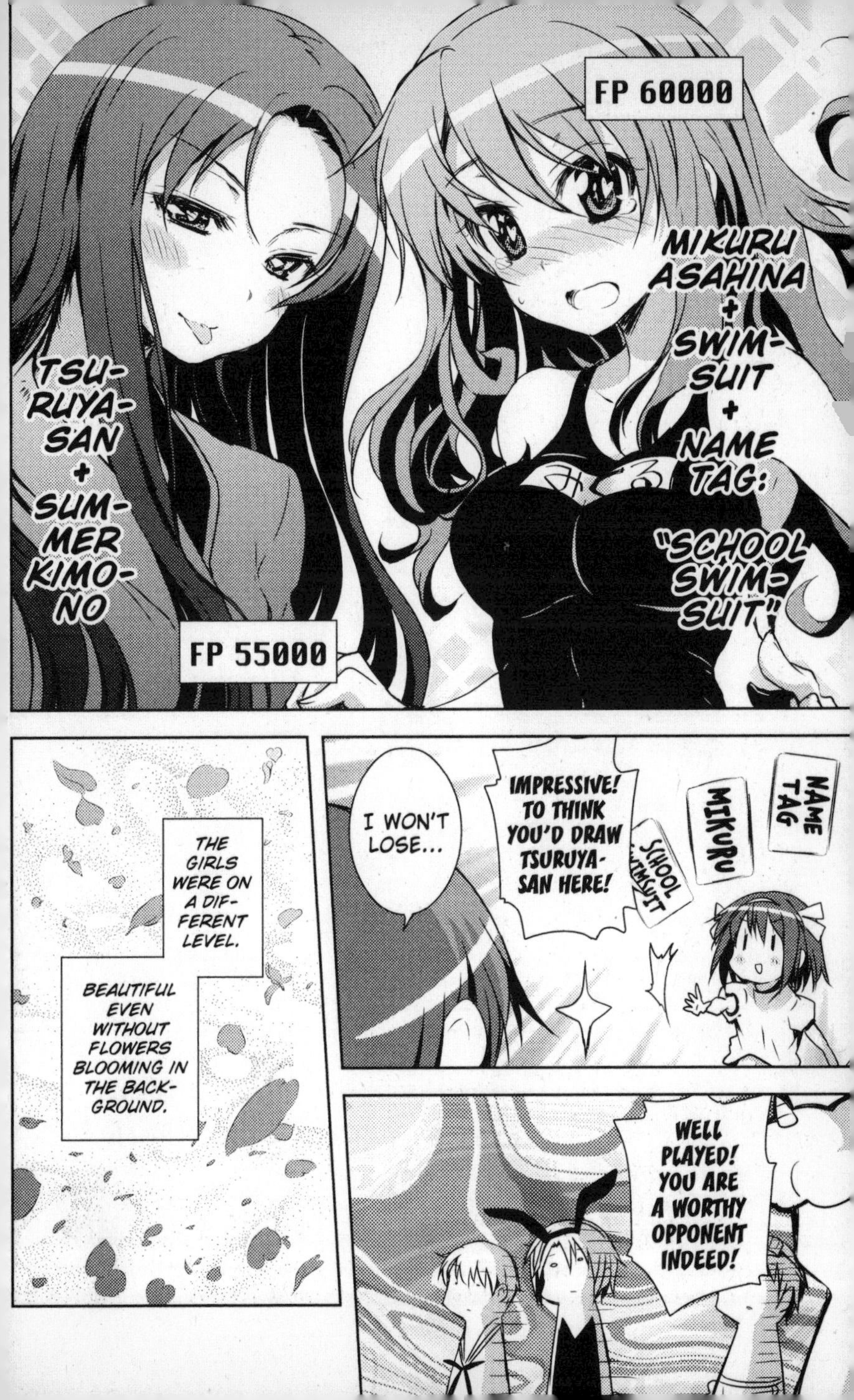
FP 60000
MIKURU ASAHINA + SWIM-SUIT + NAME TAG: "SCHOOL SWIM-SUIT"
TSU-RUYA-SAN + SUM-MER KIMO-NO
FP 55000
NAME TAG
MIKURU
SCHOOL
IMPRESSIVE! TO THINK YOU'D DRAW TSURUYA-SAN HERE!
I WON'T LOSE...
WELL PLAYED! YOU ARE A WORTHY OPPONENT INDEED!
THE GIRLS WERE ON A DIF-FERENT LEVEL.
BEAUTIFUL EVEN WITHOUT FLOWERS BLOOMING IN THE BACK-GROUND.

MAKING CHOCOLATE

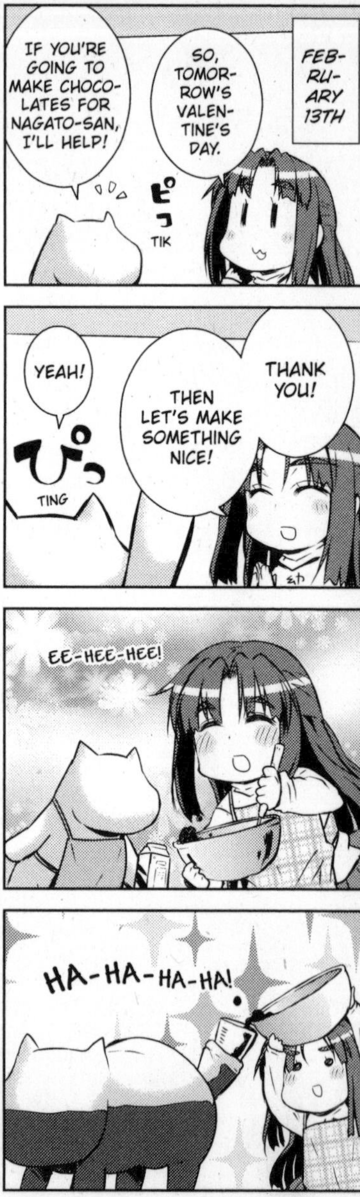
FEB-RU-ARY 13TH
SO, TOMORROW'S VALENTINE'S DAY.
ピコ
TIK
IF YOU'RE GOING TO MAKE CHOCOLATES FOR NAGATO-SAN, I'LL HELP!
THANK YOU!
THEN LET'S MAKE SOMETHING NICE!
YEAH!
TING
EE-HEE-HEE!
HA-HA-HA-HA!

MOLD

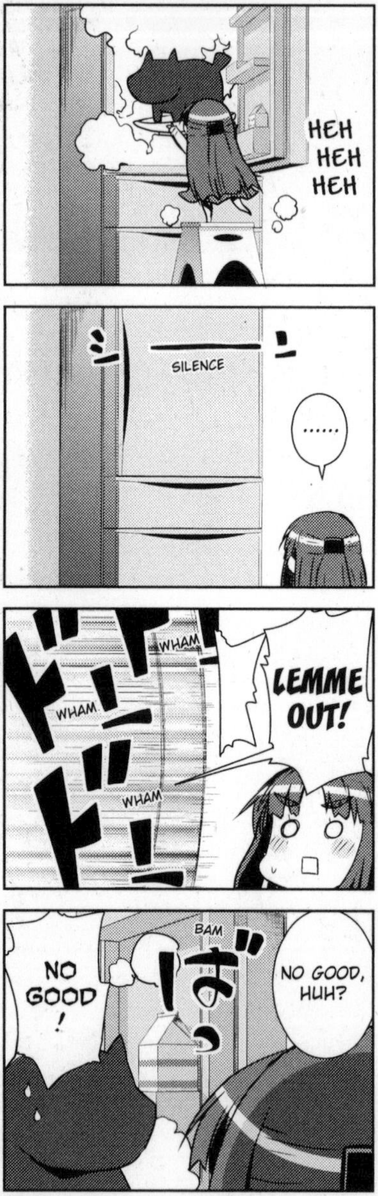
HEH HEH HEH
SILENCE
....
LEMME OUT!
WHAM
WHAM
WHAM
NO GOOD, HUH?
BAM
NO GOOD!

•Achakura-san •It's nice that she wants to make chocolates for Nagato, but... really?

•Kimidori-san •It's easy to forget that he's actually a balloon animal, but that's what he is. Yup.

KIMIDORI-SAN'S PROBLEM

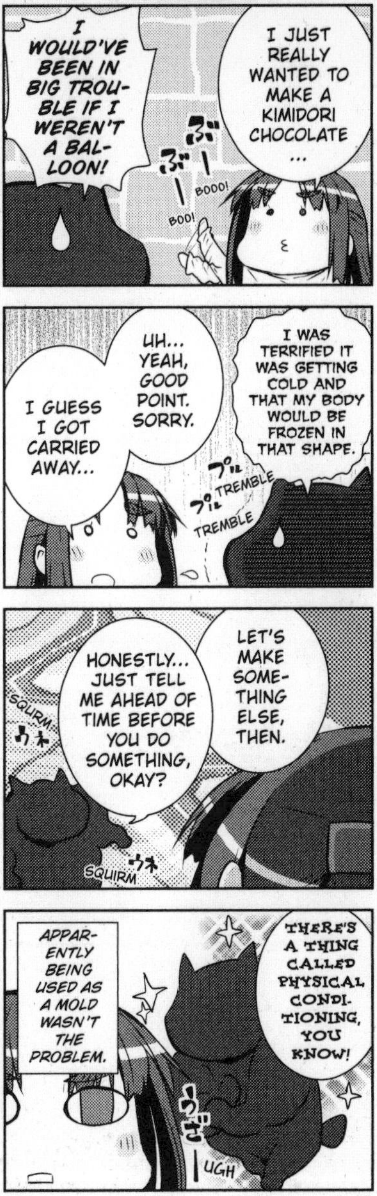
I JUST REALLY WANTED TO MAKE A KIMIDORI CHOCOLATE ...
ぶー BOOO!
ぶー BOO!
I WOULD'VE BEEN IN BIG TROU-BLE IF I WEREN'T A BAL-LOON!
I WAS TERRIFIED IT WAS GETTING COLD AND THAT MY BODY WOULD BE FROZEN IN THAT SHAPE.
プル TREMBLE
プル TREMBLE
UH... YEAH, GOOD POINT. SORRY.
I GUESS I GOT CARRIED AWAY...
LET'S MAKE SOME-THING ELSE, THEN.
HONESTLY... JUST TELL ME AHEAD OF TIME BEFORE YOU DO SOMETHING, OKAY?
ウネ SQUIRM
ウネ SQUIRM
THERE'S A THING CALLED PHYSICAL CONDI-TIONING, YOU KNOW!
うぎー UGH
APPAR-ENTLY BEING USED AS A MOLD WASN'T THE PROBLEM.

DOUBT

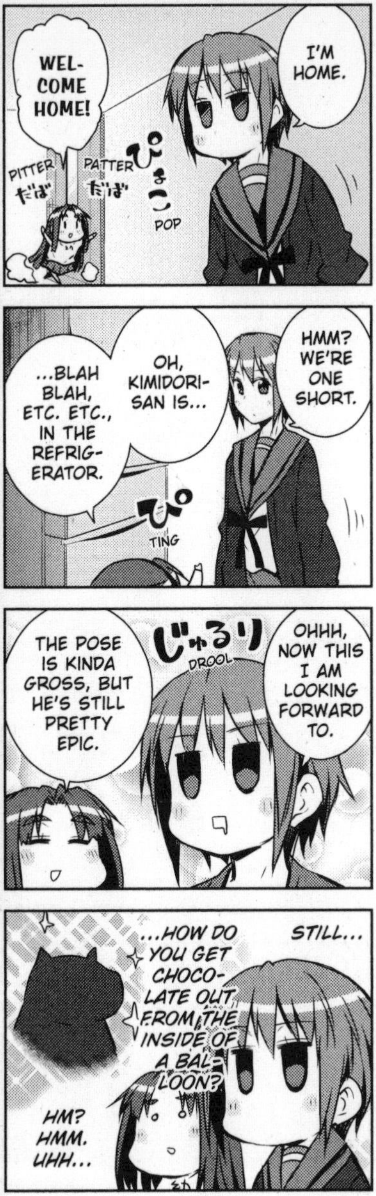
I'M HOME.
ぴょこ POP
WEL-COME HOME!
PATTER だば
PITTER だば
HMM? WE'RE ONE SHORT.
OH, KIMIDORI-SAN IS...
...BLAH BLAH, ETC. ETC., IN THE REFRIG-ERATOR.
ぴ TING
OHHH, NOW THIS I AM LOOKING FORWARD TO.
じゅるり DROOL
THE POSE IS KINDA GROSS, BUT HE'S STILL PRETTY EPIC.
STILL...
...HOW DO YOU GET CHOCO-LATE OUT FROM THE INSIDE OF A BAL-LOON?
HM? HMM. UHH...

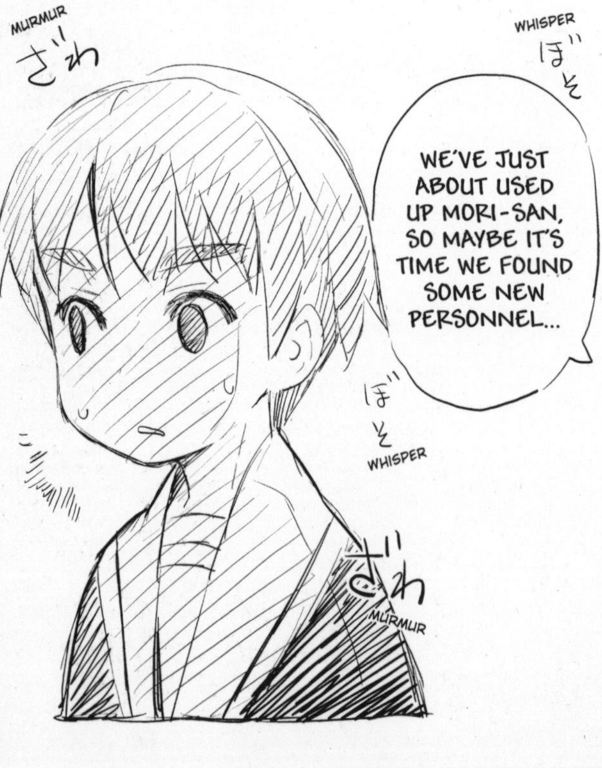
WHISPER
ぼそ
WE'VE JUST ABOUT USED UP MORI-SAN, SO MAYBE IT'S TIME WE FOUND SOME NEW PERSONNEL...
MURMUR
ざわ
ぼそ
WHISPER
ざわ
MURMUR

FOR ALL
THE DETAILS,
PLEASE READ
THE ORIGINAL
MELANCHOLY
OF HARUHI
SUZUMIYA!

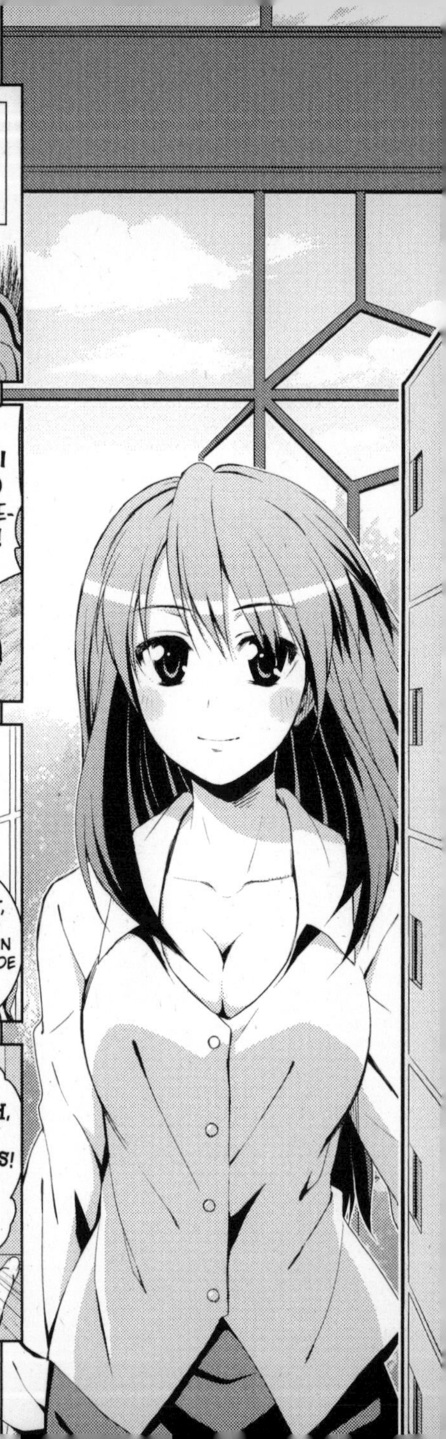

TODAY'S PROTAGONIST

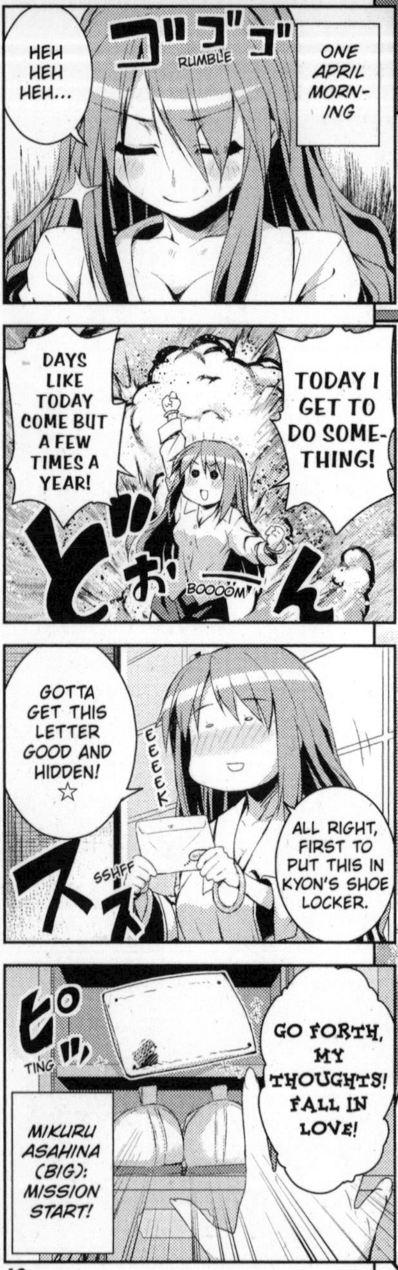
ONE APRIL MORNING
RUMBLE
HEH HEH HEH...
TODAY I GET TO DO SOMETHING!
DAYS LIKE TODAY COME BUT A FEW TIMES A YEAR!
BOOOOM
EEEEK
ALL RIGHT, FIRST TO PUT THIS IN KYON'S SHOE LOCKER.
GOTTA GET THIS LETTER GOOD AND HIDDEN! ☆
SSHFF
GO FORTH, MY THOUGHTS! FALL IN LOVE!
TING
MIKURU ASAHINA (BIG): MISSION START!

OBSTACLES

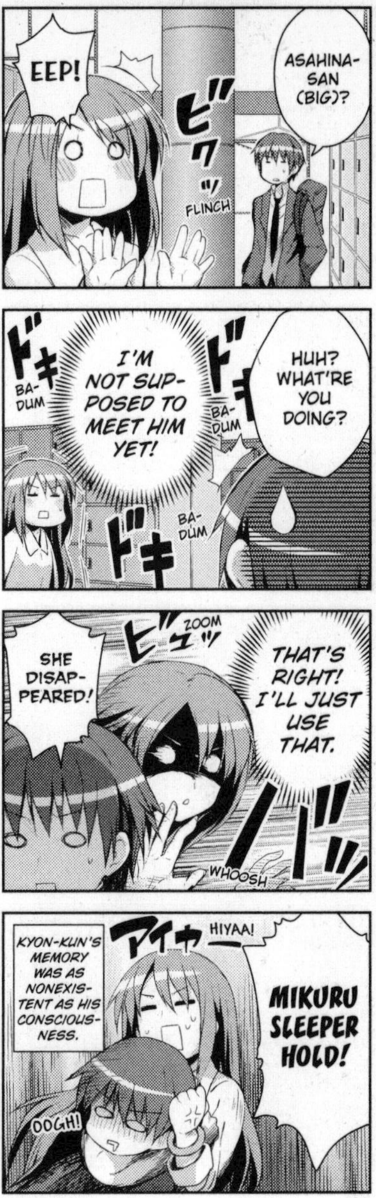
ASAHINA-SAN (BIG)?
EEP!
FLINCH
HUH? WHAT'RE YOU DOING?
BA-DUM
I'M NOT SUP-POSED TO MEET HIM YET!
BA-DUM
BA-DUM
THAT'S RIGHT! I'LL JUST USE THAT.
ZOOM
SHE DISAP-PEARED!
WHOOSH
MIKURU SLEEPER HOLD!
HIYAA!
KYON-KUN'S MEMORY WAS AS NONEXIS-TENT AS HIS CONSCIOUS-NESS.
DOGH!

WITNESS A

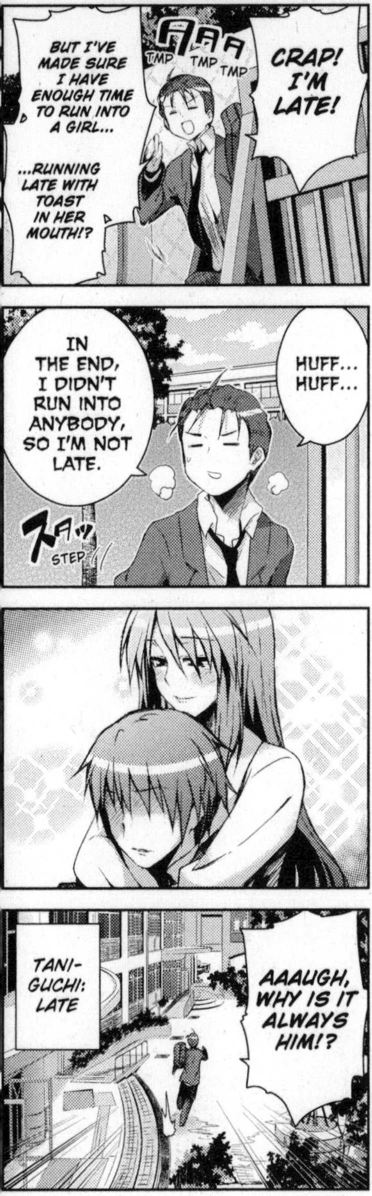
CRAP! I'M LATE!
TMP TMP TMP
BUT I'VE MADE SURE I HAVE ENOUGH TIME TO RUN INTO A GIRL...
...RUNNING LATE WITH TOAST IN HER MOUTH!?
HUFF... HUFF...
IN THE END, I DIDN'T RUN INTO ANYBODY, SO I'M NOT LATE.
STEP
AAAUGH, WHY IS IT ALWAYS HIM!?
TANI-GUCHI: LATE

•Asahina-san (Big) •An adult version of Asahina, come from the future. A bit eccentric.

•Kyon •The protagonist of this story, more or less. Gets caught up in the activities of A the Elder.

•Taniguchi •The more unfortunate of Kyon's friends. Leaves immediately when not wanted, the poor guy.

EXCUSES

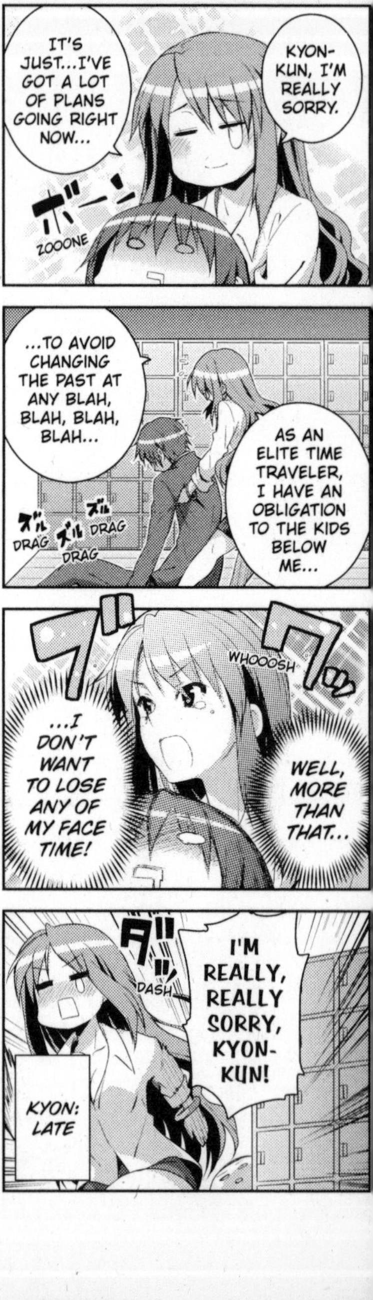
KYON-KUN, I'M REALLY SORRY.
IT'S JUST...I'VE GOT A LOT OF PLANS GOING RIGHT NOW...
ZOOONE
AS AN ELITE TIME TRAVELER, I HAVE AN OBLIGATION TO THE KIDS BELOW ME...
...TO AVOID CHANGING THE PAST AT ANY BLAH, BLAH, BLAH, BLAH...
DRAG
DRAG
DRAG
WHOOOSH
WELL, MORE THAN THAT...
...I DON'T WANT TO LOSE ANY OF MY FACE TIME!
DASH
I'M REALLY, REALLY SORRY, KYON-KUN!
KYON: LATE

HURRY

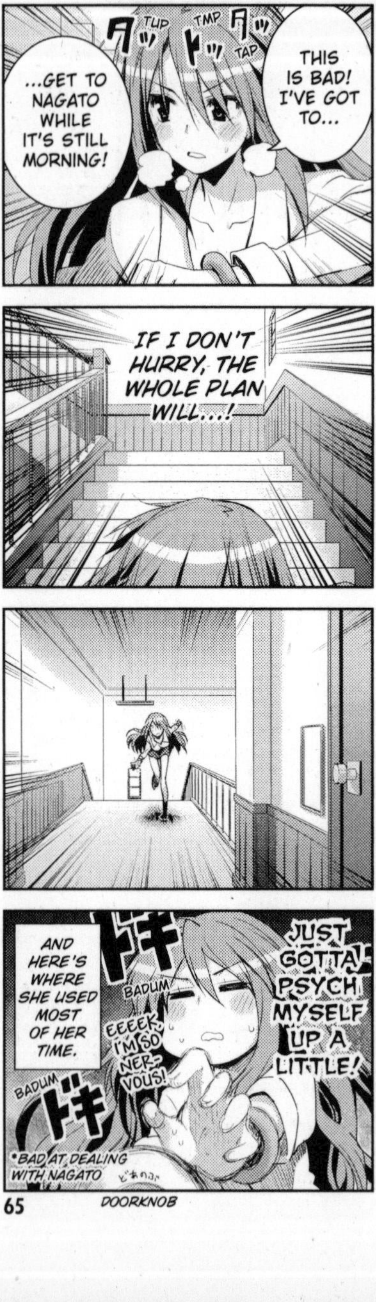
THIS IS BAD! I'VE GOT TO...
TAP
TMP
TUP
...GET TO NAGATO WHILE IT'S STILL MORNING!
IF I DON'T HURRY, THE WHOLE PLAN WILL...!
JUST GOTTA PSYCH MYSELF UP A LITTLE!
BADUM
EEEEK, I'M SO NER-VOUS!
AND HERE'S WHERE SHE USED MOST OF HER TIME.
BADUM
*BAD AT DEALING WITH NAGATO
どあのぶ

DOORKNOB

DIFFICULT PERSON

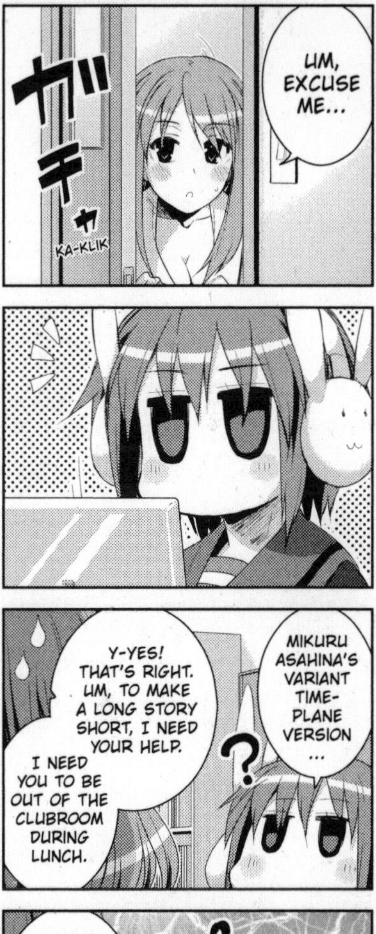
UM, EXCUSE ME...
KA-KLIK
MIKURU ASAHINA'S VARIANT TIME-PLANE VERSION ...
Y-YES! THAT'S RIGHT. UM, TO MAKE A LONG STORY SHORT, I NEED YOUR HELP.
I NEED YOU TO BE OUT OF THE CLUBROOM DURING LUNCH.
SHOCK
HUH? SHE SEEMS MORE SHOCKED THAN I WOULD'VE GUESSED!

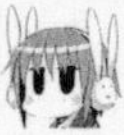

•Nagato •Alien. Apparently the clubroom is the best place for her to settle down and play video games.

COMPROMISE

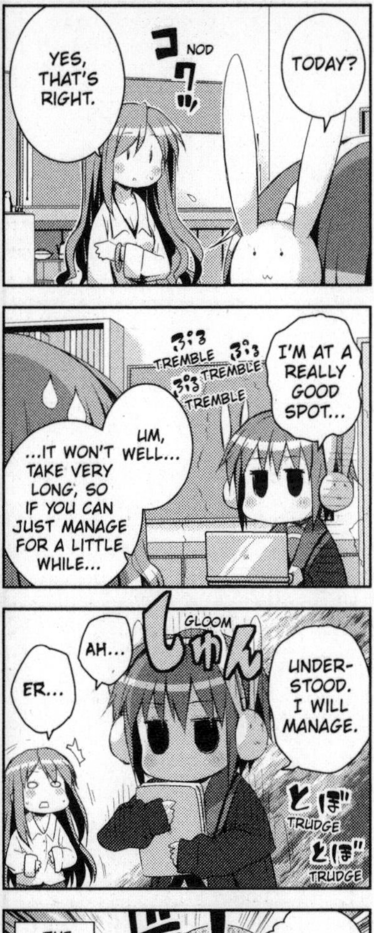
TODAY?
NOD
YES, THAT'S RIGHT.
I'M AT A REALLY GOOD SPOT...
TREMBLE TREMBLE TREMBLE
UM, WELL...
...IT WON'T TAKE VERY LONG, SO IF YOU CAN JUST MANAGE FOR A LITTLE WHILE...
UNDERSTOOD. I WILL MANAGE.
GLOOM
TRUDGE
TRUDGE
AH...
ER...
NAGATO-SAN, PLEASE STAY!
BOOM
THE PLAN CRUMBLED IMMEDIATELY.
OHHH.

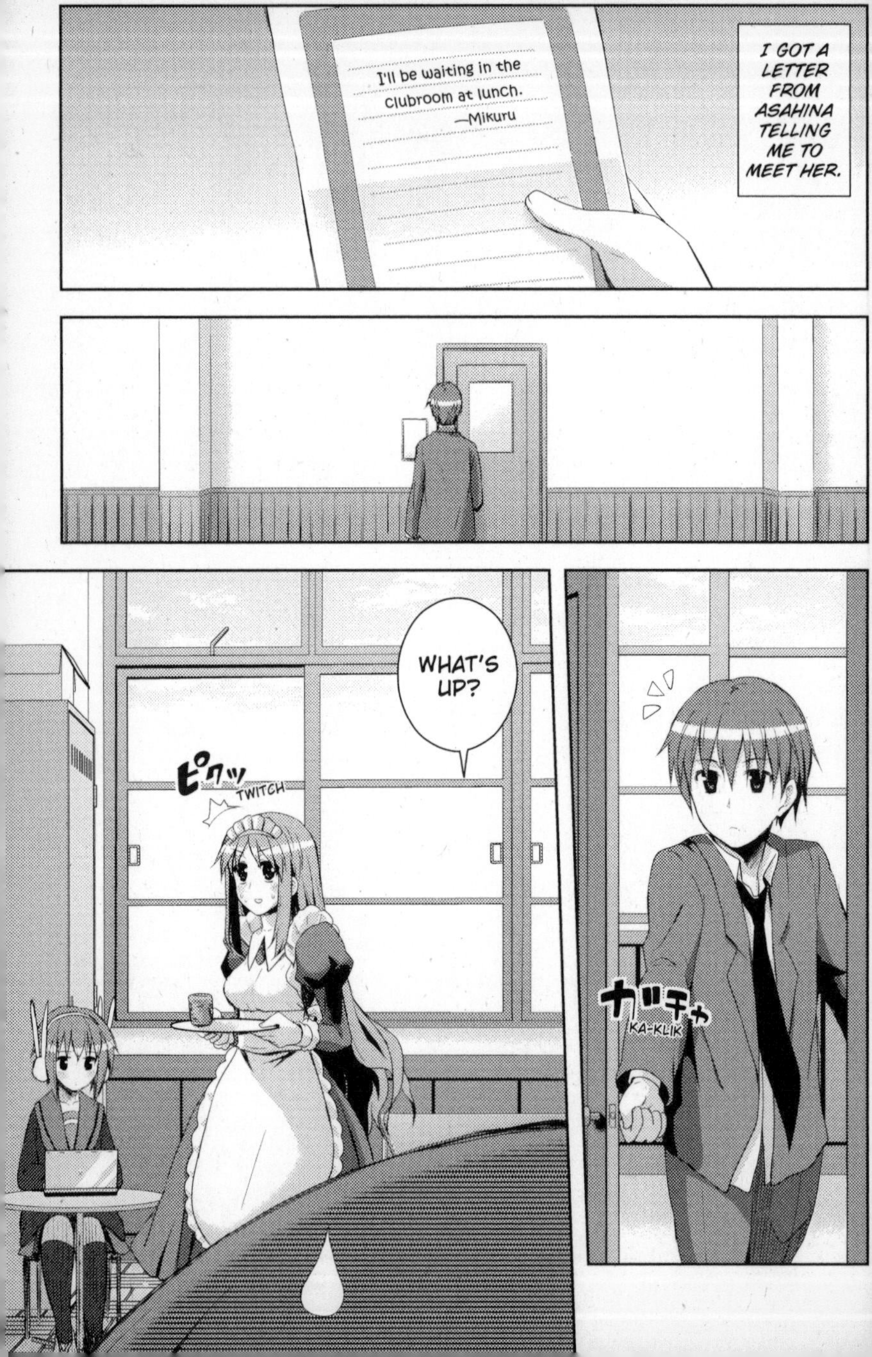

I GOT A LETTER FROM ASAHINA TELLING ME TO MEET HER.
I'll be waiting in the clubroom at lunch.
—Mikuru
ガチャ
KA-KLIK
WHAT'S UP?
ピクッ
TWITCH

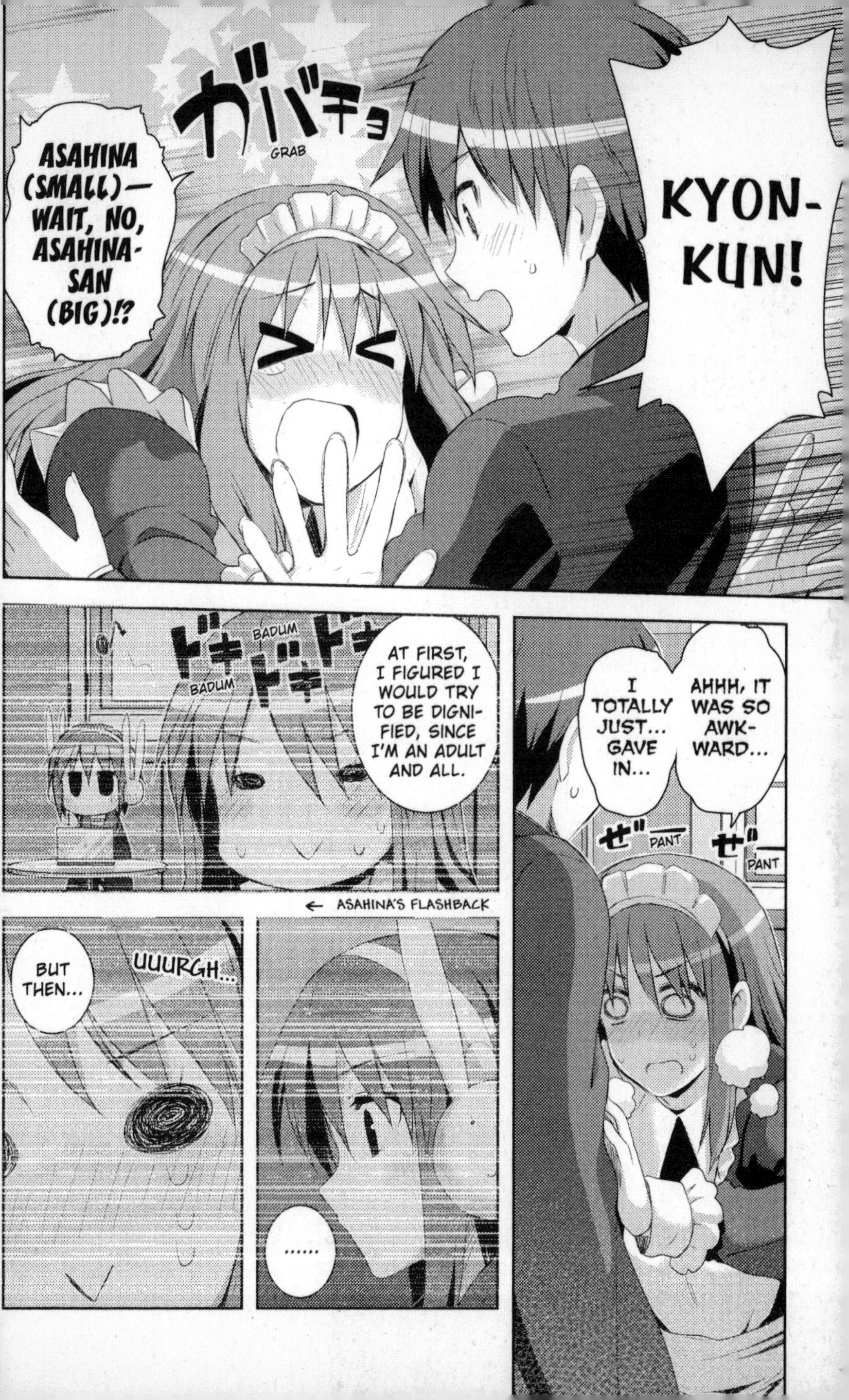
KYON-KUN!
ガバチョ
GRAB
ASAHINA (SMALL)— WAIT, NO, ASAHINA-SAN (BIG)!?
AHHH, IT WAS SO AWKWARD...
I TOTALLY JUST... GAVE IN...
ゼー PANT
ゼー PANT
AT FIRST, I FIGURED I WOULD TRY TO BE DIGNIFIED, SINCE I'M AN ADULT AND ALL.
ドキドキ BADUM
ドキドキ BADUM
← ASAHINA'S FLASHBACK
......
BUT THEN...
UUURGH...

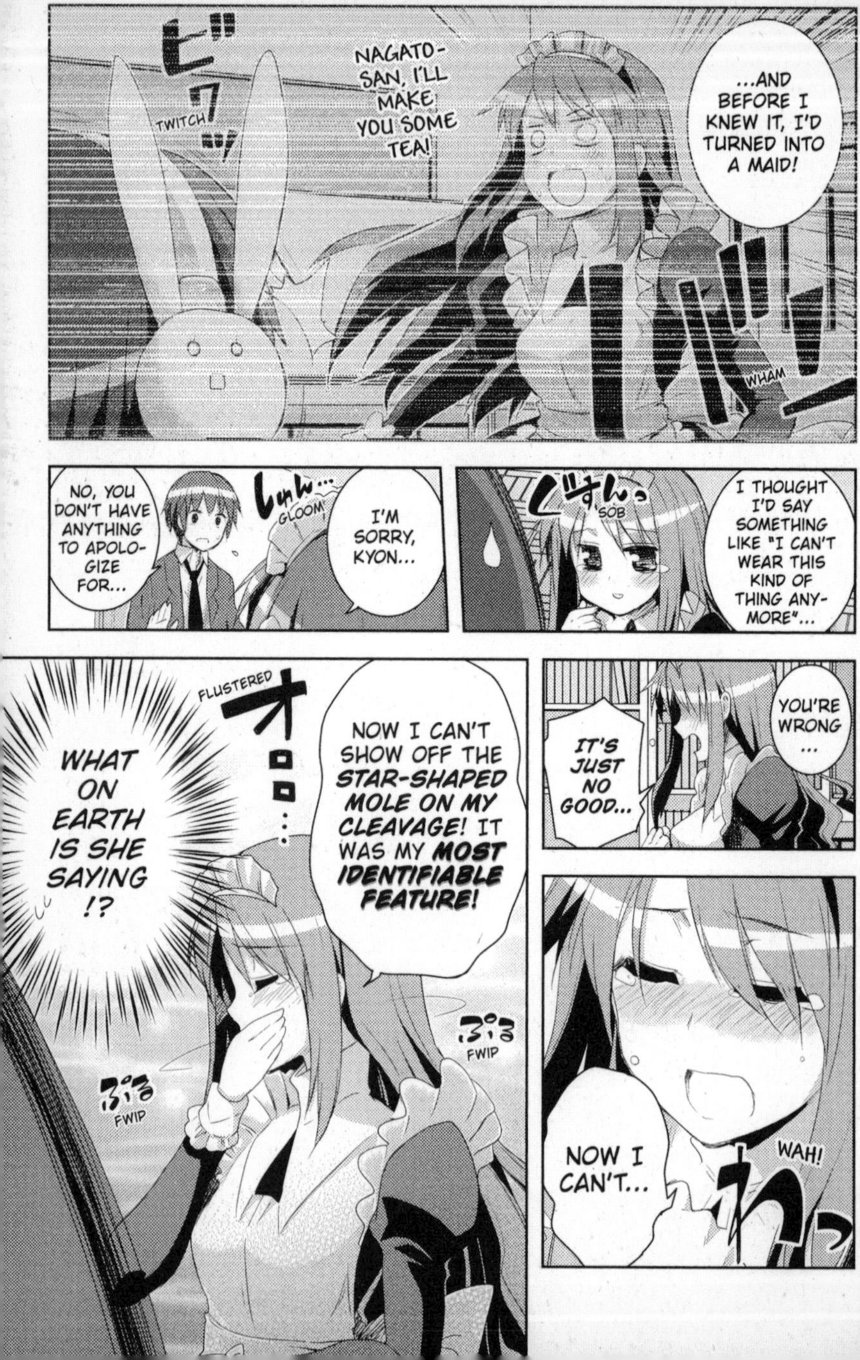
...AND BEFORE I KNEW IT, I'D TURNED INTO A MAID!
WHAM
NAGATO-SAN, I'LL MAKE YOU SOME TEA!
TWITCH
I THOUGHT I'D SAY SOMETHING LIKE "I CAN'T WEAR THIS KIND OF THING ANYMORE"...
SOB
I'M SORRY, KYON...
GLOOM
NO, YOU DON'T HAVE ANYTHING TO APOLOGIZE FOR...
YOU'RE WRONG...
IT'S JUST NO GOOD...
WAH!
NOW I CAN'T...
NOW I CAN'T SHOW OFF THE **STAR-SHAPED MOLE ON MY CLEAVAGE!** IT WAS MY **MOST IDENTIFIABLE FEATURE!**
FLUSTERED
FWIP
WHAT ON EARTH IS SHE SAYING!?
FWIP

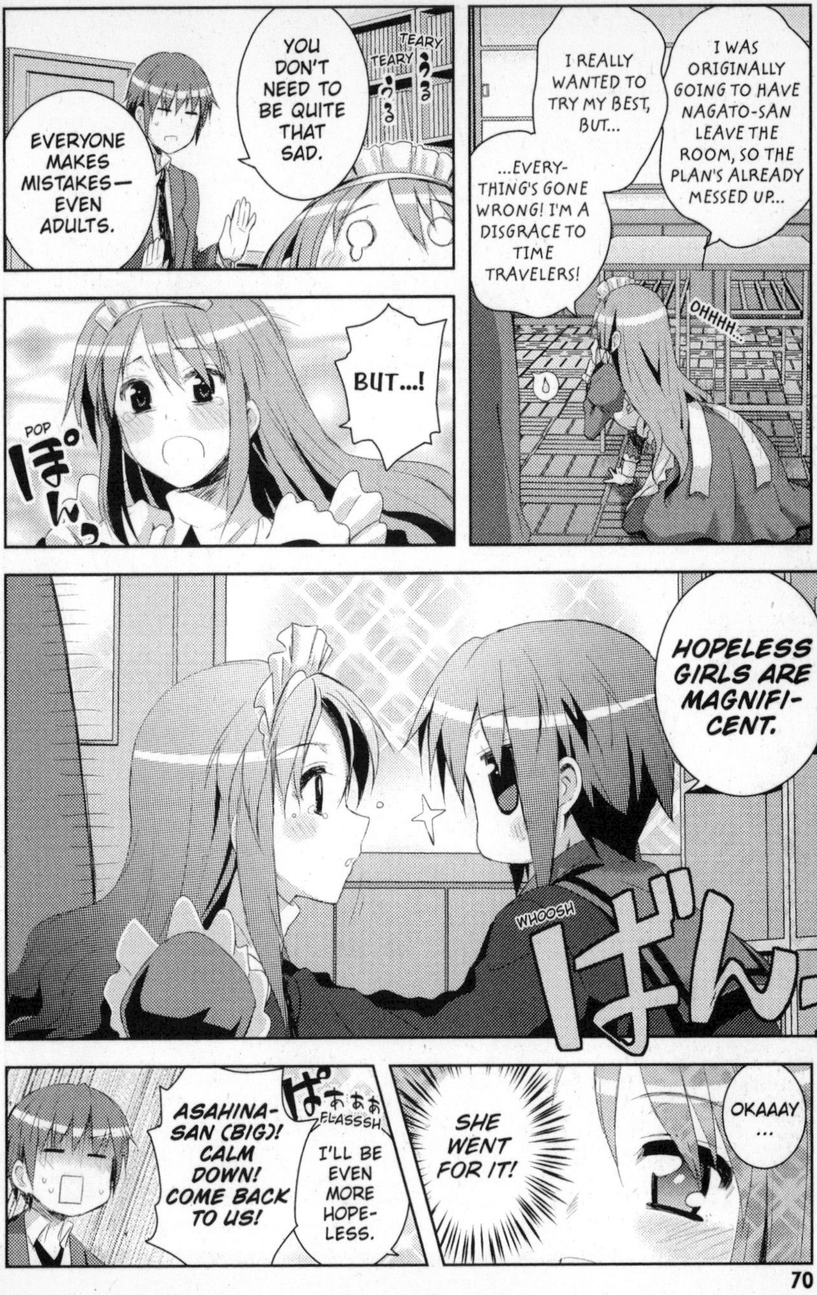
I WAS ORIGINALLY GOING TO HAVE NAGATO-SAN LEAVE THE ROOM, SO THE PLAN'S ALREADY MESSED UP...
I REALLY WANTED TO TRY MY BEST, BUT...
...EVERYTHING'S GONE WRONG! I'M A DISGRACE TO TIME TRAVELERS!
OHHHH...
TEARY うる
TEARY うる
YOU DON'T NEED TO BE QUITE THAT SAD.
EVERYONE MAKES MISTAKES— EVEN ADULTS.
BUT...!
POP ぽんっ
HOPELESS GIRLS ARE MAGNIFICENT.
WHOOSH ばんっ
OKAAAY...
SHE WENT FOR IT!
ぱあああ FLASSSH
I'LL BE EVEN MORE HOPELESS.
ASAHINA-SAN (BIG)! CALM DOWN! COME BACK TO US!

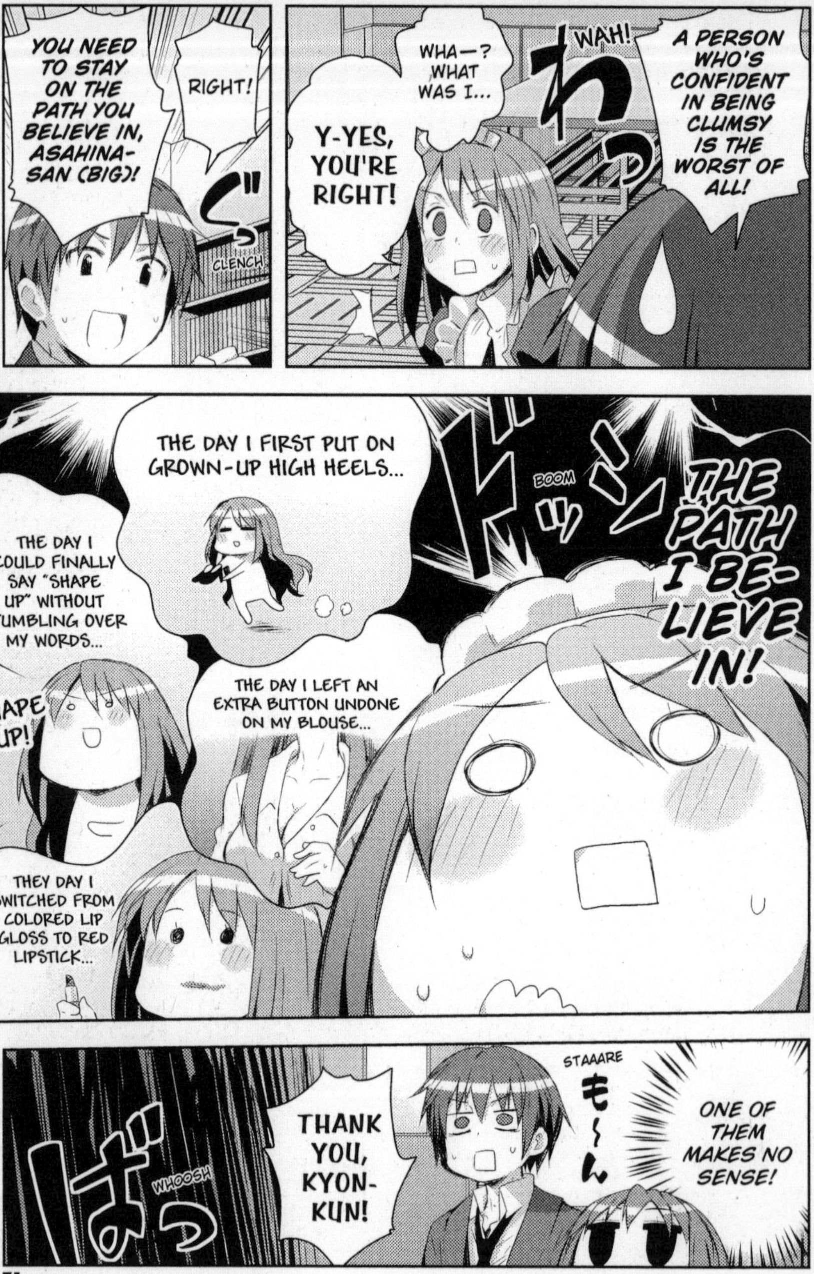
A PERSON WHO'S CONFIDENT IN BEING CLUMSY IS THE WORST OF ALL!
WAH!
WHA—? WHAT WAS I...
Y-YES, YOU'RE RIGHT!
YOU NEED TO STAY ON THE PATH YOU BELIEVE IN, ASAHINA-SAN (BIG)!
RIGHT!
CLENCH
THE PATH I BE-LIEVE IN!
BOOM
THE DAY I FIRST PUT ON GROWN-UP HIGH HEELS...
THE DAY I COULD FINALLY SAY "SHAPE UP" WITHOUT STUMBLING OVER MY WORDS...
SHAPE UP!
THE DAY I LEFT AN EXTRA BUTTON UNDONE ON MY BLOUSE...
THEY DAY I SWITCHED FROM COLORED LIP GLOSS TO RED LIPSTICK...
ONE OF THEM MAKES NO SENSE!
STAAARE
THANK YOU, KYON-KUN!
WHOOSH

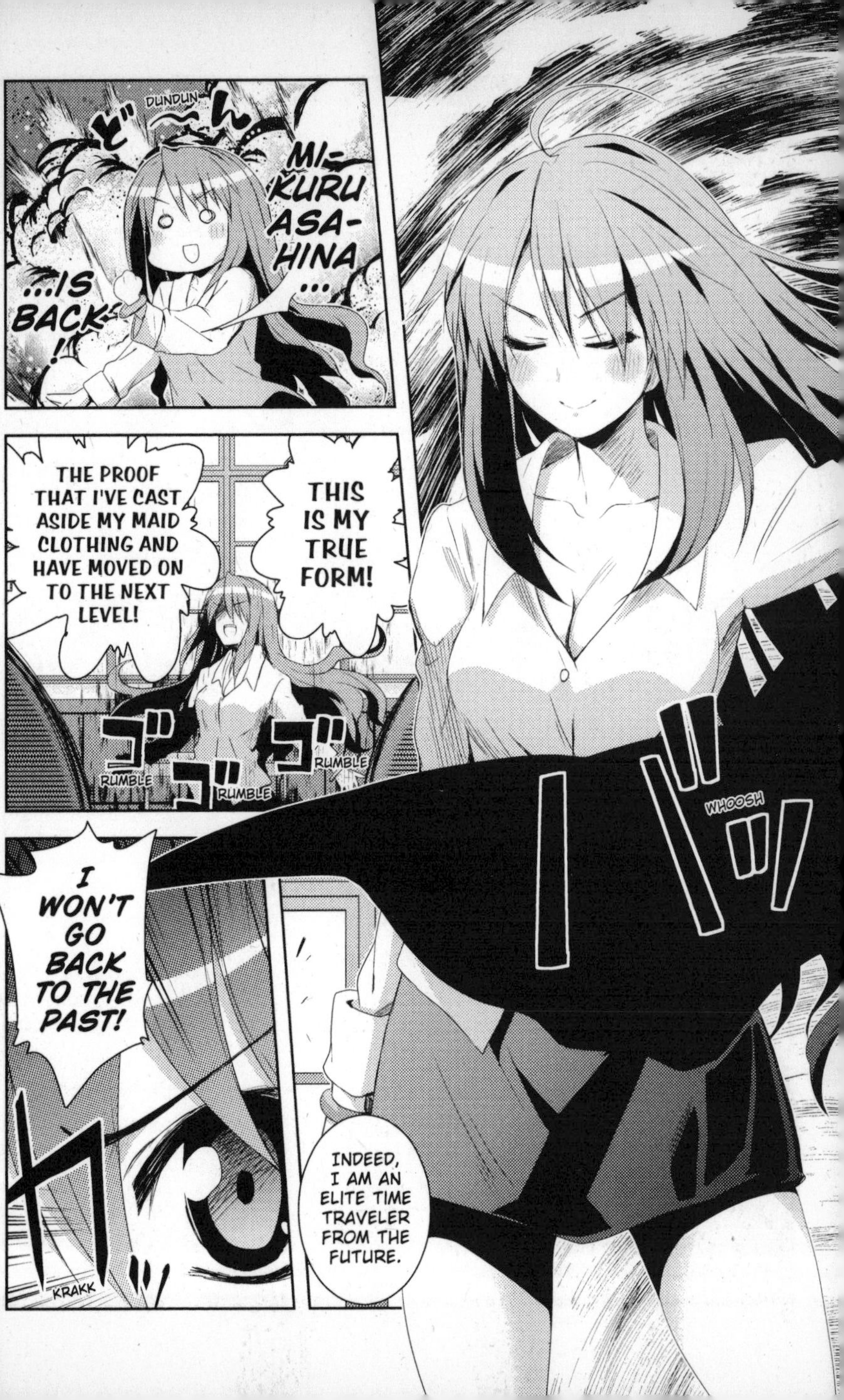
DUNDUN
MI-KURU ASA-HINA...
...IS BACK!!
THIS IS MY TRUE FORM!
THE PROOF THAT I'VE CAST ASIDE MY MAID CLOTHING AND HAVE MOVED ON TO THE NEXT LEVEL!
RUMBLE
RUMBLE
RUMBLE
I WON'T GO BACK TO THE PAST!
KRAKK
WHOOSH
INDEED, I AM AN ELITE TIME TRAVELER FROM THE FUTURE.

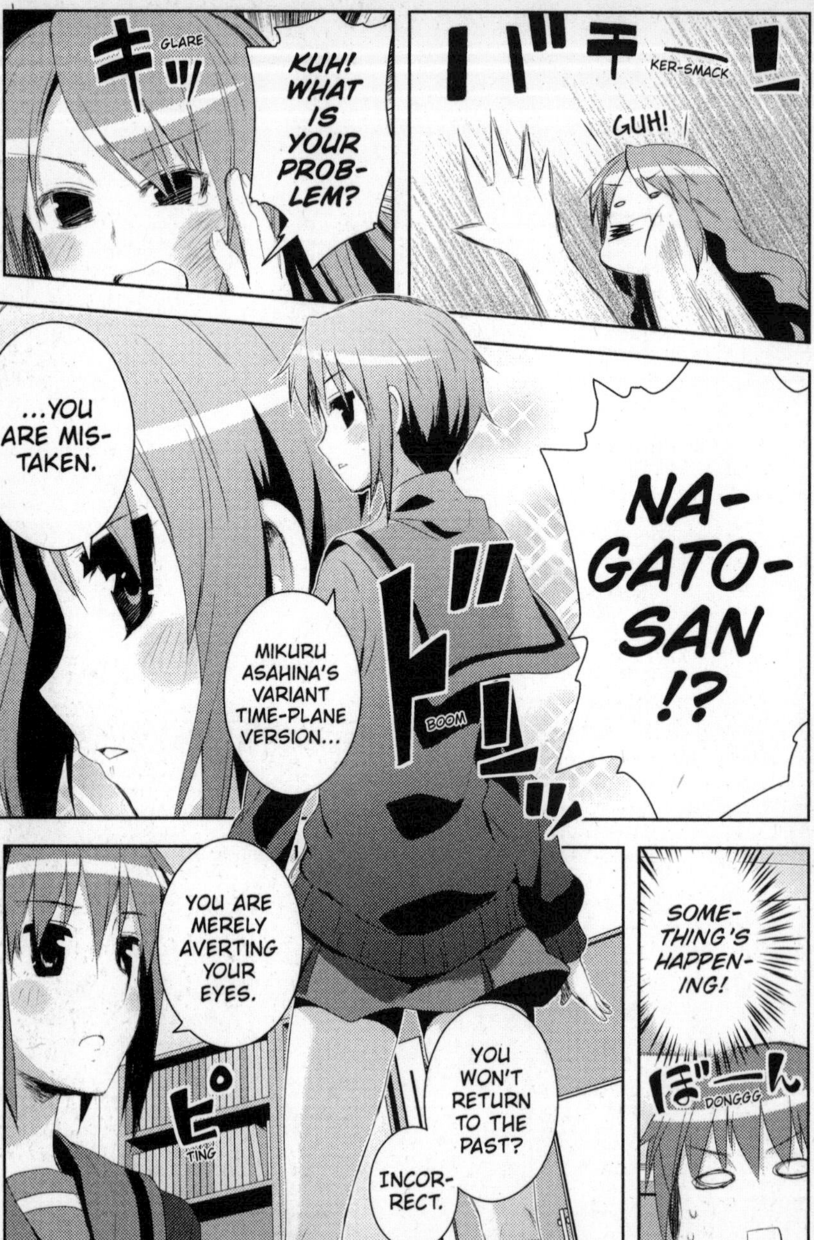
KER-SMACK
GUH!
GLARE
KUH! WHAT IS YOUR PROB-LEM?
NA-GATO-SAN!?
BOOM
MIKURU ASAHINA'S VARIANT TIME-PLANE VERSION...
...YOU ARE MIS-TAKEN.
SOME-THING'S HAPPEN-ING!
DONGGG
YOU WON'T RETURN TO THE PAST?
INCOR-RECT.
YOU ARE MERELY AVERTING YOUR EYES.
TING

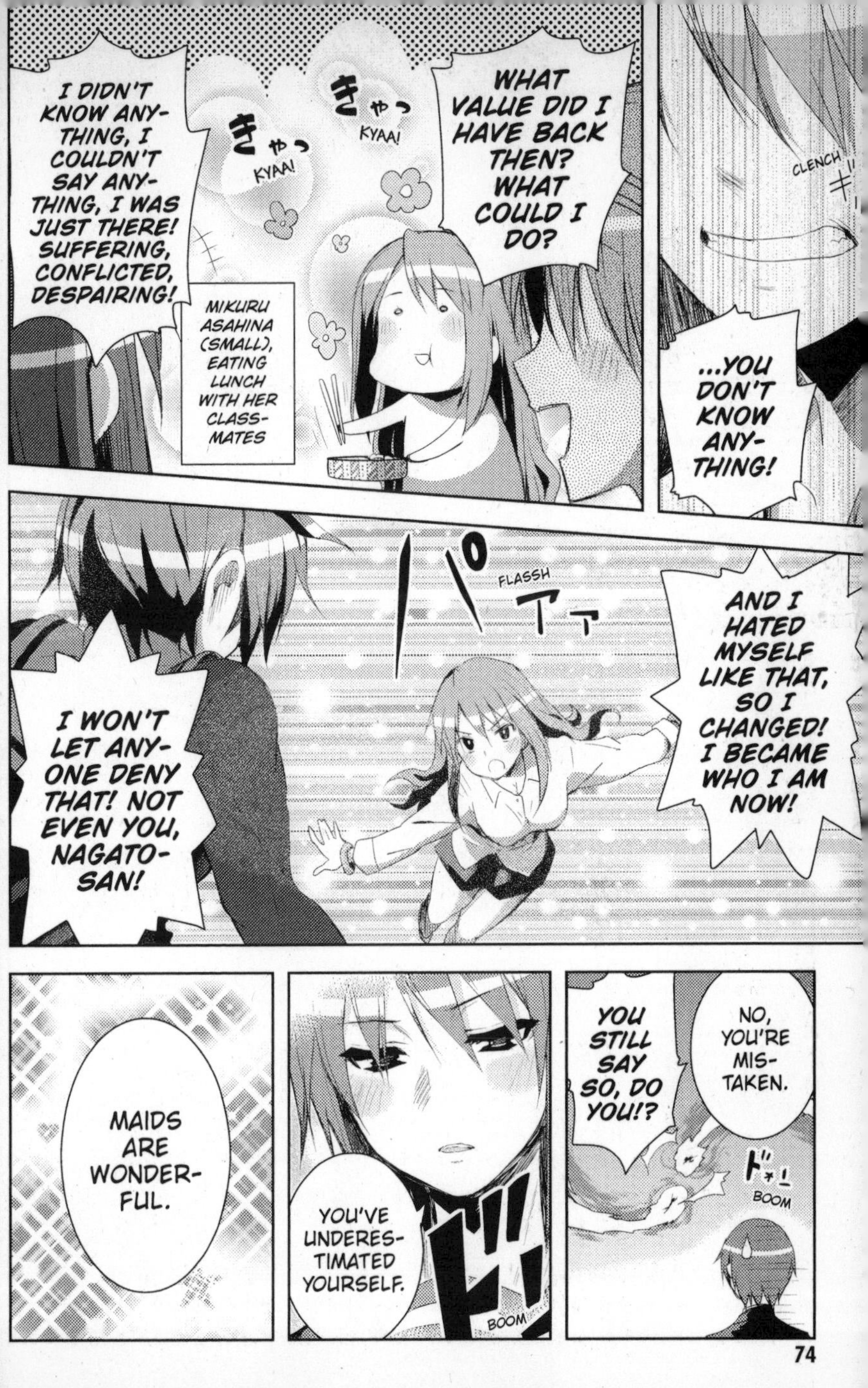
CLENCH
...YOU DON'T KNOW ANYTHING!
WHAT VALUE DID I HAVE BACK THEN? WHAT COULD I DO?
きゃっ
KYAA!
きゃっ
KYAA!
I DIDN'T KNOW ANYTHING, I COULDN'T SAY ANYTHING, I WAS JUST THERE! SUFFERING, CONFLICTED, DESPAIRING!
MIKURU ASAHINA (SMALL), EATING LUNCH WITH HER CLASSMATES
AND I HATED MYSELF LIKE THAT, SO I CHANGED! I BECAME WHO I AM NOW!
パァァ
FLASSH
I WON'T LET ANYONE DENY THAT! NOT EVEN YOU, NAGATO-SAN!
NO, YOU'RE MISTAKEN.
YOU STILL SAY SO, DO YOU!?
ドッ
BOOM
YOU'VE UNDERESTIMATED YOURSELF.
BOOM
MAIDS ARE WONDERFUL.

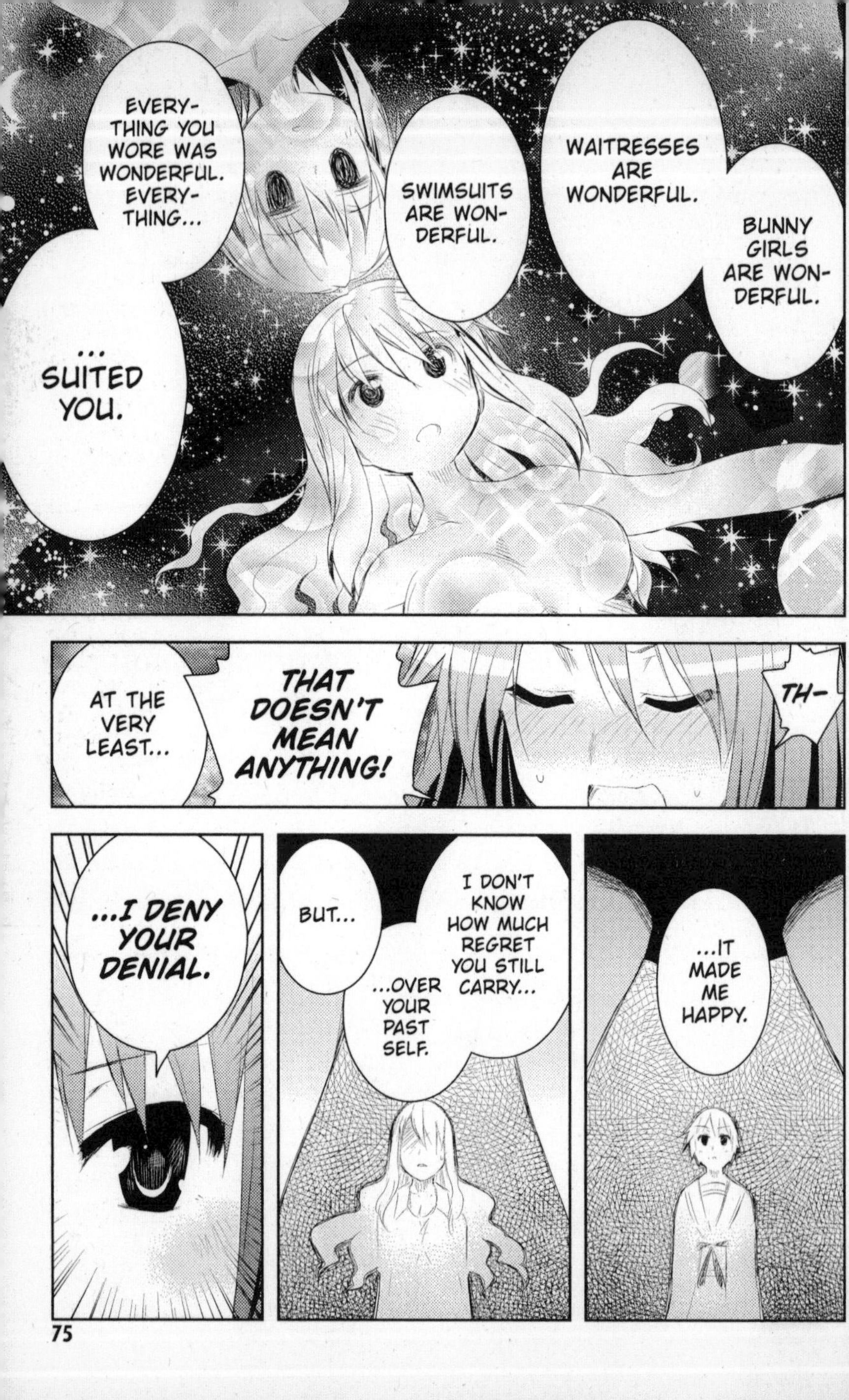
WAITRESSES ARE WONDERFUL.
BUNNY GIRLS ARE WONDERFUL.
SWIMSUITS ARE WONDERFUL.
EVERYTHING YOU WORE WAS WONDERFUL. EVERYTHING...
...SUITED YOU.
TH-
THAT DOESN'T MEAN ANYTHING!
AT THE VERY LEAST...
...IT MADE ME HAPPY.
I DON'T KNOW HOW MUCH REGRET YOU STILL CARRY...
...OVER YOUR PAST SELF.
BUT...
...I DENY YOUR DENIAL.

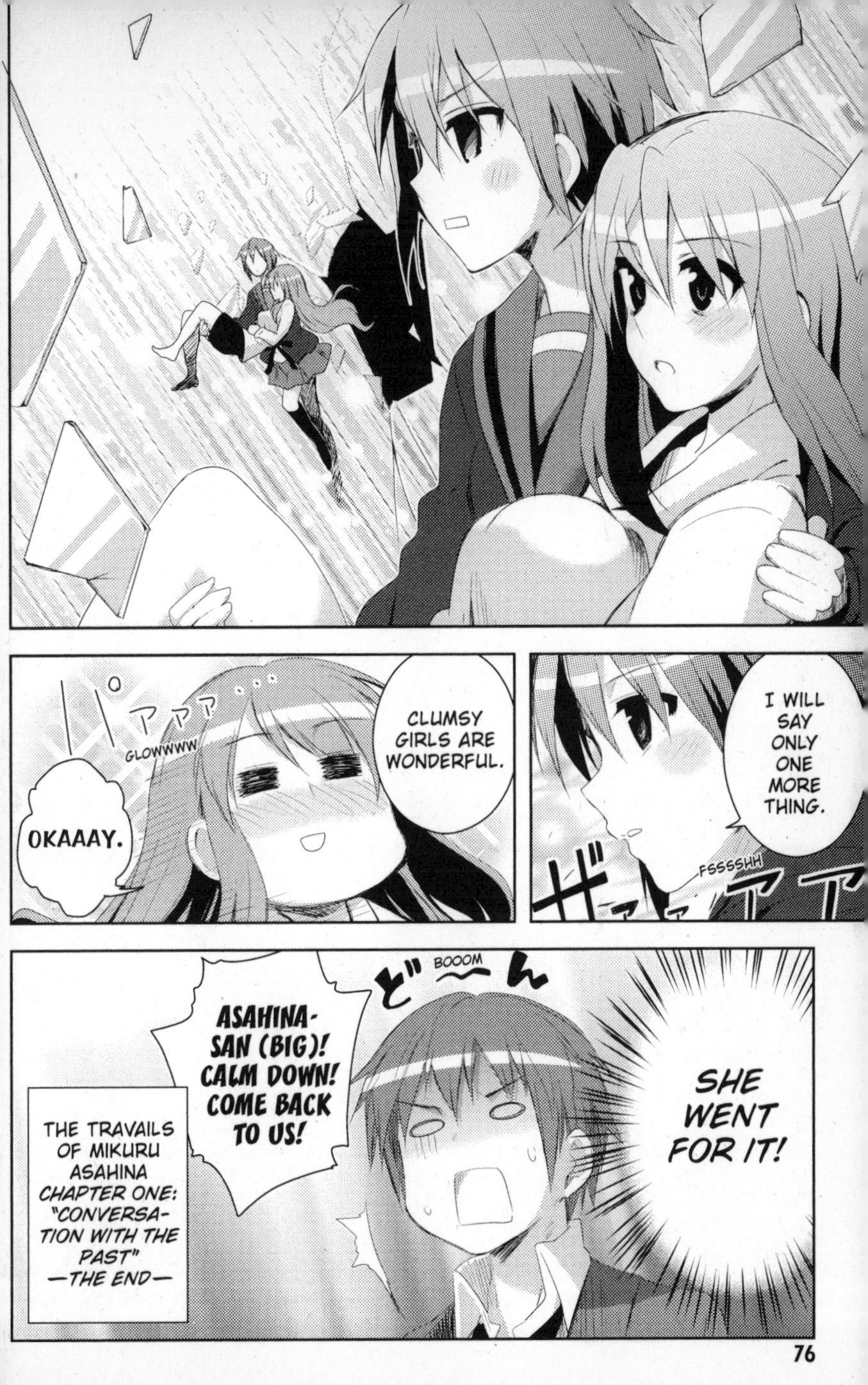
I WILL SAY ONLY ONE MORE THING.
FSSSSHH
CLUMSY GIRLS ARE WONDERFUL.
GLOWWWW
OKAAAY.
BOOOM
SHE WENT FOR IT!
ASAHINA-SAN (BIG)! CALM DOWN! COME BACK TO US!
THE TRAVAILS OF MIKURU ASAHINA CHAPTER ONE: "CONVERSATION WITH THE PAST" —THE END—

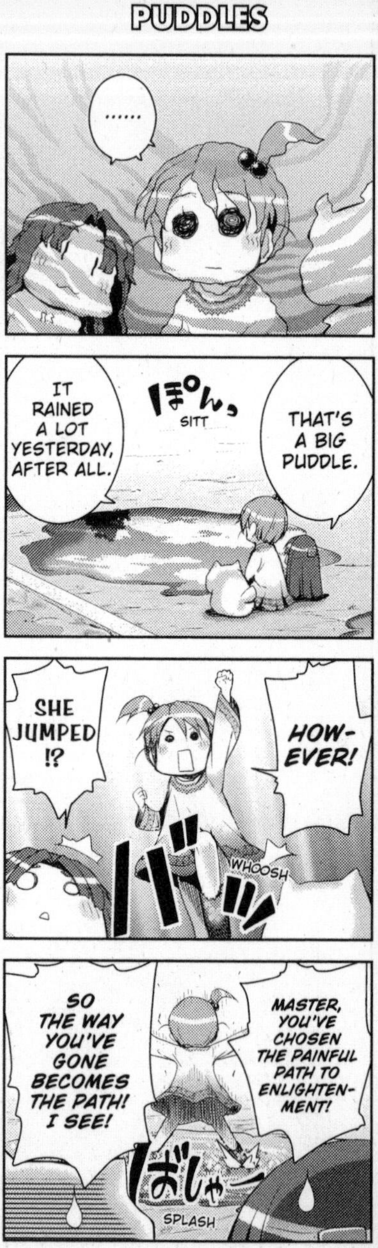
PUDDLES
......
THAT'S A BIG PUDDLE.
ぽんっ
SITT
IT RAINED A LOT YESTERDAY, AFTER ALL.
HOW-EVER!
SHE JUMPED !?
バッ
WHOOSH
MASTER, YOU'VE CHOSEN THE PAINFUL PATH TO ENLIGHTEN-MENT!
SO THE WAY YOU'VE GONE BECOMES THE PATH! I SEE!
おしゃー
SPLASH

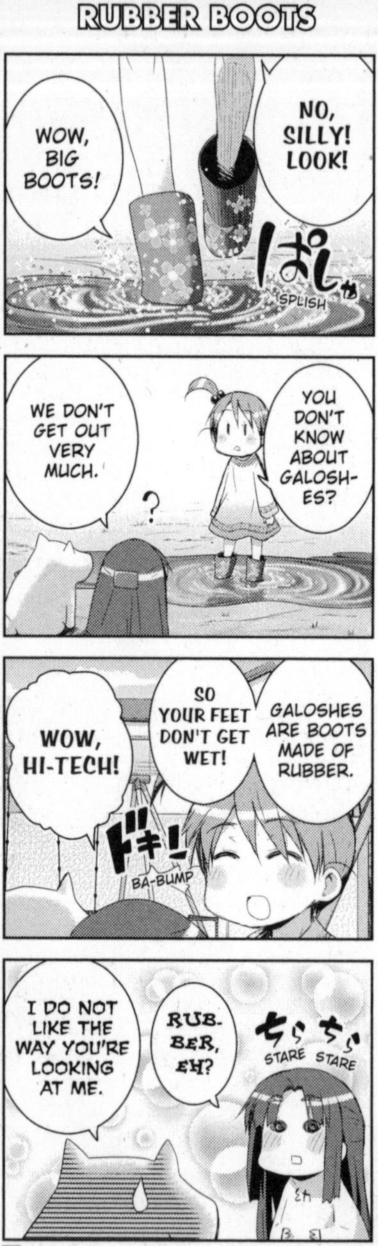
RUBBER BOOTS
NO, SILLY! LOOK!
WOW, BIG BOOTS!
ぱしゃ
SPLISH
YOU DON'T KNOW ABOUT GALOSH-ES?
WE DON'T GET OUT VERY MUCH.
?
GALOSHES ARE BOOTS MADE OF RUBBER.
SO YOUR FEET DON'T GET WET!
WOW, HI-TECH!
ドキ!
BA-BUMP
ちらちら
STARE STARE
RUB-BER, EH?
I DO NOT LIKE THE WAY YOU'RE LOOKING AT ME.

•Kyon's Sister •Protects Achakura-san and Kimidori-san from the cat.

•Achakura-san •An alien who took Kyon's sister as her master. A member of the Nagato household.

•Kimidori-san •An artificial life-form made out of a balloon. Fundamentally made of rubber.

SCIENCE FICTION

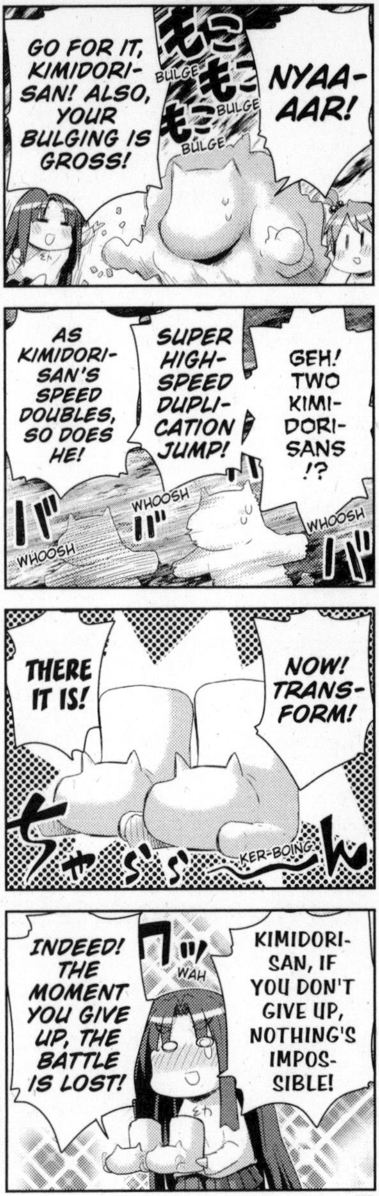
NYAAA-AAR!
BULGE
BULGE
BULGE
GO FOR IT, KIMIDORI-SAN! ALSO, YOUR BULGING IS GROSS!
GEH! TWO KIMIDORI-SANS!?
SUPER HIGH-SPEED DUPLICATION JUMP!
AS KIMIDORI-SAN'S SPEED DOUBLES, SO DOES HE!
WHOOSH
WHOOSH
WHOOSH
NOW! TRANSFORM!
THERE IT IS!
KER-BOING
KIMIDORI-SAN, IF YOU DON'T GIVE UP, NOTHING'S IMPOSSIBLE!
WAH
INDEED! THE MOMENT YOU GIVE UP, THE BATTLE IS LOST!

WORN OUT

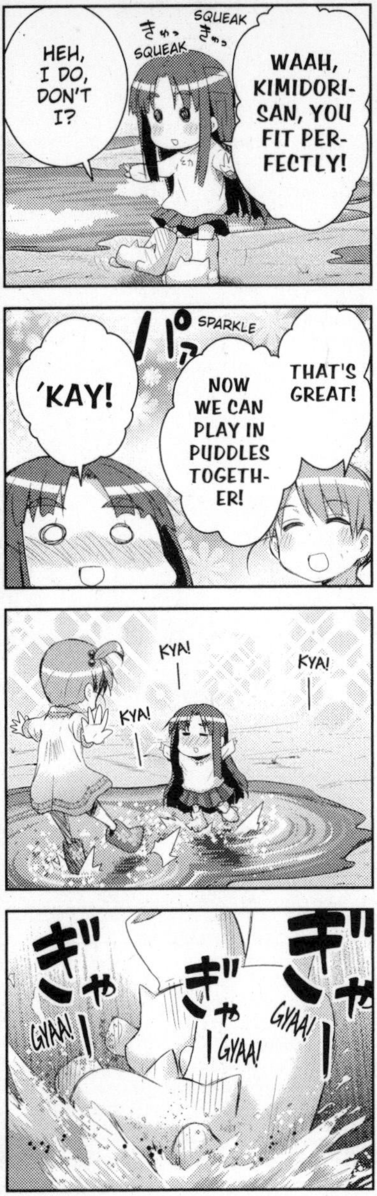
WAAH, KIMIDORI-SAN, YOU FIT PERFECTLY!
SQUEAK
SQUEAK
HEH, I DO, DON'T I?
THAT'S GREAT!
NOW WE CAN PLAY IN PUDDLES TOGETHER!
SPARKLE
'KAY!
KYA!
KYA!
KYA!
GYAA!
GYAA!
GYAA!

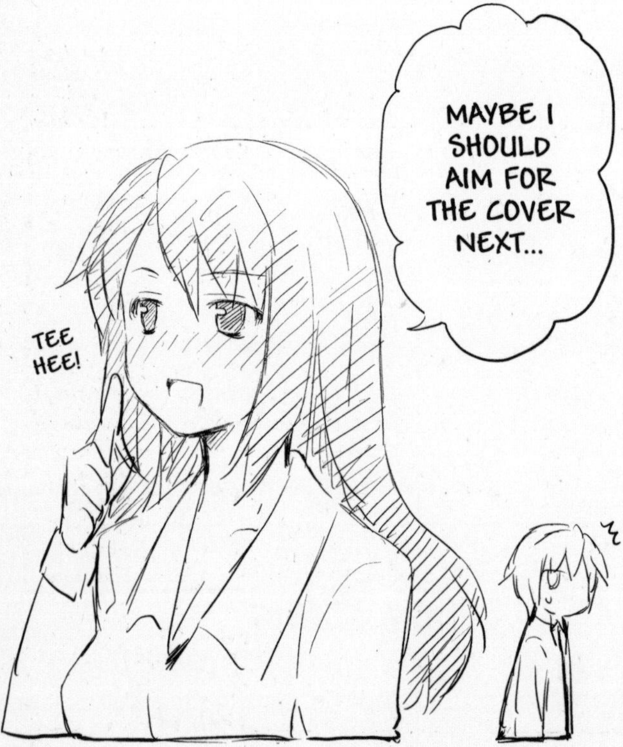
MAYBE I SHOULD AIM FOR THE COVER NEXT...
TEE HEE!

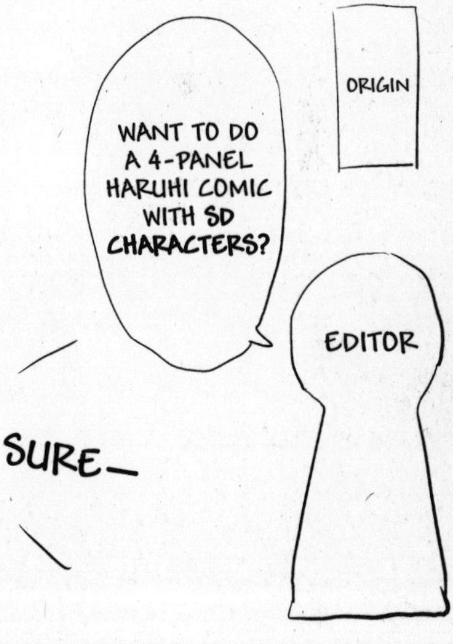
ORIGIN
WANT TO DO A 4-PANEL HARUHI COMIC WITH SD CHARACTERS?
EDITOR
SURE—

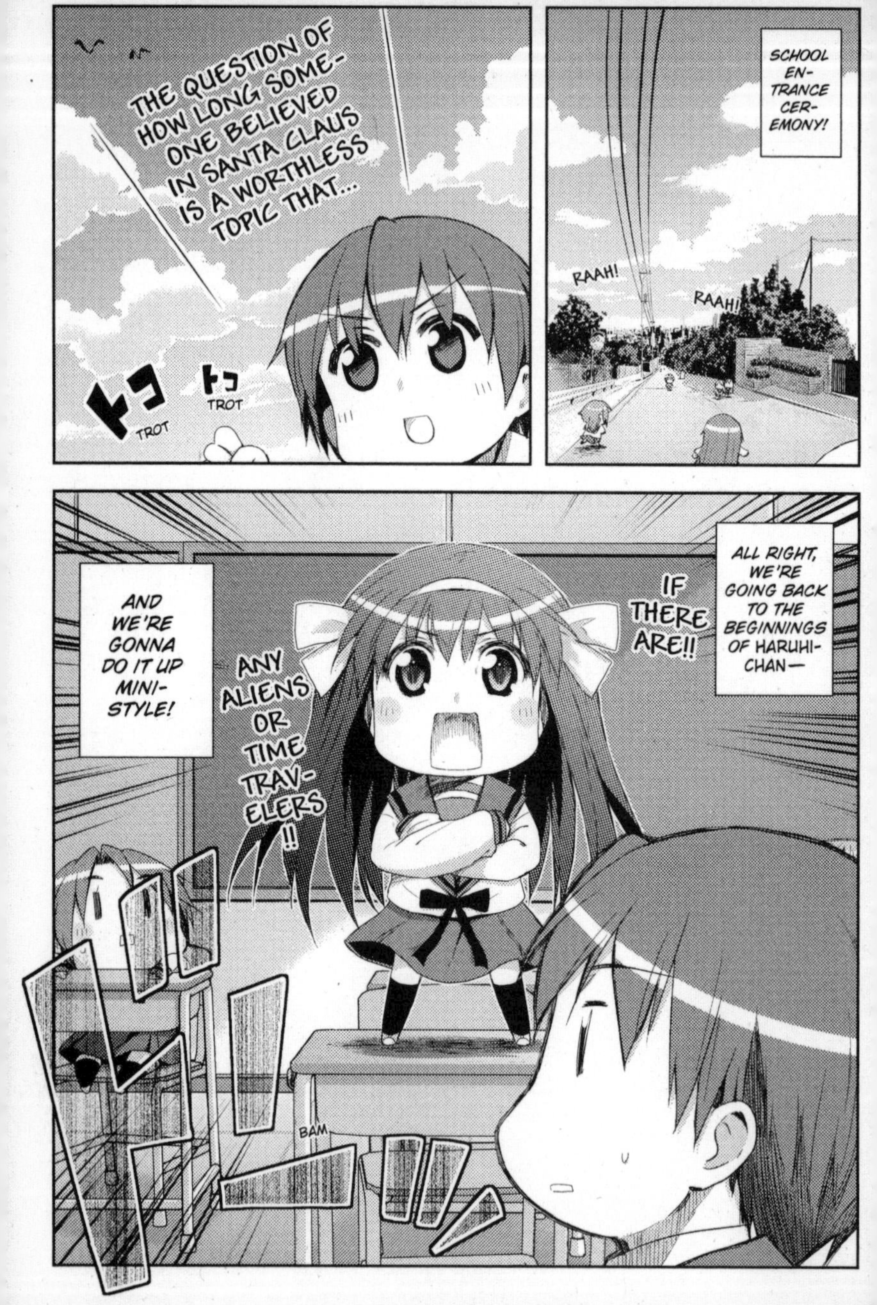
SCHOOL EN-TRANCE CER-EMONY!
RAAH!
RAAH!
THE QUESTION OF HOW LONG SOME-ONE BELIEVED IN SANTA CLAUS IS A WORTHLESS TOPIC THAT...
トコ
TROT
トコ
TROT
ALL RIGHT, WE'RE GOING BACK TO THE BEGINNINGS OF HARUHI-CHAN—
IF THERE ARE!!
ANY ALIENS OR TIME TRAV-ELERS!!
AND WE'RE GONNA DO IT UP MINI-STYLE!
BAM

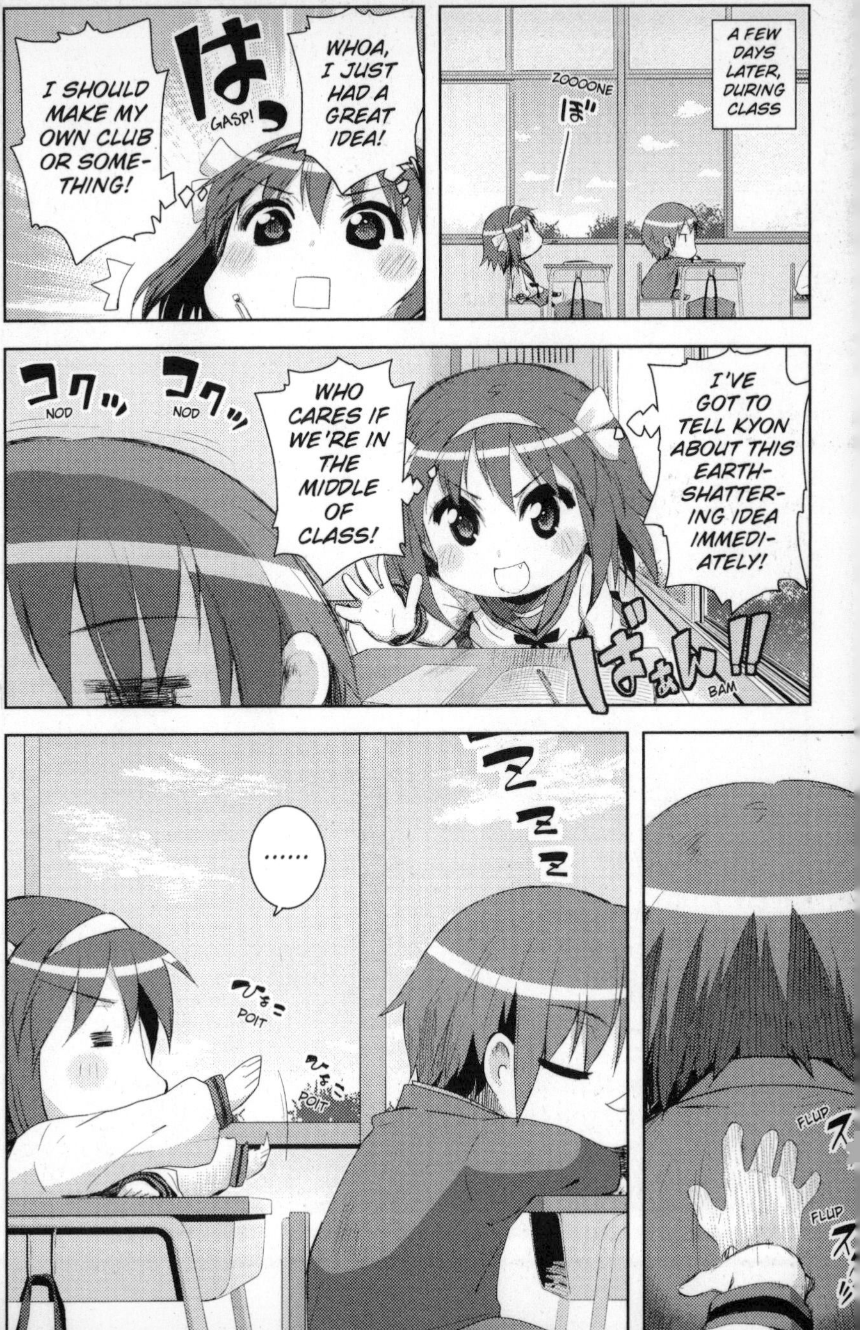
A FEW DAYS LATER, DURING CLASS
ZOOOONE
WHOA, I JUST HAD A GREAT IDEA!
GASP!
I SHOULD MAKE MY OWN CLUB OR SOMETHING!
I'VE GOT TO TELL KYON ABOUT THIS EARTH-SHATTERING IDEA IMMEDIATELY!
WHO CARES IF WE'RE IN THE MIDDLE OF CLASS!
NOD
NOD
BAM
FLUP
FLUP
......
POIT
POIT

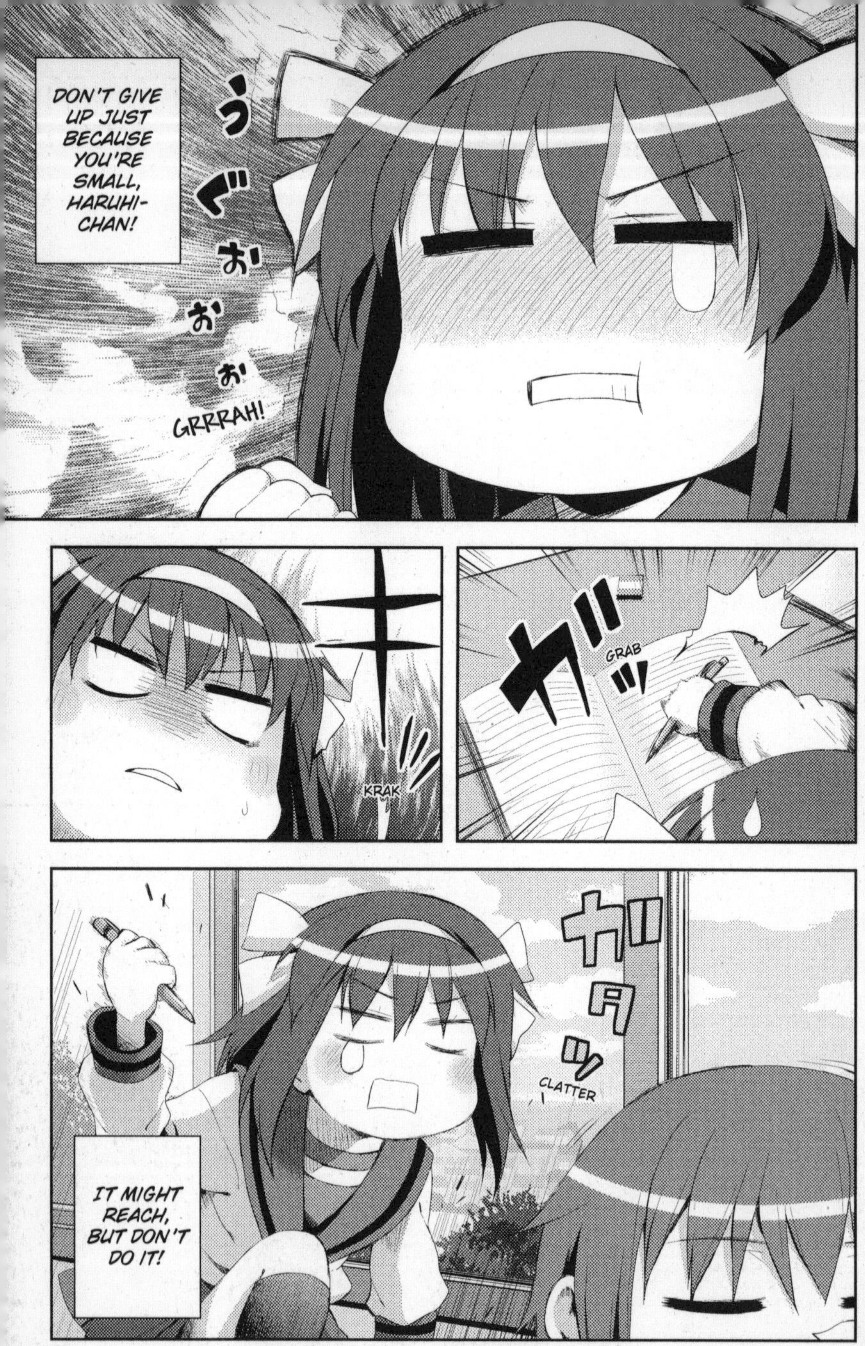
DON'T GIVE UP JUST BECAUSE YOU'RE SMALL, HARUHI-CHAN!
うぐおおお
GRRRAH!
GRAB
KRAK
ガタッ
CLATTER
IT MIGHT REACH, BUT DON'T DO IT!

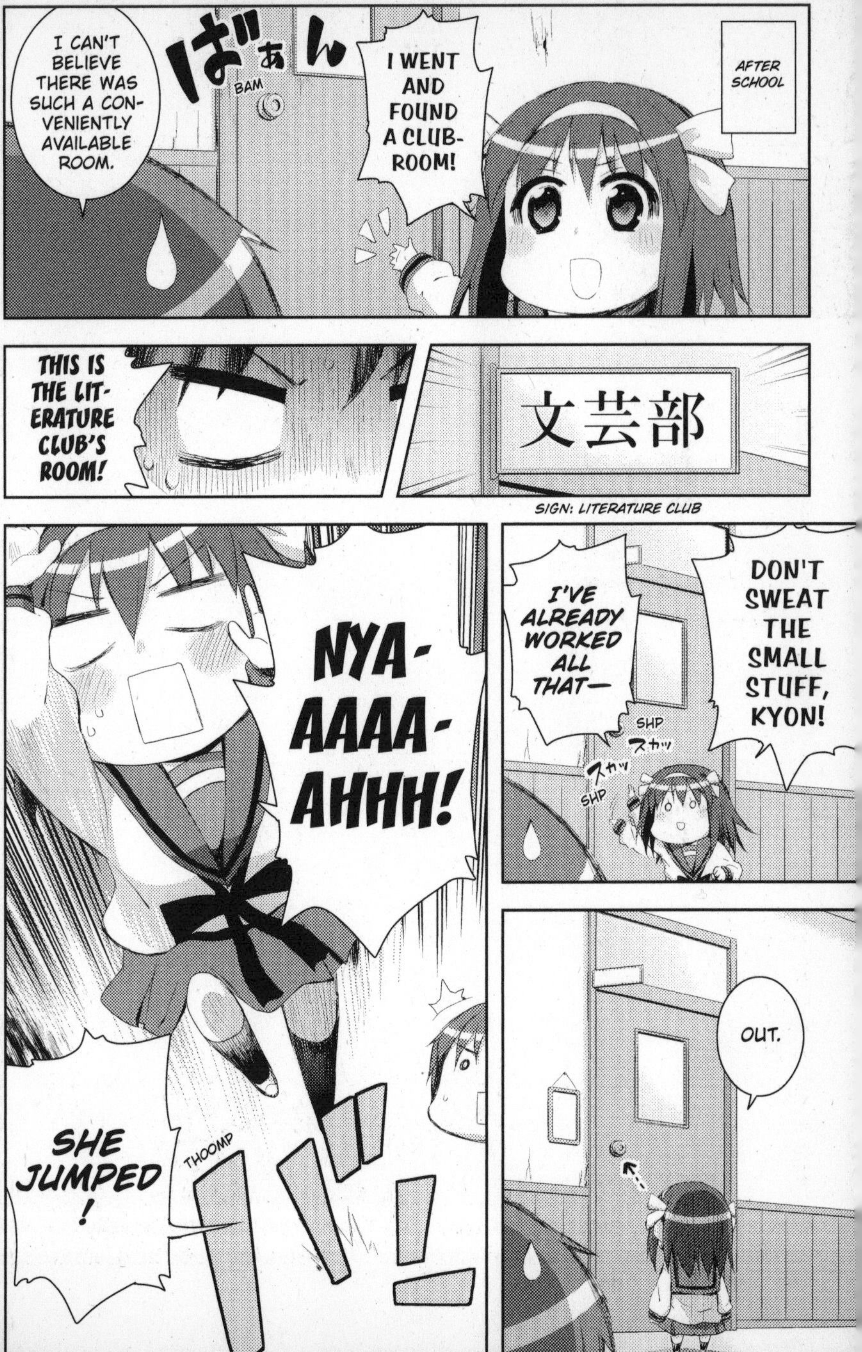
AFTER SCHOOL
I WENT AND FOUND A CLUB-ROOM!
ばぁん
BAM
I CAN'T BELIEVE THERE WAS SUCH A CON-VENIENTLY AVAILABLE ROOM.
文芸部
THIS IS THE LIT-ERATURE CLUB'S ROOM!
SIGN: LITERATURE CLUB
DON'T SWEAT THE SMALL STUFF, KYON!
I'VE ALREADY WORKED ALL THAT—
スカッ
SHP
スカッ
SHP
OUT.
NYA-AAAA-AHHH!
THOOMP
SHE JUMPED!

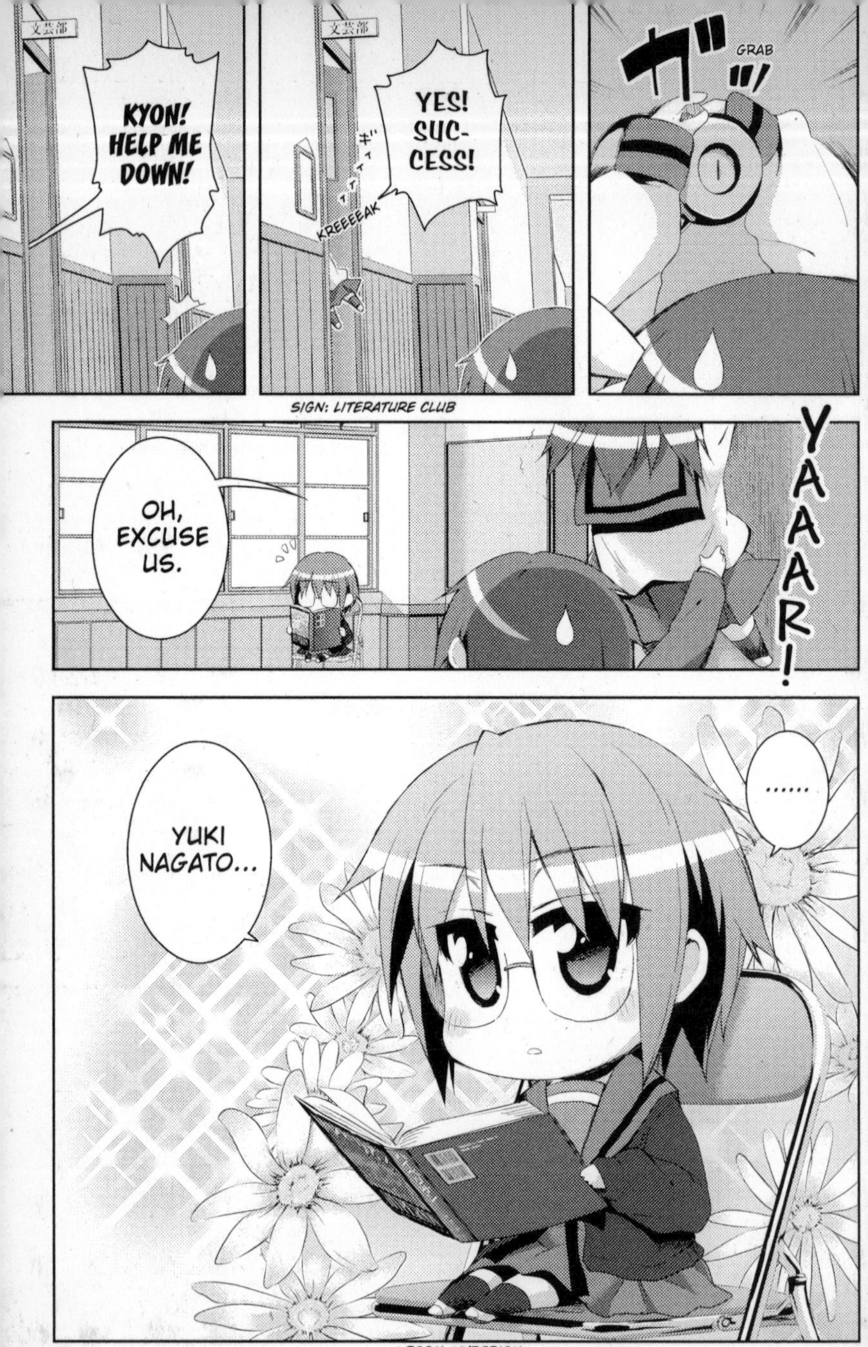
ガッ
GRAB
YES! SUC-CESS!
ギィィィ
KREEEEAK
文芸部
KYON! HELP ME DOWN!
文芸部
YAAAR!
OH, EXCUSE US.
......
YUKI NAGATO...
SIGN: LITERATURE CLUB
BOOK: HYPERION

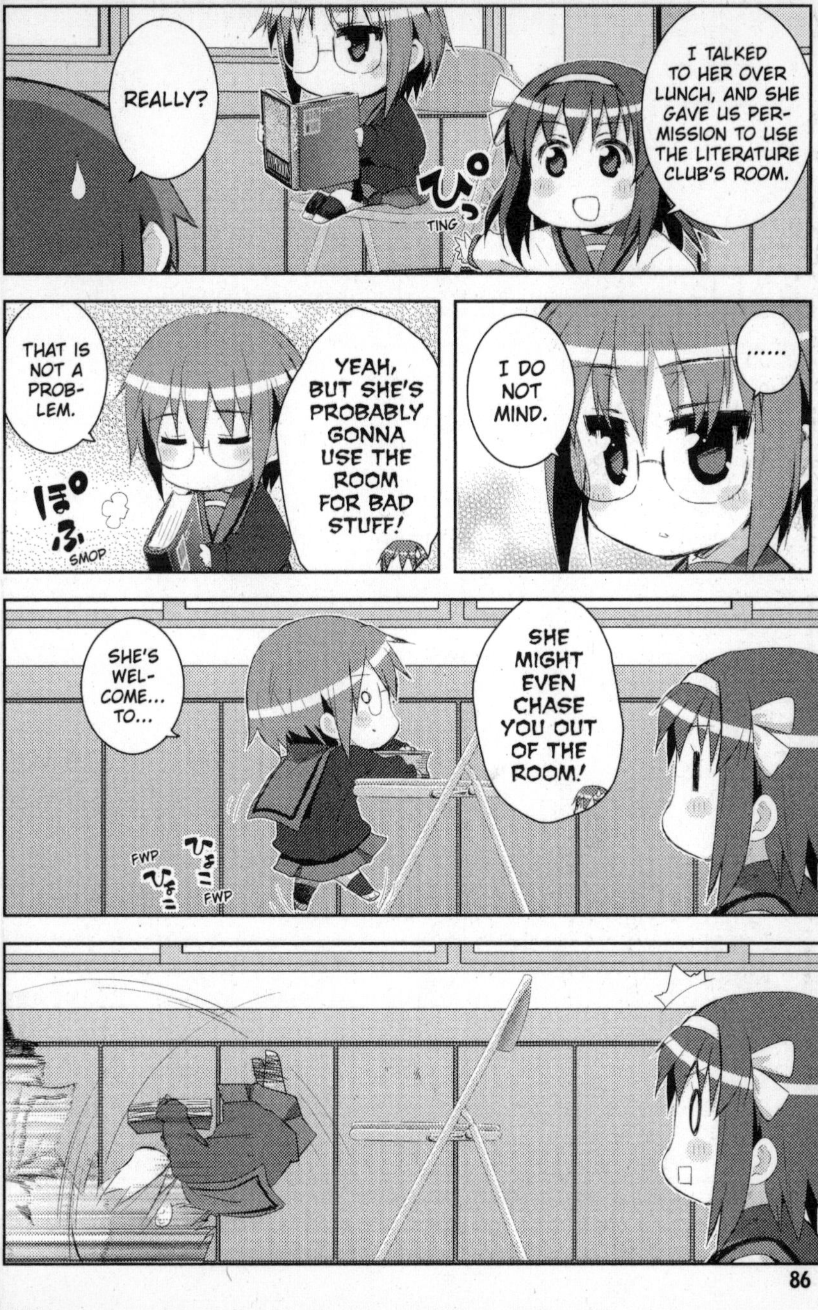
I TALKED TO HER OVER LUNCH, AND SHE GAVE US PERMISSION TO USE THE LITERATURE CLUB'S ROOM.
ぴっ
TING
REALLY?
......
I DO NOT MIND.
YEAH, BUT SHE'S PROBABLY GONNA USE THE ROOM FOR BAD STUFF!
THAT IS NOT A PROBLEM.
ぽふ
SMOP
SHE MIGHT EVEN CHASE YOU OUT OF THE ROOM!
SHE'S WELCOME... TO...
FWP
FWP

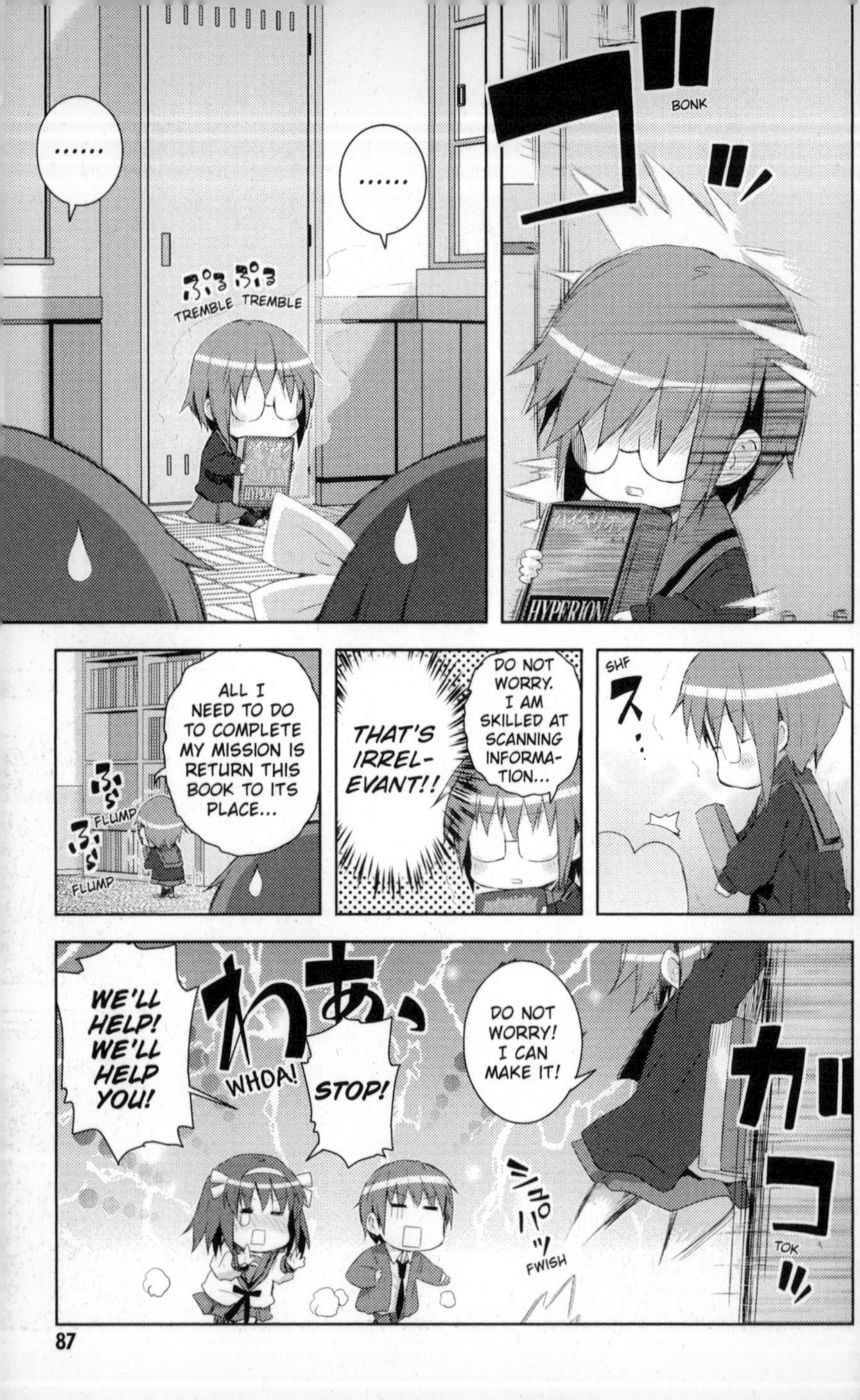
ゴッ
BONK
......
......
ぷるぷる
TREMBLE TREMBLE
HYPERION
SHF
ス
DO NOT WORRY. I AM SKILLED AT SCANNING INFORMATION...
THAT'S IRREL-EVANT!!
ALL I NEED TO DO TO COMPLETE MY MISSION IS RETURN THIS BOOK TO ITS PLACE...
FLUMP
FLUMP
カッコッ
TOK
FWISH
DO NOT WORRY! I CAN MAKE IT!
STOP!
WHOA!
わあっ
WE'LL HELP! WE'LL HELP YOU!

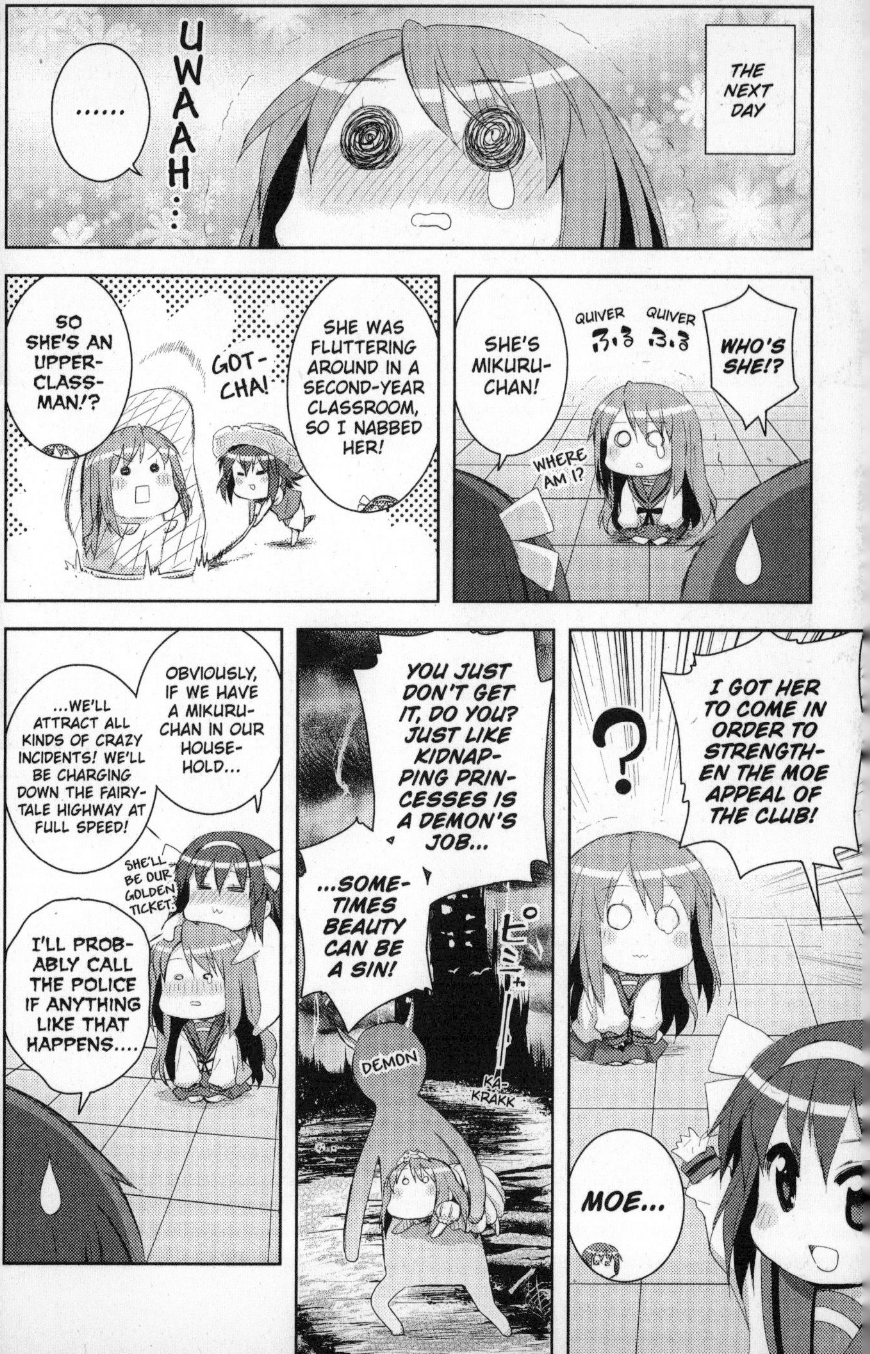
THE NEXT DAY
UWAAH...
......
WHO'S SHE!?
QUIVER QUIVER
ふるふる
SHE'S MIKURU-CHAN!
WHERE AM I?
SHE WAS FLUTTERING AROUND IN A SECOND-YEAR CLASSROOM, SO I NABBED HER!
GOT-CHA!
SO SHE'S AN UPPER-CLASSMAN!?
I GOT HER TO COME IN ORDER TO STRENGTHEN THE MOE APPEAL OF THE CLUB!
?
MOE...
YOU JUST DON'T GET IT, DO YOU? JUST LIKE KIDNAPPING PRINCESSES IS A DEMON'S JOB...
...SOMETIMES BEAUTY CAN BE A SIN!
KA-KRAKK
DEMON
OBVIOUSLY, IF WE HAVE A MIKURU-CHAN IN OUR HOUSEHOLD...
...WE'LL ATTRACT ALL KINDS OF CRAZY INCIDENTS! WE'LL BE CHARGING DOWN THE FAIRY-TALE HIGHWAY AT FULL SPEED!
SHE'LL BE OUR GOLDEN TICKET!
I'LL PROBABLY CALL THE POLICE IF ANYTHING LIKE THAT HAPPENS....

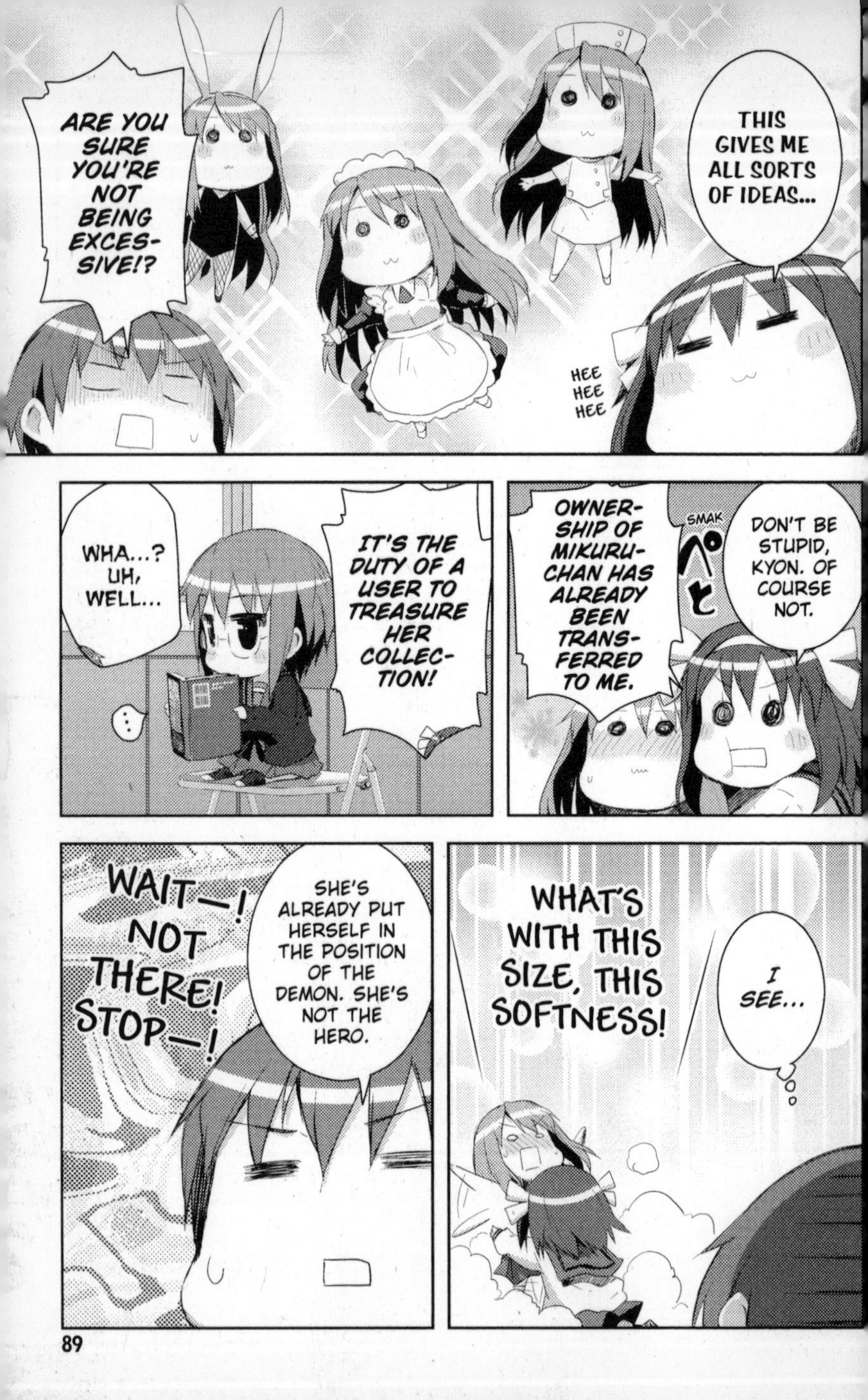
THIS GIVES ME ALL SORTS OF IDEAS...
HEE HEE HEE
ARE YOU SURE YOU'RE NOT BEING EXCES-SIVE!?
DON'T BE STUPID, KYON. OF COURSE NOT.
SMAK
OWNER-SHIP OF MIKURU-CHAN HAS ALREADY BEEN TRANS-FERRED TO ME.
IT'S THE DUTY OF A USER TO TREASURE HER COLLEC-TION!
WHA...? UH, WELL...
...
I SEE...
WHAT'S WITH THIS SIZE, THIS SOFTNESS!
SHE'S ALREADY PUT HERSELF IN THE POSITION OF THE DEMON. SHE'S NOT THE HERO.
WAIT—! NOT THERE! STOP—!

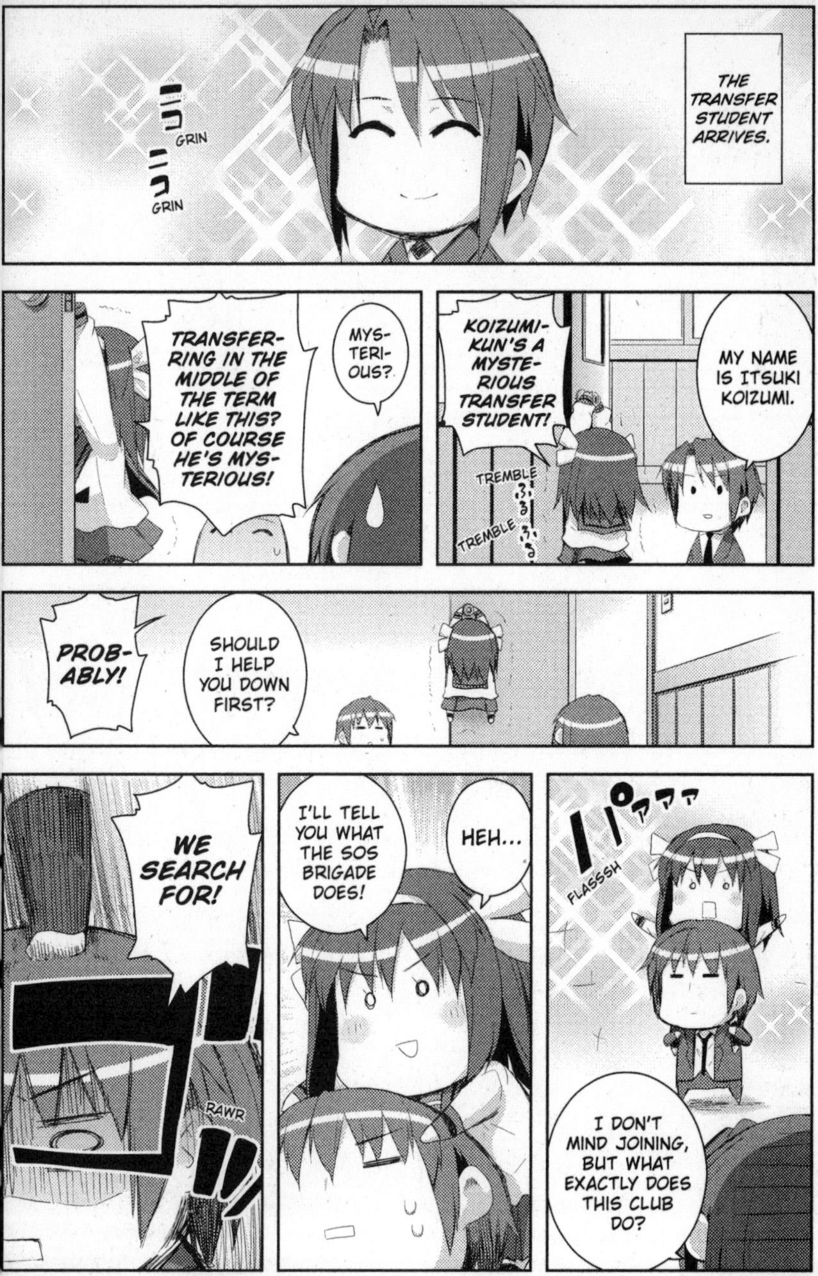
THE TRANSFER STUDENT ARRIVES.
GRIN
GRIN
MY NAME IS ITSUKI KOIZUMI.
KOIZUMI-KUN'S A MYSTERIOUS TRANSFER STUDENT!
TREMBLE
TREMBLE
MYSTERIOUS?
TRANSFERRING IN THE MIDDLE OF THE TERM LIKE THIS? OF COURSE HE'S MYSTERIOUS!
SHOULD I HELP YOU DOWN FIRST?
PROBABLY!
FLASSSH
I DON'T MIND JOINING, BUT WHAT EXACTLY DOES THIS CLUB DO?
HEH...
I'LL TELL YOU WHAT THE SOS BRIGADE DOES!
WE SEARCH FOR!
RAWR

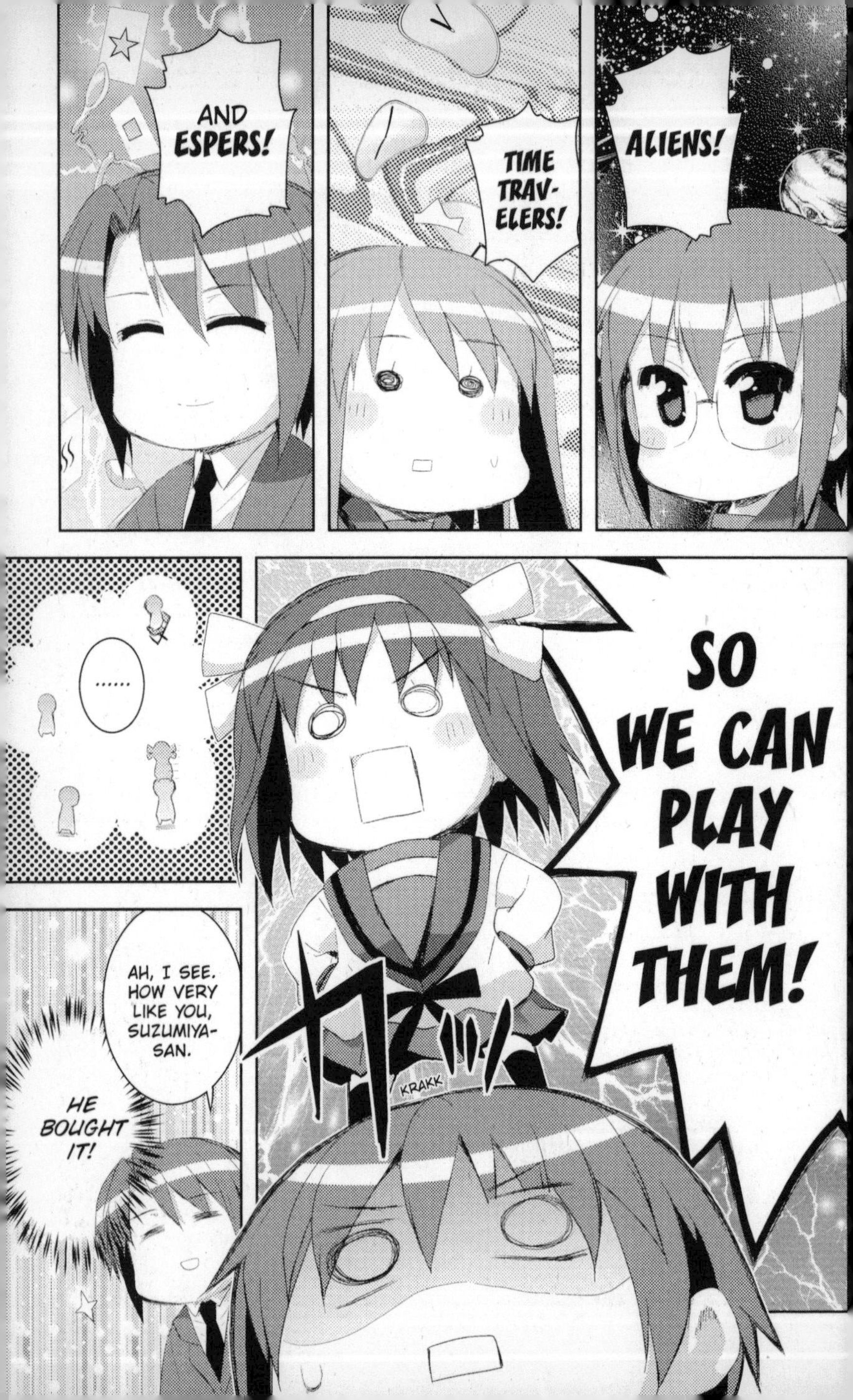
ALIENS!
TIME TRAVELERS!
AND ESPERS!
SO WE CAN PLAY WITH THEM!
KRAKK
......
AH, I SEE. HOW VERY LIKE YOU, SUZUMIYA-SAN.
HE BOUGHT IT!

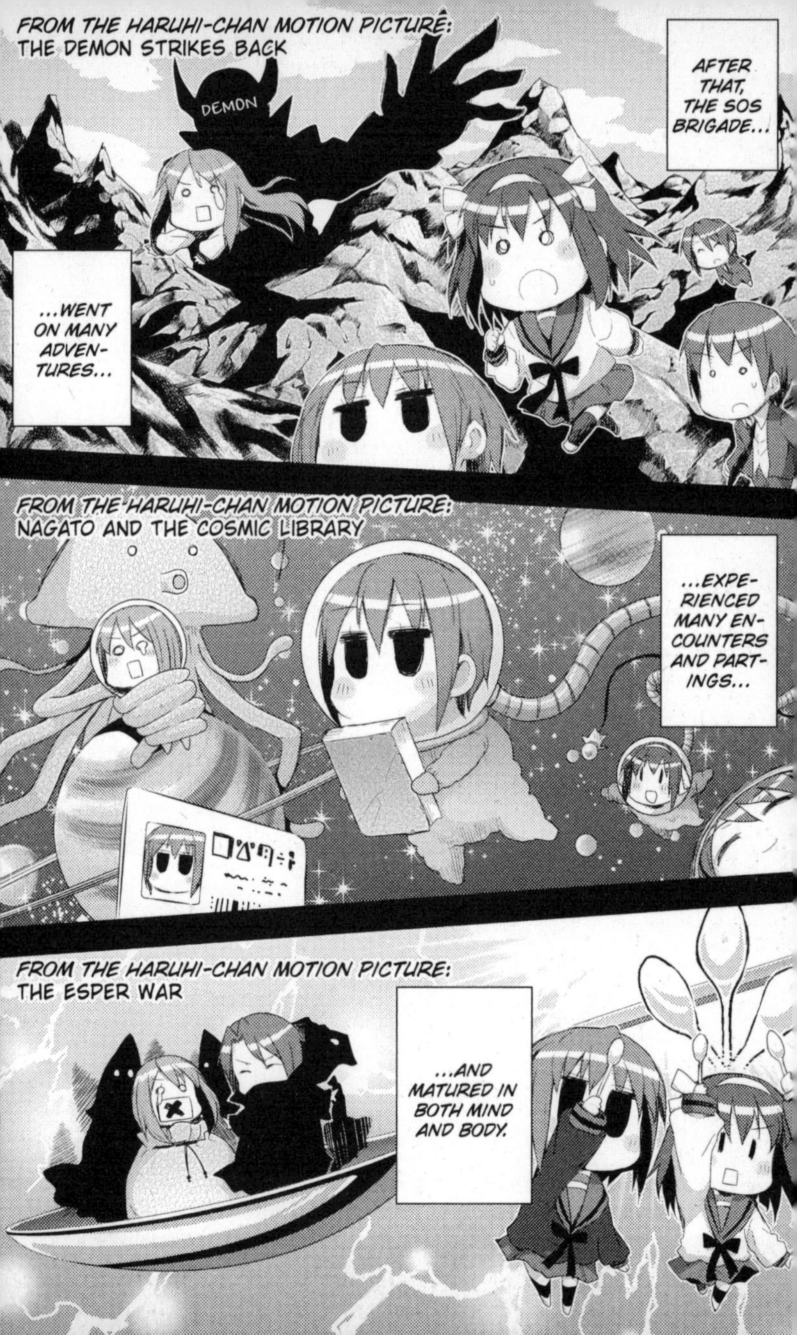
FROM THE HARUHI-CHAN MOTION PICTURE: THE DEMON STRIKES BACK
AFTER THAT, THE SOS BRIGADE...
DEMON
...WENT ON MANY ADVEN-TURES...
FROM THE HARUHI-CHAN MOTION PICTURE: NAGATO AND THE COSMIC LIBRARY
...EXPE-RIENCED MANY EN-COUNTERS AND PART-INGS...
FROM THE HARUHI-CHAN MOTION PICTURE: THE ESPER WAR
...AND MATURED IN BOTH MIND AND BODY.

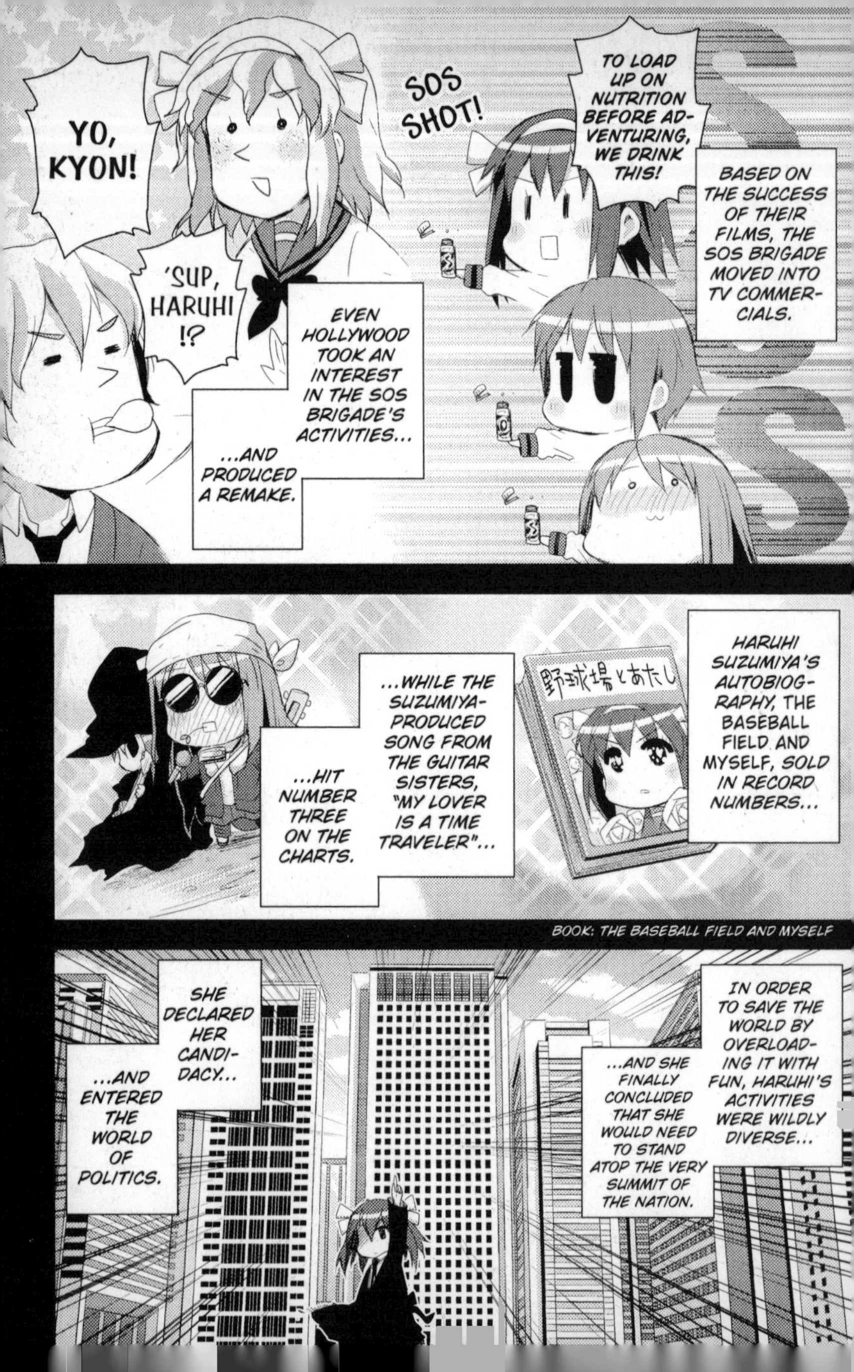
BASED ON THE SUCCESS OF THEIR FILMS, THE SOS BRIGADE MOVED INTO TV COMMER-CIALS.
TO LOAD UP ON NUTRITION BEFORE AD-VENTURING, WE DRINK THIS!
SOS SHOT!
YO, KYON!
'SUP, HARUHI!?
EVEN HOLLYWOOD TOOK AN INTEREST IN THE SOS BRIGADE'S ACTIVITIES...
...AND PRODUCED A REMAKE.
HARUHI SUZUMIYA'S AUTOBIOG-RAPHY, THE BASEBALL FIELD AND MYSELF, SOLD IN RECORD NUMBERS...
野球場とあたし
...WHILE THE SUZUMIYA-PRODUCED SONG FROM THE GUITAR SISTERS, "MY LOVER IS A TIME TRAVELER"...
...HIT NUMBER THREE ON THE CHARTS.
BOOK: THE BASEBALL FIELD AND MYSELF
IN ORDER TO SAVE THE WORLD BY OVERLOAD-ING IT WITH FUN, HARUHI'S ACTIVITIES WERE WILDLY DIVERSE...
...AND SHE FINALLY CONCLUDED THAT SHE WOULD NEED TO STAND ATOP THE VERY SUMMIT OF THE NATION.
SHE DECLARED HER CANDI-DACY...
...AND ENTERED THE WORLD OF POLITICS.

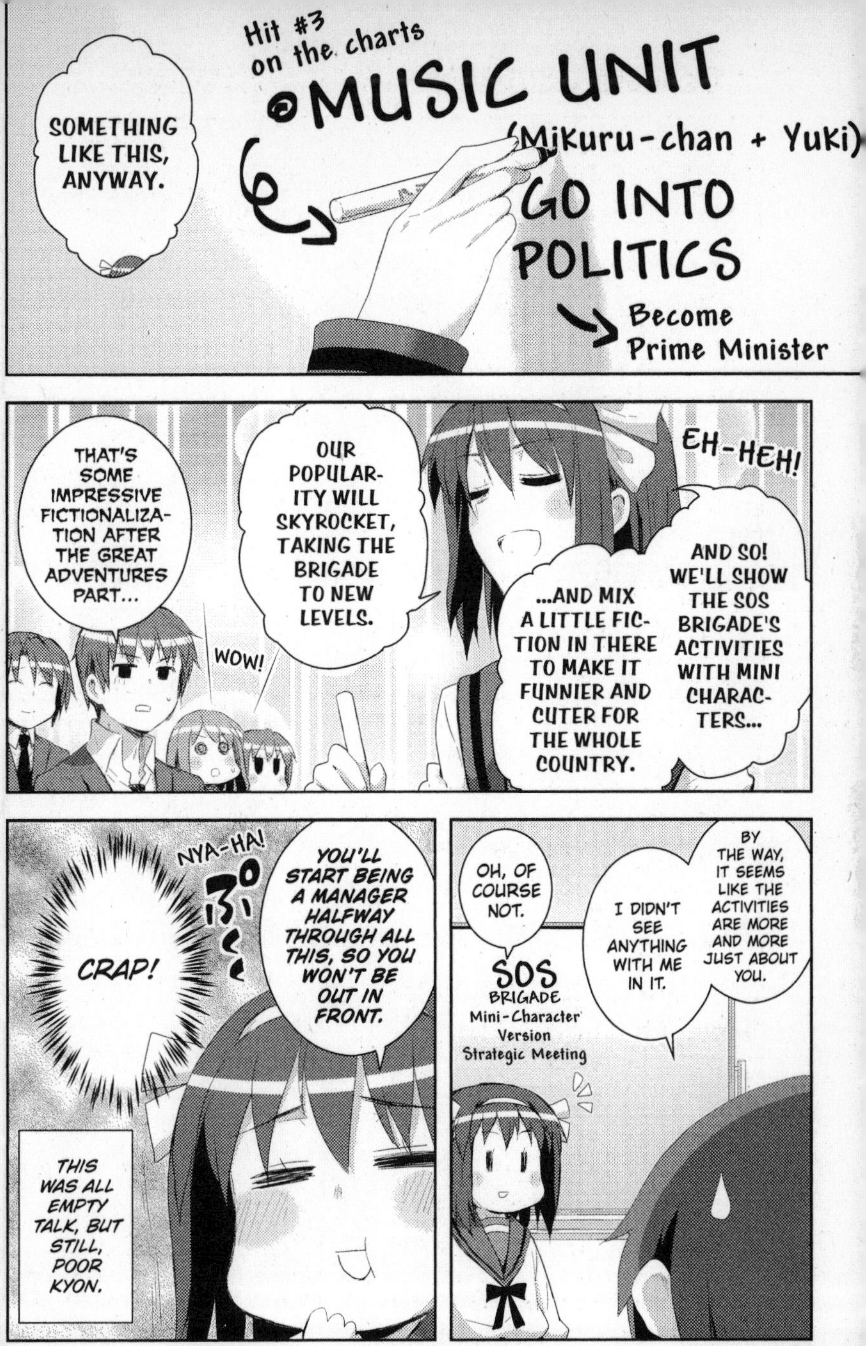
Hit #3 on the charts
MUSIC UNIT
(Mikuru-chan + Yuki)
GO INTO POLITICS
Become Prime Minister
SOMETHING LIKE THIS, ANYWAY.
EH-HEH!
AND SO! WE'LL SHOW THE SOS BRIGADE'S ACTIVITIES WITH MINI CHARACTERS...
...AND MIX A LITTLE FICTION IN THERE TO MAKE IT FUNNIER AND CUTER FOR THE WHOLE COUNTRY.
OUR POPULARITY WILL SKYROCKET, TAKING THE BRIGADE TO NEW LEVELS.
WOW!
THAT'S SOME IMPRESSIVE FICTIONALIZATION AFTER THE GREAT ADVENTURES PART...
BY THE WAY, IT SEEMS LIKE THE ACTIVITIES ARE MORE AND MORE JUST ABOUT YOU.
I DIDN'T SEE ANYTHING WITH ME IN IT.
OH, OF COURSE NOT.
SOS BRIGADE Mini-Character Version Strategic Meeting
NYA-HA!
YOU'LL START BEING A MANAGER HALFWAY THROUGH ALL THIS, SO YOU WON'T BE OUT IN FRONT.
CRAP!
THIS WAS ALL EMPTY TALK, BUT STILL, POOR KYON.

INCIDENT

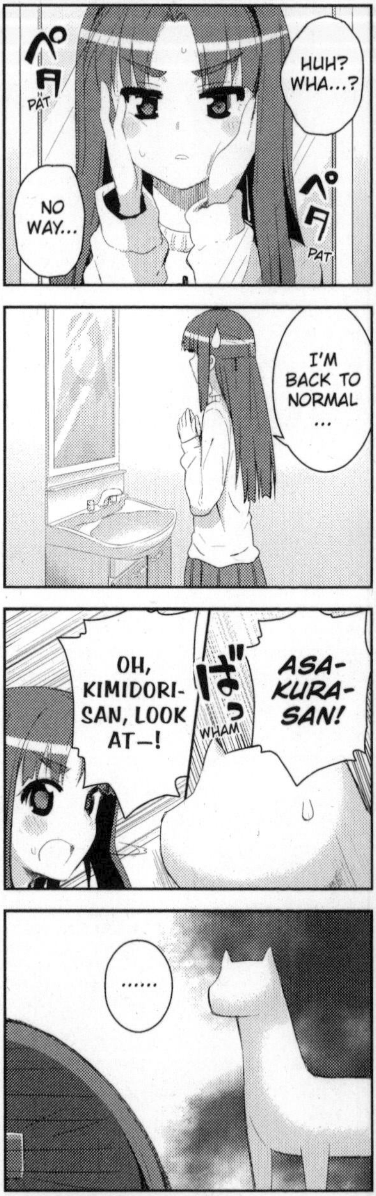
ペタ
PAT
HUH? WHA...?
ペタ
PAT
NO WAY...
I'M BACK TO NORMAL ...
ASA-KURA-SAN!
ばっ
WHAM
OH, KIMIDORI-SAN, LOOK AT—!
......

SERIOUS INCIDENT

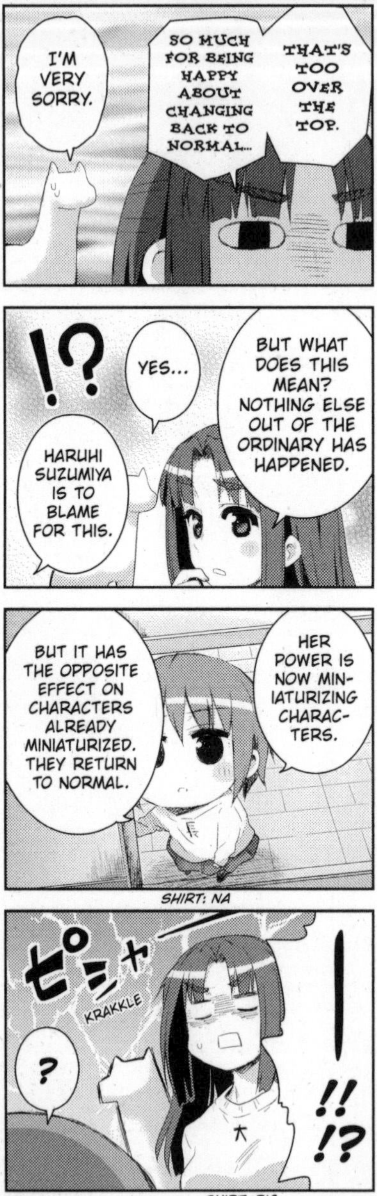
THAT'S TOO OVER THE TOP.
SO MUCH FOR BEING HAPPY ABOUT CHANGING BACK TO NORMAL...
I'M VERY SORRY.
BUT WHAT DOES THIS MEAN? NOTHING ELSE OUT OF THE ORDINARY HAS HAPPENED.
YES...
!?
HARUHI SUZUMIYA IS TO BLAME FOR THIS.
HER POWER IS NOW MINIATURIZING CHARACTERS.
BUT IT HAS THE OPPOSITE EFFECT ON CHARACTERS ALREADY MINIATURIZED. THEY RETURN TO NORMAL.
—!!!?
ピシャ
KRAKKLE
?

SHIRT: NA

SHIRT: BIG

OUT OF CONTROL SITUATION

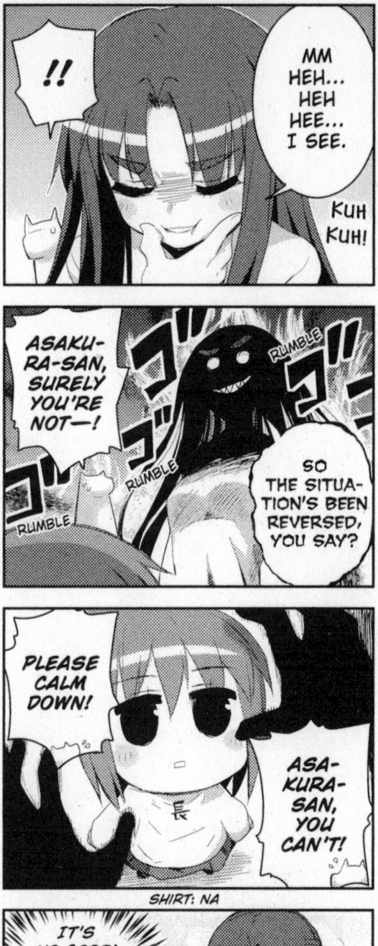
!!
MM HEH... HEH HEE... I SEE.
KUH KUH!
ASAKURA-SAN, SURELY YOU'RE NOT—!
RUMBLE
RUMBLE
RUMBLE
SO THE SITUATION'S BEEN REVERSED, YOU SAY?
PLEASE CALM DOWN!
ASAKURA-SAN, YOU CAN'T!
SHIRT: NA
IT'S NO GOOD! ASAKURA'S MATERNAL INSTINCTS ARE EXPLODING!
SQUEEEEEZE
きゅ~

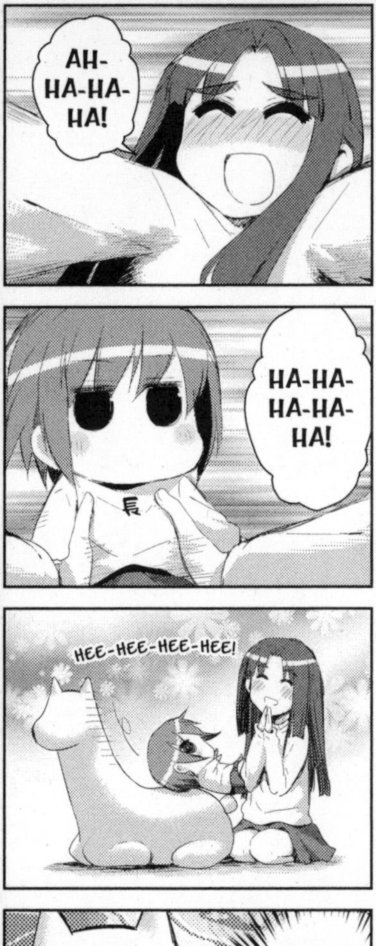
AH-HA-HA-HA!
HA-HA-HA-HA-HA!
HEE-HEE-HEE-HEE!
ASAKURA-SAN, SNAP OUT OF IT!
THIS CONTINUED UNTIL HER BODY RETURNED TO NORMAL.
も~ん
STAAARE

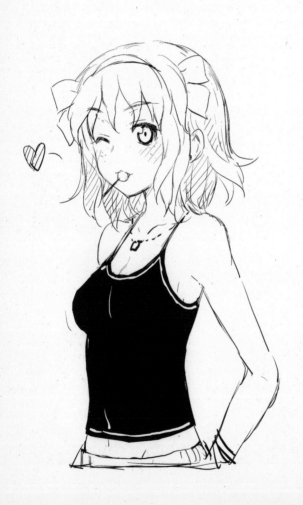

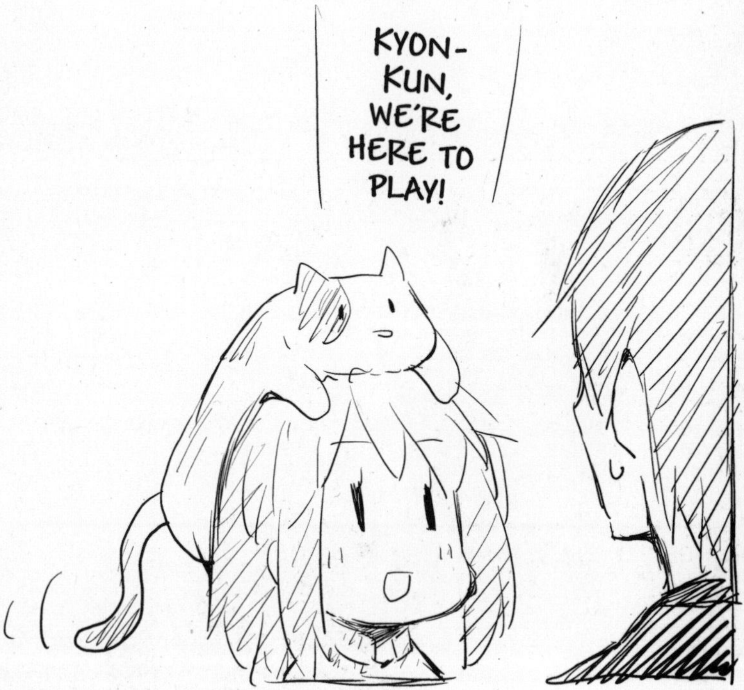
KYON-KUN, WE'RE HERE TO PLAY!

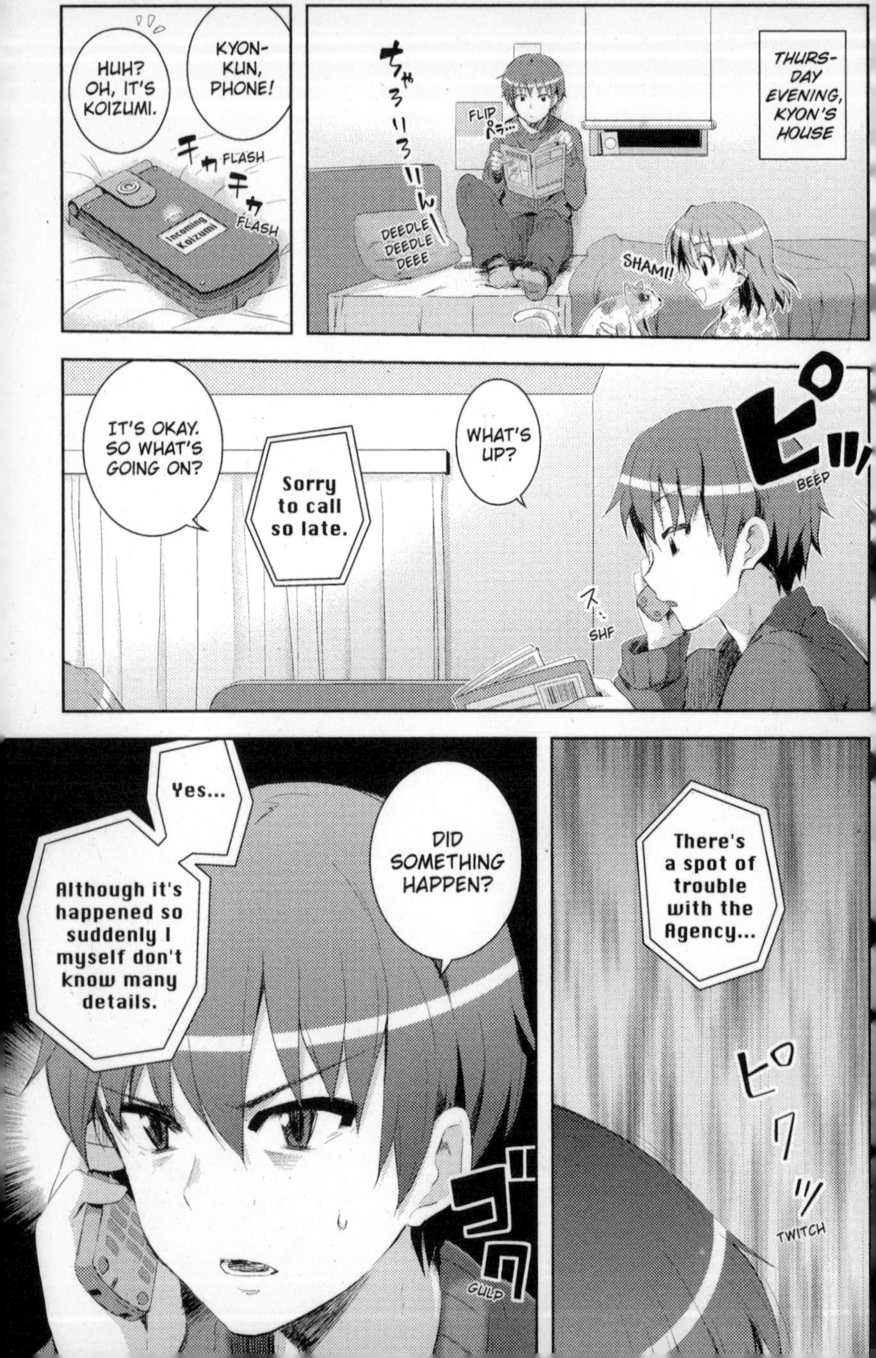
THURSDAY EVENING, KYON'S HOUSE
FLIP
DEEDLE DEEDLE DEEE
SHAMI!
KYON-KUN, PHONE!
HUH? OH, IT'S KOIZUMI.
FLASH
FLASH
Incoming Koizumi
BEEP
WHAT'S UP?
SHF
Sorry to call so late.
IT'S OKAY. SO WHAT'S GOING ON?
There's a spot of trouble with the Agency...
TWITCH
DID SOMETHING HAPPEN?
GULP
Yes...
Although it's happened so suddenly I myself don't know many details.

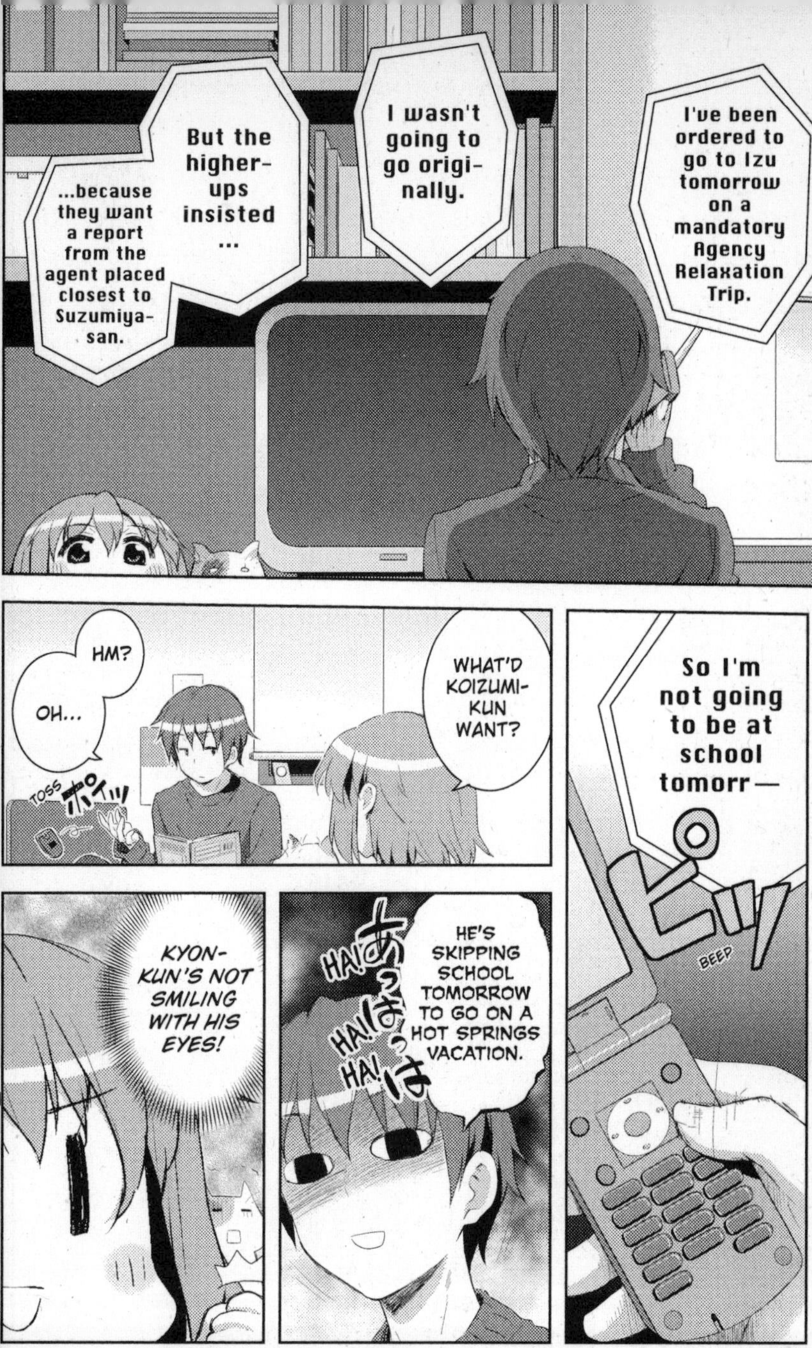
I've been ordered to go to Izu tomorrow on a mandatory Agency Relaxation Trip.
I wasn't going to go originally.
But the higher-ups insisted...
...because they want a report from the agent placed closest to Suzumiya-san.
So I'm not going to be at school tomorr—
ピッ
BEEP
WHAT'D KOIZUMI-KUN WANT?
HM?
OH...
ポイッ
TOSS
HE'S SKIPPING SCHOOL TOMORROW TO GO ON A HOT SPRINGS VACATION.
あっはっは
HA! HA! HA!
KYON-KUN'S NOT SMILING WITH HIS EYES!

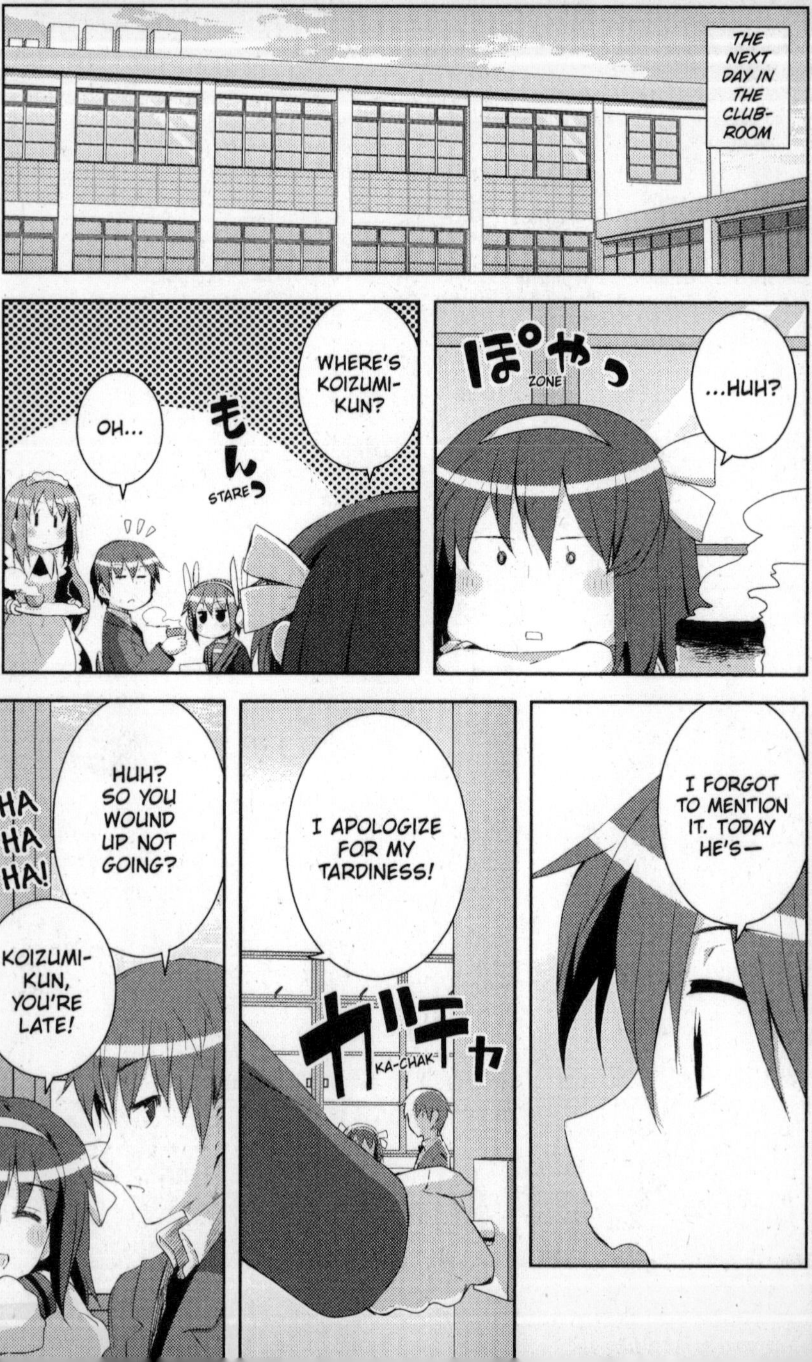
THE NEXT DAY IN THE CLUB-ROOM
ぽやっ
ZONE
...HUH?
WHERE'S KOIZUMI-KUN?
もんっ
STARE
OH...
I FORGOT TO MENTION IT. TODAY HE'S—
I APOLOGIZE FOR MY TARDINESS!
ガチャ
KA-CHAK
HUH? SO YOU WOUND UP NOT GOING?
HA HA HA!
KOIZUMI-KUN, YOU'RE LATE!

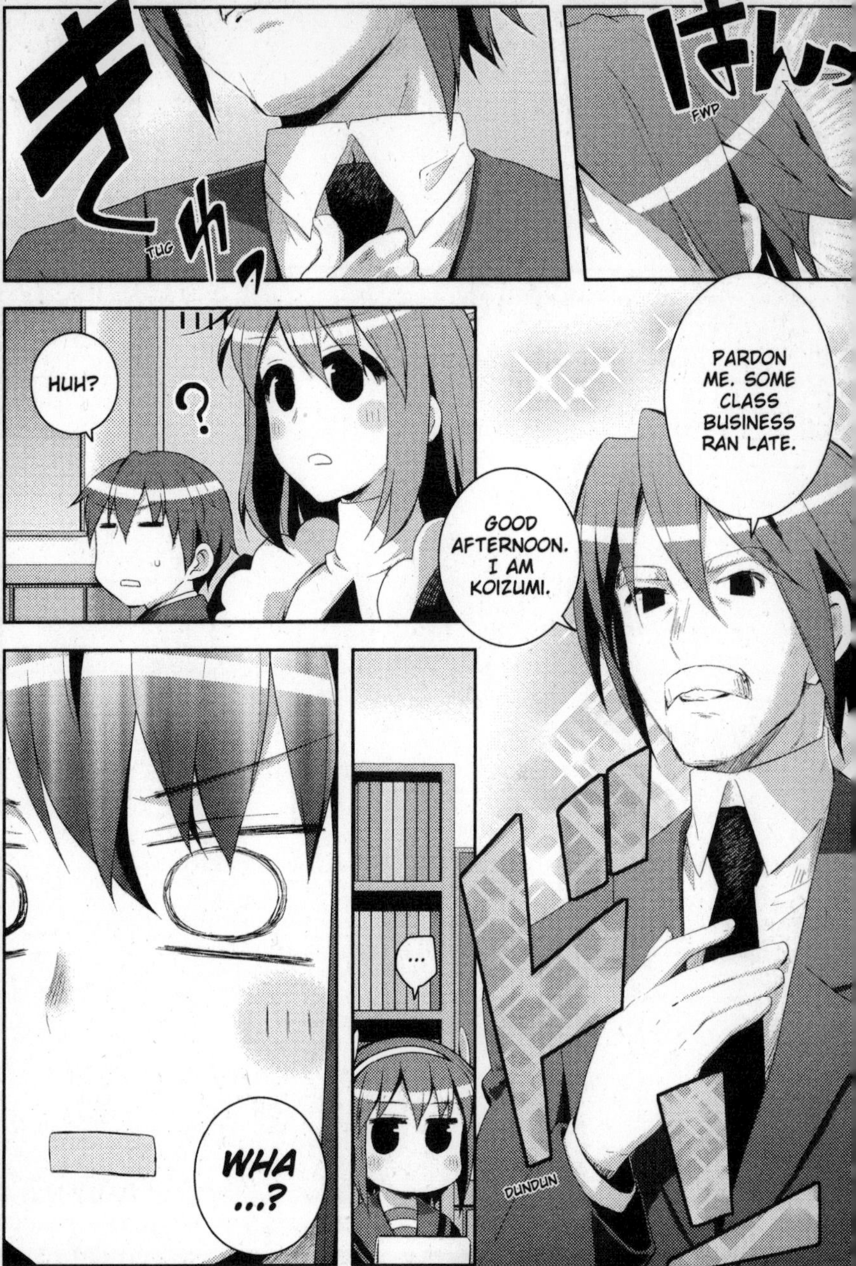
ばんっ
FWP
ぎゅっ
TUG
PARDON ME. SOME CLASS BUSINESS RAN LATE.
GOOD AFTERNOON. I AM KOIZUMI.
DUNDUN
HUH?
?
...
WHA ...?

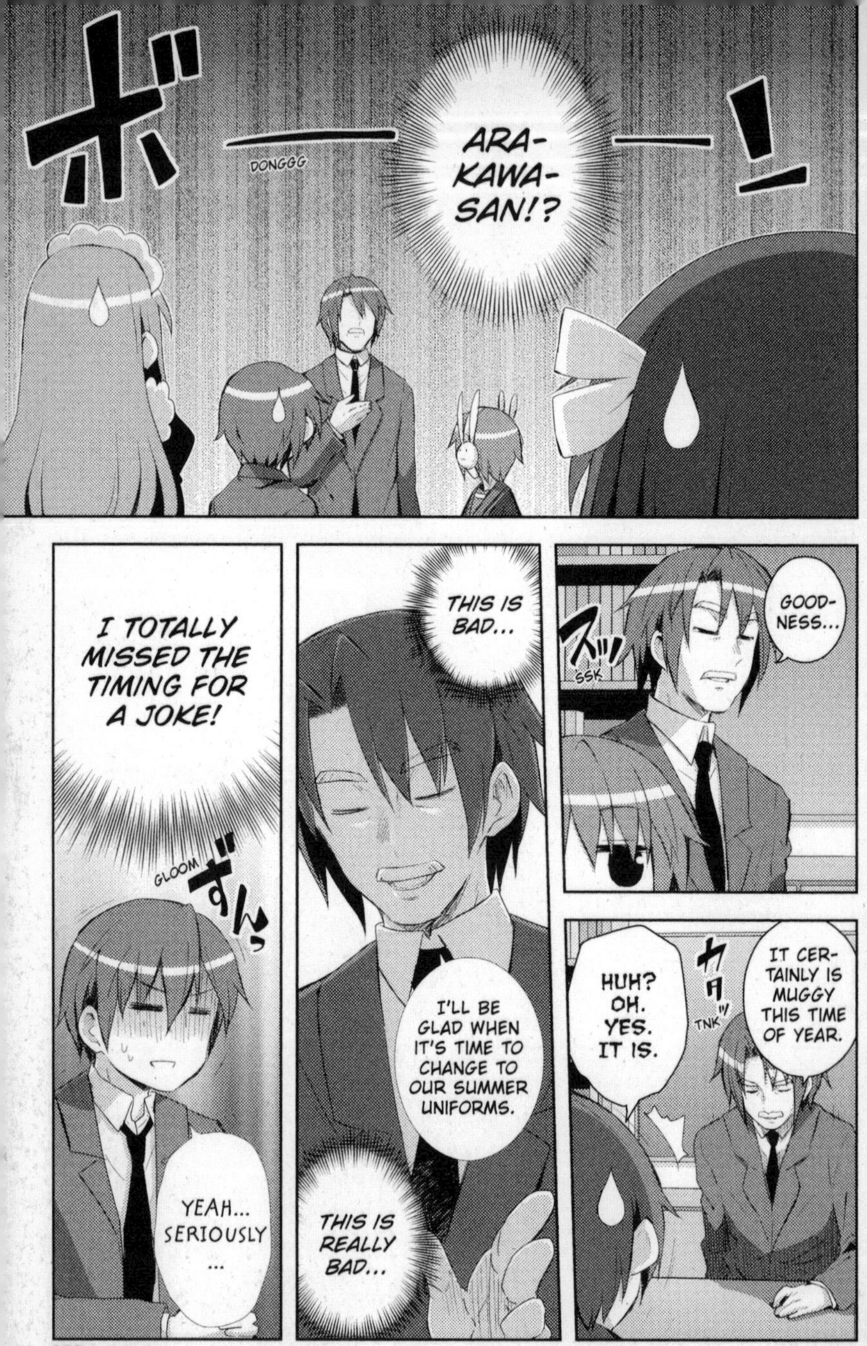
ボー
DONGGG
ARA-KAWA-SAN!?
ー!
GOODNESS...
ズッ
SSK
IT CERTAINLY IS MUGGY THIS TIME OF YEAR.
カタッ
TNK
HUH? OH. YES. IT IS.
THIS IS BAD...
I'LL BE GLAD WHEN IT'S TIME TO CHANGE TO OUR SUMMER UNIFORMS.
THIS IS REALLY BAD...
I TOTALLY MISSED THE TIMING FOR A JOKE!
GLOOM
ずんっ
YEAH... SERIOUSLY ...

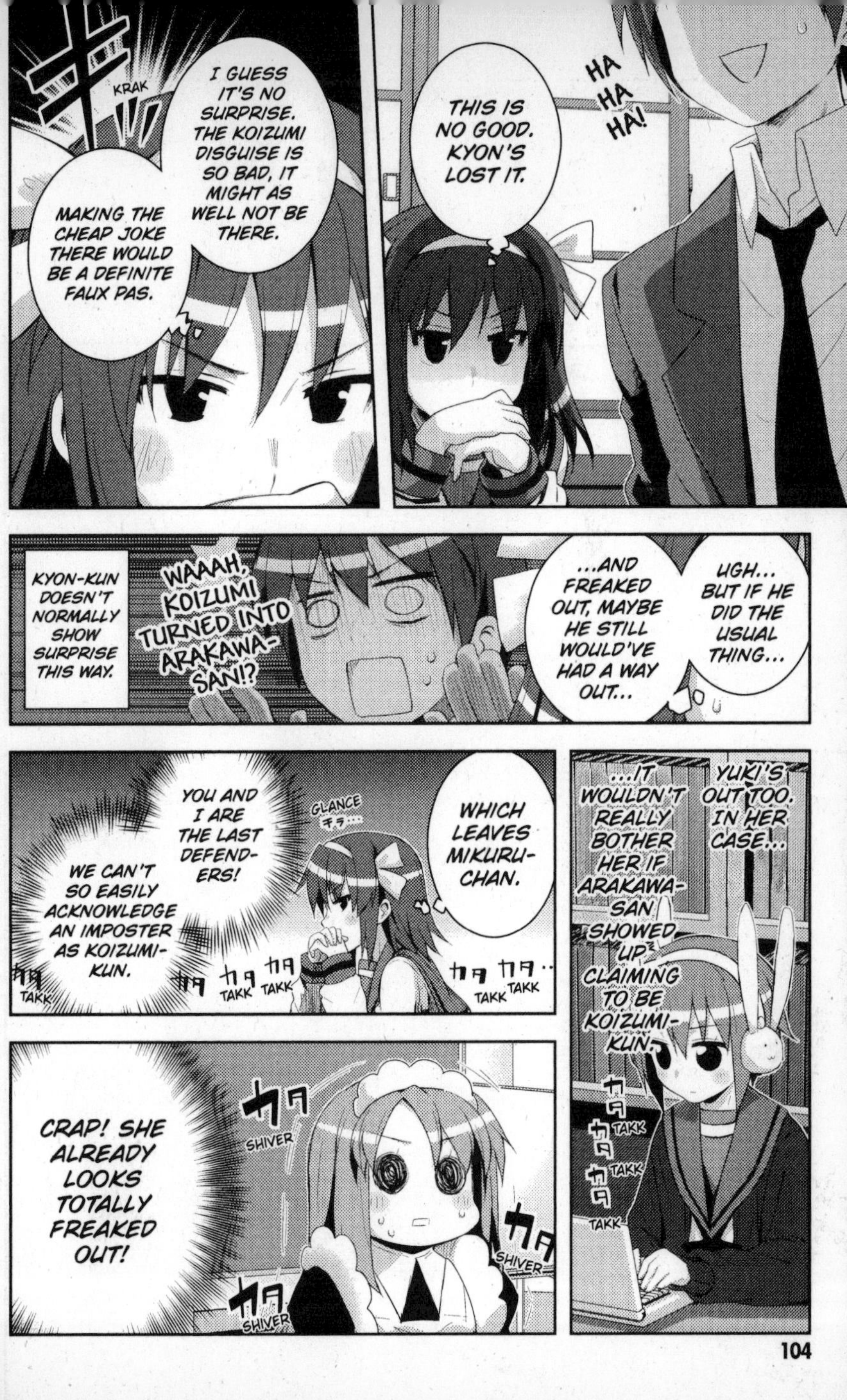
HA HA HA!
THIS IS NO GOOD. KYON'S LOST IT.
KRAK
I GUESS IT'S NO SURPRISE. THE KOIZUMI DISGUISE IS SO BAD, IT MIGHT AS WELL NOT BE THERE.
MAKING THE CHEAP JOKE THERE WOULD BE A DEFINITE FAUX PAS.
UGH... BUT IF HE DID THE USUAL THING...
...AND FREAKED OUT, MAYBE HE STILL WOULD'VE HAD A WAY OUT...
WAAAH, KOIZUMI TURNED INTO ARAKAWA-SAN!?
KYON-KUN DOESN'T NORMALLY SHOW SURPRISE THIS WAY.
YUKI'S OUT TOO. IN HER CASE...
...IT WOULDN'T REALLY BOTHER HER IF ARAKAWA-SAN SHOWED UP CLAIMING TO BE KOIZUMI-KUN.
カタ TAKK
カタ TAKK
カタ TAKK
WHICH LEAVES MIKURU-CHAN.
GLANCE チラ…
YOU AND I ARE THE LAST DEFENDERS!
WE CAN'T SO EASILY ACKNOWLEDGE AN IMPOSTER AS KOIZUMI-KUN.
カタ カタ… TAKK TAKK
カタ カタ TAKK TAKK
カタ TAKK
カタ SHIVER
CRAP! SHE ALREADY LOOKS TOTALLY FREAKED OUT!
カタ SHIVER
カタ SHIVER

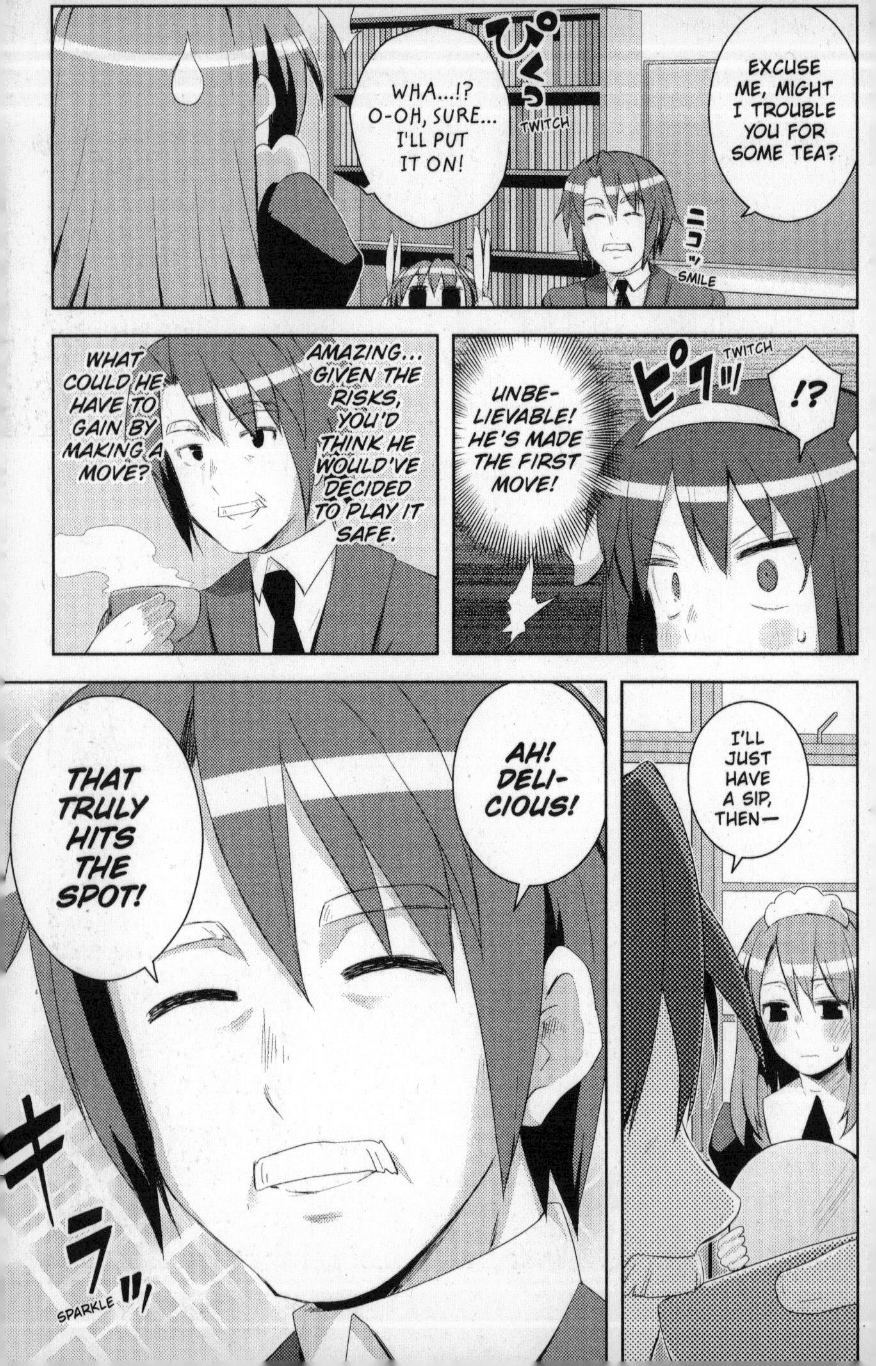
EXCUSE ME, MIGHT I TROUBLE YOU FOR SOME TEA?
ニコッ
SMILE
ぴくっ
TWITCH
WHA...!? O-OH, SURE... I'LL PUT IT ON!
ピクッ
TWITCH
!?
UNBE-LIEVABLE! HE'S MADE THE FIRST MOVE!
AMAZING... GIVEN THE RISKS, YOU'D THINK HE WOULD'VE DECIDED TO PLAY IT SAFE.
WHAT COULD HE HAVE TO GAIN BY MAKING A MOVE?
I'LL JUST HAVE A SIP, THEN—
AH! DELI-CIOUS!
THAT TRULY HITS THE SPOT!
キラッ
SPARKLE

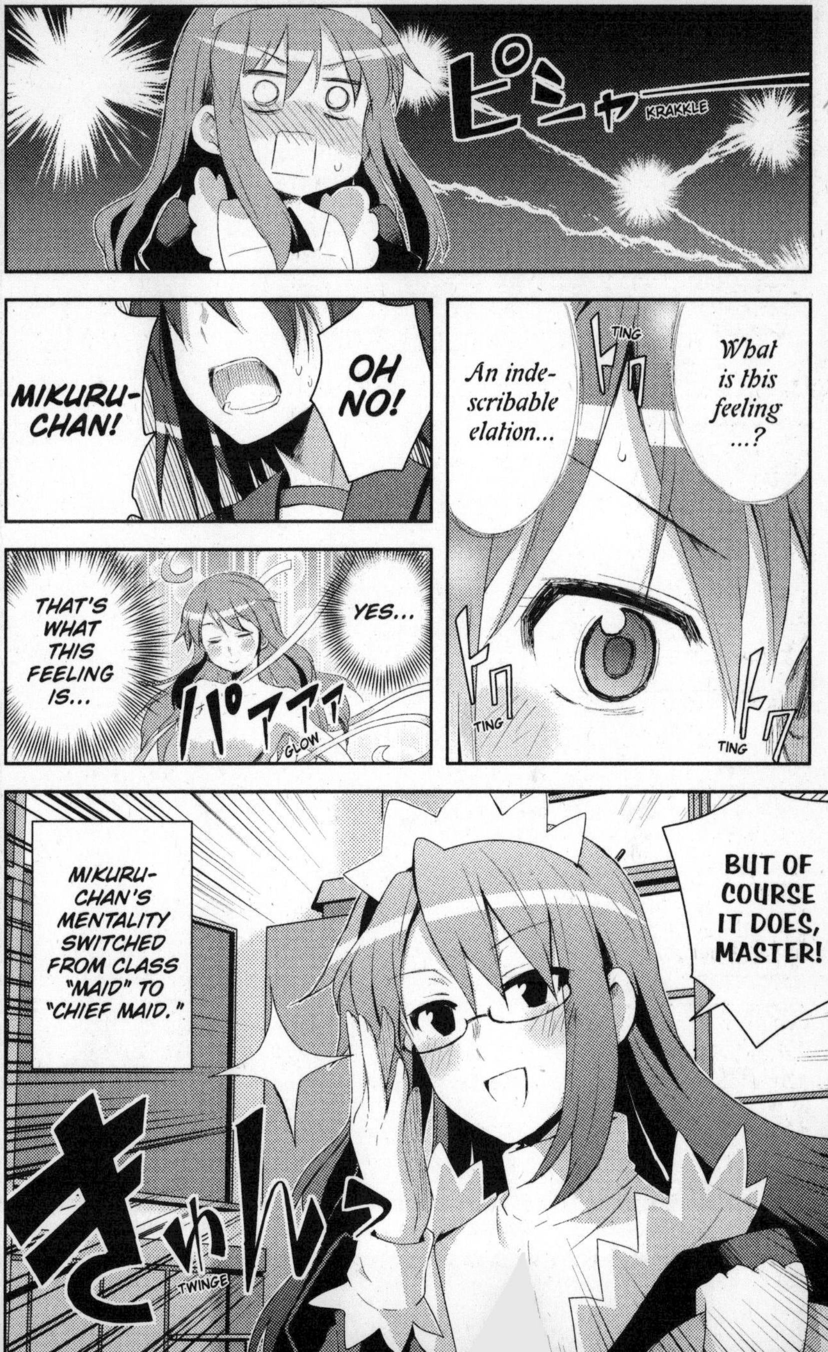

ピシャー
KRAKKLE
What is this feeling ...?
An inde-scribable elation...
TING
TING
TING
OH NO!
MIKURU-CHAN!
YES...
THAT'S WHAT THIS FEELING IS...
GLOW
BUT OF COURSE IT DOES, MASTER!
MIKURU-CHAN'S MENTALITY SWITCHED FROM CLASS "MAID" TO "CHIEF MAID."
TWINGE

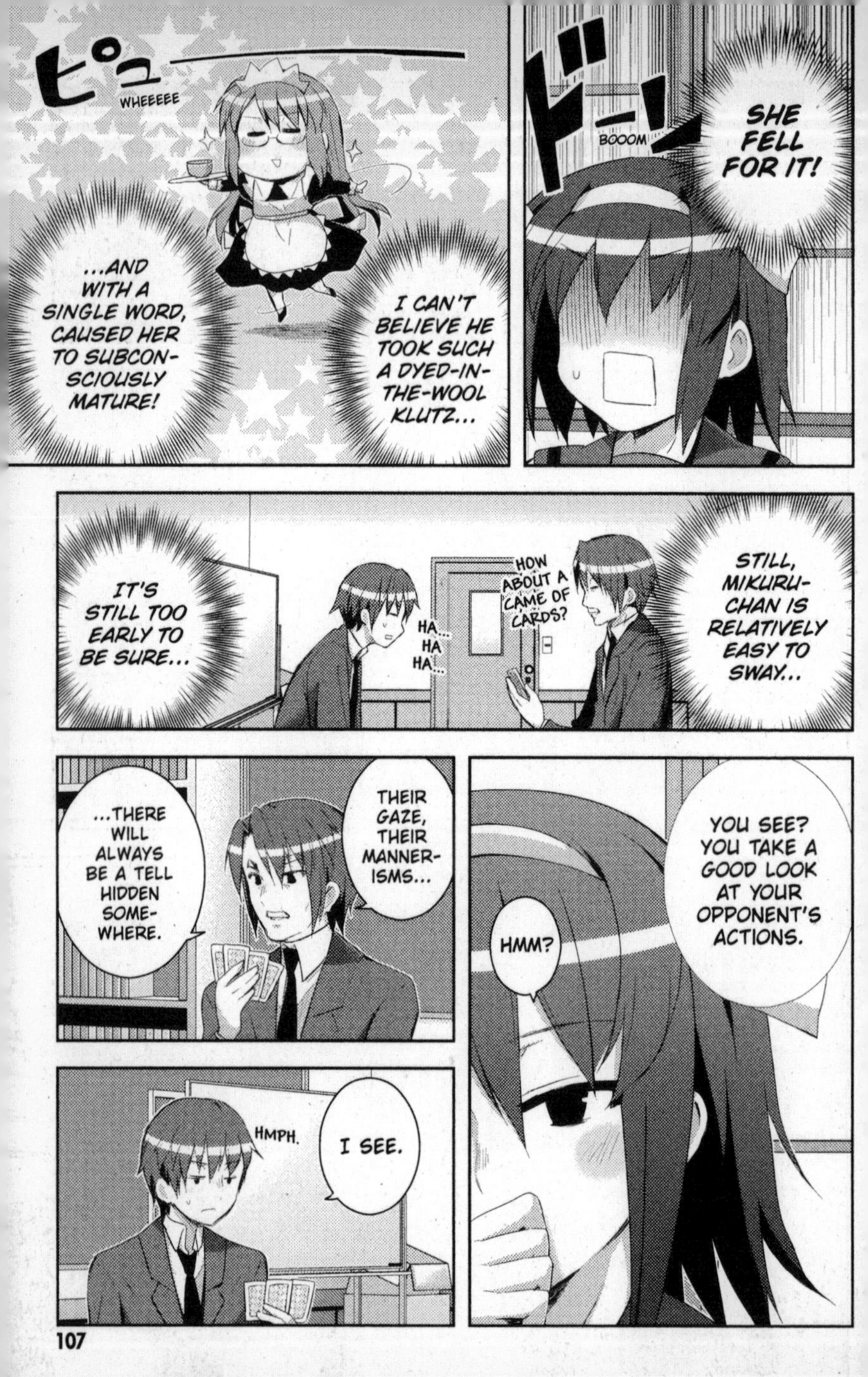
ドーン
BOOOM
SHE FELL FOR IT!
ピュ
WHEEEEE
I CAN'T BELIEVE HE TOOK SUCH A DYED-IN-THE-WOOL KLUTZ...
...AND WITH A SINGLE WORD, CAUSED HER TO SUBCON-SCIOUSLY MATURE!
STILL, MIKURU-CHAN IS RELATIVELY EASY TO SWAY...
HOW ABOUT A CAME OF CARDS?
HA... HA HA...
IT'S STILL TOO EARLY TO BE SURE...
YOU SEE? YOU TAKE A GOOD LOOK AT YOUR OPPONENT'S ACTIONS.
HMM?
THEIR GAZE, THEIR MANNER-ISMS...
...THERE WILL ALWAYS BE A TELL HIDDEN SOME-WHERE.
I SEE.
HMPH.

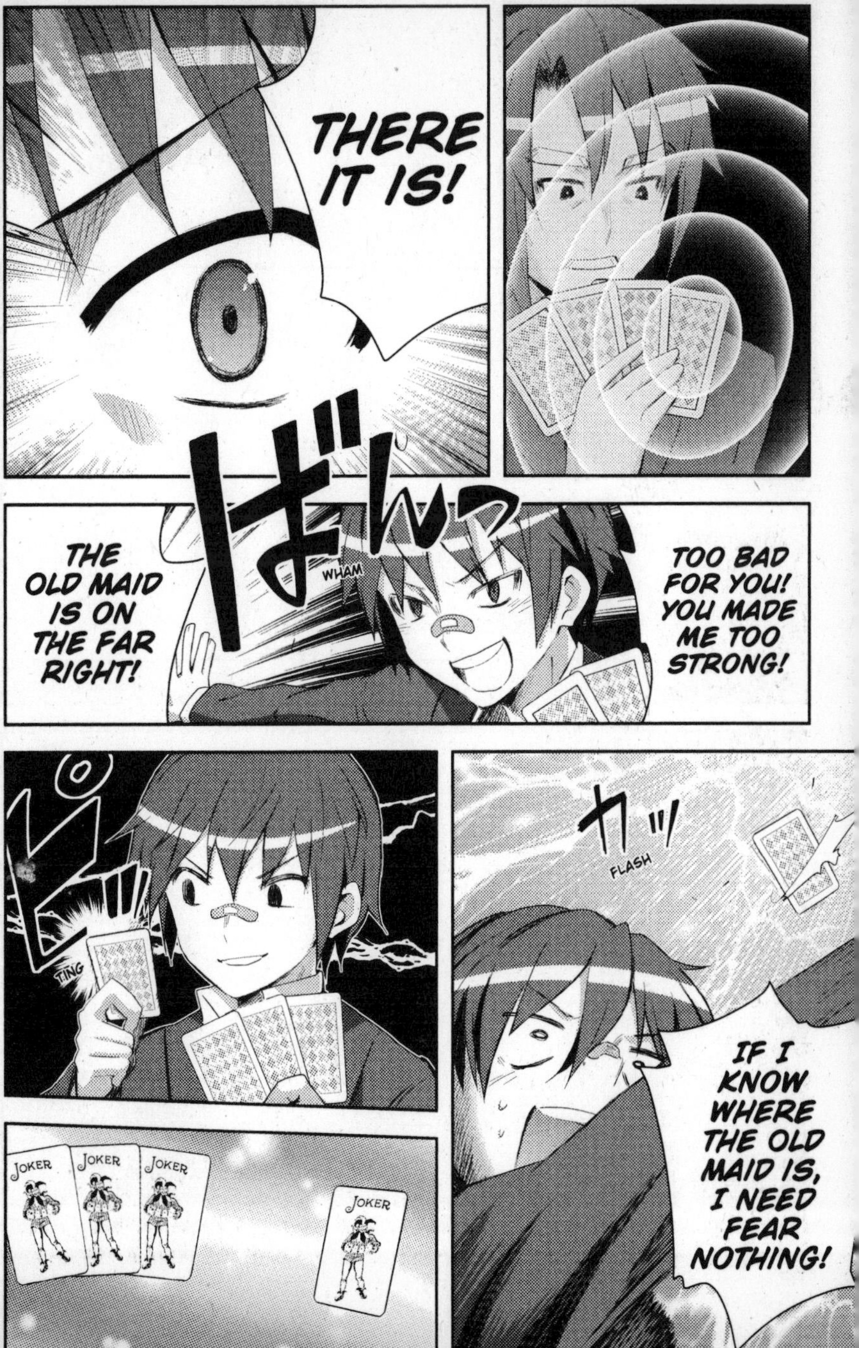
THERE IT IS!
ばんっ
WHAM
TOO BAD FOR YOU! YOU MADE ME TOO STRONG!
THE OLD MAID IS ON THE FAR RIGHT!
カッ
FLASH
IF I KNOW WHERE THE OLD MAID IS, I NEED FEAR NOTHING!
TING
JOKER
JOKER
JOKER
JOKER

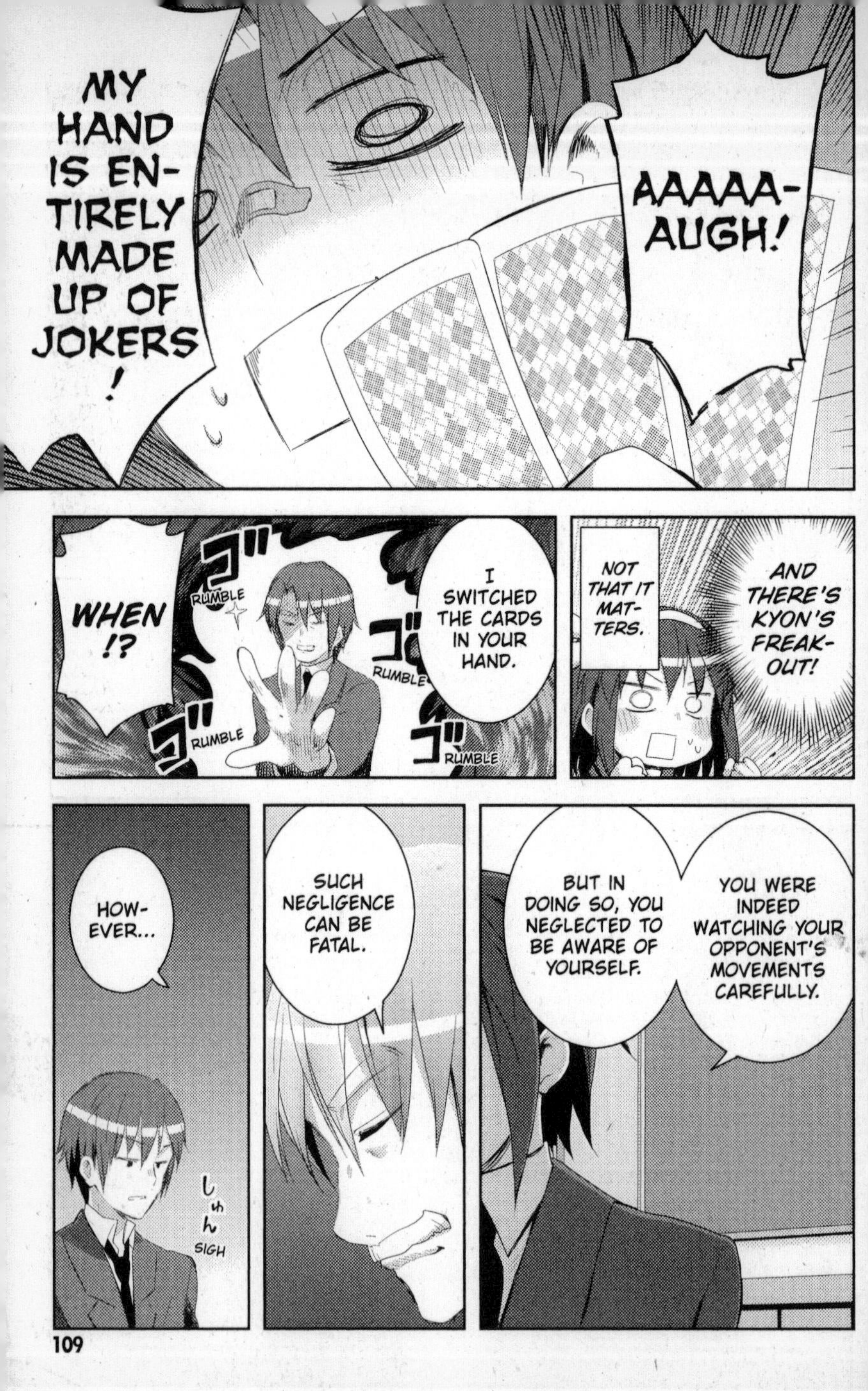
AAAAA-AUGH!
MY HAND IS ENTIRELY MADE UP OF JOKERS!
AND THERE'S KYON'S FREAK-OUT!
NOT THAT IT MATTERS.
I SWITCHED THE CARDS IN YOUR HAND.
RUMBLE
RUMBLE
RUMBLE
RUMBLE
WHEN!?
YOU WERE INDEED WATCHING YOUR OPPONENT'S MOVEMENTS CAREFULLY.
BUT IN DOING SO, YOU NEGLECTED TO BE AWARE OF YOURSELF.
SUCH NEGLIGENCE CAN BE FATAL.
HOWEVER...
SIGH

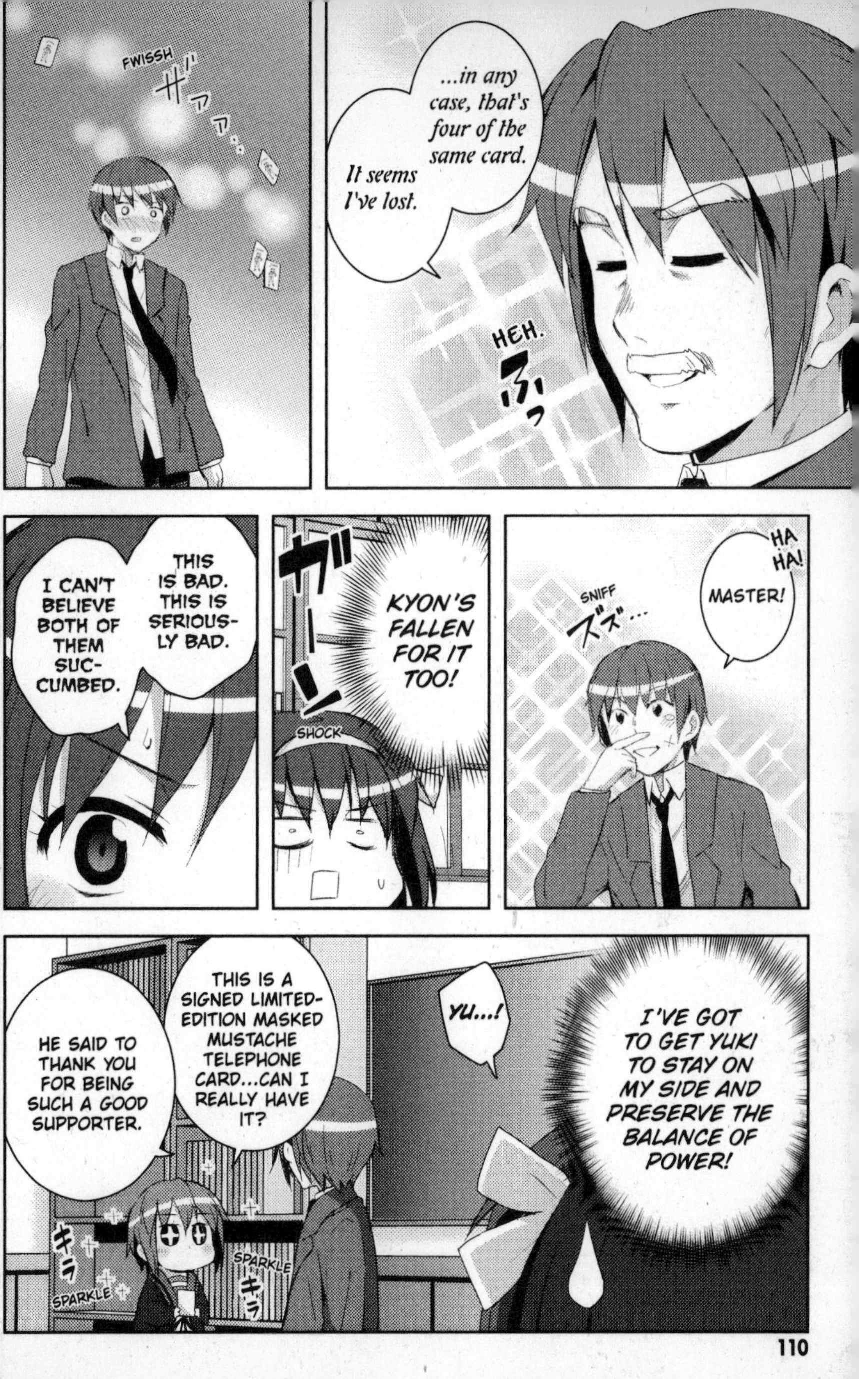
...in any case, that's four of the same card.
It seems I've lost.
HEH.
ふっ
FWISSH
ザァア...
HA HA! MASTER!
SNIFF
ズズ...
KYON'S FALLEN FOR IT TOO!
ガーン
SHOCK
THIS IS BAD. THIS IS SERIOUS-LY BAD.
I CAN'T BELIEVE BOTH OF THEM SUC-CUMBED.
I'VE GOT TO GET YUKI TO STAY ON MY SIDE AND PRESERVE THE BALANCE OF POWER!
YU...!
THIS IS A SIGNED LIMITED-EDITION MASKED MUSTACHE TELEPHONE CARD...CAN I REALLY HAVE IT?
HE SAID TO THANK YOU FOR BEING SUCH A GOOD SUPPORTER.
SPARKLE
キラ
SPARKLE
キラ

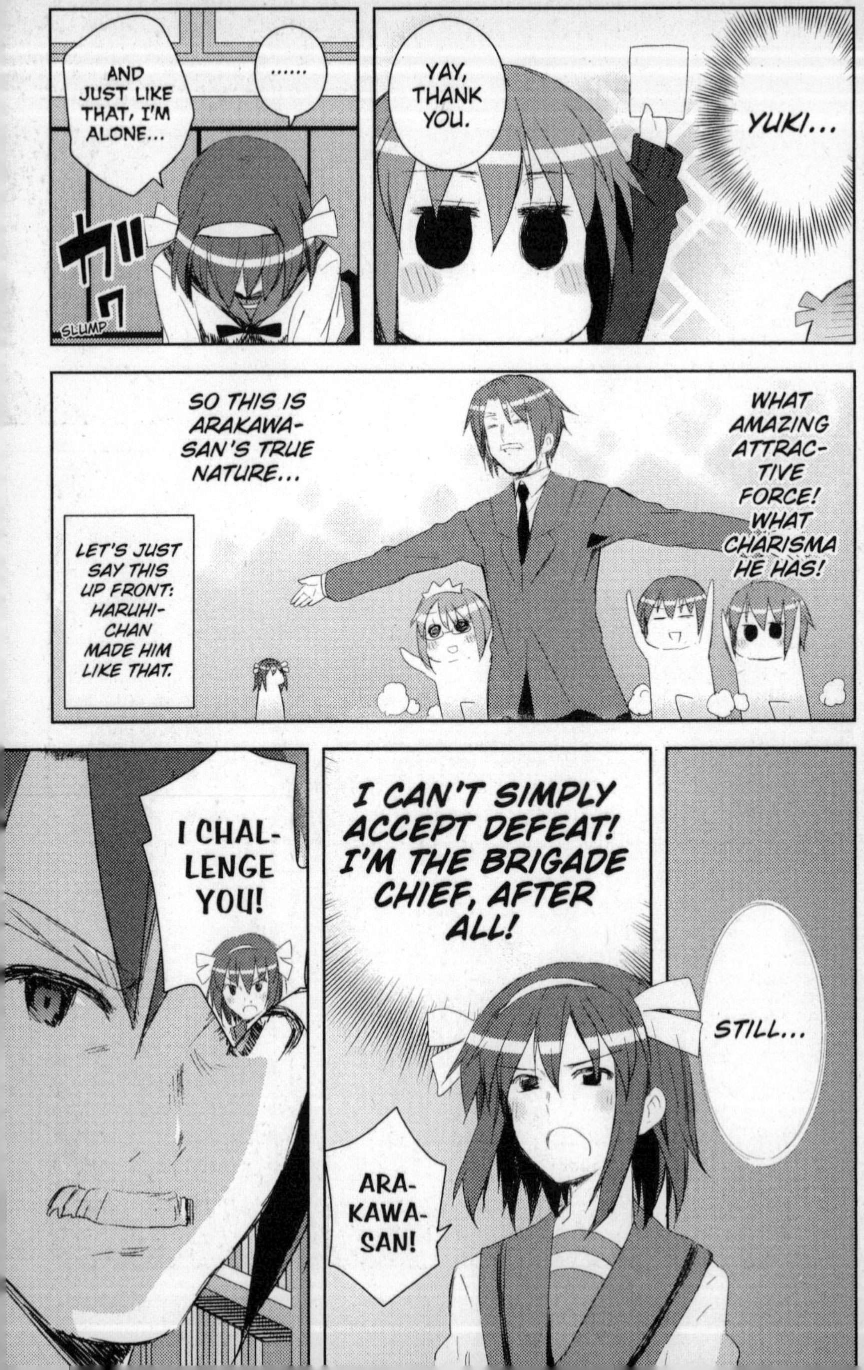
YAY, THANK YOU.
YUKI...
......
AND JUST LIKE THAT, I'M ALONE...
SLUMP
WHAT AMAZING ATTRAC-TIVE FORCE! WHAT CHARISMA HE HAS!
SO THIS IS ARAKAWA-SAN'S TRUE NATURE...
LET'S JUST SAY THIS UP FRONT: HARUHI-CHAN MADE HIM LIKE THAT.
STILL...
ARA-KAWA-SAN!
I CAN'T SIMPLY ACCEPT DEFEAT! I'M THE BRIGADE CHIEF, AFTER ALL!
I CHAL-LENGE YOU!

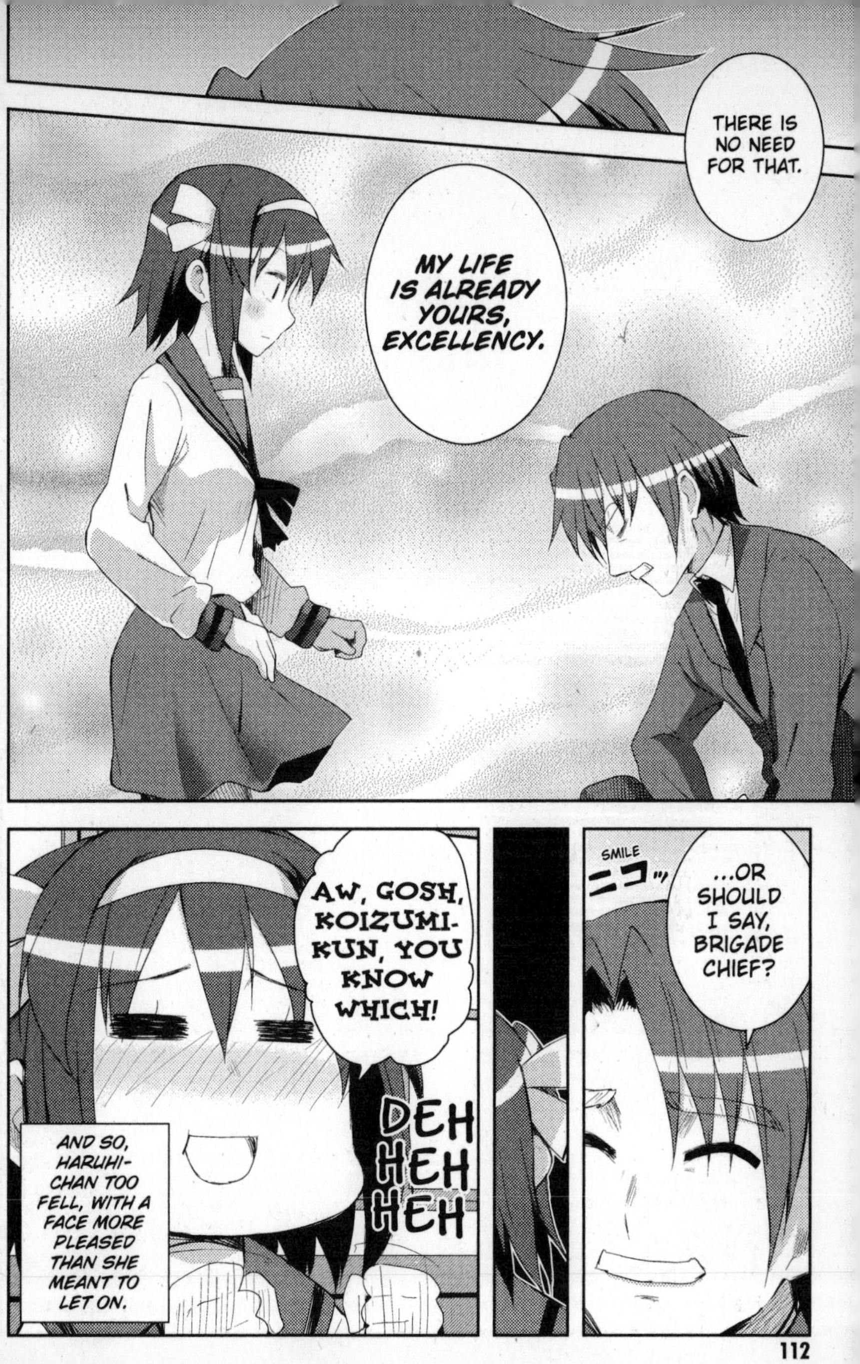
THERE IS NO NEED FOR THAT.
MY LIFE IS ALREADY YOURS, EXCELLENCY.
SMILE
ニコッ
...OR SHOULD I SAY, BRIGADE CHIEF?
AW, GOSH, KOIZUMI-KUN, YOU KNOW WHICH!
DEH HEH HEH
AND SO, HARUHI-CHAN TOO FELL, WITH A FACE MORE PLEASED THAN SHE MEANT TO LET ON.

REGRETS

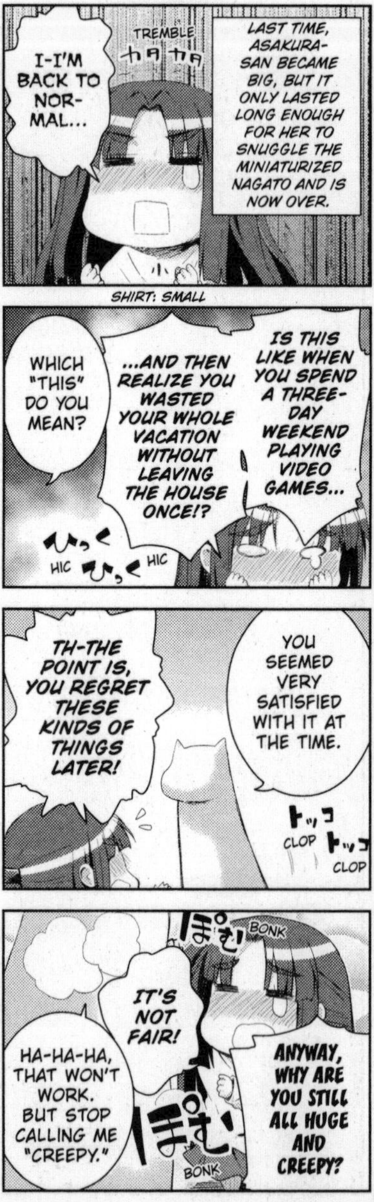
LAST TIME, ASAKURA-SAN BECAME BIG, BUT IT ONLY LASTED LONG ENOUGH FOR HER TO SNUGGLE THE MINIATURIZED NAGATO AND IS NOW OVER.
TREMBLE
I-I'M BACK TO NORMAL...
SHIRT: SMALL
IS THIS LIKE WHEN YOU SPEND A THREE-DAY WEEKEND PLAYING VIDEO GAMES...
...AND THEN REALIZE YOU WASTED YOUR WHOLE VACATION WITHOUT LEAVING THE HOUSE ONCE!?
WHICH "THIS" DO YOU MEAN?
HIC
HIC
YOU SEEMED VERY SATISFIED WITH IT AT THE TIME.
TH-THE POINT IS, YOU REGRET THESE KINDS OF THINGS LATER!
CLOP
CLOP
BONK
ANYWAY, WHY ARE YOU STILL ALL HUGE AND CREEPY?
IT'S NOT FAIR!
HA-HA-HA, THAT WON'T WORK. BUT STOP CALLING ME "CREEPY."
BONK

FEELING STYLISH

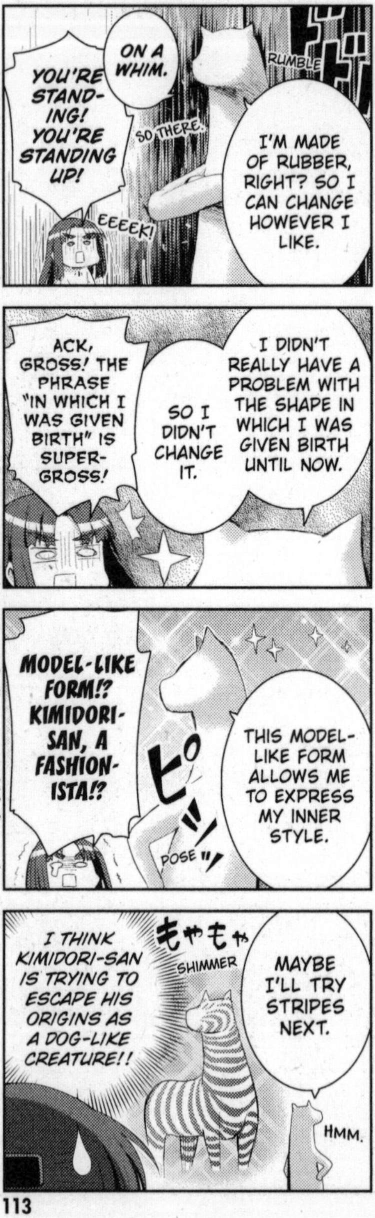
RUMBLE
I'M MADE OF RUBBER, RIGHT? SO I CAN CHANGE HOWEVER I LIKE.
ON A WHIM.
SO THERE.
YOU'RE STANDING! YOU'RE STANDING UP!
EEEEK!
I DIDN'T REALLY HAVE A PROBLEM WITH THE SHAPE IN WHICH I WAS GIVEN BIRTH UNTIL NOW.
SO I DIDN'T CHANGE IT.
ACK, GROSS! THE PHRASE "IN WHICH I WAS GIVEN BIRTH" IS SUPER-GROSS!
THIS MODEL-LIKE FORM ALLOWS ME TO EXPRESS MY INNER STYLE.
MODEL-LIKE FORM!? KIMIDORI-SAN, A FASHIONISTA!?
POSE
MAYBE I'LL TRY STRIPES NEXT.
SHIMMER
I THINK KIMIDORI-SAN IS TRYING TO ESCAPE HIS ORIGINS AS A DOG-LIKE CREATURE!!
HMM.

•Achakura-san •An alien who sometimes grows and sometimes shrinks. Kyon's Sister's disciple.

•Kimidori-san •A balloon animal life-form who's trying to escape his canine origins and move to the next stage of evolution.

PEGASUS

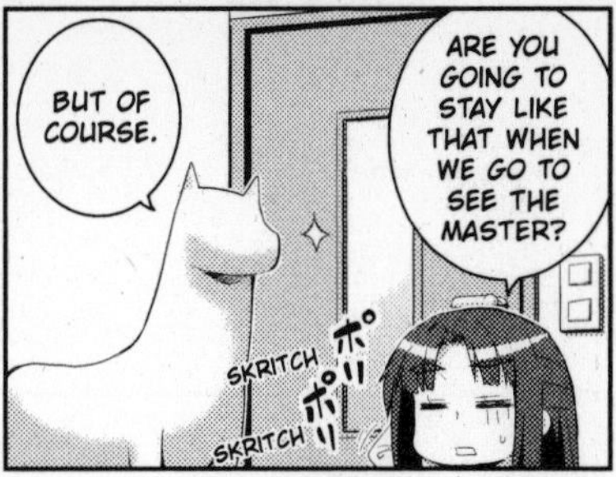
ARE YOU GOING TO STAY LIKE THAT WHEN WE GO TO SEE THE MASTER?
BUT OF COURSE.
ポリ SKRITCH
ポリ SKRITCH

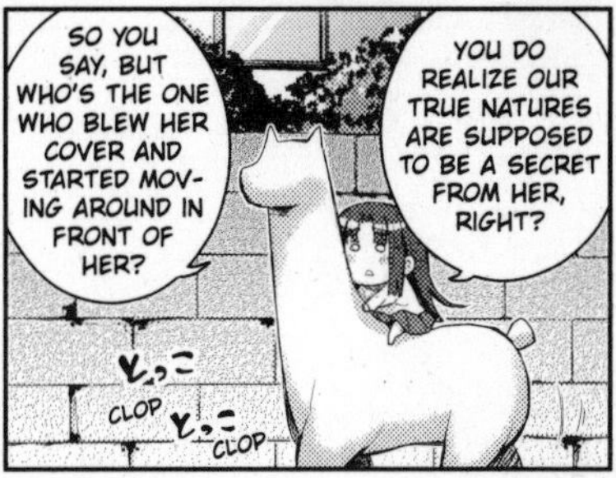
YOU DO REALIZE OUR TRUE NATURES ARE SUPPOSED TO BE A SECRET FROM HER, RIGHT?
SO YOU SAY, BUT WHO'S THE ONE WHO BLEW HER COVER AND STARTED MOVING AROUND IN FRONT OF HER?
とっこ CLOP
とっこ CLOP

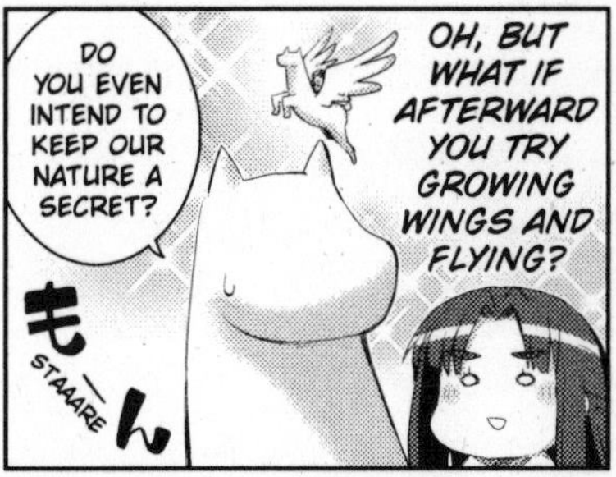
OH, BUT WHAT IF AFTERWARD YOU TRY GROWING WINGS AND FLYING?
DO YOU EVEN INTEND TO KEEP OUR NATURE A SECRET?
もーん STAAARE

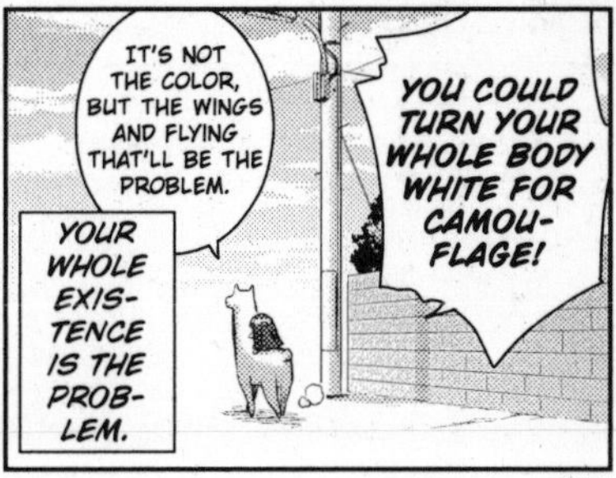
YOU COULD TURN YOUR WHOLE BODY WHITE FOR CAMOUFLAGE!
IT'S NOT THE COLOR, BUT THE WINGS AND FLYING THAT'LL BE THE PROBLEM.
YOUR WHOLE EXISTENCE IS THE PROBLEM.

WAIT, WAIT, DON'T TELL ME

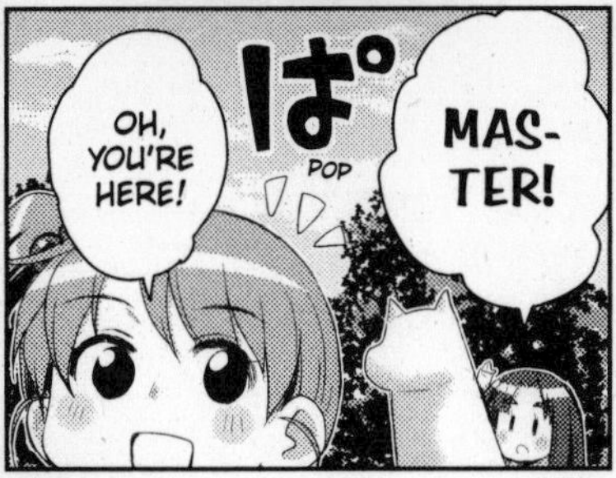
MASTER!
ぱ POP
OH, YOU'RE HERE!

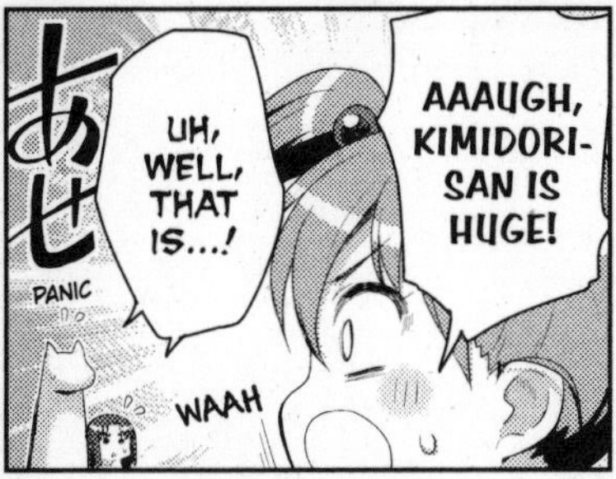
AAAUGH, KIMIDORI-SAN IS HUGE!
UH, WELL, THAT IS...!
あせ PANIC
WAAH

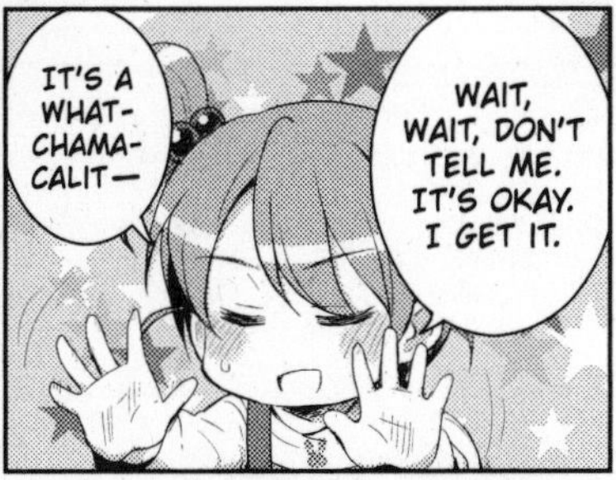
WAIT, WAIT, DON'T TELL ME. IT'S OKAY. I GET IT.
IT'S A WHATCHAMACALIT—

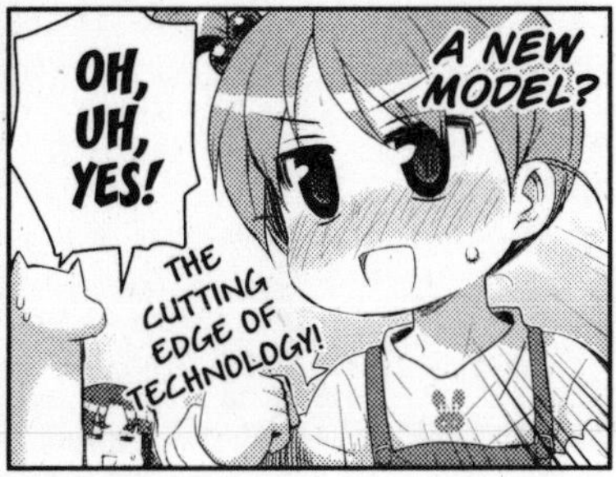
A NEW MODEL?
OH, UH, YES!
THE CUTTING EDGE OF TECHNOLOGY!

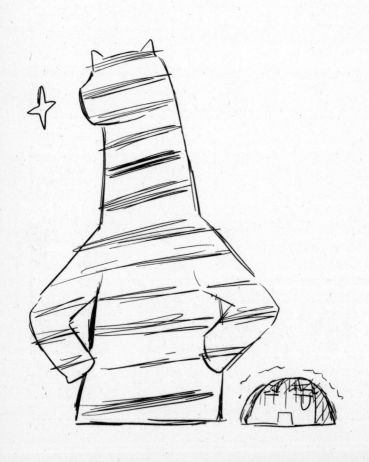

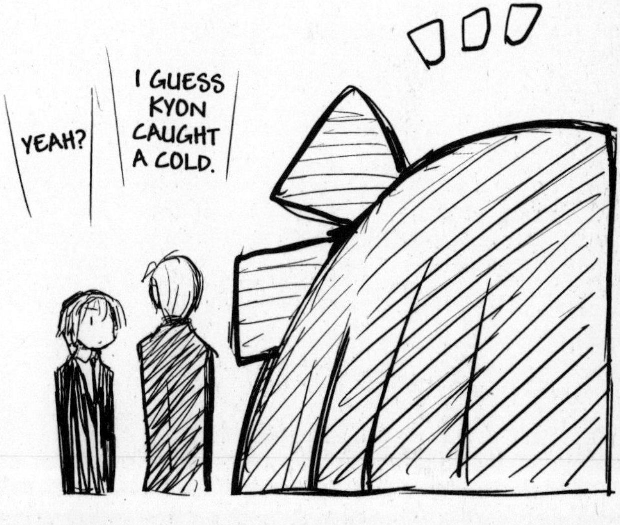
I GUESS KYON CAUGHT A COLD.
YEAH?

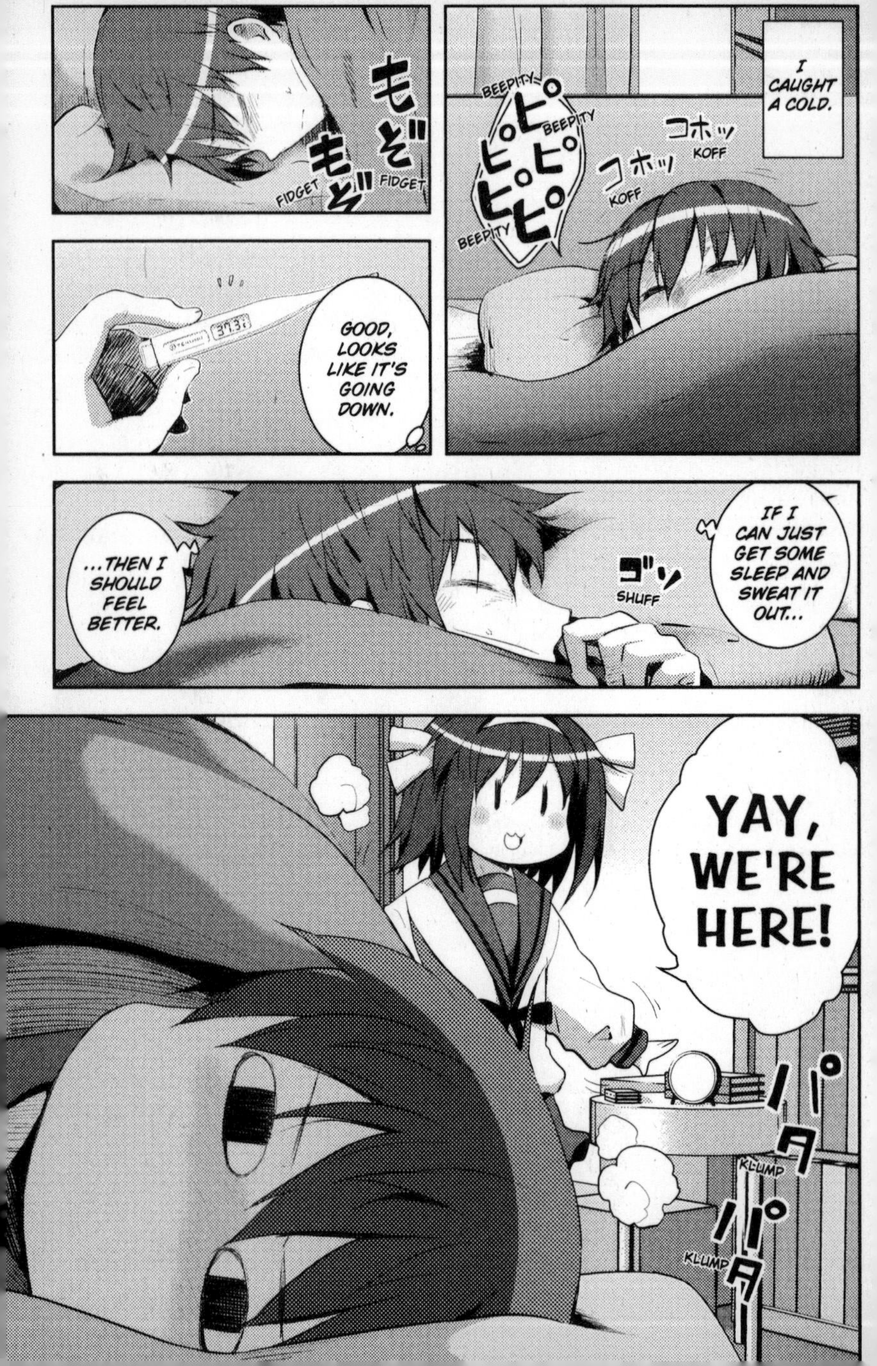
I CAUGHT A COLD.
コホッ
KOFF
コホッ
KOFF
ピピピピピピ
BEEPITY BEEPITY BEEPITY
もぞもぞ
FIDGET FIDGET
GOOD, LOOKS LIKE IT'S GOING DOWN.
IF I CAN JUST GET SOME SLEEP AND SWEAT IT OUT...
ゴッ
SHUFF
...THEN I SHOULD FEEL BETTER.
YAY, WE'RE HERE!
パタパタ
KLUMP KLUMP

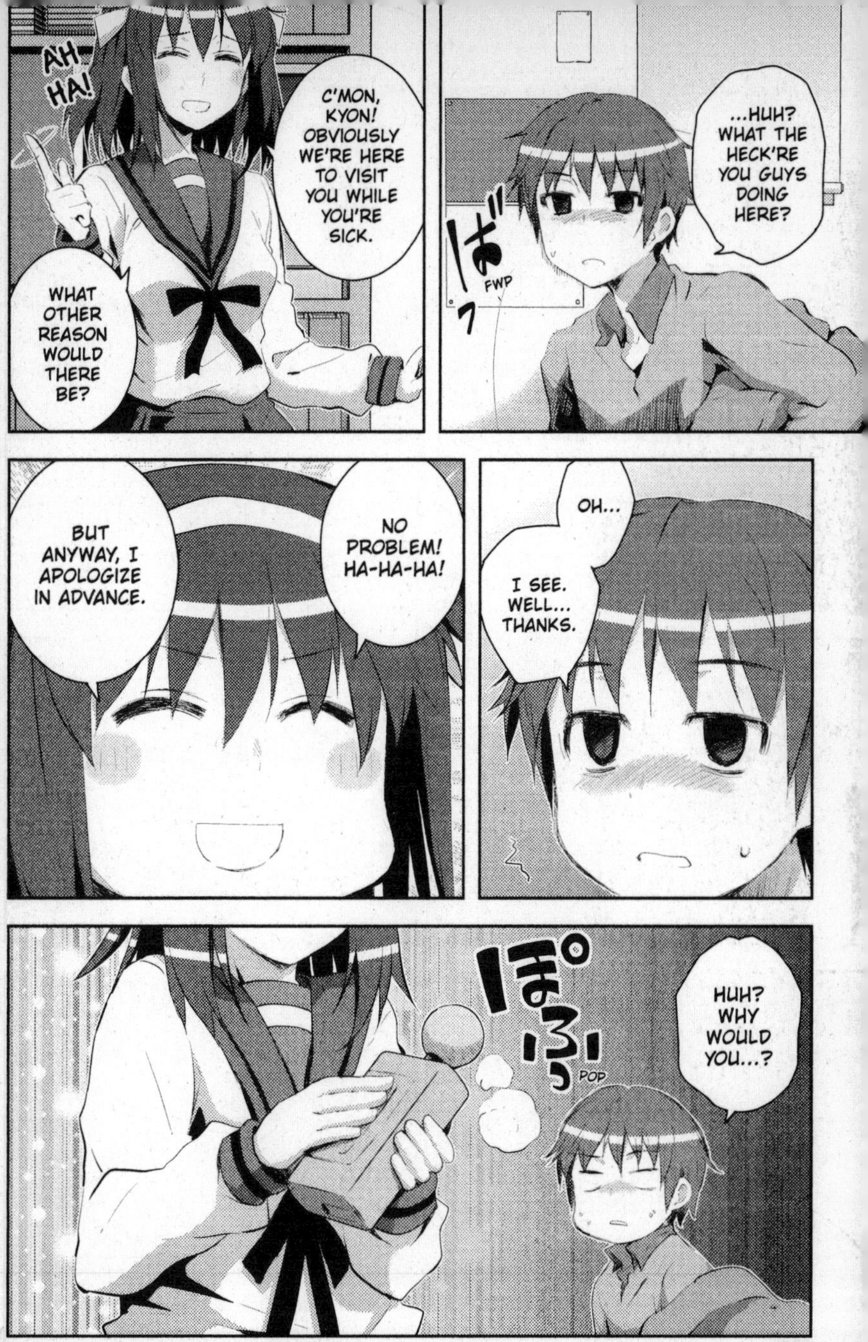
...HUH? WHAT THE HECK'RE YOU GUYS DOING HERE?
FWP
AH HA!
C'MON, KYON! OBVIOUSLY WE'RE HERE TO VISIT YOU WHILE YOU'RE SICK.
WHAT OTHER REASON WOULD THERE BE?
OH...
I SEE. WELL... THANKS.
NO PROBLEM! HA-HA-HA!
BUT ANYWAY, I APOLOGIZE IN ADVANCE.
POP
HUH? WHY WOULD YOU...?

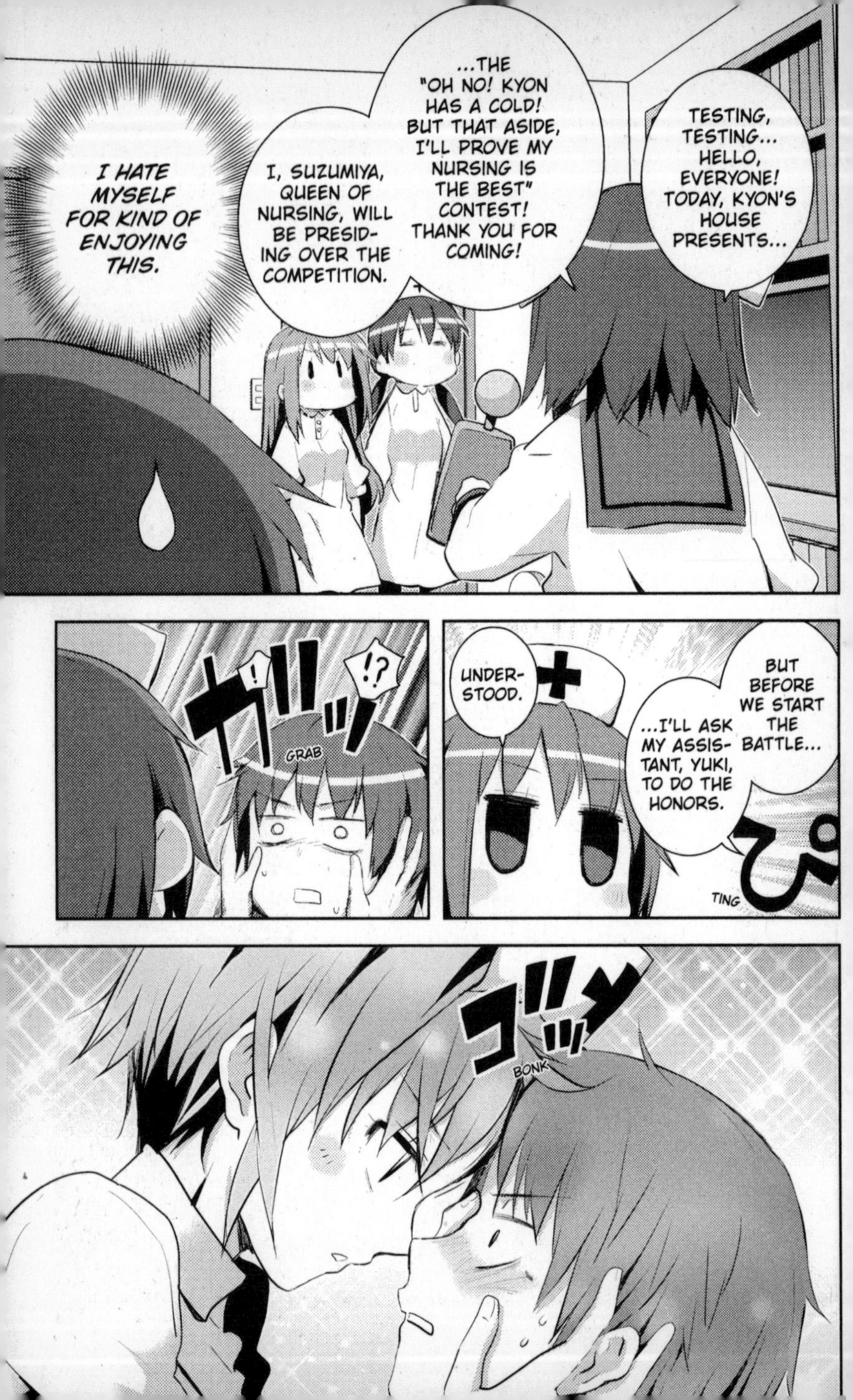
TESTING, TESTING... HELLO, EVERYONE! TODAY, KYON'S HOUSE PRESENTS...
..."THE "OH NO! KYON HAS A COLD! BUT THAT ASIDE, I'LL PROVE MY NURSING IS THE BEST" CONTEST! THANK YOU FOR COMING!
I, SUZUMIYA, QUEEN OF NURSING, WILL BE PRESID-ING OVER THE COMPETITION.
I HATE MYSELF FOR KIND OF ENJOYING THIS.
BUT BEFORE WE START THE BATTLE...
...I'LL ASK MY ASSIS-TANT, YUKI, TO DO THE HONORS.
TING
UNDER-STOOD.
!?
!
GRAB
BONK

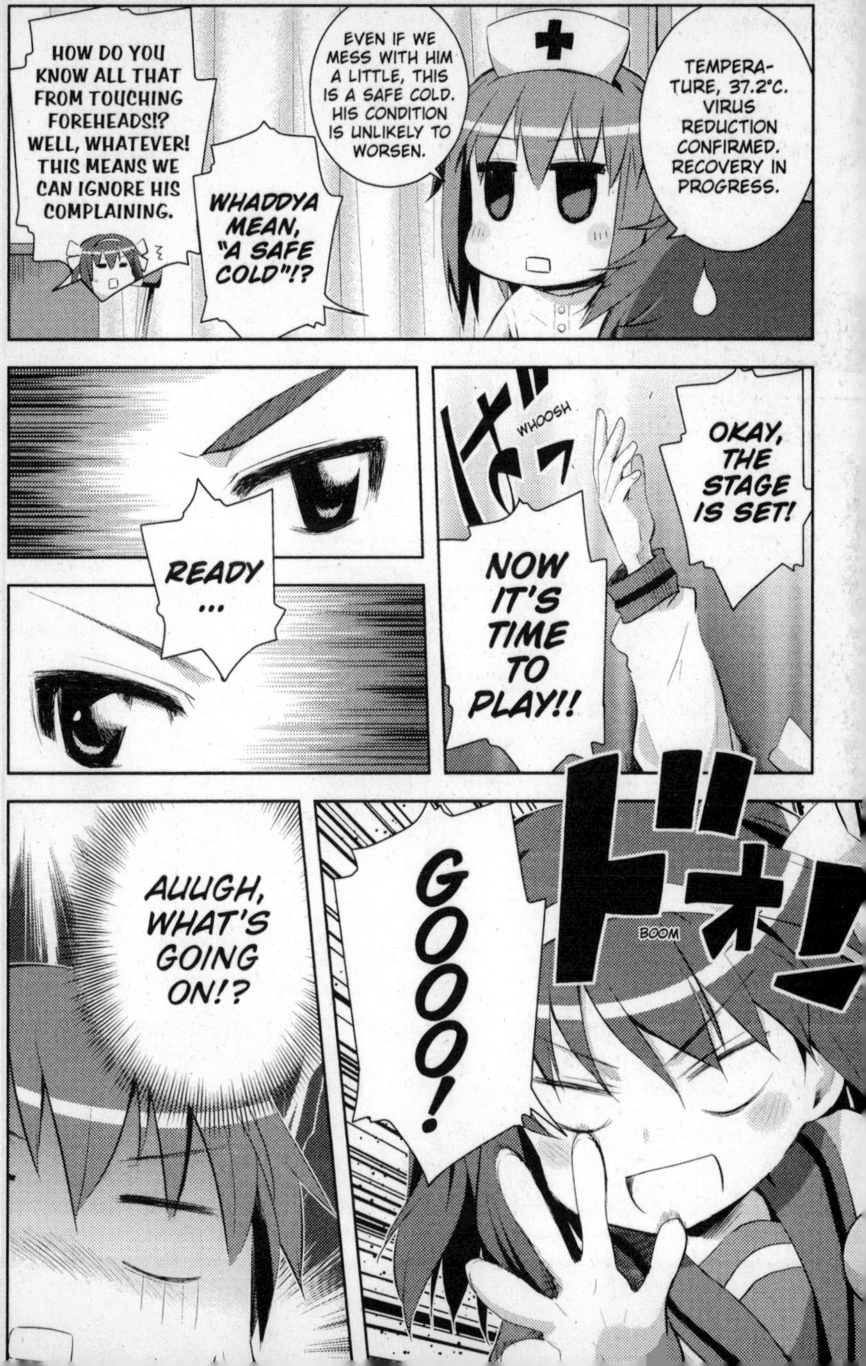
TEMPERATURE, 37.2°C. VIRUS REDUCTION CONFIRMED. RECOVERY IN PROGRESS.
EVEN IF WE MESS WITH HIM A LITTLE, THIS IS A SAFE COLD. HIS CONDITION IS UNLIKELY TO WORSEN.
WHADDYA MEAN, "A SAFE COLD"!?
HOW DO YOU KNOW ALL THAT FROM TOUCHING FOREHEADS!? WELL, WHATEVER! THIS MEANS WE CAN IGNORE HIS COMPLAINING.
WHOOSH
OKAY, THE STAGE IS SET!
NOW IT'S TIME TO PLAY!!
READY...
BOOM
GOOOO!
AUUGH, WHAT'S GOING ON!?

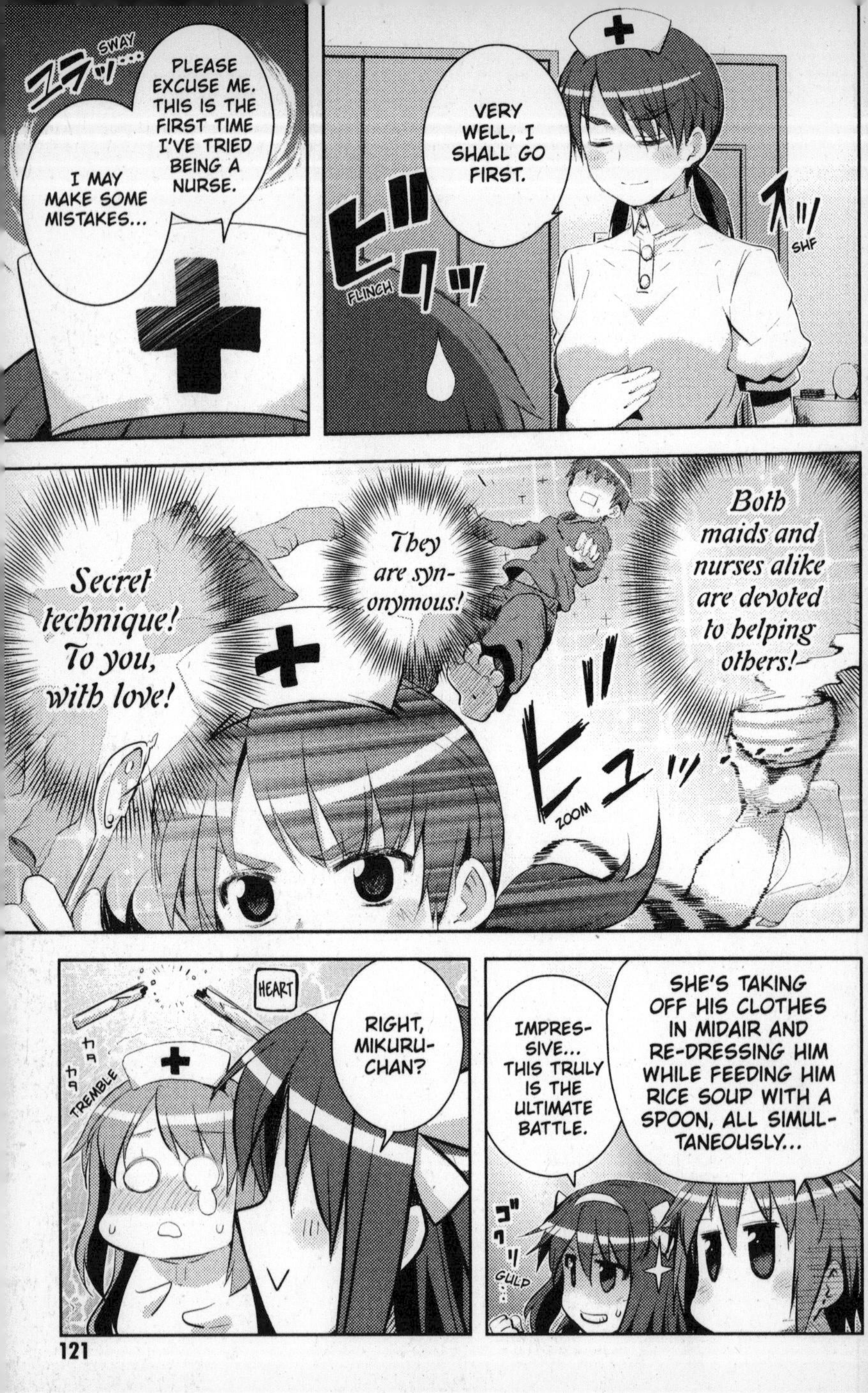
VERY WELL, I SHALL GO FIRST.
SHF
FLINCH
SWAY
PLEASE EXCUSE ME. THIS IS THE FIRST TIME I'VE TRIED BEING A NURSE.
I MAY MAKE SOME MISTAKES...
Both maids and nurses alike are devoted to helping others!
They are synonymous!
Secret technique! To you, with love!
ZOOM
SHE'S TAKING OFF HIS CLOTHES IN MIDAIR AND RE-DRESSING HIM WHILE FEEDING HIM RICE SOUP WITH A SPOON, ALL SIMULTANEOUSLY...
IMPRESSIVE... THIS TRULY IS THE ULTIMATE BATTLE.
GULP
RIGHT, MIKURU-CHAN?
HEART
TREMBLE

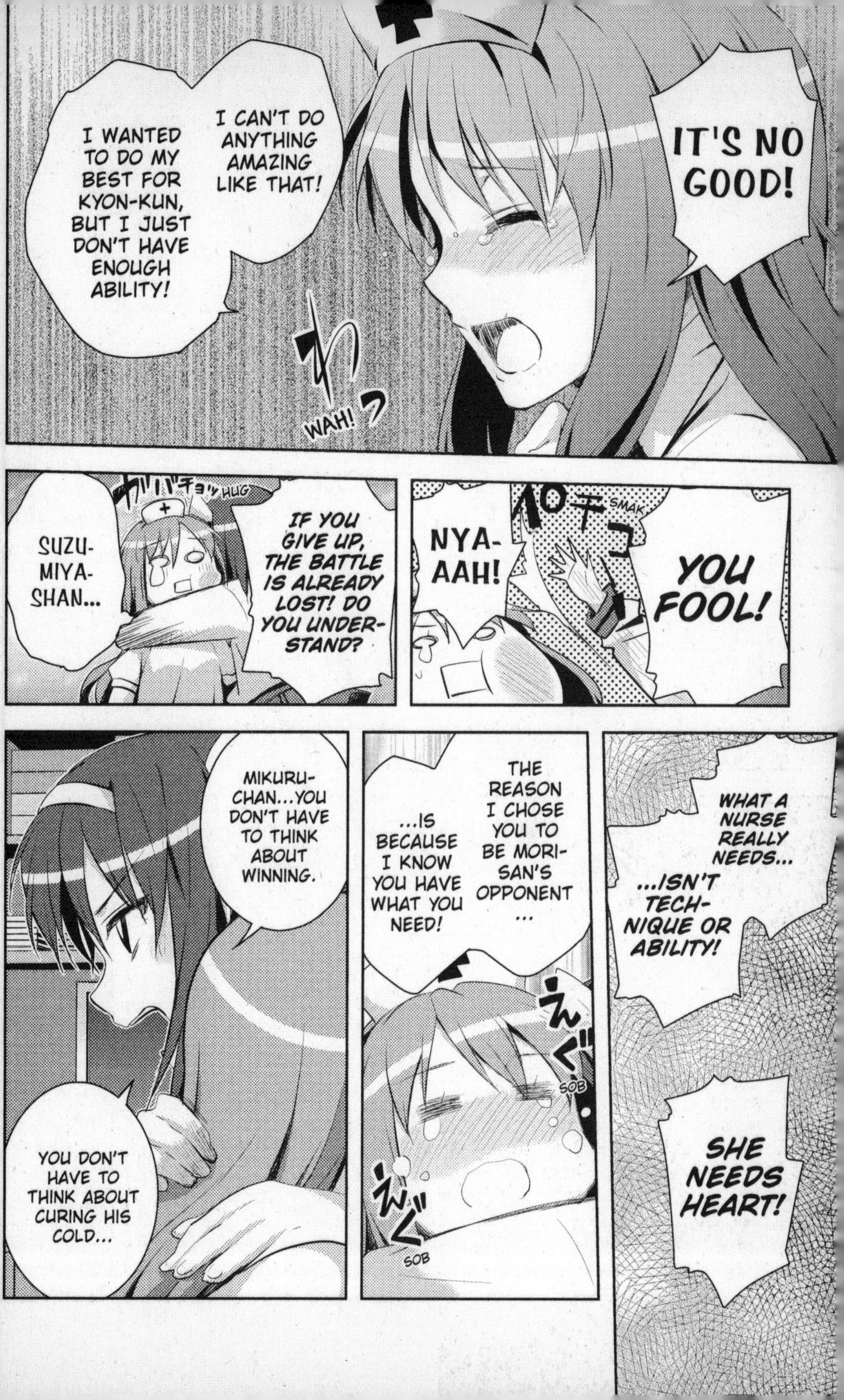
IT'S NO GOOD!
I CAN'T DO ANYTHING AMAZING LIKE THAT!
I WANTED TO DO MY BEST FOR KYON-KUN, BUT I JUST DON'T HAVE ENOUGH ABILITY!
WAH!
YOU FOOL!
SMAK
NYA-AAH!
IF YOU GIVE UP, THE BATTLE IS ALREADY LOST! DO YOU UNDERSTAND?
HUG
SUZU-MIYA-SHAN...
WHAT A NURSE REALLY NEEDS...
...ISN'T TECH-NIQUE OR ABILITY!
SHE NEEDS HEART!
THE REASON I CHOSE YOU TO BE MORI-SAN'S OPPONENT...
...IS BECAUSE I KNOW YOU HAVE WHAT YOU NEED!
SOB
SOB
MIKURU-CHAN...YOU DON'T HAVE TO THINK ABOUT WINNING.
YOU DON'T HAVE TO THINK ABOUT CURING HIS COLD...

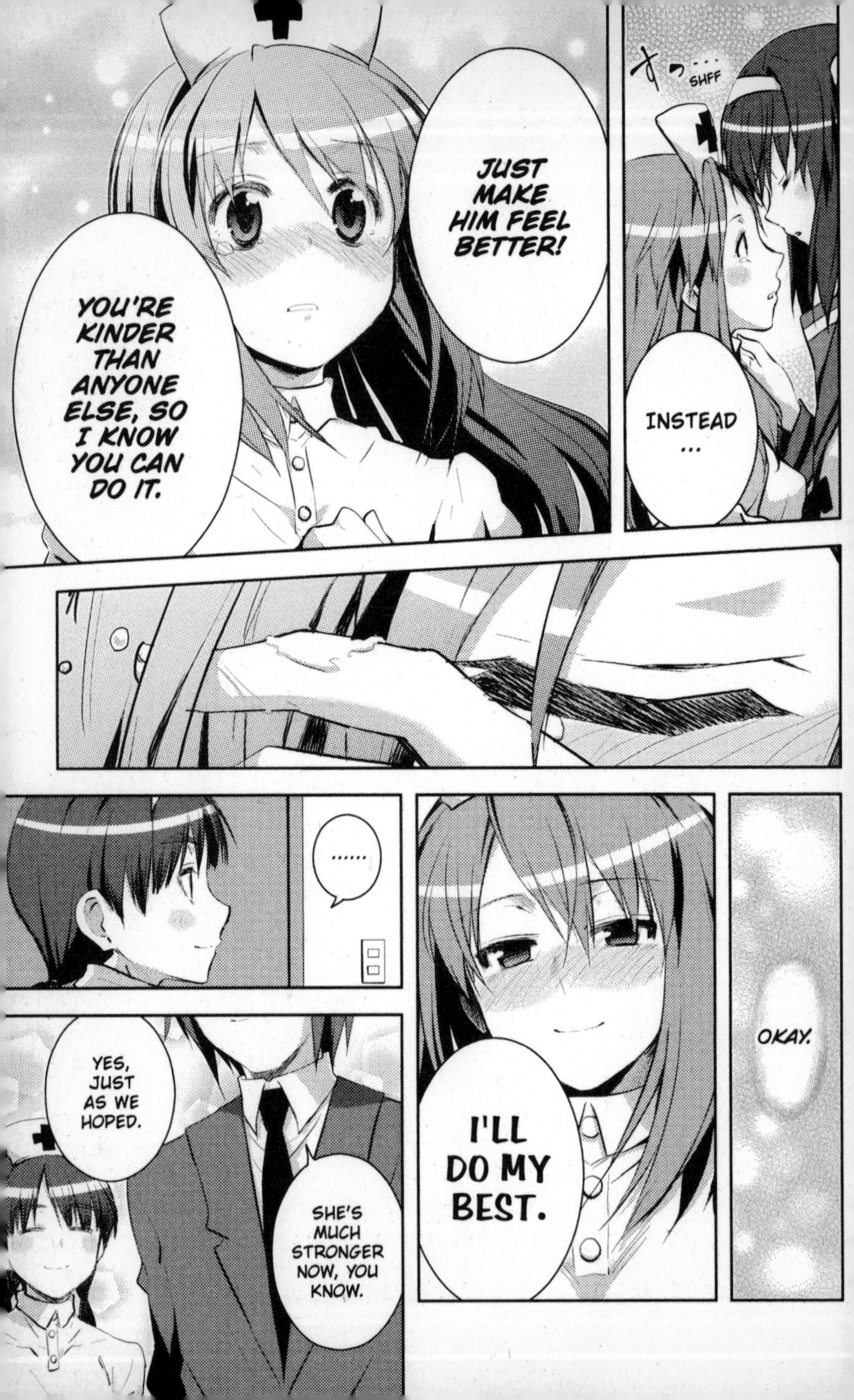
すっ…
SHFF
INSTEAD ...
JUST MAKE HIM FEEL BETTER!
YOU'RE KINDER THAN ANYONE ELSE, SO I KNOW YOU CAN DO IT.
OKAY.
I'LL DO MY BEST.
......
YES, JUST AS WE HOPED.
SHE'S MUCH STRONGER NOW, YOU KNOW.

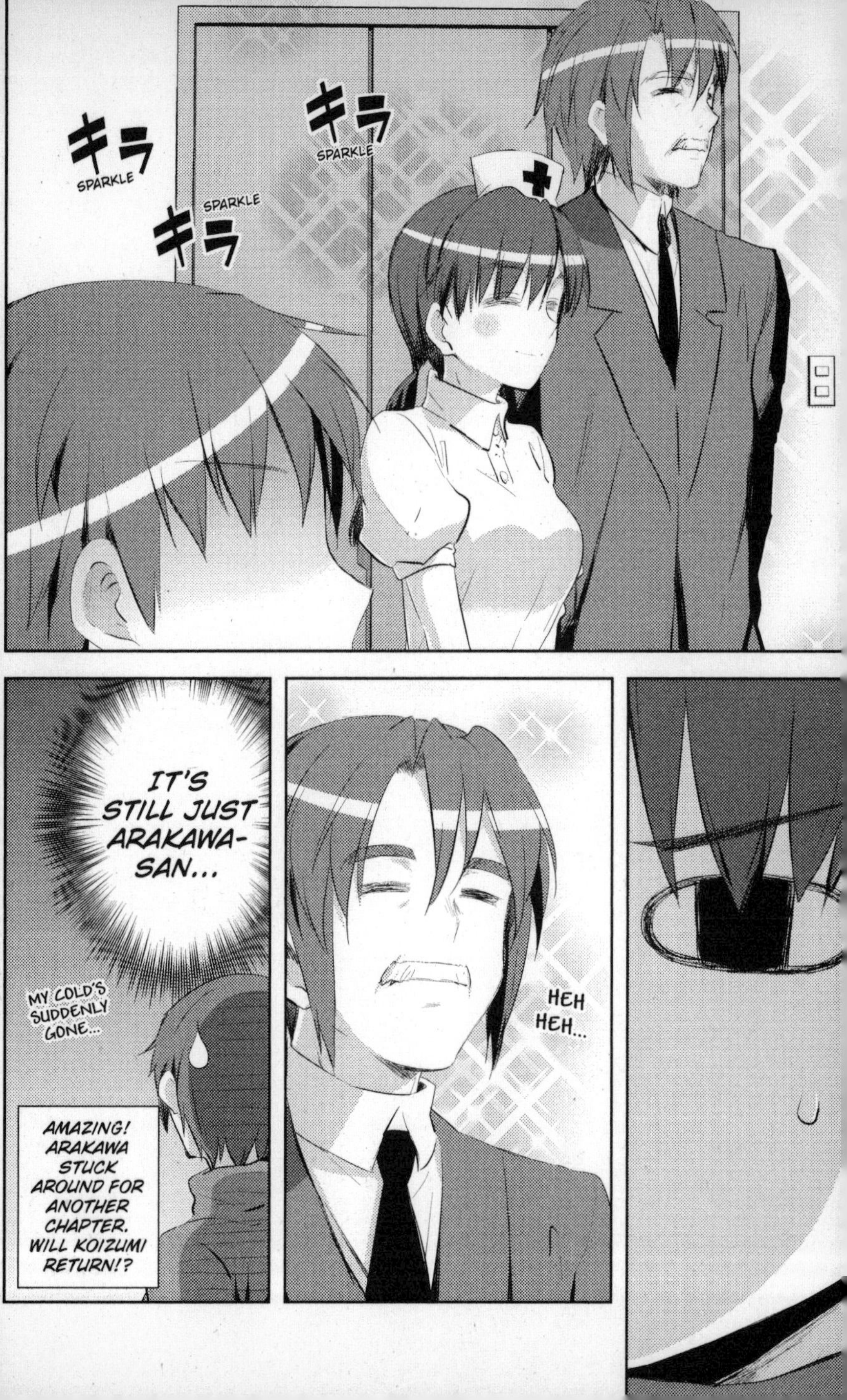
キラ
SPARKLE
キラ
SPARKLE
SPARKLE
キラ
HEH HEH...
IT'S STILL JUST ARAKAWA-SAN...
MY COLD'S SUDDENLY GONE...
AMAZING! ARAKAWA STUCK AROUND FOR ANOTHER CHAPTER. WILL KOIZUMI RETURN!?

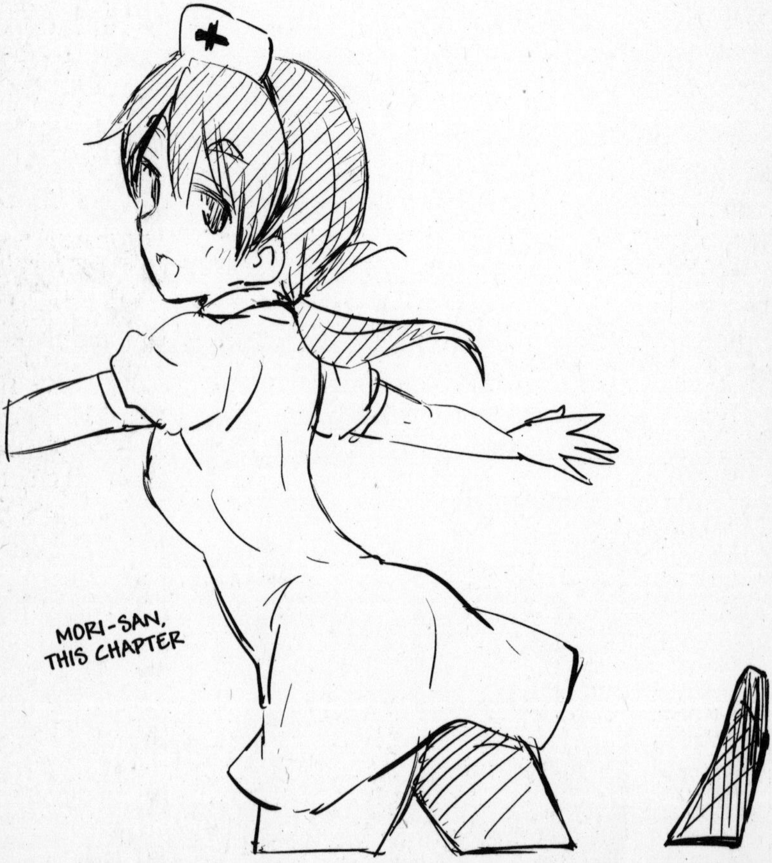
MORI-SAN,
THIS CHAPTER

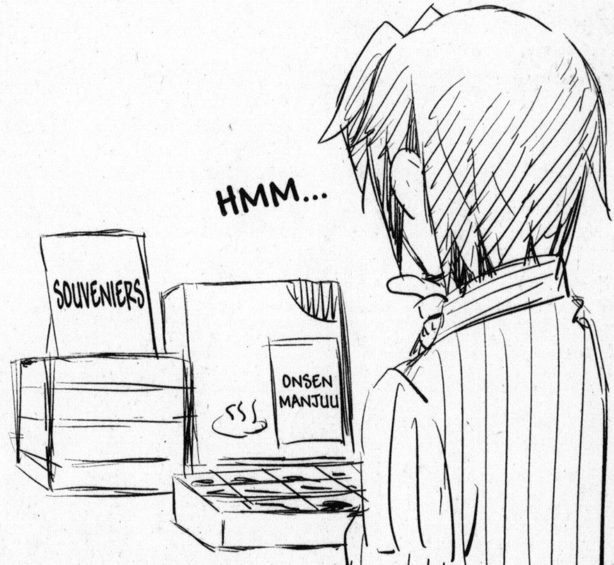
HMM...
SOUVENIERS
ONSEN MANJUU

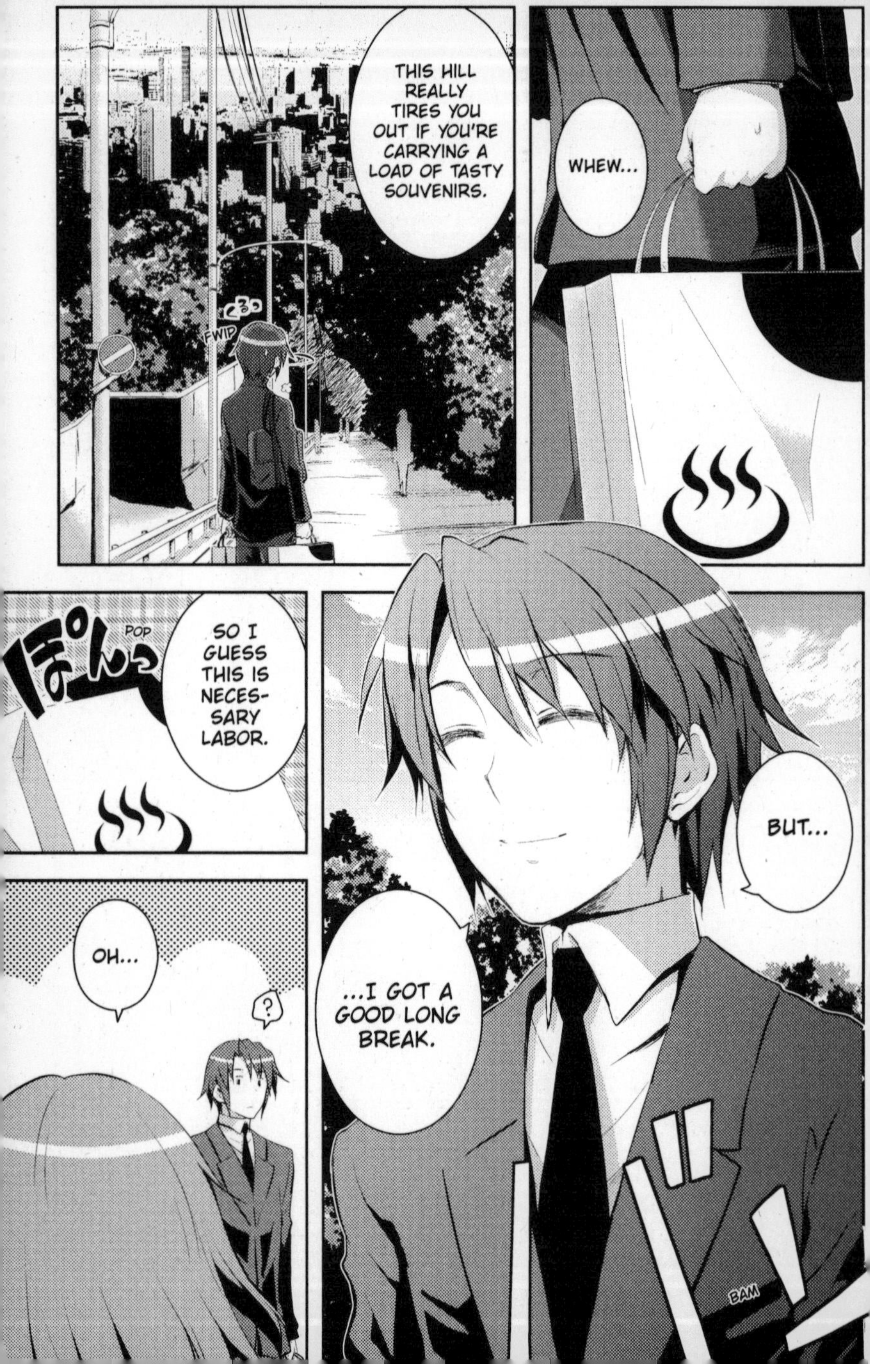
WHEW...
THIS HILL REALLY TIRES YOU OUT IF YOU'RE CARRYING A LOAD OF TASTY SOUVENIRS.
くるっ
FWIP
BUT...
...I GOT A GOOD LONG BREAK.
BAM
ぽんっ
POP
SO I GUESS THIS IS NECES-SARY LABOR.
OH...
?

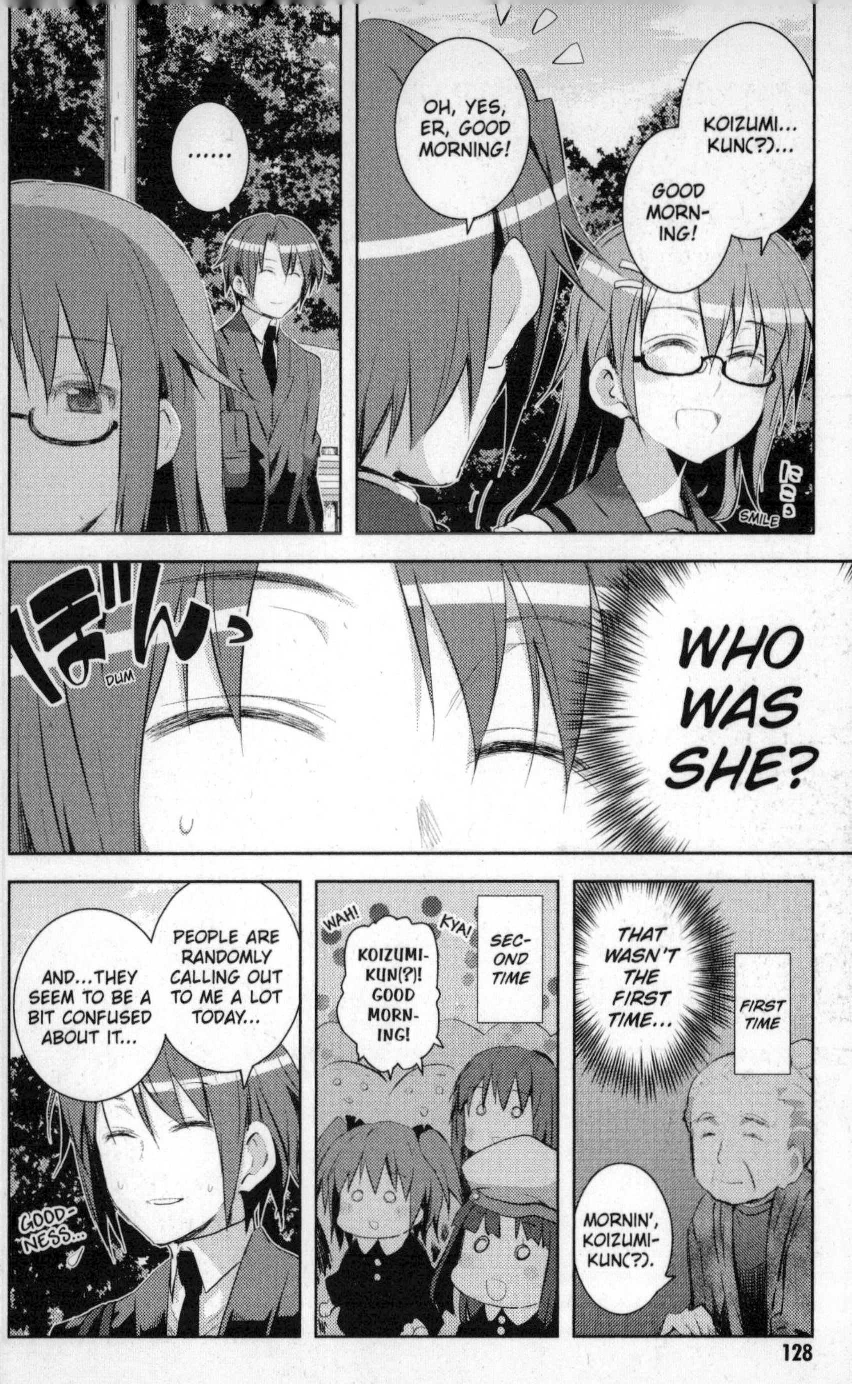
KOIZUMI... KUN(?)...
GOOD MORN-ING!
SMILE
OH, YES, ER, GOOD MORNING!
......
WHO WAS SHE?
DUM
THAT WASN'T THE FIRST TIME...
FIRST TIME
MORNIN', KOIZUMI-KUN(?).
SEC-OND TIME
KYA!
WAH!
KOIZUMI-KUN(?)! GOOD MORN-ING!
PEOPLE ARE RANDOMLY CALLING OUT TO ME A LOT TODAY...
AND...THEY SEEM TO BE A BIT CONFUSED ABOUT IT...
GOOD-NESS...

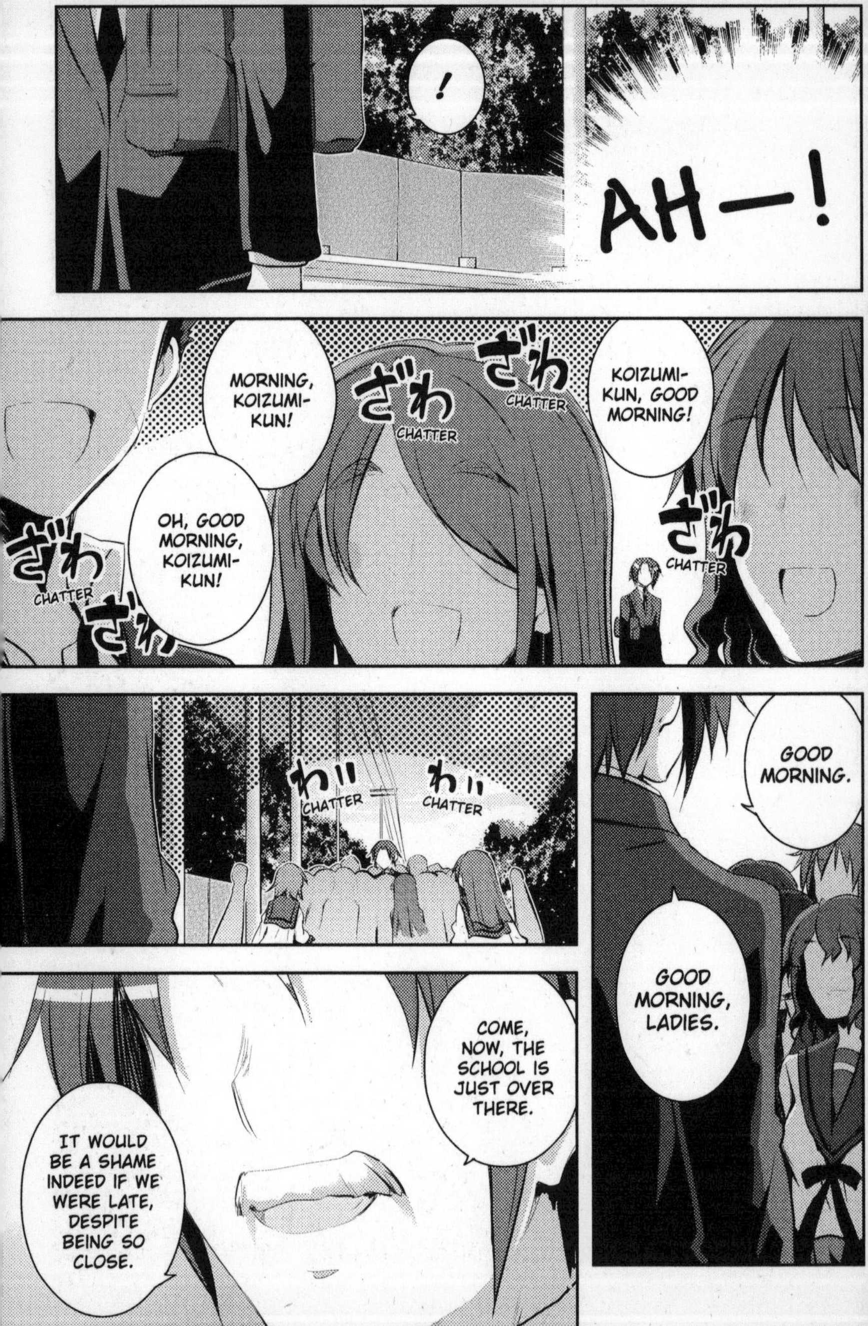
AH—!
!
KOIZUMI-KUN, GOOD MORNING!
ざわ CHATTER
ざわ CHATTER
MORNING, KOIZUMI-KUN!
ざわ CHATTER
OH, GOOD MORNING, KOIZUMI-KUN!
ざわ CHATTER
ざわ
GOOD MORNING.
GOOD MORNING, LADIES.
わい CHATTER
わい CHATTER
COME, NOW, THE SCHOOL IS JUST OVER THERE.
IT WOULD BE A SHAME INDEED IF WE WERE LATE, DESPITE BEING SO CLOSE.

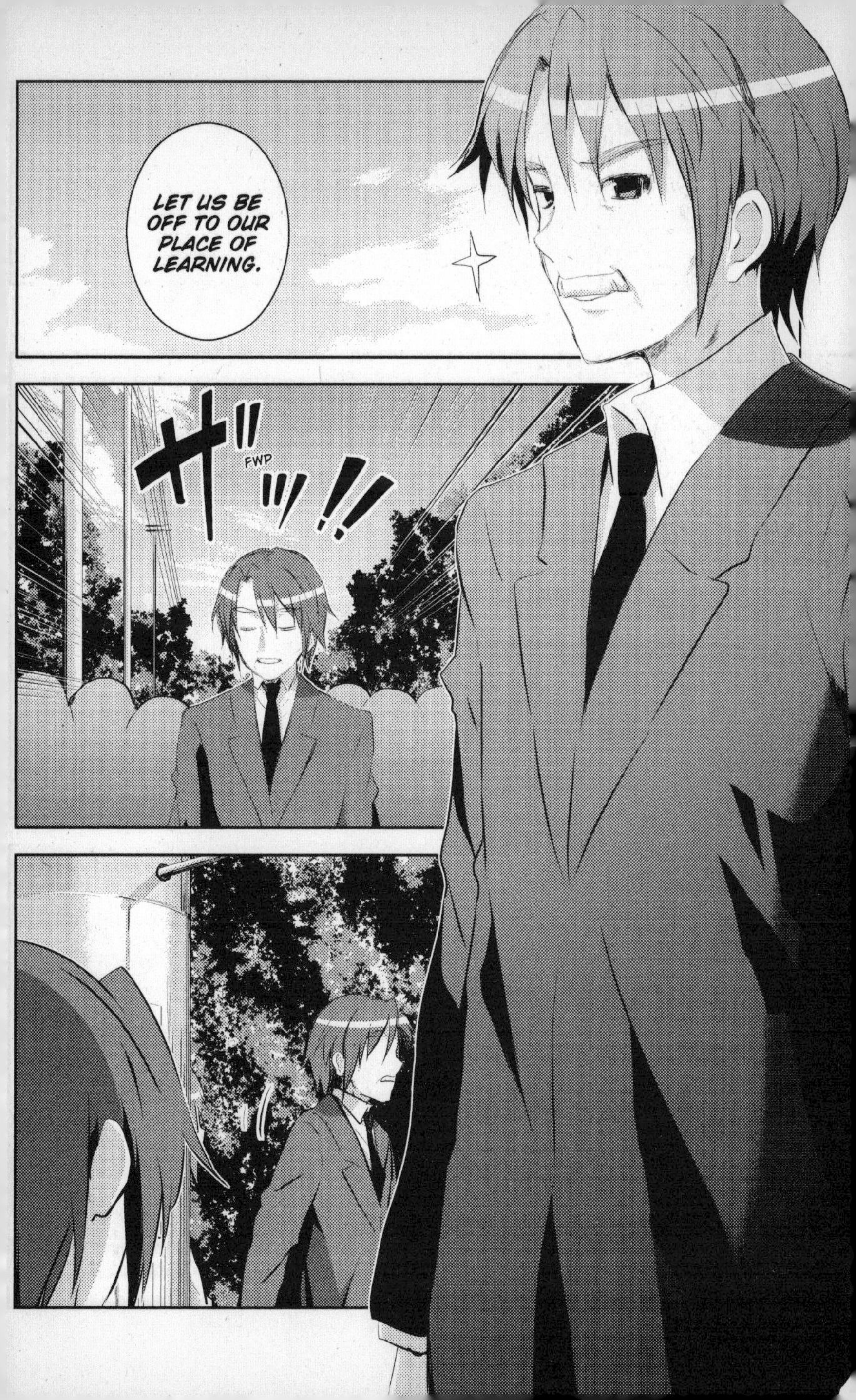
LET US BE OFF TO OUR PLACE OF LEARNING.
FWP

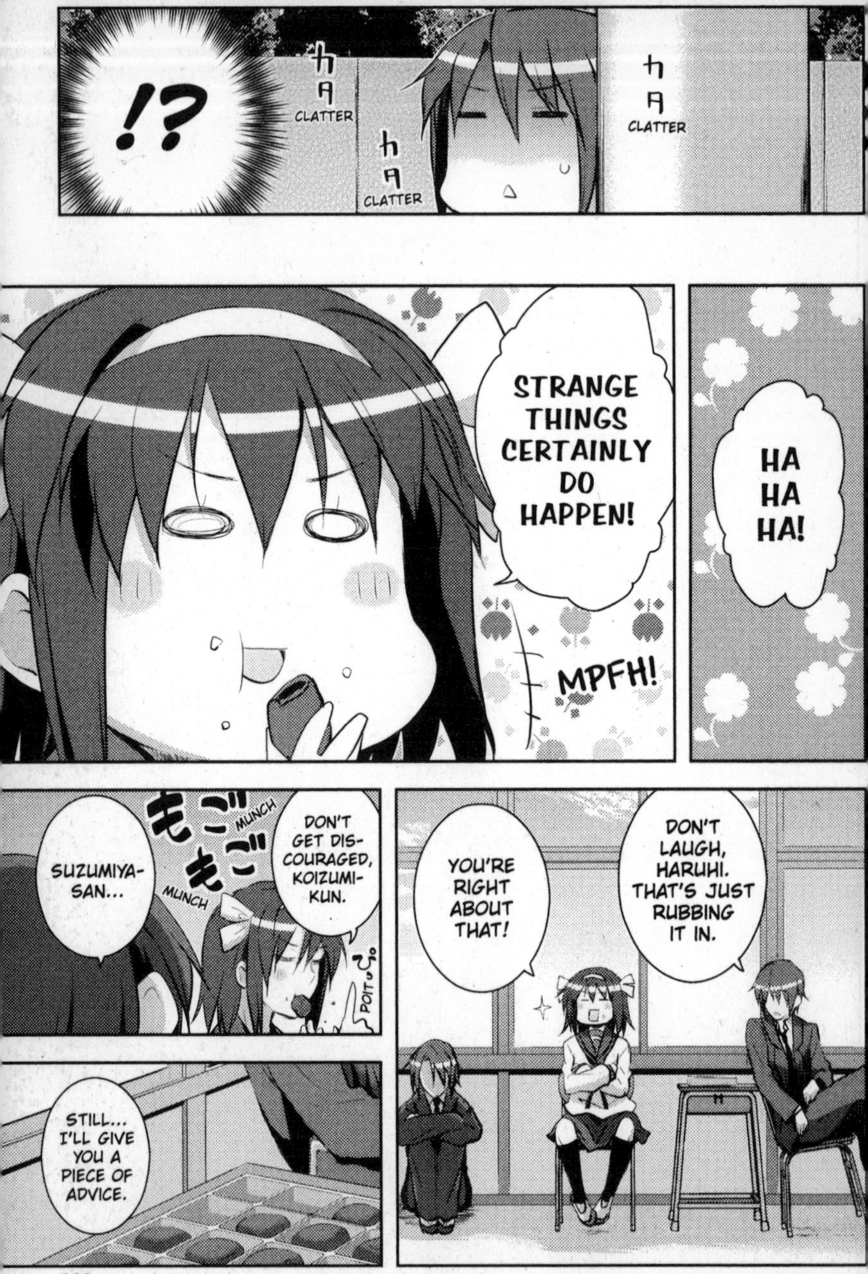
カタ
CLATTER
カタ
CLATTER
カタ
CLATTER
!?
HA HA HA!
STRANGE THINGS CERTAINLY DO HAPPEN!
MPFH!
DON'T LAUGH, HARUHI. THAT'S JUST RUBBING IT IN.
YOU'RE RIGHT ABOUT THAT!
DON'T GET DIS-COURAGED, KOIZUMI-KUN.
もご
MUNCH
もご
MUNCH
SUZUMIYA-SAN...
POIT
STILL... I'LL GIVE YOU A PIECE OF ADVICE.

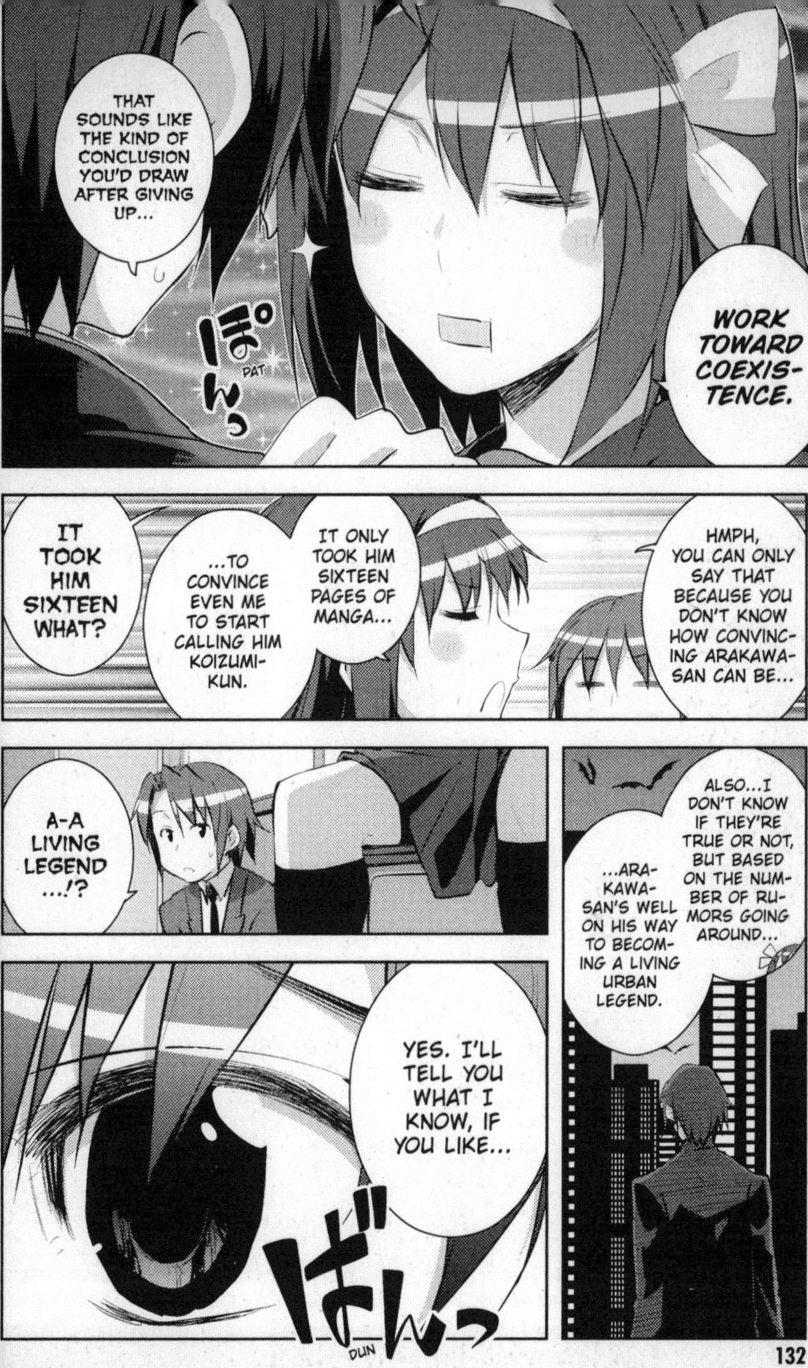
WORK TOWARD COEXISTENCE.
THAT SOUNDS LIKE THE KIND OF CONCLUSION YOU'D DRAW AFTER GIVING UP...
ぽんっ
PAT
HMPH, YOU CAN ONLY SAY THAT BECAUSE YOU DON'T KNOW HOW CONVINCING ARAKAWA-SAN CAN BE...
IT ONLY TOOK HIM SIXTEEN PAGES OF MANGA...
...TO CONVINCE EVEN ME TO START CALLING HIM KOIZUMI-KUN.
IT TOOK HIM SIXTEEN WHAT?
ALSO...I DON'T KNOW IF THEY'RE TRUE OR NOT, BUT BASED ON THE NUMBER OF RUMORS GOING AROUND...
...ARAKAWA-SAN'S WELL ON HIS WAY TO BECOMING A LIVING URBAN LEGEND.
A-A LIVING LEGEND...!?
YES. I'LL TELL YOU WHAT I KNOW, IF YOU LIKE...
ばんっ
DUN

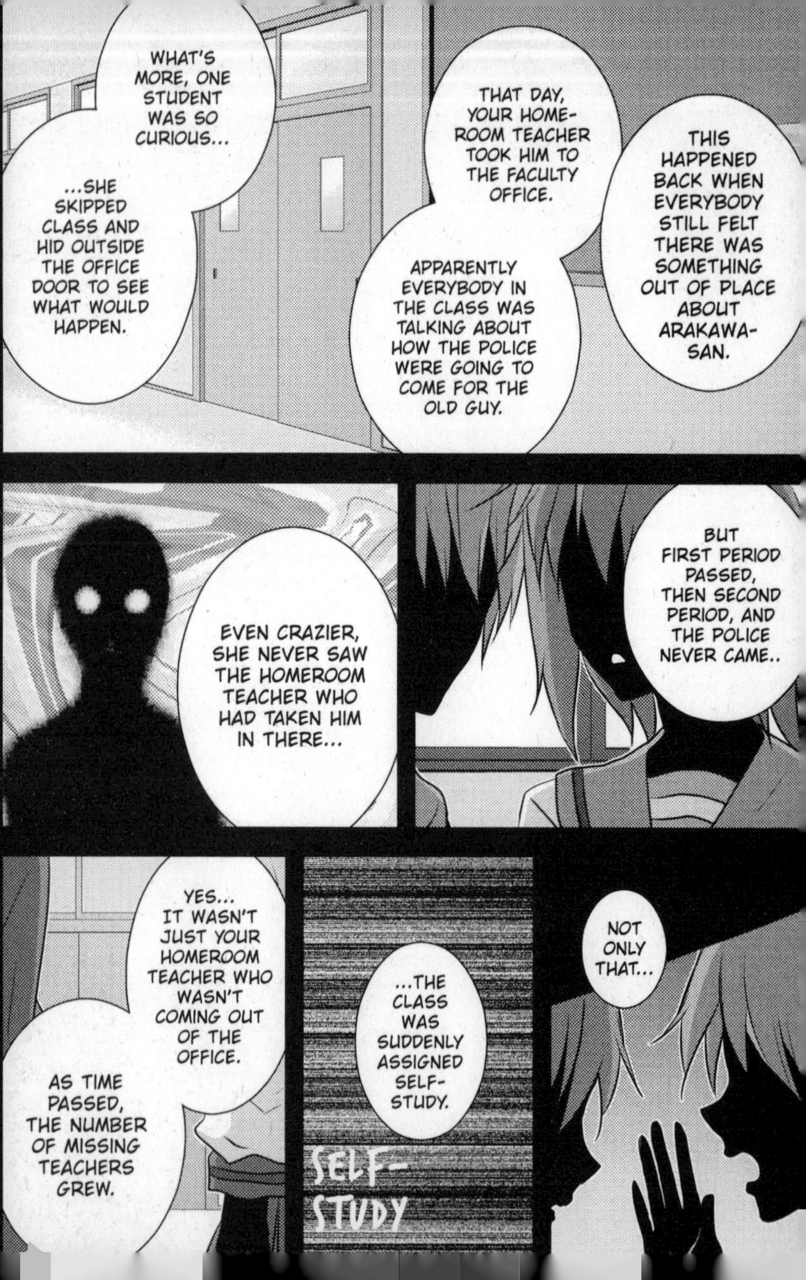
THIS HAPPENED BACK WHEN EVERYBODY STILL FELT THERE WAS SOMETHING OUT OF PLACE ABOUT ARAKAWA-SAN.
THAT DAY, YOUR HOME-ROOM TEACHER TOOK HIM TO THE FACULTY OFFICE.
APPARENTLY EVERYBODY IN THE CLASS WAS TALKING ABOUT HOW THE POLICE WERE GOING TO COME FOR THE OLD GUY.
WHAT'S MORE, ONE STUDENT WAS SO CURIOUS...
...SHE SKIPPED CLASS AND HID OUTSIDE THE OFFICE DOOR TO SEE WHAT WOULD HAPPEN.
BUT FIRST PERIOD PASSED, THEN SECOND PERIOD, AND THE POLICE NEVER CAME..
EVEN CRAZIER, SHE NEVER SAW THE HOMEROOM TEACHER WHO HAD TAKEN HIM IN THERE...
NOT ONLY THAT...
...THE CLASS WAS SUDDENLY ASSIGNED SELF-STUDY.
SELF-STUDY
YES... IT WASN'T JUST YOUR HOMEROOM TEACHER WHO WASN'T COMING OUT OF THE OFFICE.
AS TIME PASSED, THE NUMBER OF MISSING TEACHERS GREW.

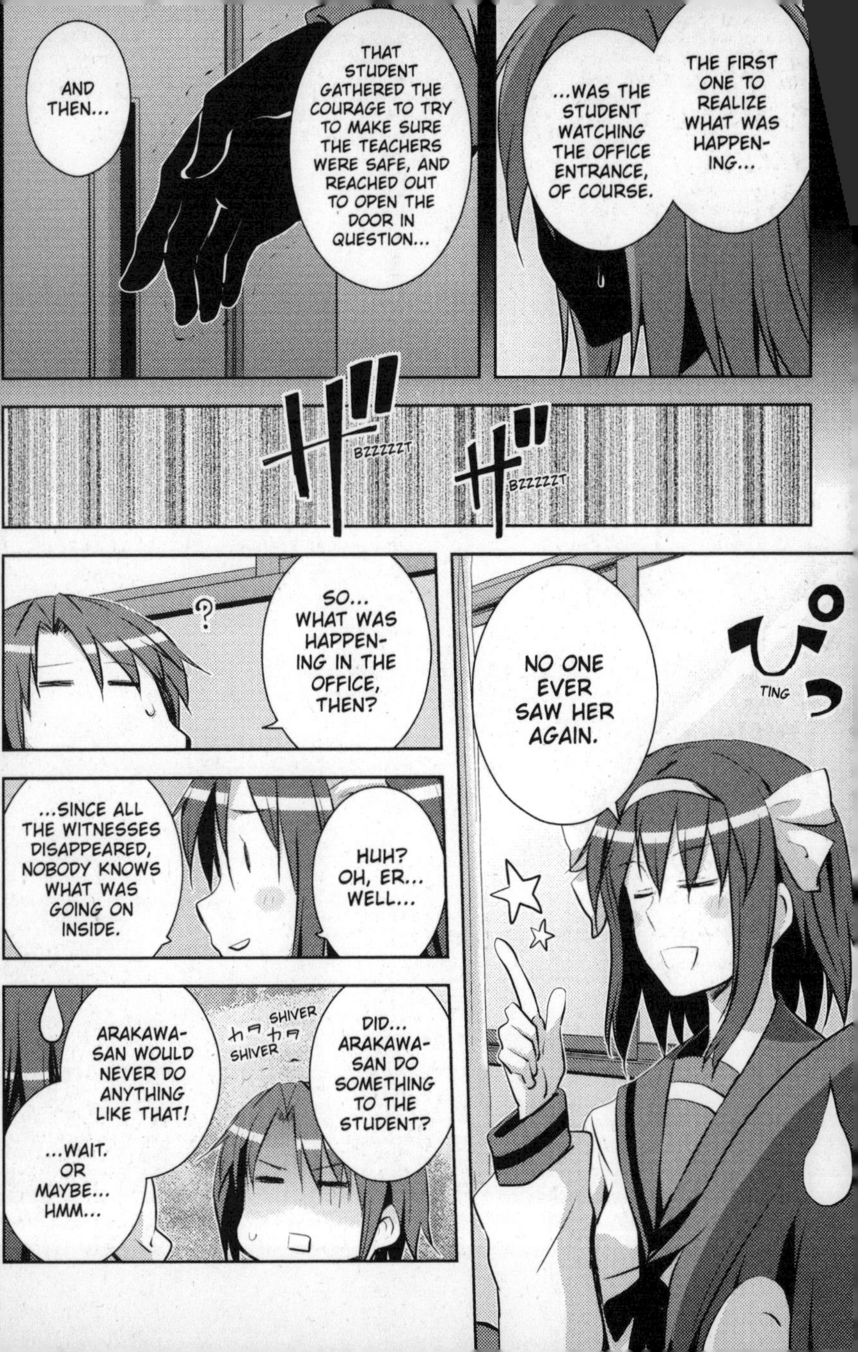
THE FIRST ONE TO REALIZE WHAT WAS HAPPENING...
...WAS THE STUDENT WATCHING THE OFFICE ENTRANCE, OF COURSE.
THAT STUDENT GATHERED THE COURAGE TO TRY TO MAKE SURE THE TEACHERS WERE SAFE, AND REACHED OUT TO OPEN THE DOOR IN QUESTION...
AND THEN...
ザ BZZZZZT
ザ BZZZZZT
NO ONE EVER SAW HER AGAIN.
ぴっ TING
SO... WHAT WAS HAPPENING IN THE OFFICE, THEN?
?
HUH? OH, ER... WELL...
...SINCE ALL THE WITNESSES DISAPPEARED, NOBODY KNOWS WHAT WAS GOING ON INSIDE.
DID... ARAKAWA-SAN DO SOMETHING TO THE STUDENT?
カタカタ SHIVER SHIVER
ARAKAWA-SAN WOULD NEVER DO ANYTHING LIKE THAT!
...WAIT. OR MAYBE... HMM...

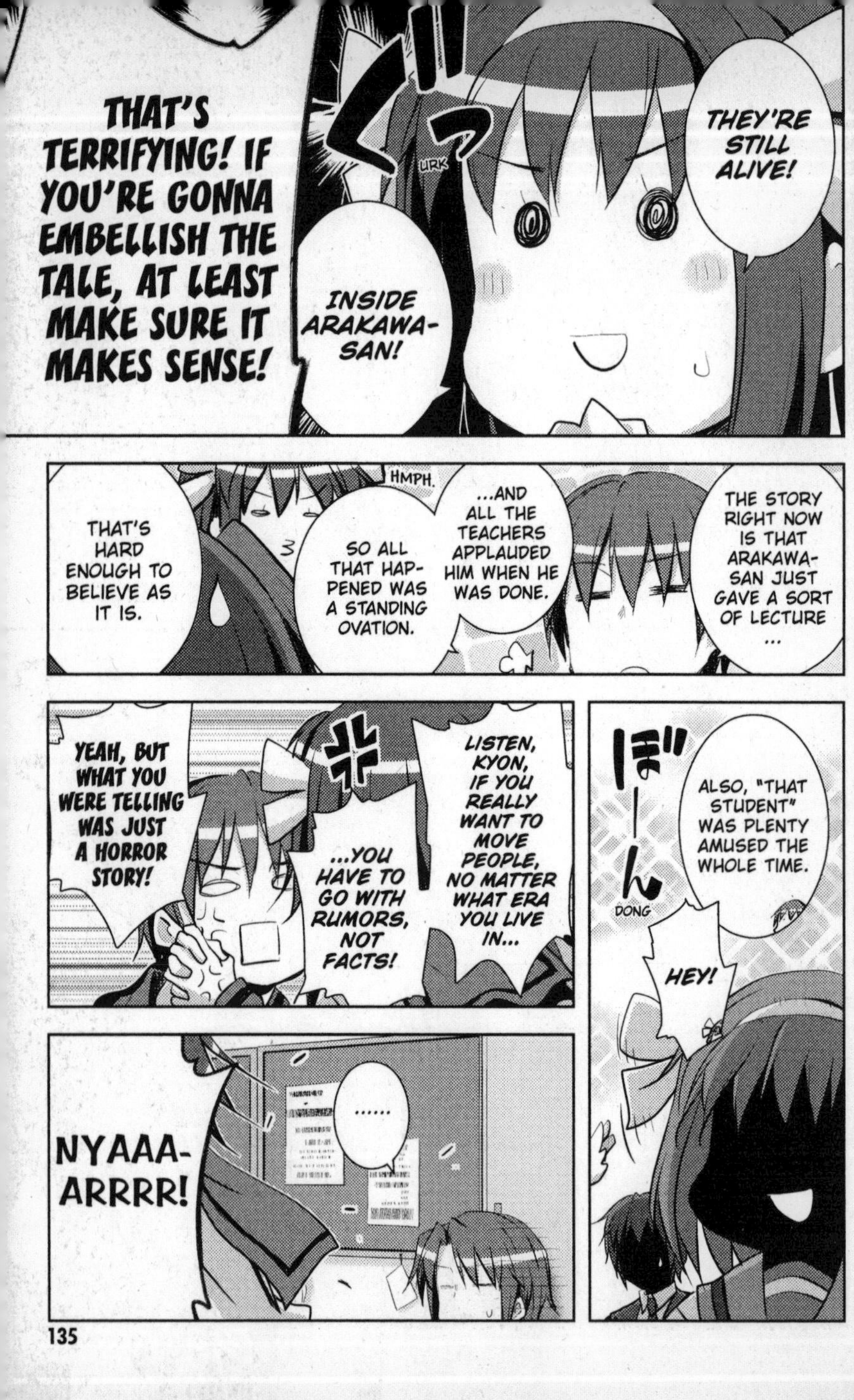
THEY'RE STILL ALIVE!
URK
INSIDE ARAKAWA-SAN!
THAT'S TERRIFYING! IF YOU'RE GONNA EMBELLISH THE TALE, AT LEAST MAKE SURE IT MAKES SENSE!
THE STORY RIGHT NOW IS THAT ARAKAWA-SAN JUST GAVE A SORT OF LECTURE ...
...AND ALL THE TEACHERS APPLAUDED HIM WHEN HE WAS DONE.
HMPH.
SO ALL THAT HAPPENED WAS A STANDING OVATION.
THAT'S HARD ENOUGH TO BELIEVE AS IT IS.
ALSO, "THAT STUDENT" WAS PLENTY AMUSED THE WHOLE TIME.
ぼーん
DONG
HEY!
LISTEN, KYON, IF YOU REALLY WANT TO MOVE PEOPLE, NO MATTER WHAT ERA YOU LIVE IN...
...YOU HAVE TO GO WITH RUMORS, NOT FACTS!
YEAH, BUT WHAT YOU WERE TELLING WAS JUST A HORROR STORY!
......
NYAAA-ARRRR!

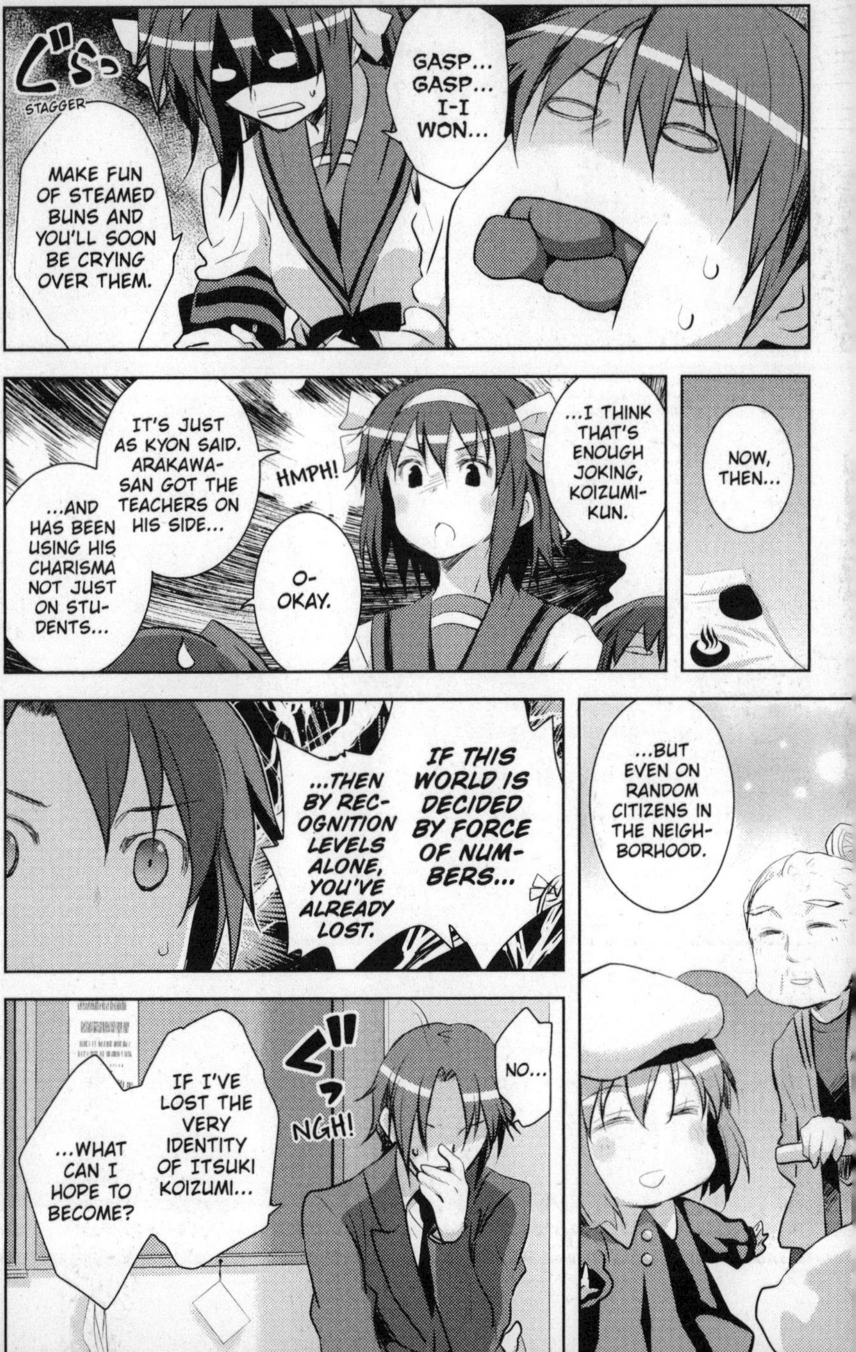
GASP... GASP... I-I WON...
ぐらっ
STAGGER
MAKE FUN OF STEAMED BUNS AND YOU'LL SOON BE CRYING OVER THEM.
NOW, THEN...
...I THINK THAT'S ENOUGH JOKING, KOIZUMI-KUN.
HMPH!
O-OKAY.
IT'S JUST AS KYON SAID. ARAKAWA-SAN GOT THE TEACHERS ON HIS SIDE...
...AND HAS BEEN USING HIS CHARISMA NOT JUST ON STUDENTS...
...BUT EVEN ON RANDOM CITIZENS IN THE NEIGHBORHOOD.
IF THIS WORLD IS DECIDED BY FORCE OF NUMBERS...
...THEN BY RECOGNITION LEVELS ALONE, YOU'VE ALREADY LOST.
NO...
ぐっ
NGH!
IF I'VE LOST THE VERY IDENTITY OF ITSUKI KOIZUMI...
...WHAT CAN I HOPE TO BECOME?

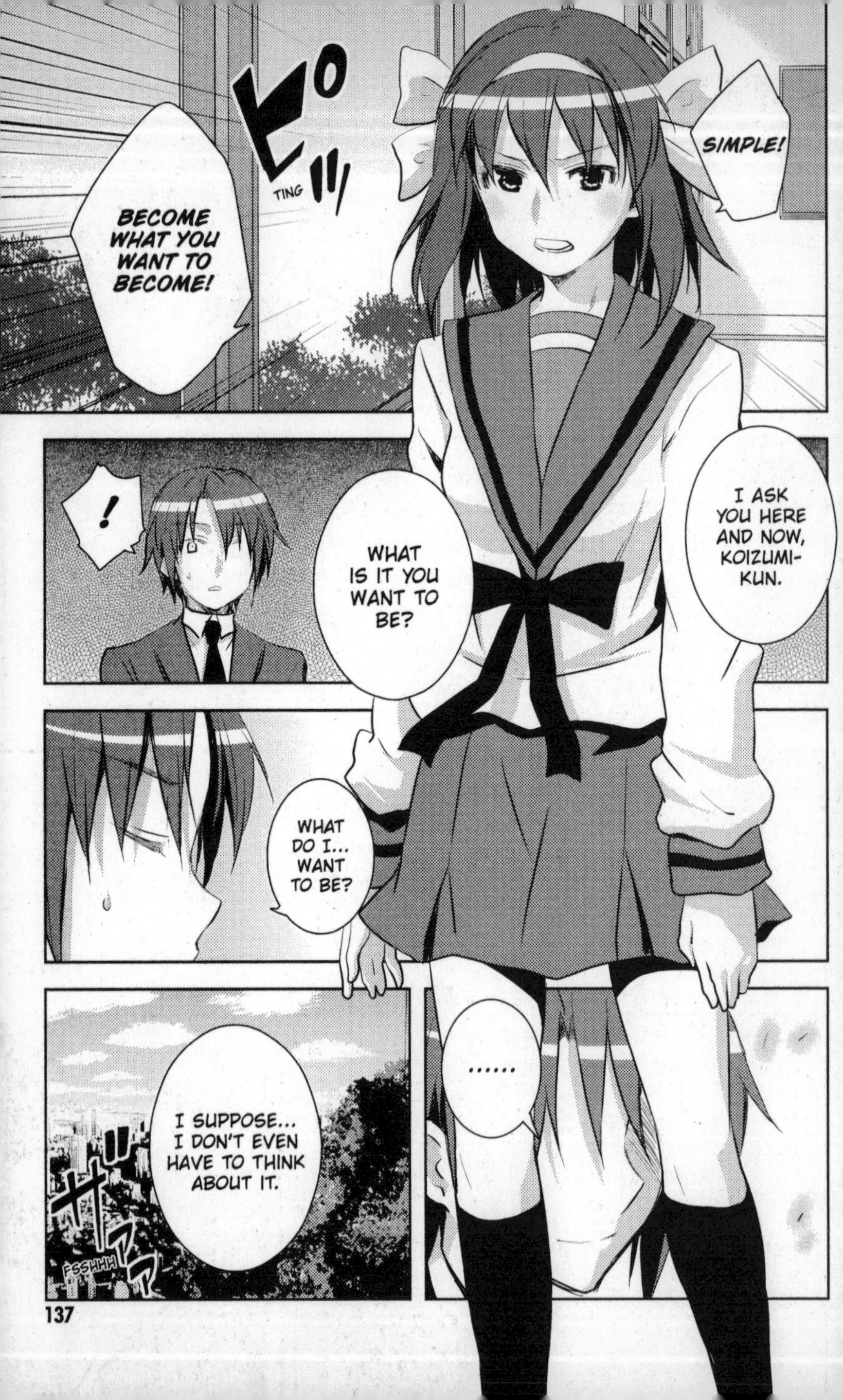
SIMPLE!
TING
BECOME WHAT YOU WANT TO BECOME!
I ASK YOU HERE AND NOW, KOIZUMI-KUN.
WHAT IS IT YOU WANT TO BE?
!
WHAT DO I... WANT TO BE?
......
I SUPPOSE... I DON'T EVEN HAVE TO THINK ABOUT IT.
FSSHHH

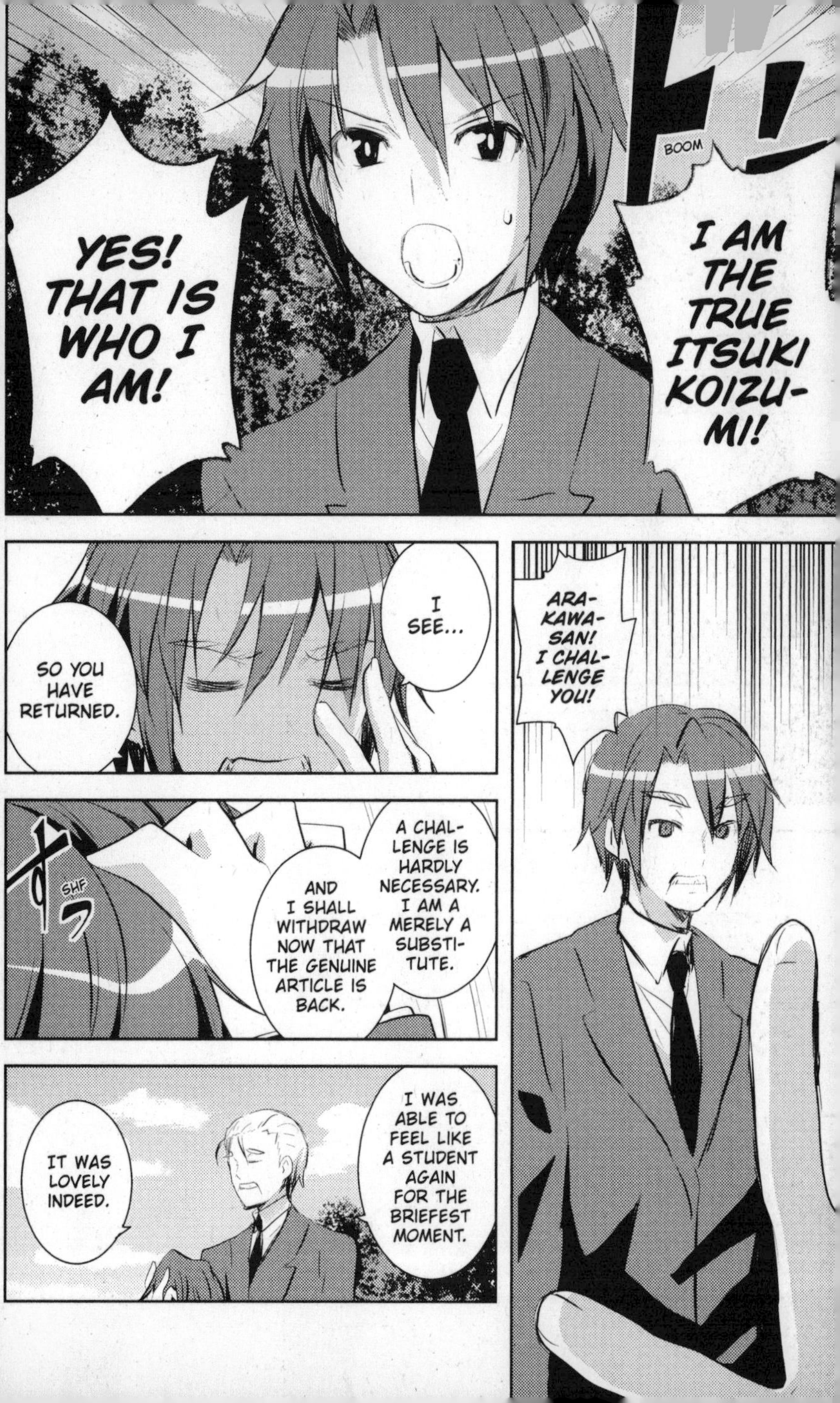
BOOM
I AM THE TRUE ITSUKI KOIZUMI!
YES! THAT IS WHO I AM!
ARAKAWA-SAN! I CHALLENGE YOU!
I SEE...
SO YOU HAVE RETURNED.
SHF
A CHALLENGE IS HARDLY NECESSARY. I AM A MERELY A SUBSTITUTE.
AND I SHALL WITHDRAW NOW THAT THE GENUINE ARTICLE IS BACK.
I WAS ABLE TO FEEL LIKE A STUDENT AGAIN FOR THE BRIEFEST MOMENT.
IT WAS LOVELY INDEED.

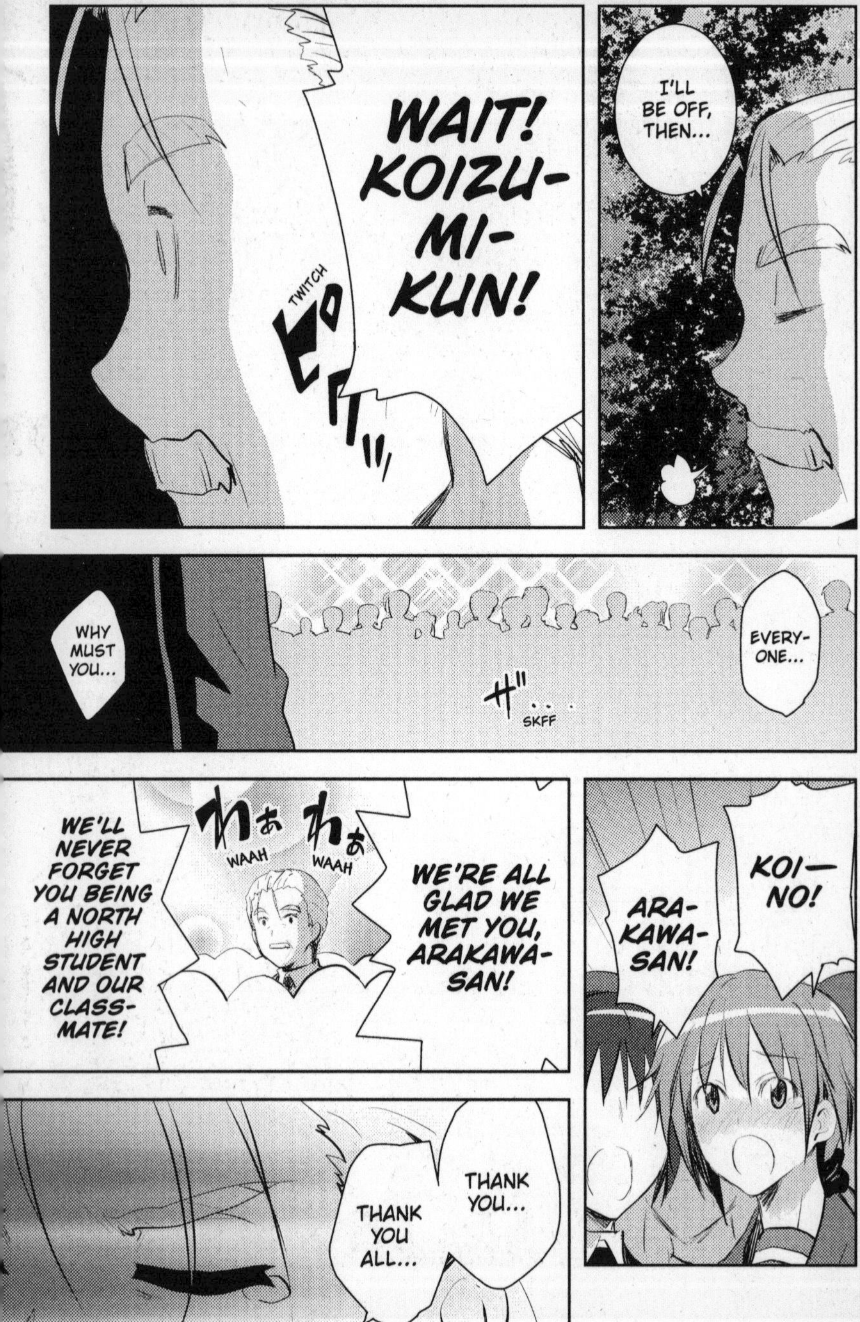
I'LL BE OFF, THEN...
WAIT! KOIZUMI-KUN!
TWITCH
EVERYONE...
SKFF
WHY MUST YOU...
KOI—NO!
ARAKAWA-SAN!
WE'RE ALL GLAD WE MET YOU, ARAKAWA-SAN!
WAAH WAAH
WE'LL NEVER FORGET YOU BEING A NORTH HIGH STUDENT AND OUR CLASSMATE!
THANK YOU...
THANK YOU ALL...

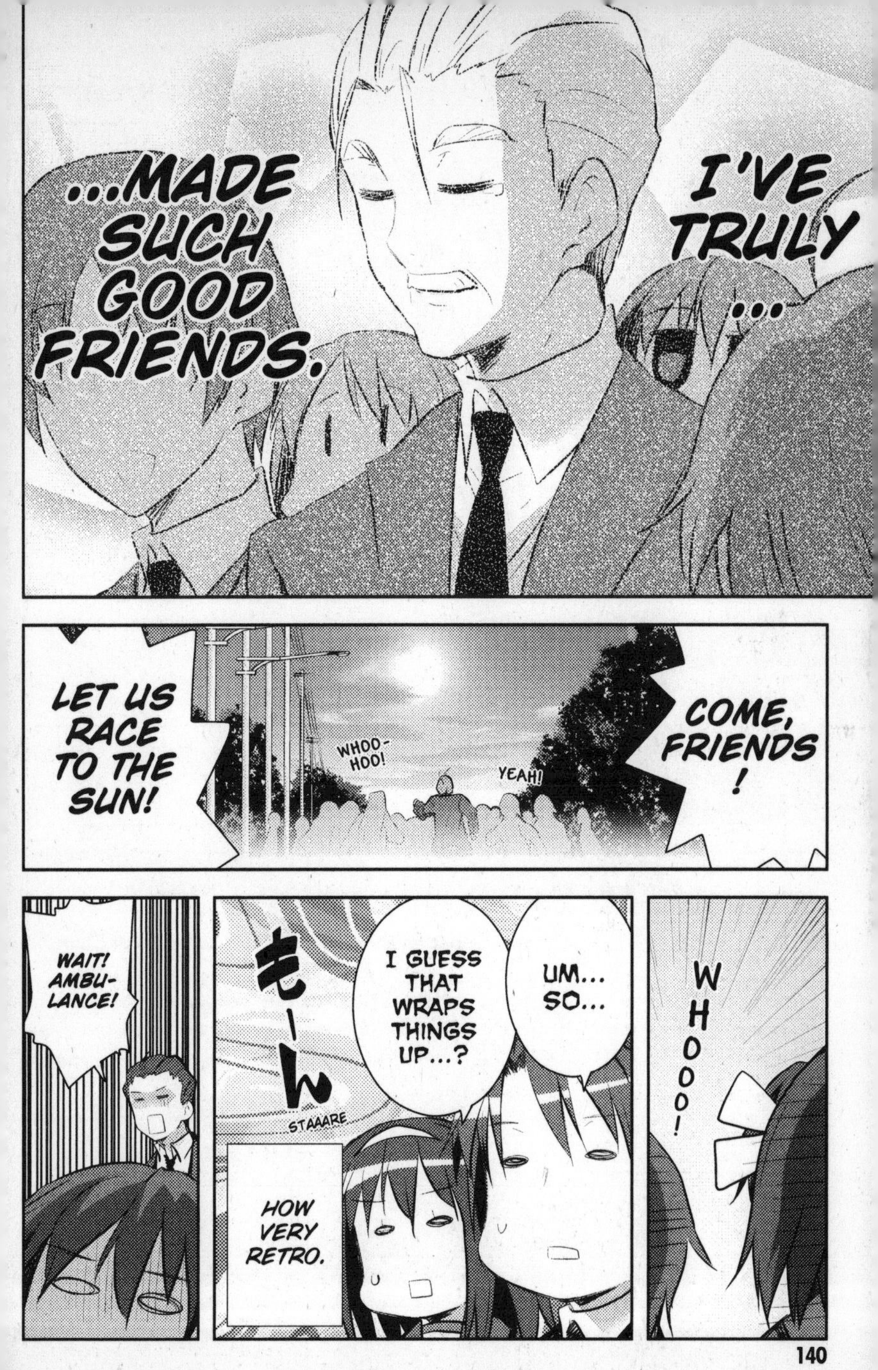
I'VE TRULY ...
...MADE SUCH GOOD FRIENDS.
COME, FRIENDS!
YEAH!
WHOO-HOO!
LET US RACE TO THE SUN!
WHOOOO!
UM... SO...
I GUESS THAT WRAPS THINGS UP...?
きーん
STAAARE
HOW VERY RETRO.
WAIT! AMBULANCE!

INHERITED TALE

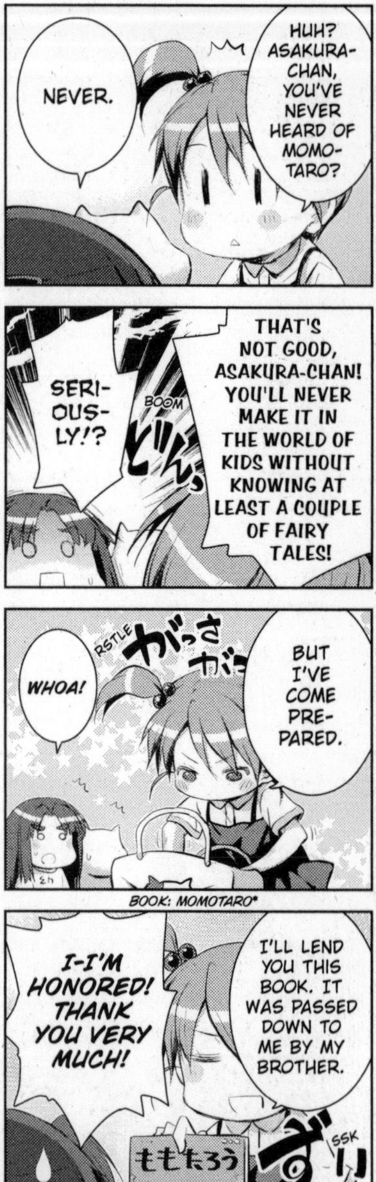
HUH? ASAKURA-CHAN, YOU'VE NEVER HEARD OF MOMOTARO?
NEVER.
THAT'S NOT GOOD, ASAKURA-CHAN! YOU'LL NEVER MAKE IT IN THE WORLD OF KIDS WITHOUT KNOWING AT LEAST A COUPLE OF FAIRY TALES!
SERI-OUS-LY!?
BOOM
BUT I'VE COME PRE-PARED.
RSTLE
WHOA!
BOOK: MOMOTARO*
I'LL LEND YOU THIS BOOK. IT WAS PASSED DOWN TO ME BY MY BROTHER.
I-I'M HONORED! THANK YOU VERY MUCH!
ももたろう
SSK

BANNED BOOK

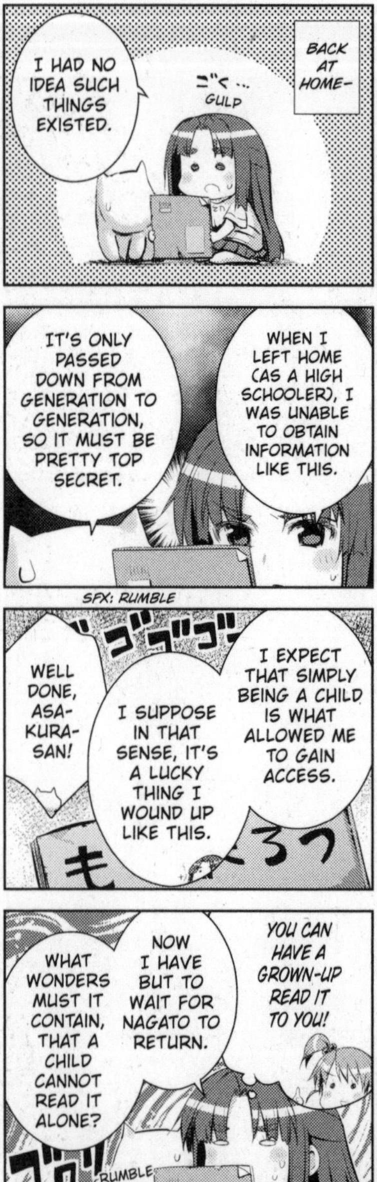
BACK AT HOME-
GULP
I HAD NO IDEA SUCH THINGS EXISTED.
WHEN I LEFT HOME (AS A HIGH SCHOOLER), I WAS UNABLE TO OBTAIN INFORMATION LIKE THIS.
IT'S ONLY PASSED DOWN FROM GENERATION TO GENERATION, SO IT MUST BE PRETTY TOP SECRET.
SFX: RUMBLE
I EXPECT THAT SIMPLY BEING A CHILD IS WHAT ALLOWED ME TO GAIN ACCESS.
I SUPPOSE IN THAT SENSE, IT'S A LUCKY THING I WOUND UP LIKE THIS.
WELL DONE, ASA-KURA-SAN!
YOU CAN HAVE A GROWN-UP READ IT TO YOU!
NOW I HAVE BUT TO WAIT FOR NAGATO TO RETURN.
WHAT WONDERS MUST IT CONTAIN, THAT A CHILD CANNOT READ IT ALONE?
RUMBLE

*MOMOTARO, LITERALLY "PEACH BOY," IS A CLASSIC JAPANESE FOLK TALE. AFTER AN OLD WOMAN DISCOVERS A GIANT PEACH FLOATING DOWN THE RIVER, SHE AND HER ELDERLY HUSBAND ARE SURPRISED WHEN A BOY LEAPS FROM THE FRUIT, SENT FROM HEAVEN TO BE THEIR SON, AND THEY NAME HIM MOMOTARO. YEARS LATER, MOMOTARO LEAVES HIS PARENTS TO CHALLENGE DEMONS ON A DISTANT ISLAND, AIDED ON HIS QUEST BY A NUMBER OF ANIMAL COMRADES.

FAMILY

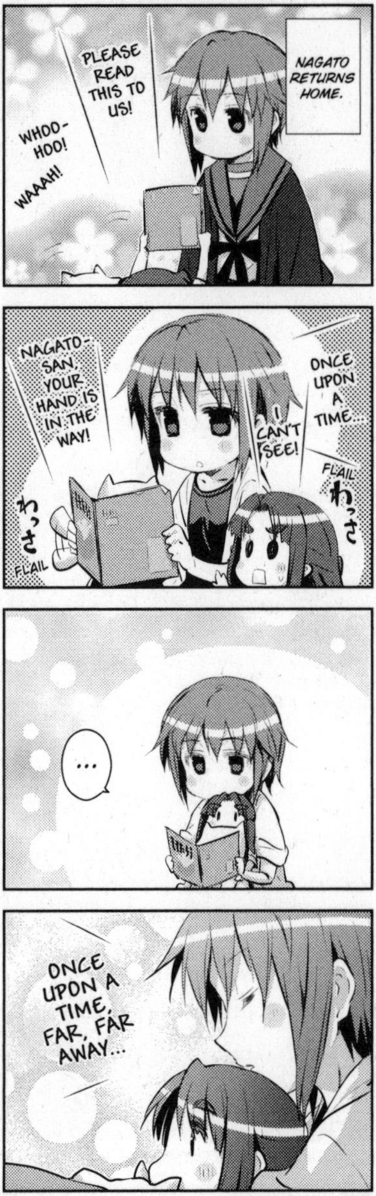
NAGATO RETURNS HOME.
PLEASE READ THIS TO US!
WHOO-HOO!
WAAAH!
ONCE UPON A TIME...
I CAN'T SEE!
NAGATO-SAN, YOUR HAND IS IN THE WAY!
FLAIL わっさ
FLAIL わっさ
...
ONCE UPON A TIME, FAR, FAR AWAY...

CONJECTURE

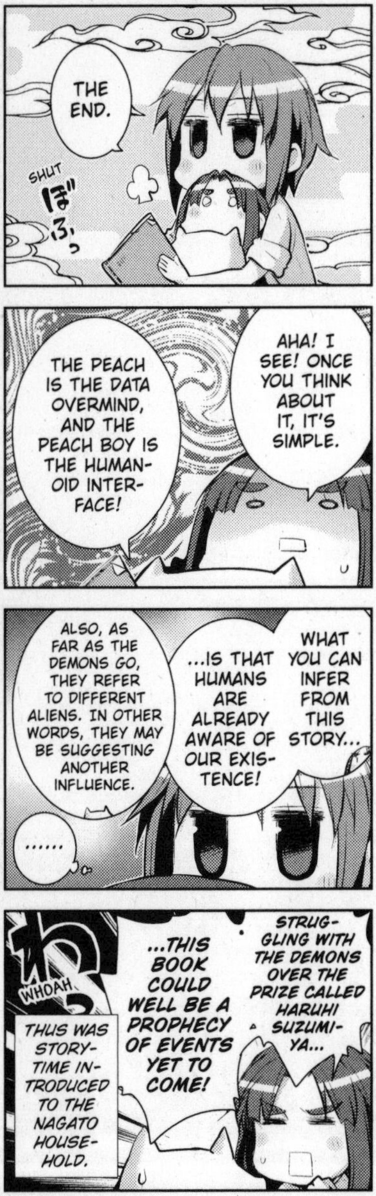
THE END.
SHUT ぼふっ
AHA! I SEE! ONCE YOU THINK ABOUT IT, IT'S SIMPLE.
THE PEACH IS THE DATA OVERMIND, AND THE PEACH BOY IS THE HUMAN-OID INTER-FACE!
WHAT YOU CAN INFER FROM THIS STORY...
...IS THAT HUMANS ARE ALREADY AWARE OF OUR EXIS-TENCE!
ALSO, AS FAR AS THE DEMONS GO, THEY REFER TO DIFFERENT ALIENS. IN OTHER WORDS, THEY MAY BE SUGGESTING ANOTHER INFLUENCE.
......
STRUG-GLING WITH THE DEMONS OVER THE PRIZE CALLED HARUHI SUZUMI-YA...
...THIS BOOK COULD WELL BE A PROPHECY OF EVENTS YET TO COME!
WHOAH わっ
THUS WAS STORY-TIME IN-TRODUCED TO THE NAGATO HOUSE-HOLD.

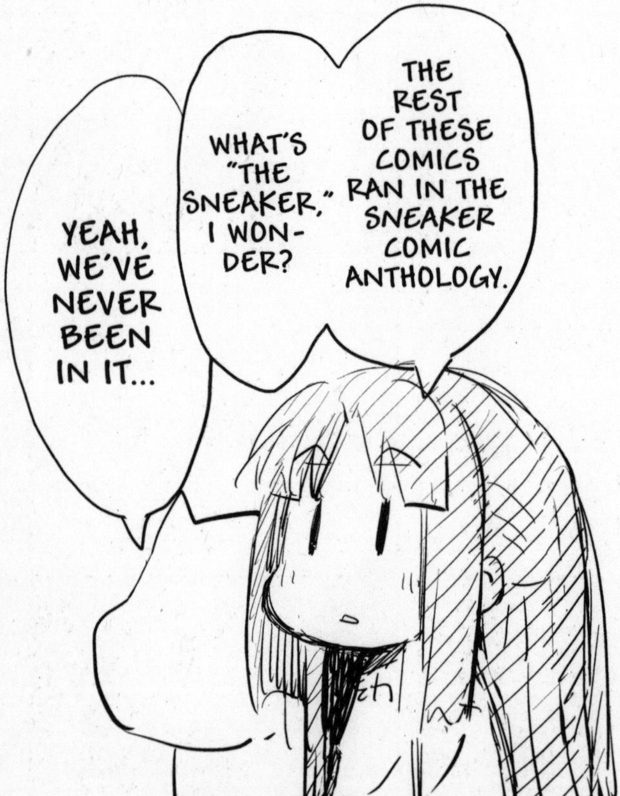
THE REST OF THESE COMICS RAN IN THE SNEAKER COMIC ANTHOLOGY.
WHAT'S "THE SNEAKER," I WONDER?
YEAH, WE'VE NEVER BEEN IN IT...

FEELING OUT OF PLACE

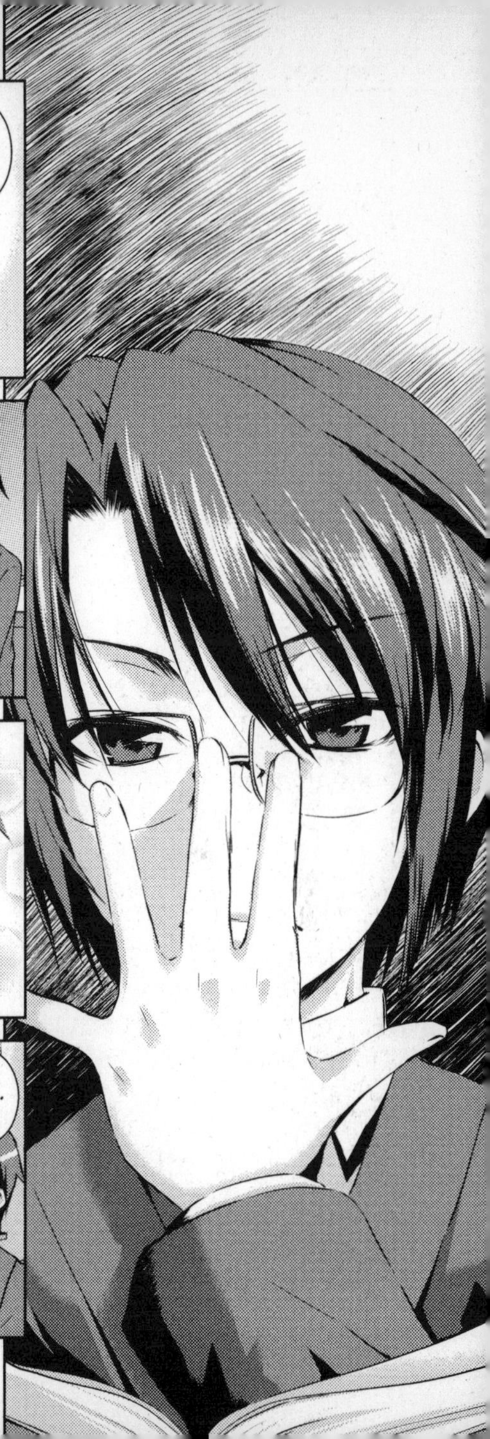

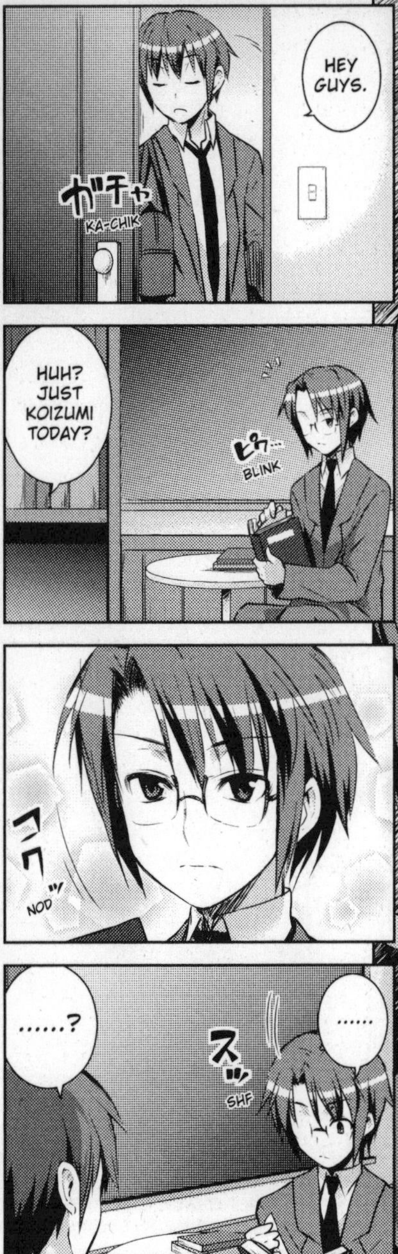
HEY GUYS.
ガチャ
KA-CHIK
HUH? JUST KOIZUMI TODAY?
ピク…
BLINK
コクッ
NOD
......
......?
スッ
SHF

FEELING OUT OF PLACE 2

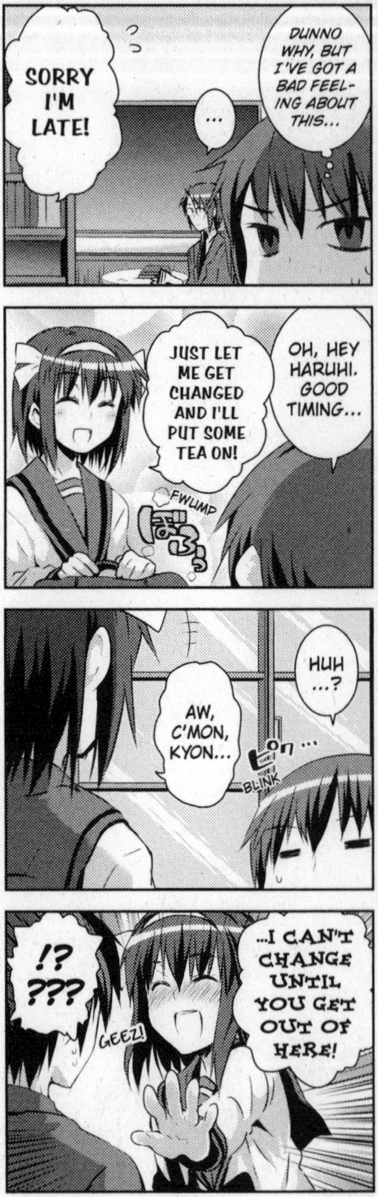
DUNNO WHY, BUT I'VE GOT A BAD FEEL-ING ABOUT THIS...
...
SORRY I'M LATE!
OH, HEY HARUHI. GOOD TIMING...
JUST LET ME GET CHANGED AND I'LL PUT SOME TEA ON!
FWUMP
HUH ...?
BLINK
AW, C'MON, KYON...
...I CAN'T CHANGE UNTIL YOU GET OUT OF HERE!
GEEZ!
!? ???

FEELING OUT OF PLACE 3

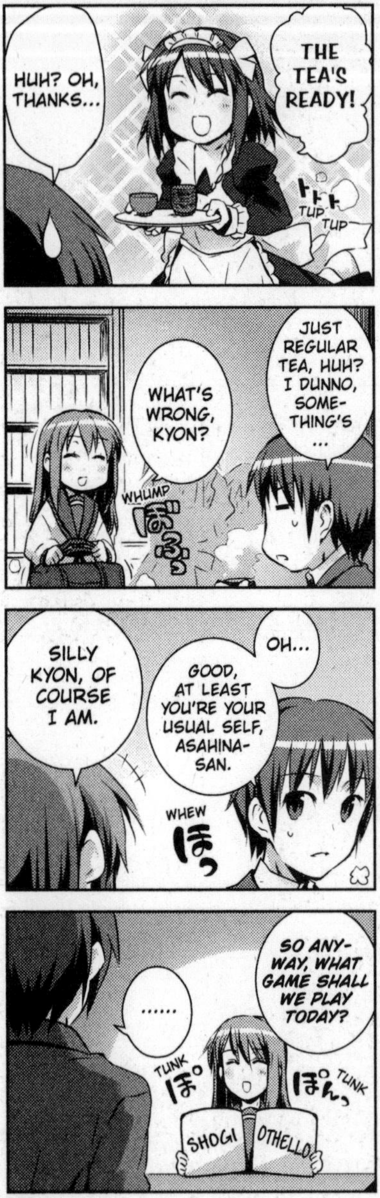
THE TEA'S READY!
TUP TUP
HUH? OH, THANKS...
JUST REGULAR TEA, HUH? I DUNNO, SOME-THING'S ...
WHAT'S WRONG, KYON?
WHUMP
OH...
GOOD, AT LEAST YOU'RE YOUR USUAL SELF, ASAHINA-SAN.
SILLY KYON, OF COURSE I AM.
WHEW
SO ANY-WAY, WHAT GAME SHALL WE PLAY TODAY?
......
TUNK
TUNK
SHOGI
OTHELLO

FEELING OUT OF PLACE 4

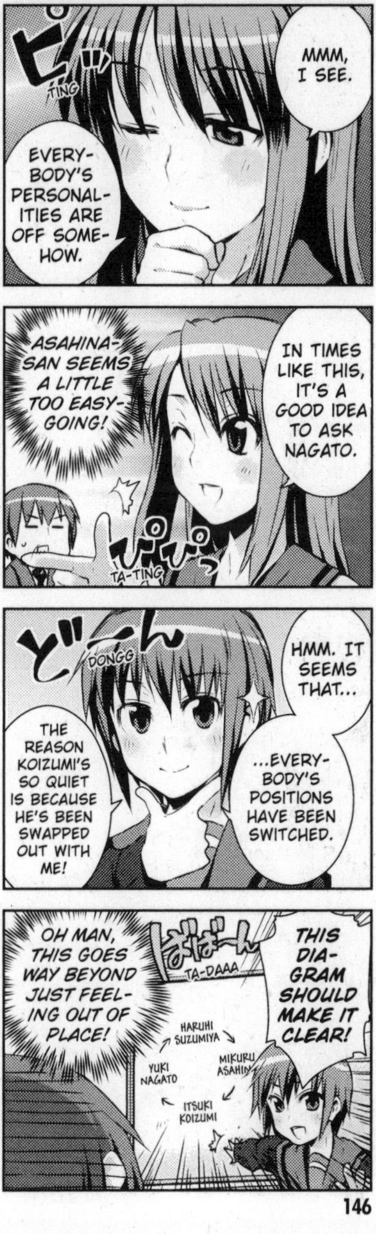
MMM, I SEE.
TING
EVERYBODY'S PERSONALITIES ARE OFF SOMEHOW.
IN TIMES LIKE THIS, IT'S A GOOD IDEA TO ASK NAGATO.
ASAHINA-SAN SEEMS A LITTLE TOO EASY-GOING!
TA-TING
HMM. IT SEEMS THAT...
DONGG
...EVERYBODY'S POSITIONS HAVE BEEN SWITCHED.
THE REASON KOIZUMI'S SO QUIET IS BECAUSE HE'S BEEN SWAPPED OUT WITH ME!
THIS DIAGRAM SHOULD MAKE IT CLEAR!
TA-DAAA
OH MAN, THIS GOES WAY BEYOND JUST FEELING OUT OF PLACE!
HARUHI SUZUMIYA
MIKURU ASAHINA
YUKI NAGATO
ITSUKI KOIZUMI

BEYOND THE FEELING

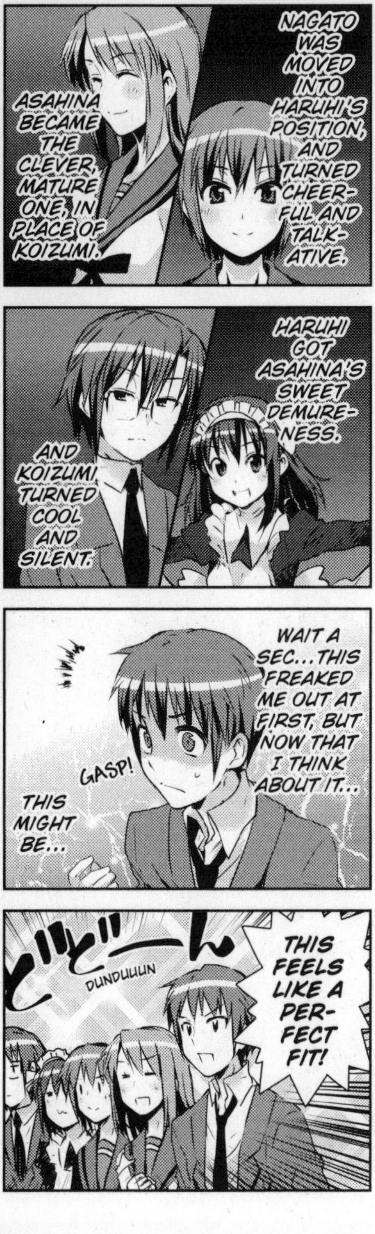
NAGATO WAS MOVED INTO HARUHI'S POSITION, AND TURNED CHEERFUL AND TALKATIVE.
ASAHINA BECAME THE CLEVER, MATURE ONE, IN PLACE OF KOIZUMI.
HARUHI GOT ASAHINA'S SWEET DEMURENESS.
AND KOIZUMI TURNED COOL AND SILENT.
WAIT A SEC...THIS FREAKED ME OUT AT FIRST, BUT NOW THAT I THINK ABOUT IT...
GASP!
THIS MIGHT BE...
THIS FEELS LIKE A PERFECT FIT!
DUNDUUUN

NORMAL DAYS

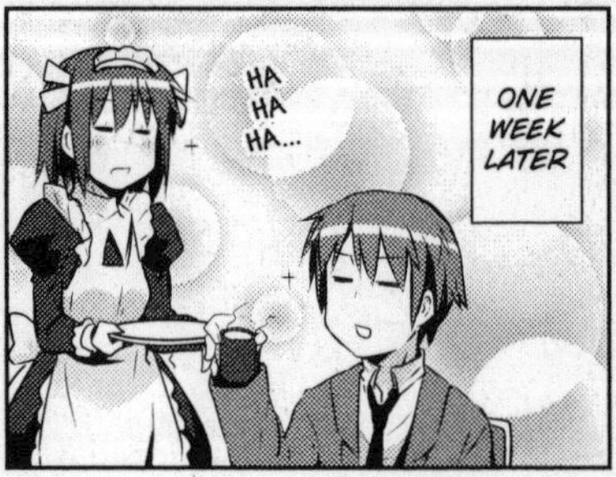
ONE WEEK LATER
HA HA HA...

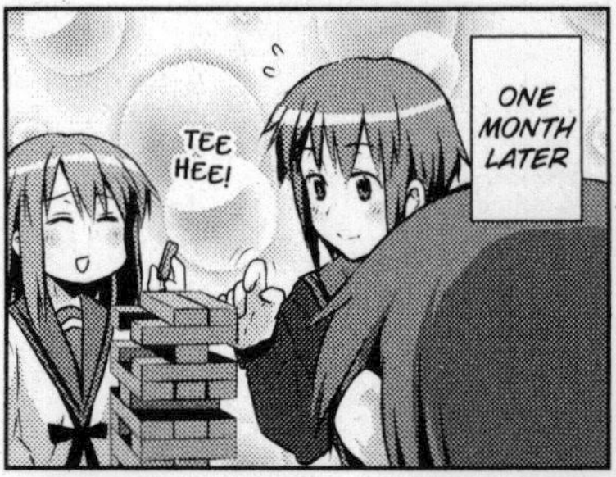
ONE MONTH LATER
TEE HEE!

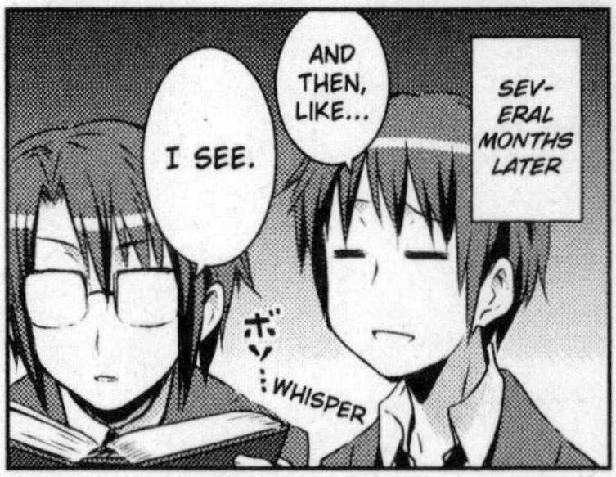
SEV-ERAL MONTHS LATER
AND THEN, LIKE...
I SEE.
ボソ
WHISPER

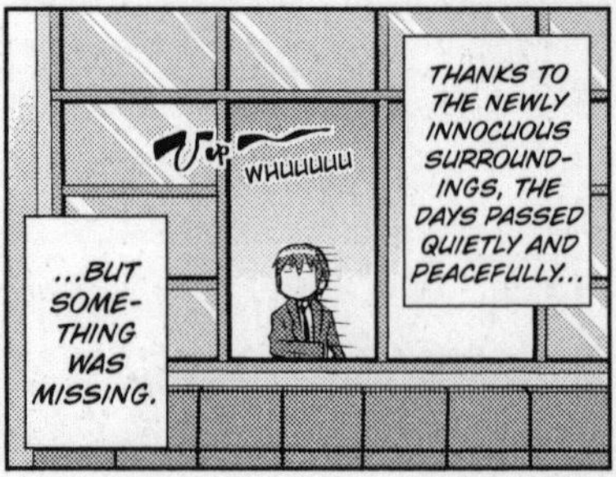
THANKS TO THE NEWLY INNOCUOUS SURROUND-INGS, THE DAYS PASSED QUIETLY AND PEACEFULLY...
ひゅ～
WHUUUUU
...BUT SOME-THING WAS MISSING.

SATISFACTION

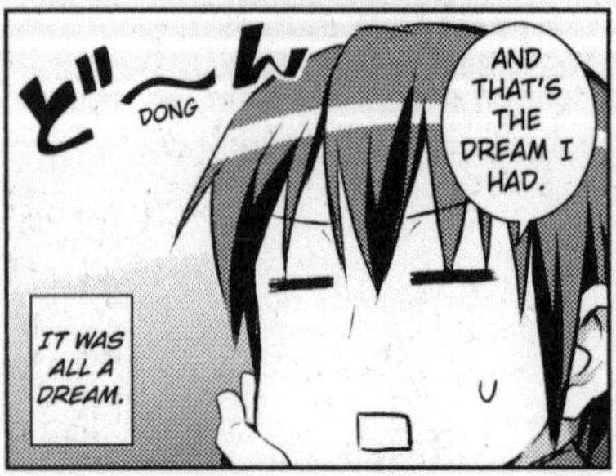
AND THAT'S THE DREAM I HAD.
ど～ん
DONG
IT WAS ALL A DREAM.

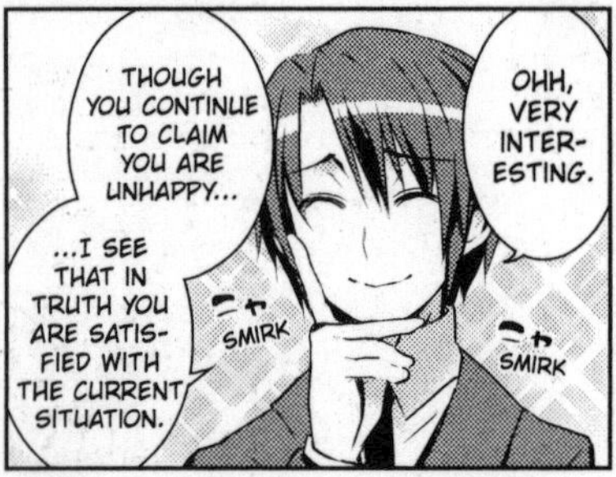
OHH, VERY INTER-ESTING.
ニヤ
SMIRK
THOUGH YOU CONTINUE TO CLAIM YOU ARE UNHAPPY...
...I SEE THAT IN TRUTH YOU ARE SATIS-FIED WITH THE CURRENT SITUATION.
ニヤ
SMIRK

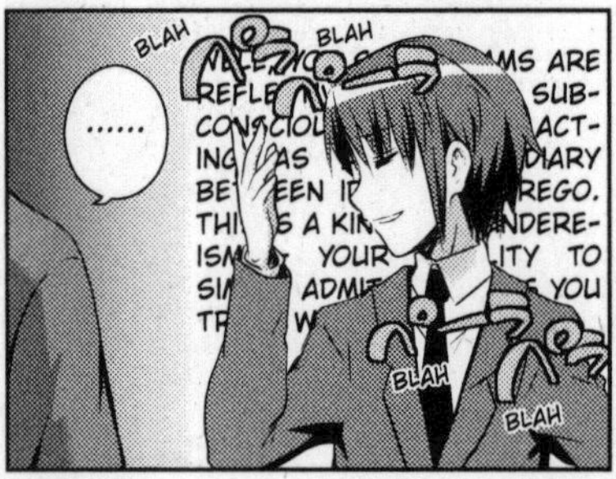
BLAH
BLAH
......
BLAH
BLAH

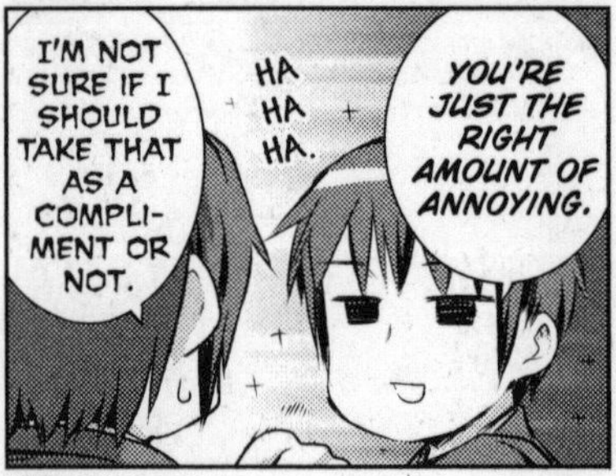
YOU'RE JUST THE RIGHT AMOUNT OF ANNOYING.
HA HA HA.
I'M NOT SURE IF I SHOULD TAKE THAT AS A COMPLI-MENT OR NOT.

THE FIXER

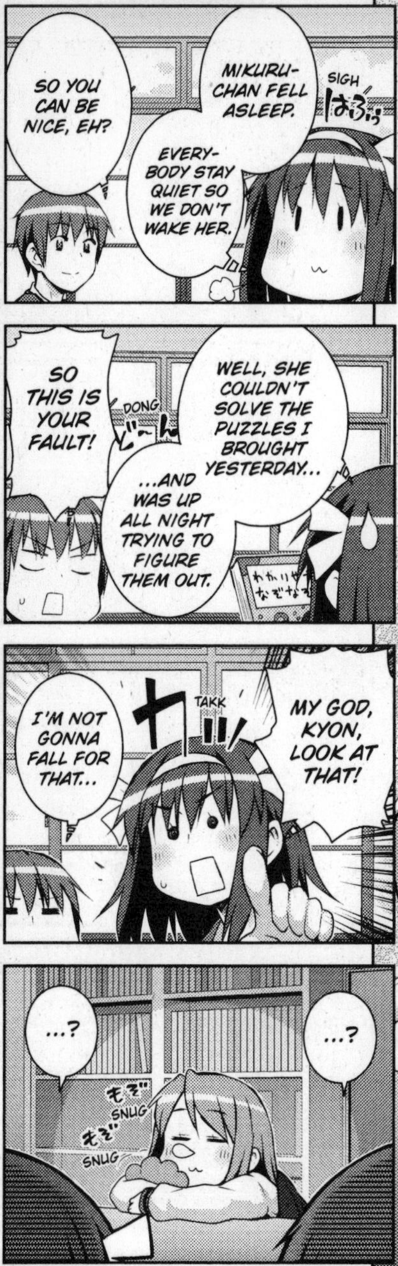
MIKURU-CHAN FELL ASLEEP.
SIGH
EVERYBODY STAY QUIET SO WE DON'T WAKE HER.
SO YOU CAN BE NICE, EH?
WELL, SHE COULDN'T SOLVE THE PUZZLES I BROUGHT YESTERDAY...
...AND WAS UP ALL NIGHT TRYING TO FIGURE THEM OUT.
DONG
SO THIS IS YOUR FAULT!
MY GOD, KYON, LOOK AT THAT!
TAKK
I'M NOT GONNA FALL FOR THAT...
...?
...?
もぞ
SNUG
もぞ
SNUG

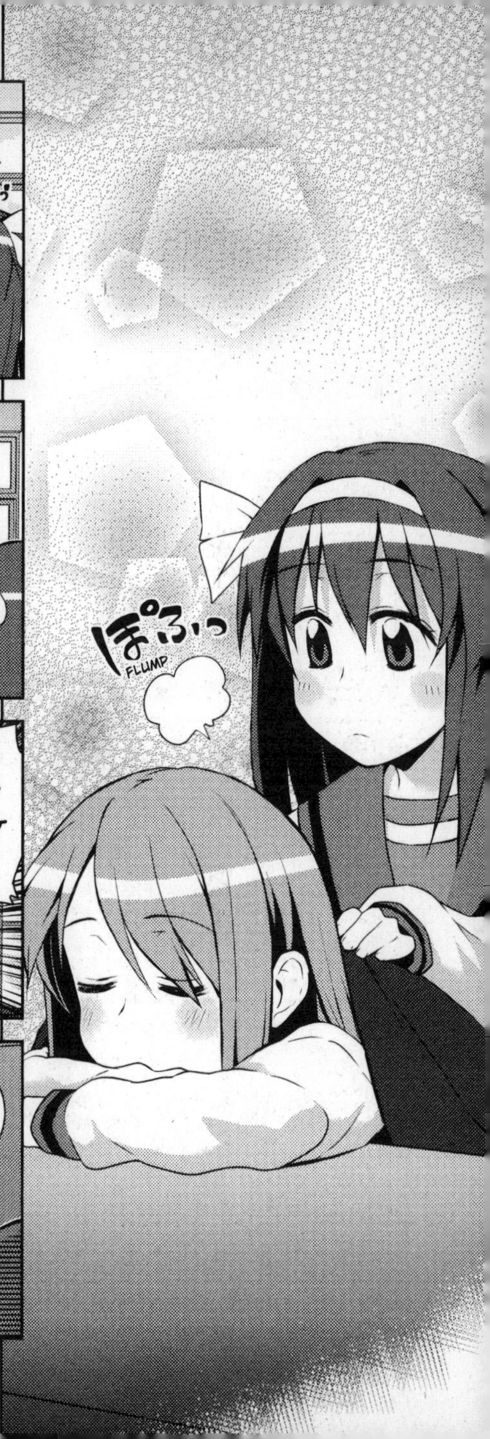
ぽふっ
FLUMP

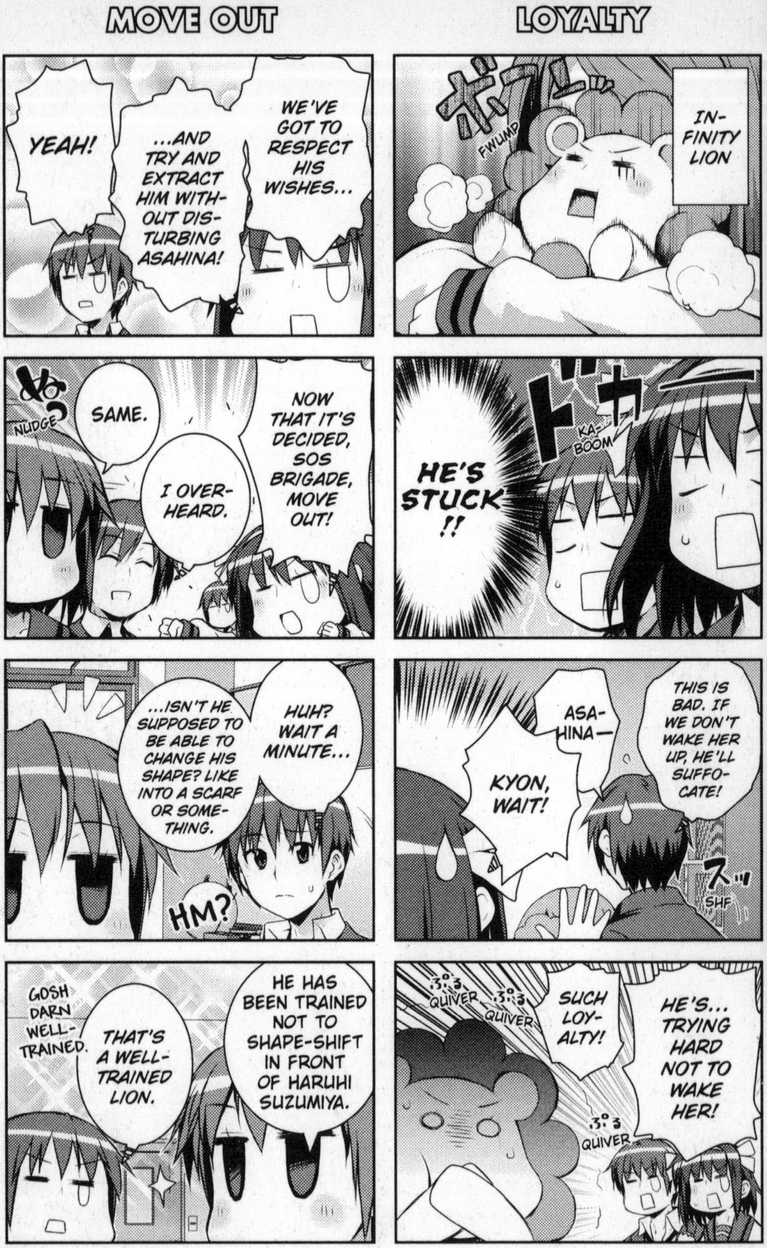
LOYALTY
FWUMP
IN-FINITY LION
KA-BOOM
HE'S STUCK!!
THIS IS BAD. IF WE DON'T WAKE HER UP, HE'LL SUFFO-CATE!
ASA-HINA—
KYON, WAIT!
SHF
HE'S... TRYING HARD NOT TO WAKE HER!
SUCH LOY-ALTY!
QUIVER
QUIVER
QUIVER
MOVE OUT
WE'VE GOT TO RESPECT HIS WISHES...
...AND TRY AND EXTRACT HIM WITH-OUT DIS-TURBING ASAHINA!
YEAH!
NOW THAT IT'S DECIDED, SOS BRIGADE, MOVE OUT!
I OVER-HEARD.
SAME.
NUDGE
HUH? WAIT A MINUTE...
...ISN'T HE SUPPOSED TO BE ABLE TO CHANGE HIS SHAPE? LIKE INTO A SCARF OR SOME-THING.
HM?
HE HAS BEEN TRAINED NOT TO SHAPE-SHIFT IN FRONT OF HARUHI SUZUMIYA.
THAT'S A WELL-TRAINED LION.
GOSH DARN WELL-TRAINED.

•Haruhi-chan •SOS Brigade brigade chief. Currently leading the charge to let Mikuru-chan sleep well.

•Kyon •The protagonist of this story, more or less. Also trying to let Mikuru-chan sleep.

•Nagato •Actually an alien. Possesses fantastic cosmic powers, but rarely uses them.

OPERATION IMPORTANT POINTS

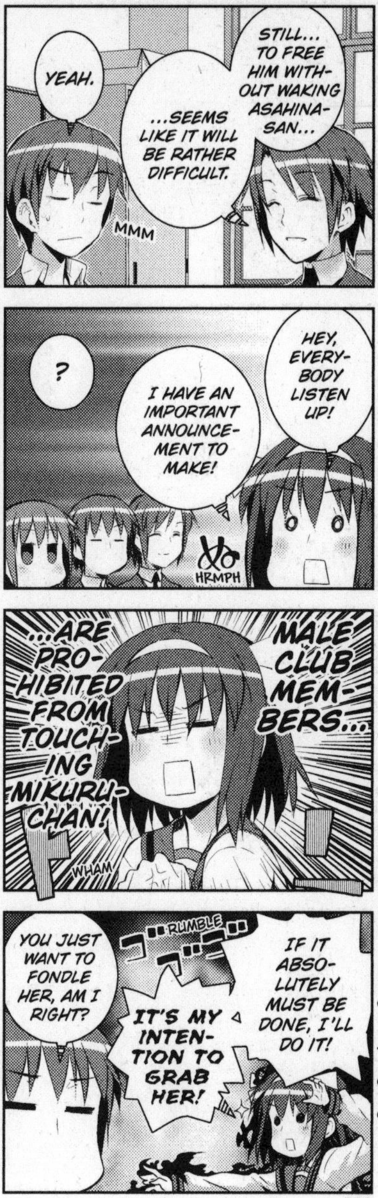
STILL... TO FREE HIM WITHOUT WAKING ASAHINA-SAN...
...SEEMS LIKE IT WILL BE RATHER DIFFICULT.
YEAH.
MMM
HEY, EVERYBODY LISTEN UP!
I HAVE AN IMPORTANT ANNOUNCEMENT TO MAKE!
?
HRMPH
MALE CLUB MEMBERS...
...ARE PROHIBITED FROM TOUCHING MIKURU-CHAN!
WHAM
IF IT ABSOLUTELY MUST BE DONE, I'LL DO IT!
RUMBLE
IT'S MY INTENTION TO GRAB HER!
YOU JUST WANT TO FONDLE HER, AM I RIGHT?

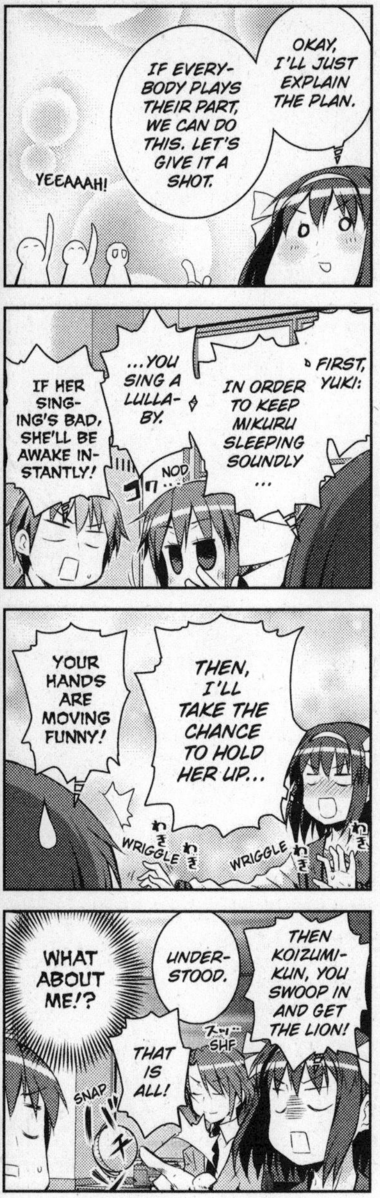
OKAY, I'LL JUST EXPLAIN THE PLAN.
IF EVERYBODY PLAYS THEIR PART, WE CAN DO THIS. LET'S GIVE IT A SHOT.
YEEAAAH!
FIRST, YUKI:
IN ORDER TO KEEP MIKURU SLEEPING SOUNDLY...
...YOU SING A LULLABY.
NOD
IF HER SINGING'S BAD, SHE'LL BE AWAKE INSTANTLY!
THEN, I'LL TAKE THE CHANCE TO HOLD HER UP...
WRIGGLE
WRIGGLE
YOUR HANDS ARE MOVING FUNNY!
THEN KOIZUMI-KUN, YOU SWOOP IN AND GET THE LION!
UNDERSTOOD.
SHF
THAT IS ALL!
SNAP
WHAT ABOUT ME!?

•Mikuru-chan •Actually a time traveler. Accidentally fell asleep in the club room.

•Infinity Lion •An alien life-form, trained to act normally in front of Haruhi.

•Koizumi •Enigmatic transfer student and esper. Watches Kyon from afar when he thinks something funny is going on.

DRAMATIC ESCAPE

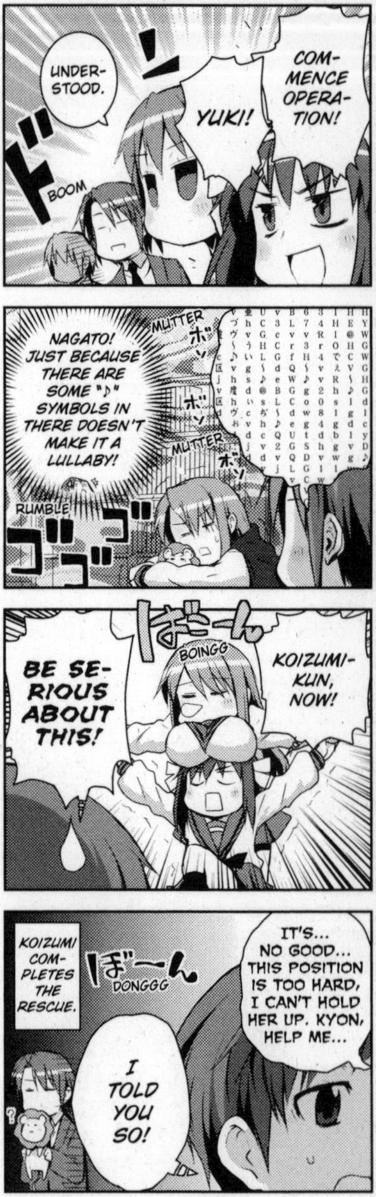
COM-MENCE OPERA-TION!
YUKI!
UNDER-STOOD.
BOOM
NAGATO! JUST BECAUSE THERE ARE SOME "♪" SYMBOLS IN THERE DOESN'T MAKE IT A LULLABY!
MUTTER
MUTTER
RUMBLE
KOIZUMI-KUN, NOW!
BOINGG
BE SE-RIOUS ABOUT THIS!
IT'S... NO GOOD... THIS POSITION IS TOO HARD, I CAN'T HOLD HER UP. KYON, HELP ME...
DONGGG
KOIZUMI COM-PLETES THE RESCUE.
I TOLD YOU SO!

WARMLY

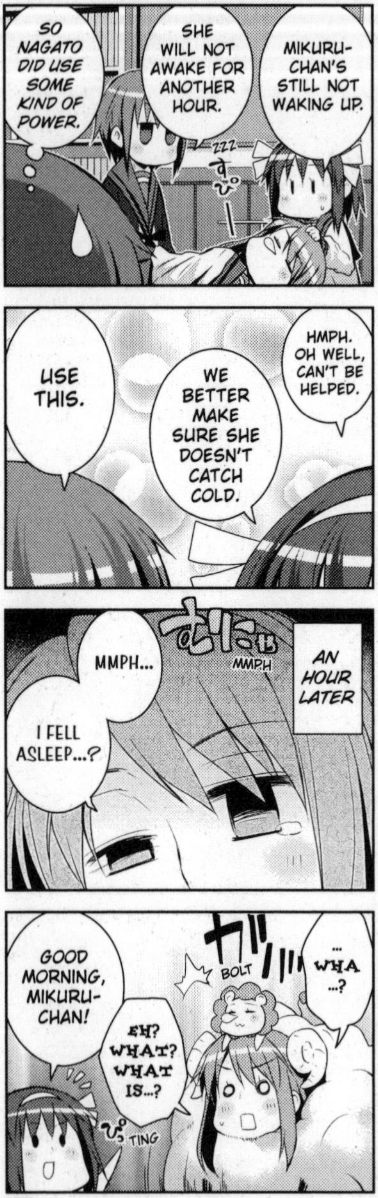
MIKURU-CHAN'S STILL NOT WAKING UP.
SHE WILL NOT AWAKE FOR ANOTHER HOUR.
ZZZ
SO NAGATO DID USE SOME KIND OF POWER.
HMPH. OH WELL, CAN'T BE HELPED.
WE BETTER MAKE SURE SHE DOESN'T CATCH COLD.
USE THIS.
AN HOUR LATER
MMPH
MMPH...
I FELL ASLEEP...?
... WHA ...?
BOLT
EH? WHAT? WHAT IS...?
GOOD MORNING, MIKURU-CHAN!
TING

THANKSGIVING

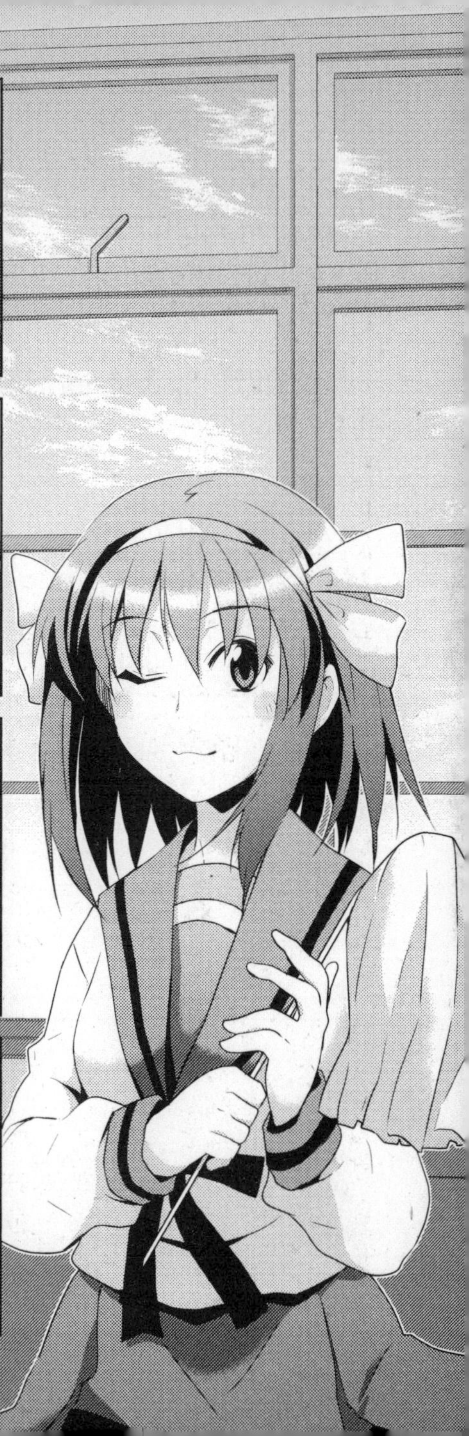

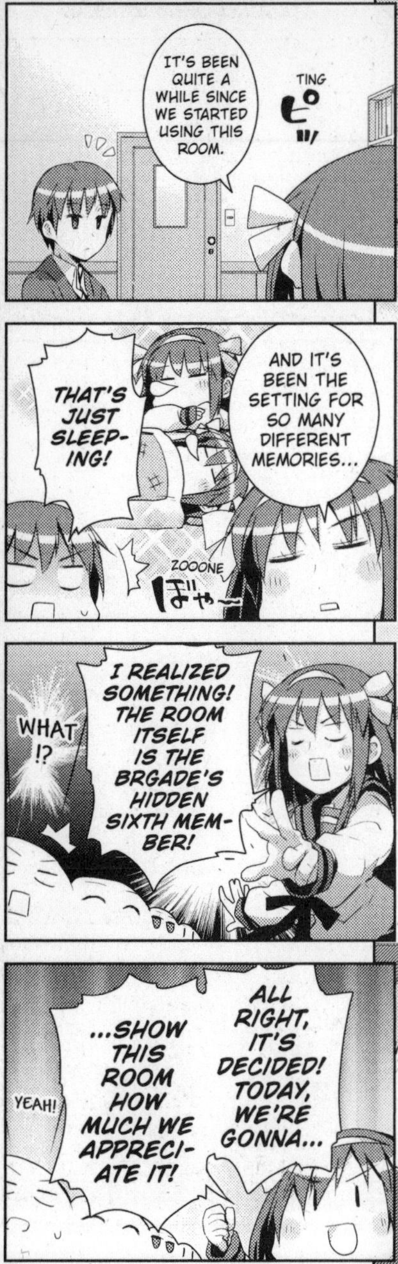
IT'S BEEN QUITE A WHILE SINCE WE STARTED USING THIS ROOM.
TING
ピッ
AND IT'S BEEN THE SETTING FOR SO MANY DIFFERENT MEMORIES...
THAT'S JUST SLEEP-ING!
ZOOONE
ぼやー
I REALIZED SOMETHING! THE ROOM ITSELF IS THE BRGADE'S HIDDEN SIXTH MEM-BER!
WHAT !?
ALL RIGHT, IT'S DECIDED! TODAY, WE'RE GONNA...
...SHOW THIS ROOM HOW MUCH WE APPRECI-ATE IT!
YEAH!

USUAL PLACES

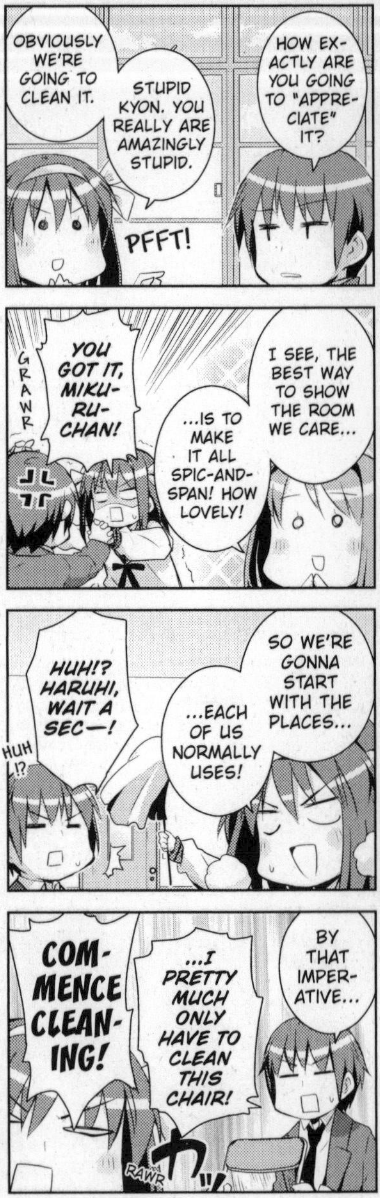
HOW EXACTLY ARE YOU GOING TO "APPRECIATE" IT?
OBVIOUSLY WE'RE GOING TO CLEAN IT.
STUPID KYON. YOU REALLY ARE AMAZINGLY STUPID.
PFFT!
I SEE, THE BEST WAY TO SHOW THE ROOM WE CARE...
...IS TO MAKE IT ALL SPIC-AND-SPAN! HOW LOVELY!
YOU GOT IT, MIKURU-CHAN!
GRAWR
SO WE'RE GONNA START WITH THE PLACES...
...EACH OF US NORMALLY USES!
HUH!? HARUHI, WAIT A SEC—!
HUH !?
BY THAT IMPERATIVE...
...I PRETTY MUCH ONLY HAVE TO CLEAN THIS CHAIR!
COMMENCE CLEANING!
RAWR

NAGATO'S TREASURE

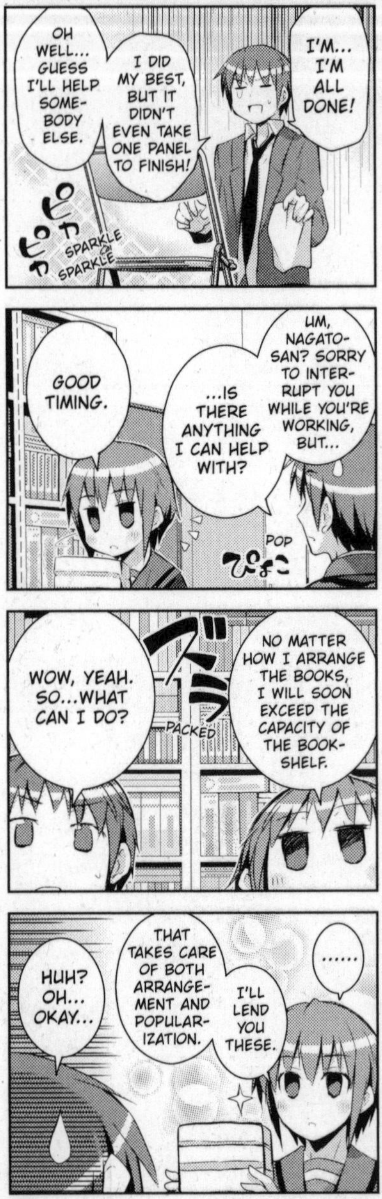
I'M... I'M ALL DONE!
I DID MY BEST, BUT IT DIDN'T EVEN TAKE ONE PANEL TO FINISH!
OH WELL... GUESS I'LL HELP SOMEBODY ELSE.
SPARKLE SPARKLE
UM, NAGATO-SAN? SORRY TO INTERRUPT YOU WHILE YOU'RE WORKING, BUT...
...IS THERE ANYTHING I CAN HELP WITH?
GOOD TIMING.
POP
NO MATTER HOW I ARRANGE THE BOOKS, I WILL SOON EXCEED THE CAPACITY OF THE BOOKSHELF.
PACKED
WOW, YEAH. SO...WHAT CAN I DO?
......
I'LL LEND YOU THESE.
THAT TAKES CARE OF BOTH ARRANGEMENT AND POPULARIZATION.
HUH? OH... OKAY...

MIKURU'S TREASURE

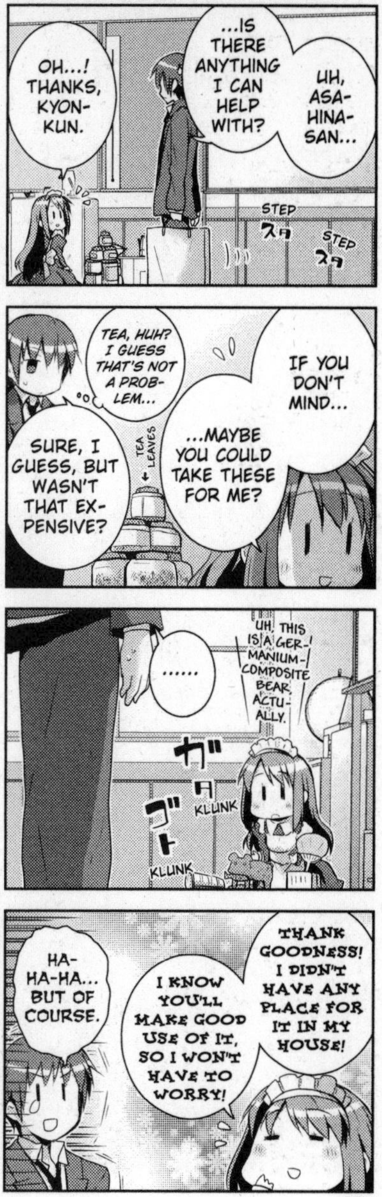
UH, ASAHINA-SAN...
...IS THERE ANYTHING I CAN HELP WITH?
OH...! THANKS, KYON-KUN.
STEP
STEP
IF YOU DON'T MIND...
...MAYBE YOU COULD TAKE THESE FOR ME?
TEA, HUH? I GUESS THAT'S NOT A PROBLEM...
SURE, I GUESS, BUT WASN'T THAT EXPENSIVE?
TEA LEAVES
UH, THIS IS A GERMANIUM-COMPOSITE BEAR, ACTUALLY.
......
KLUNK
KLUNK
THANK GOODNESS! I DIDN'T HAVE ANY PLACE FOR IT IN MY HOUSE!
I KNOW YOU'LL MAKE GOOD USE OF IT, SO I WON'T HAVE TO WORRY!
HA-HA-HA... BUT OF COURSE.

INCITEMENT

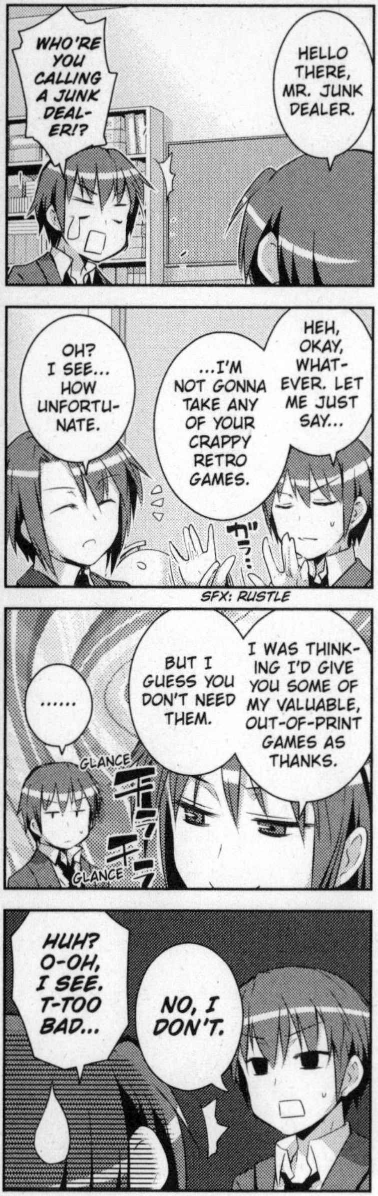
HELLO THERE, MR. JUNK DEALER.
WHO'RE YOU CALLING A JUNK DEALER!?
HEH, OKAY, WHATEVER. LET ME JUST SAY...
...I'M NOT GONNA TAKE ANY OF YOUR CRAPPY RETRO GAMES.
OH? I SEE... HOW UNFORTUNATE.
SFX: RUSTLE
I WAS THINKING I'D GIVE YOU SOME OF MY VALUABLE, OUT-OF-PRINT GAMES AS THANKS.
BUT I GUESS YOU DON'T NEED THEM.
......
GLANCE
GLANCE
NO, I DON'T.
HUH? O-OH, I SEE. T-TOO BAD...

PROGRESSION

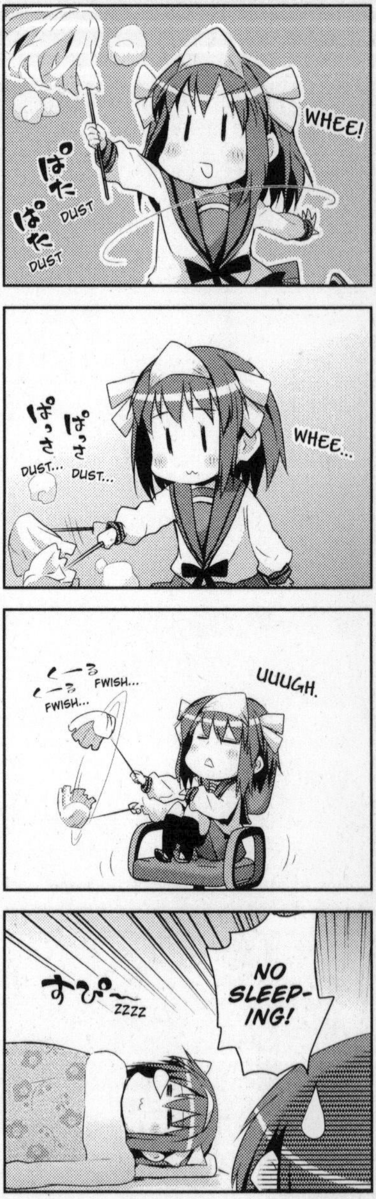
WHEE!
ぱた ぱた
DUST DUST
WHEE...
ぱっさ ぱっさ
DUST... DUST...
UUUGH.
くーる くーる
FWISH... FWISH...
NO SLEEPING!
すぴ~
ZZZZ

AS BRIGADE CHIEF...

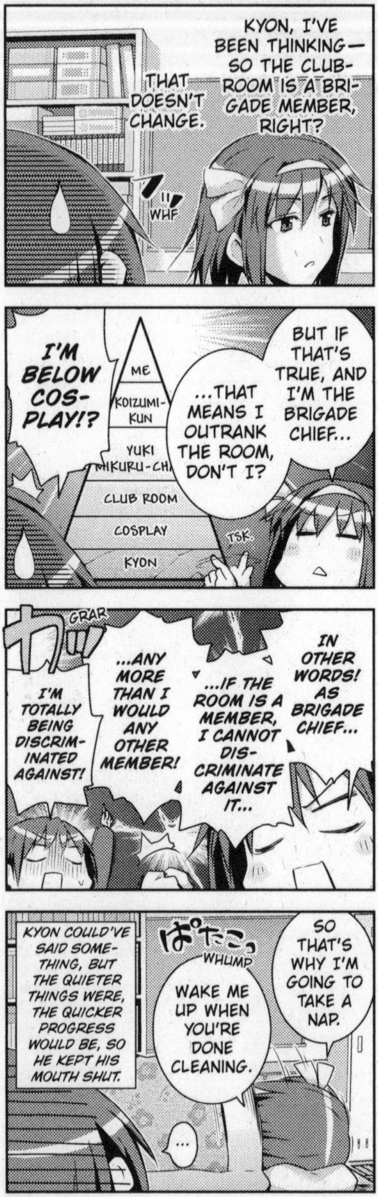
KYON, I'VE BEEN THINKING— SO THE CLUB-ROOM IS A BRIGADE MEMBER, RIGHT?
WHF
THAT DOESN'T CHANGE.
BUT IF THAT'S TRUE, AND I'M THE BRIGADE CHIEF...
...THAT MEANS I OUTRANK THE ROOM, DON'T I?
TSK
ME
KOIZUMI-KUN
YUKI
MIKURU-CHA
CLUB ROOM
COSPLAY
KYON
I'M BELOW COSPLAY!?
IN OTHER WORDS! AS BRIGADE CHIEF...
...IF THE ROOM IS A MEMBER, I CANNOT DISCRIMINATE AGAINST IT...
...ANY MORE THAN I WOULD ANY OTHER MEMBER!
ワッ
GRAR
I'M TOTALLY BEING DISCRIMINATED AGAINST!
SO THAT'S WHY I'M GOING TO TAKE A NAP.
ぱたこ
WHUMP
WAKE ME UP WHEN YOU'RE DONE CLEANING.
KYON COULD'VE SAID SOMETHING, BUT THE QUIETER THINGS WERE, THE QUICKER PROGRESS WOULD BE, SO HE KEPT HIS MOUTH SHUT.
...

PERSONAL RULES

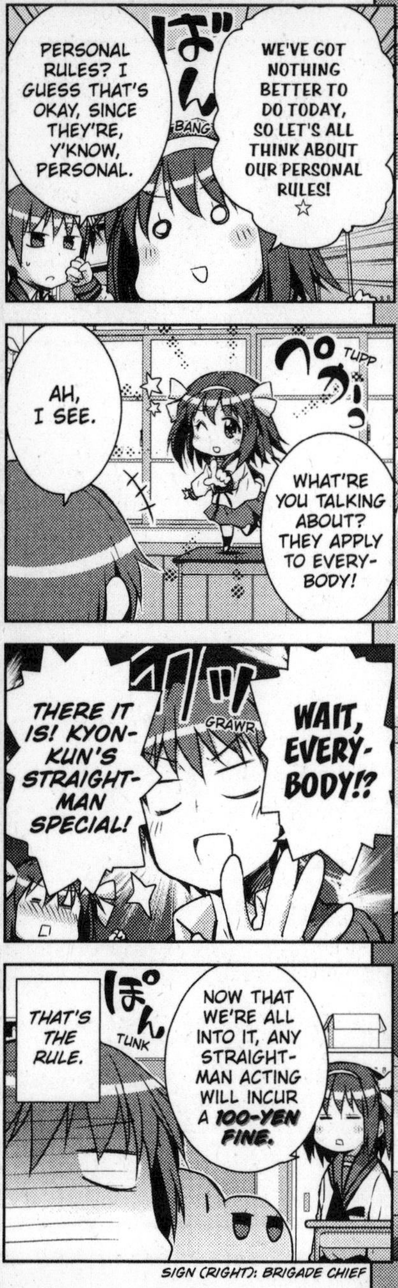

WE'VE GOT NOTHING BETTER TO DO TODAY, SO LET'S ALL THINK ABOUT OUR PERSONAL RULES! ☆
ばん
BANG
PERSONAL RULES? I GUESS THAT'S OKAY, SINCE THEY'RE, Y'KNOW, PERSONAL.
TUPP
WHAT'RE YOU TALKING ABOUT? THEY APPLY TO EVERY-BODY!
AH, I SEE.
GRAWR
WAIT, EVERY-BODY!?
THERE IT IS! KYON-KUN'S STRAIGHT-MAN SPECIAL!
ぽん
TUNK
NOW THAT WE'RE ALL INTO IT, ANY STRAIGHT-MAN ACTING WILL INCUR A 100-YEN FINE.
THAT'S THE RULE.

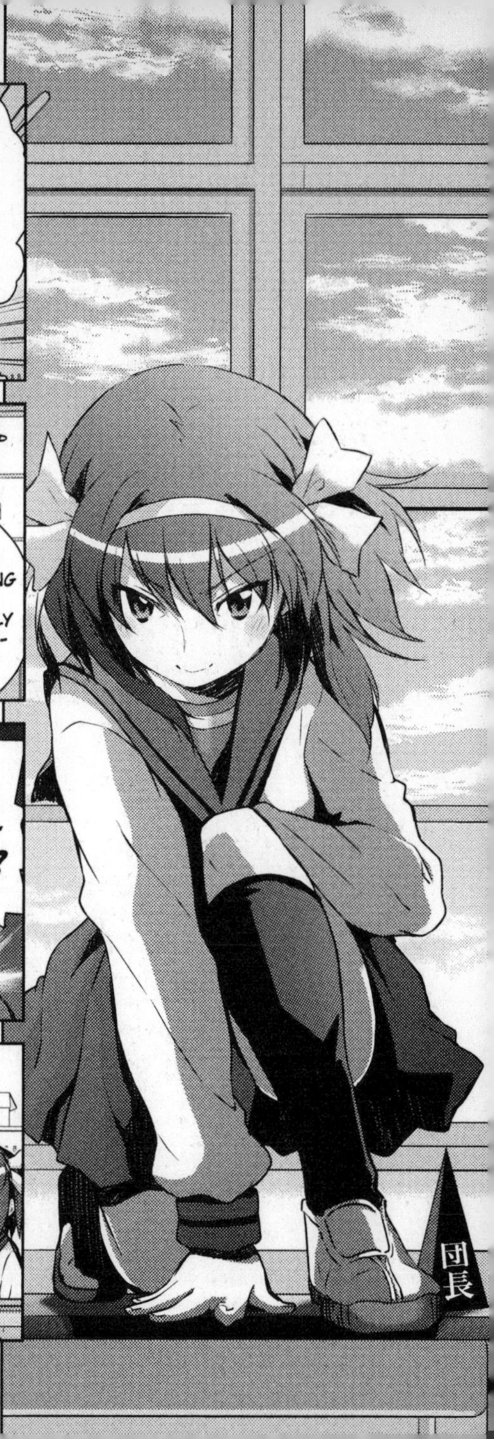

団長

SIGN (RIGHT): BRIGADE CHIEF

SPIRIT

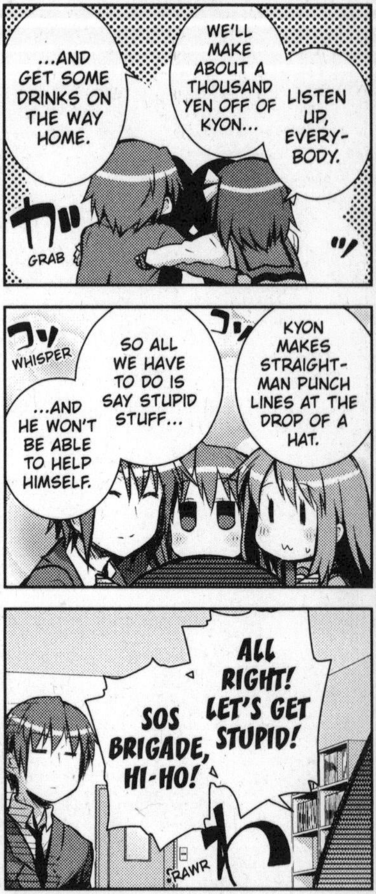
LISTEN UP, EVERY-BODY.
WE'LL MAKE ABOUT A THOUSAND YEN OFF OF KYON...
...AND GET SOME DRINKS ON THE WAY HOME.
GRAB
KYON MAKES STRAIGHT-MAN PUNCH LINES AT THE DROP OF A HAT.
SO ALL WE HAVE TO DO IS SAY STUPID STUFF...
...AND HE WON'T BE ABLE TO HELP HIMSELF.
WHISPER
ALL RIGHT! LET'S GET STUPID!
SOS BRIGADE, HI-HO!
RAWR
......

KOIZUMI THE VANGUARD

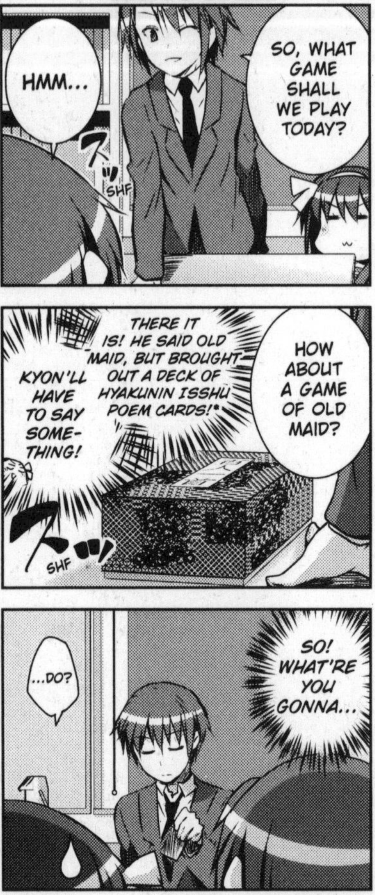
SO, WHAT GAME SHALL WE PLAY TODAY?
HMM...
SHF
HOW ABOUT A GAME OF OLD MAID?
THERE IT IS! HE SAID OLD MAID, BUT BROUGHT OUT A DECK OF HYAKUNIN ISSHU POEM CARDS!*
KYON'LL HAVE TO SAY SOME-THING!
SHF
SO! WHAT'RE YOU GONNA...
...DO?
AAAUGH! HE'S JUST STANDING THEM UP!
RUMBLE
RUMBLE

•Haruhi-chan •SOS Brigade brigade chief. Applies personal rules to other people. That's why she's the Chief.

•Kyon •The protagonist of this story, more or less. What will he do now that he can't be the straight man?

•Nagato •Actually an alien. Will she now act as Haruhi's assassin and attack Kyon...?

*THESE CARDS, WHICH FEATURE POETRY TAKEN FROM A HYAKUNIN ISSHU (POETRY ANTHOLOGY), ARE CALLED KARUTA CARDS. IN KARUTA, PLAYERS MUST MATCH THE FIRST PART OF A POEM OR PROVERB WITH ITS LATTER HALF.

NEXT STRIKE: SUZUMIYA

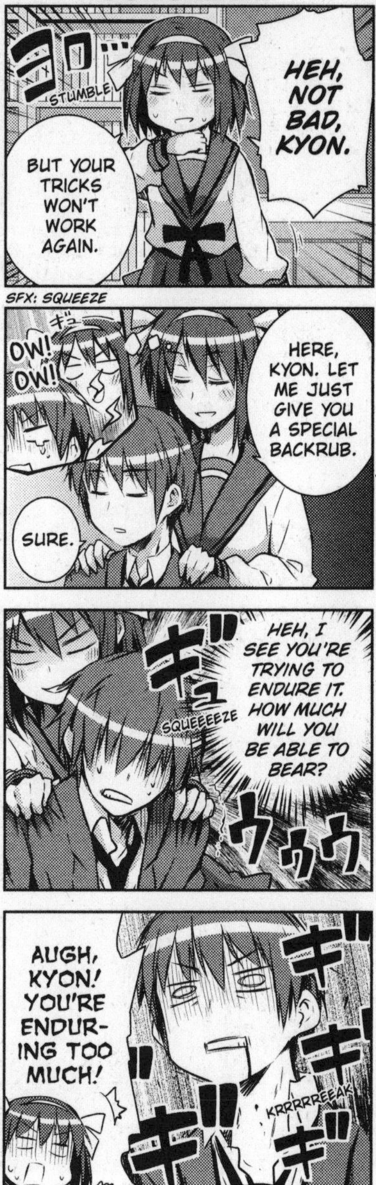
STUMBLE
HEH, NOT BAD, KYON.
BUT YOUR TRICKS WON'T WORK AGAIN.
SFX: SQUEEZE
HERE, KYON. LET ME JUST GIVE YOU A SPECIAL BACKRUB.
OW! OW!
SURE.
HEH, I SEE YOU'RE TRYING TO ENDURE IT. HOW MUCH WILL YOU BE ABLE TO BEAR?
SQUEEEEZE
AUGH, KYON! YOU'RE ENDUR-ING TOO MUCH!
KRRRRREEAK

TRAP

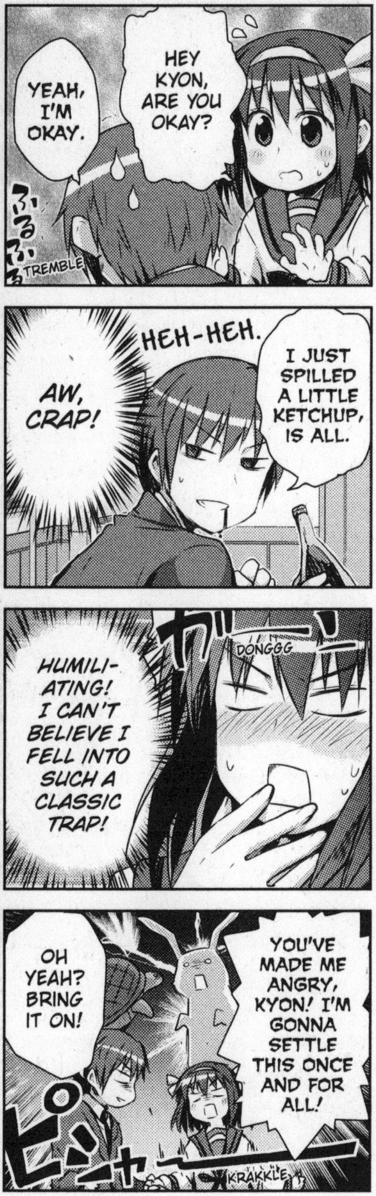
HEY KYON, ARE YOU OKAY?
YEAH, I'M OKAY.
TREMBLE
I JUST SPILLED A LITTLE KETCHUP, IS ALL.
HEH-HEH.
AW, CRAP!
DONGGG
HUMILI-ATING! I CAN'T BELIEVE I FELL INTO SUCH A CLASSIC TRAP!
YOU'VE MADE ME ANGRY, KYON! I'M GONNA SETTLE THIS ONCE AND FOR ALL!
OH YEAH? BRING IT ON!
KRAKKLE

•Mikuru-chan •Actually a time traveler. Apparently Mu-chan's out on urgent teapot business today.

•Koizumi •Enigmatic transfer student and esper. His vanguard attack on Kyon failed.

PETITION

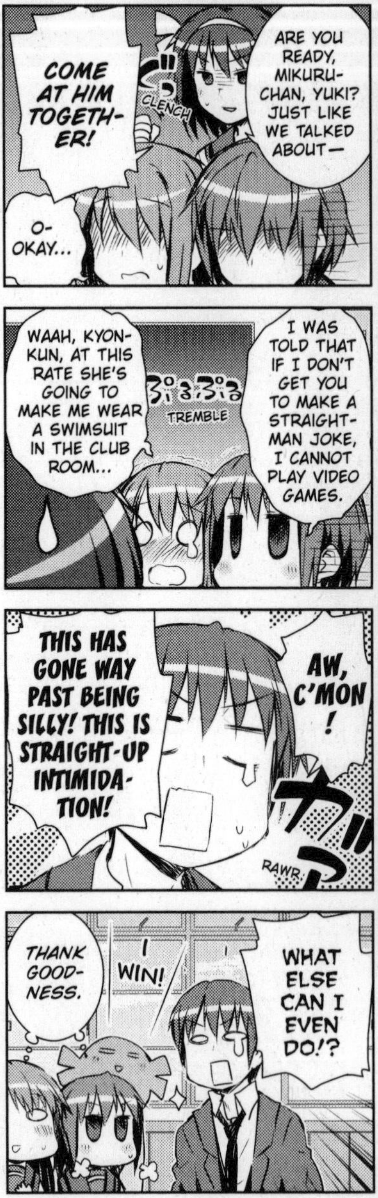
ARE YOU READY, MIKURU-CHAN, YUKI? JUST LIKE WE TALKED ABOUT—
CLENCH
COME AT HIM TOGETHER!
O- OKAY...
I WAS TOLD THAT IF I DON'T GET YOU TO MAKE A STRAIGHT-MAN JOKE, I CANNOT PLAY VIDEO GAMES.
TREMBLE
WAAH, KYON-KUN, AT THIS RATE SHE'S GOING TO MAKE ME WEAR A SWIMSUIT IN THE CLUB ROOM...
AW, C'MON!
RAWR.
THIS HAS GONE WAY PAST BEING SILLY! THIS IS STRAIGHT-UP INTIMIDATION!
WHAT ELSE CAN I EVEN DO!?
I WIN!
THANK GOODNESS.

IN THE END

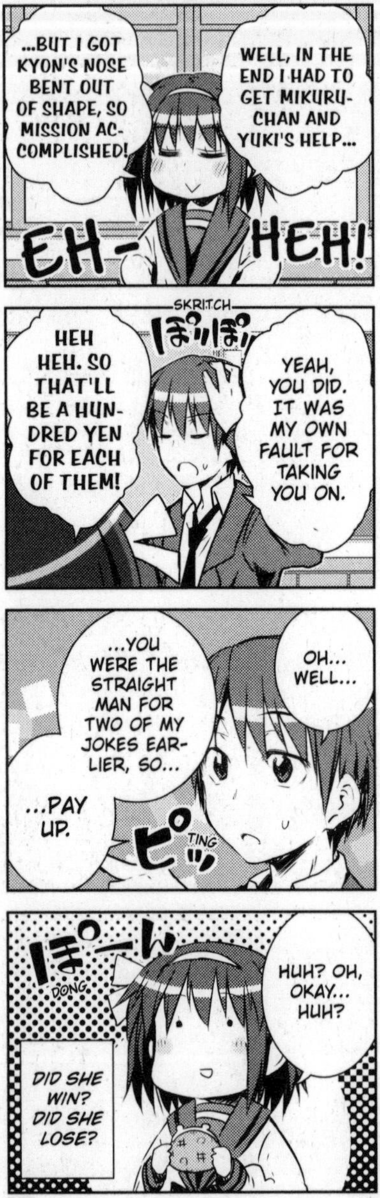
WELL, IN THE END I HAD TO GET MIKURU-CHAN AND YUKI'S HELP...
...BUT I GOT KYON'S NOSE BENT OUT OF SHAPE, SO MISSION ACCOMPLISHED!
EH-HEH!
YEAH, YOU DID. IT WAS MY OWN FAULT FOR TAKING YOU ON.
SKRITCH
HEH HEH. SO THAT'LL BE A HUNDRED YEN FOR EACH OF THEM!
OH... WELL...
...YOU WERE THE STRAIGHT MAN FOR TWO OF MY JOKES EARLIER, SO...
TING
...PAY UP.
HUH? OH, OKAY... HUH?
DONG
DID SHE WIN? DID SHE LOSE?

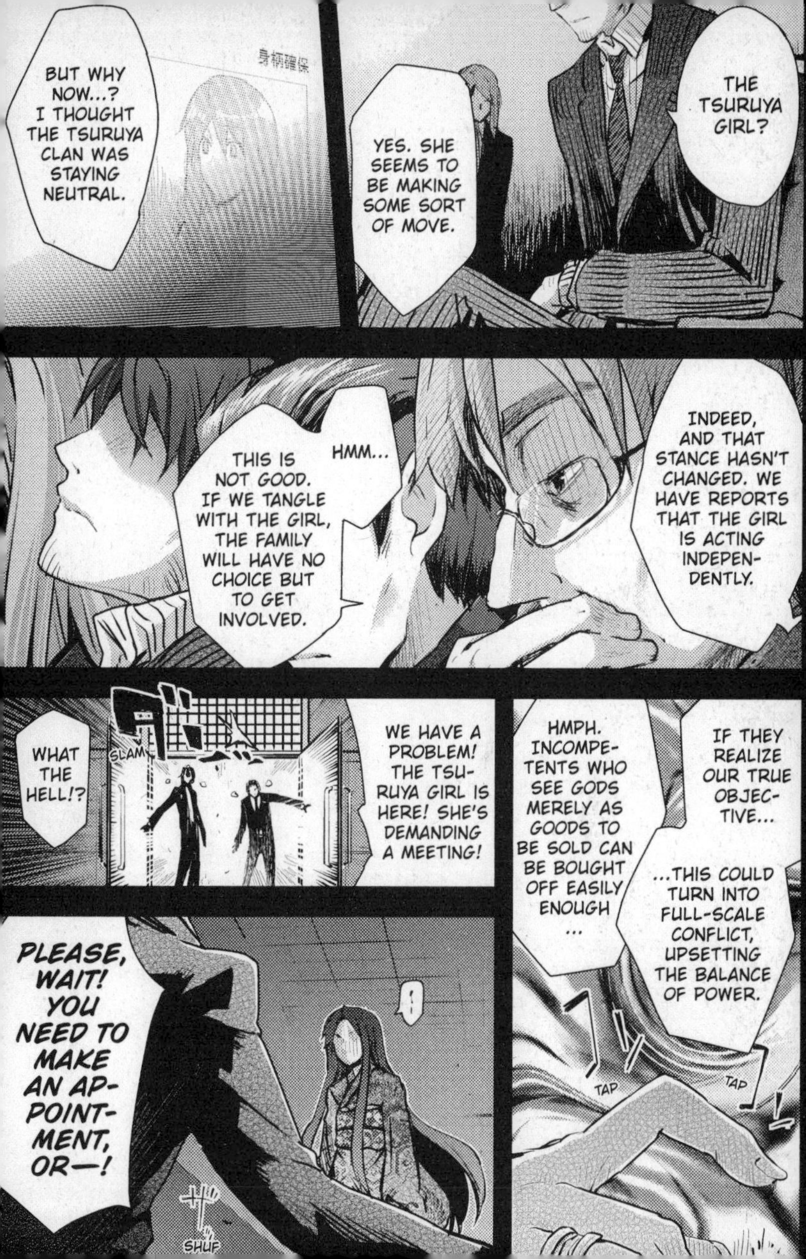
THE TSURUYA GIRL?
YES. SHE SEEMS TO BE MAKING SOME SORT OF MOVE.
身柄確保
BUT WHY NOW...? I THOUGHT THE TSURUYA CLAN WAS STAYING NEUTRAL.
INDEED, AND THAT STANCE HASN'T CHANGED. WE HAVE REPORTS THAT THE GIRL IS ACTING INDEPEN-DENTLY.
HMM...
THIS IS NOT GOOD. IF WE TANGLE WITH THE GIRL, THE FAMILY WILL HAVE NO CHOICE BUT TO GET INVOLVED.
IF THEY REALIZE OUR TRUE OBJEC-TIVE...
...THIS COULD TURN INTO FULL-SCALE CONFLICT, UPSETTING THE BALANCE OF POWER.
HMPH. INCOMPE-TENTS WHO SEE GODS MERELY AS GOODS TO BE SOLD CAN BE BOUGHT OFF EASILY ENOUGH ...
TAP
TAP
WE HAVE A PROBLEM! THE TSU-RUYA GIRL IS HERE! SHE'S DEMANDING A MEETING!
SLAM
WHAT THE HELL!?
!
PLEASE, WAIT! YOU NEED TO MAKE AN AP-POINT-MENT, OR—!
SHUF

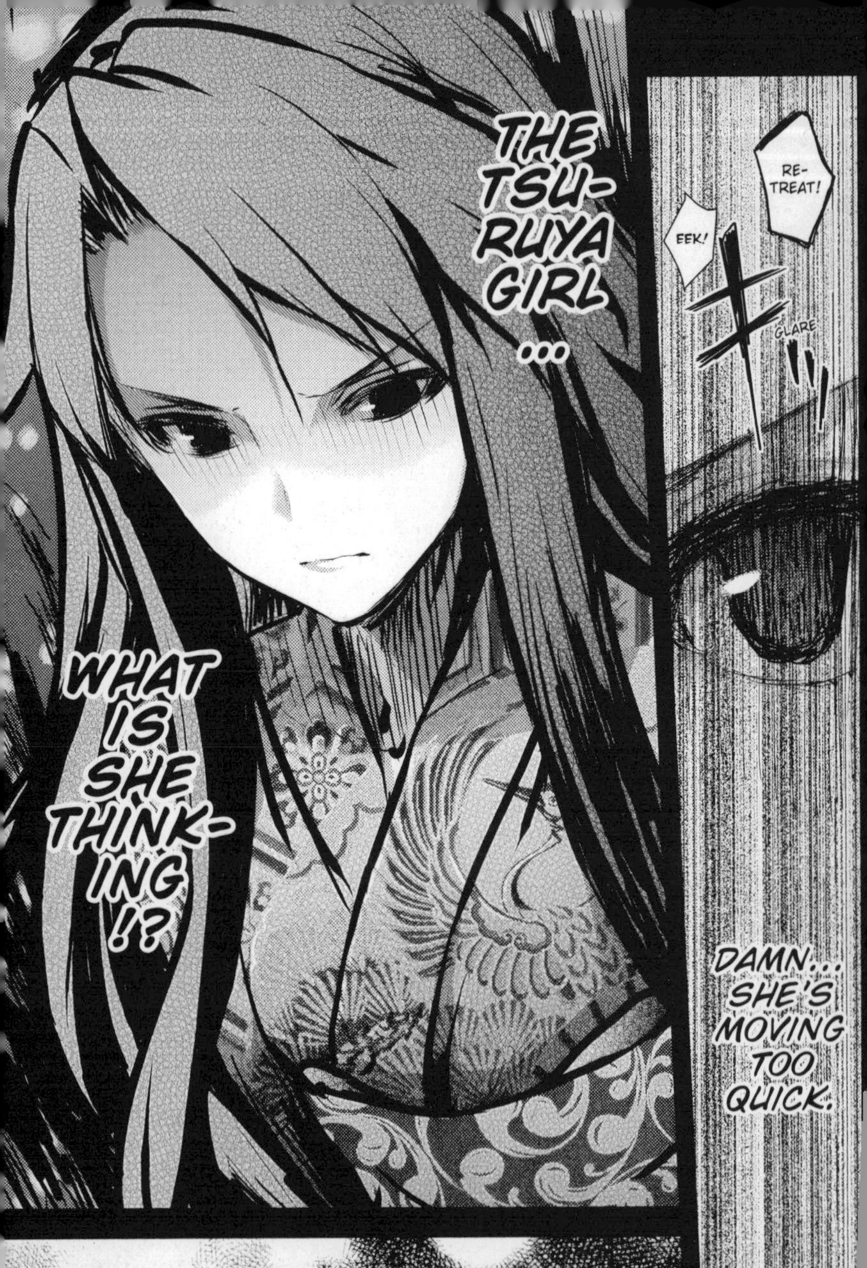
RE-TREAT!
EEK!
GLARE
DAMN... SHE'S MOVING TOO QUICK.
THE TSU-RUYA GIRL...
WHAT IS SHE THINK-ING!?
......THE DISAPPEARANCE OF MIKURU ASAHINA

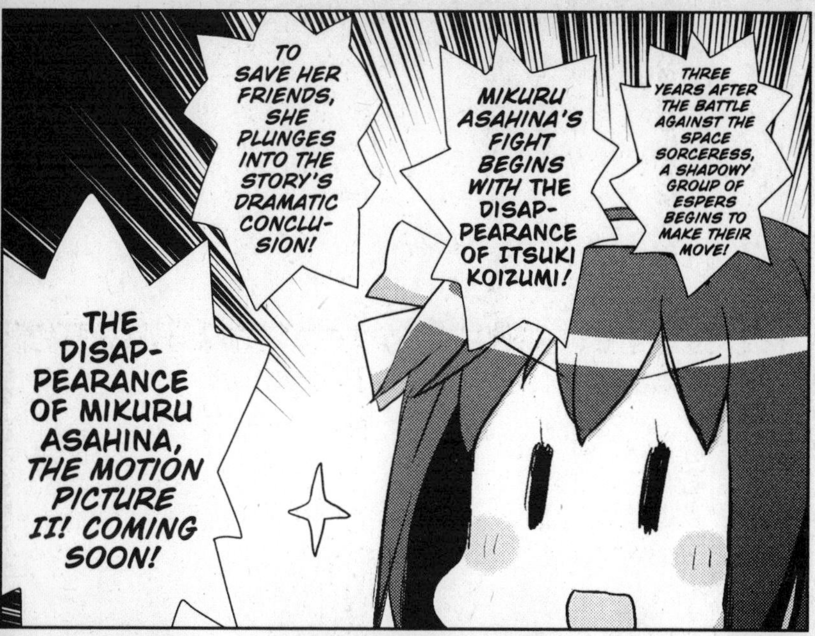
THREE YEARS AFTER THE BATTLE AGAINST THE SPACE SORCERESS, A SHADOWY GROUP OF ESPERS BEGINS TO MAKE THEIR MOVE!
MIKURU ASAHINA'S FIGHT BEGINS WITH THE DISAPPEARANCE OF ITSUKI KOIZUMI!
TO SAVE HER FRIENDS, SHE PLUNGES INTO THE STORY'S DRAMATIC CONCLUSION!
THE DISAPPEARANCE OF MIKURU ASAHINA, THE MOTION PICTURE II! COMING SOON!

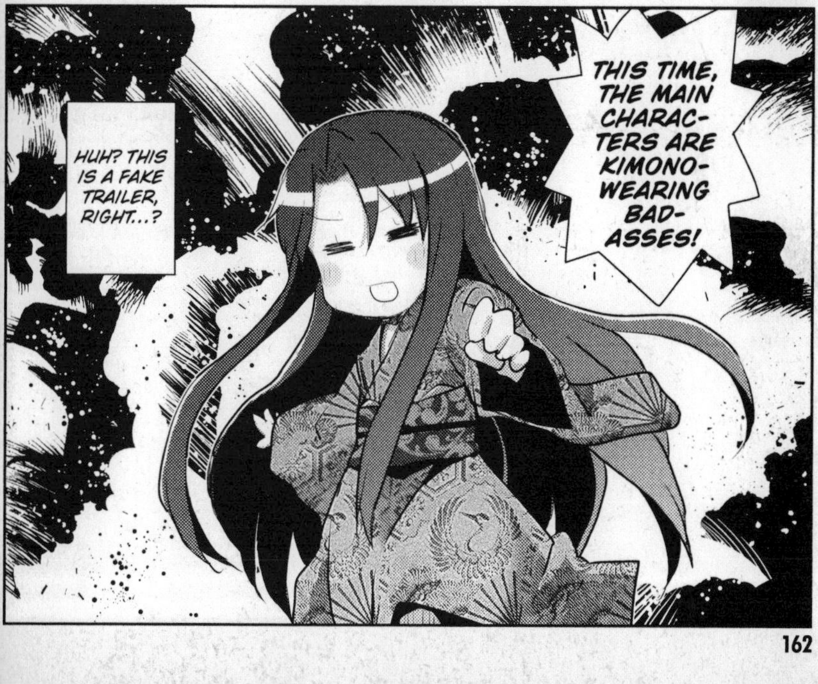
THIS TIME, THE MAIN CHARACTERS ARE KIMONO-WEARING BADASSES!
HUH? THIS IS A FAKE TRAILER, RIGHT...?

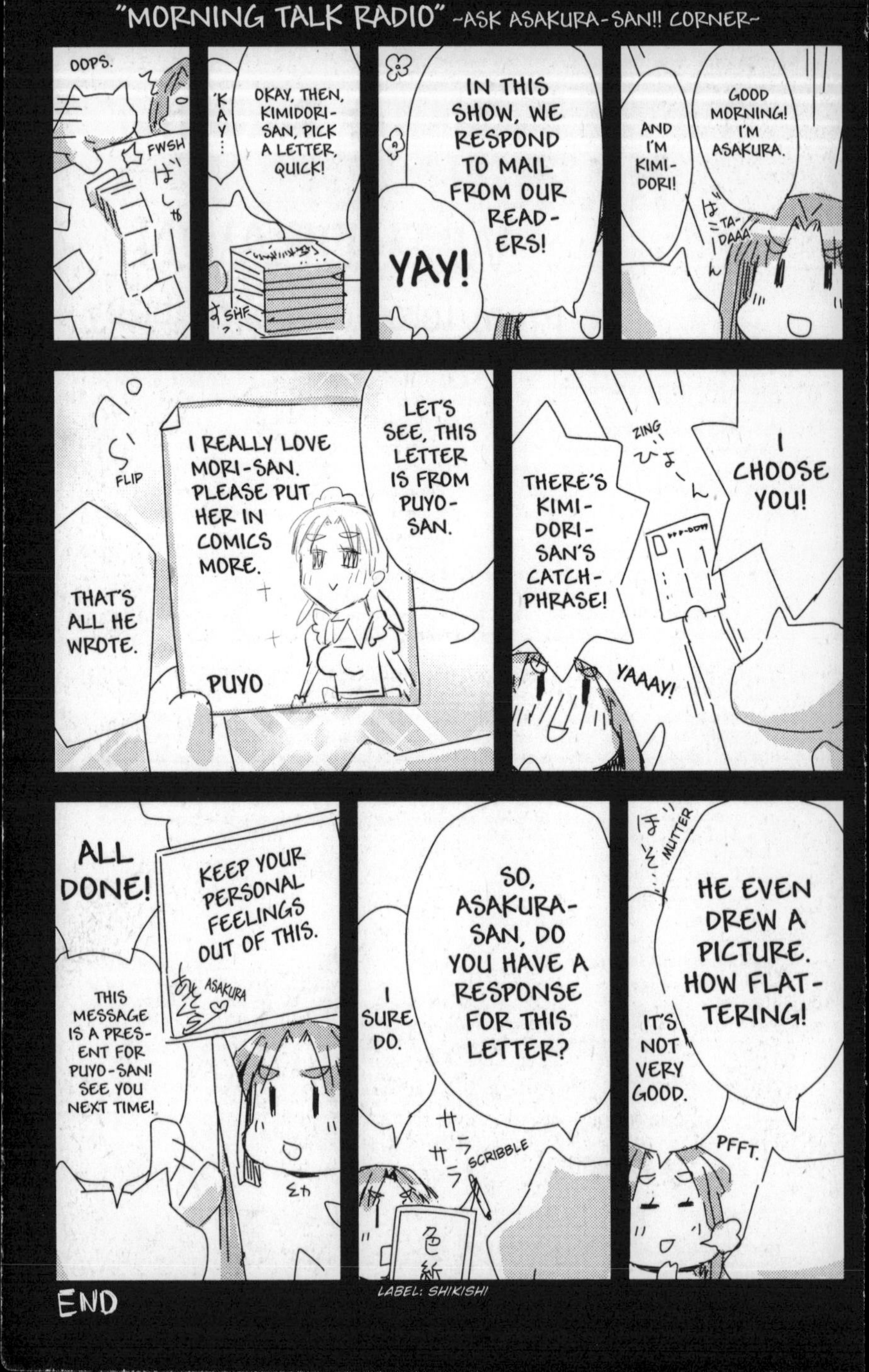
"MORNING TALK RADIO" ~ASK ASAKURA-SAN!! CORNER~
GOOD MORNING! I'M ASAKURA.
AND I'M KIMIDORI!
TA-DAAA
IN THIS SHOW, WE RESPOND TO MAIL FROM OUR READERS!
YAY!
OKAY, THEN, KIMIDORI-SAN, PICK A LETTER, QUICK!
'KAY...
SHF
OOPS.
FWSH
I CHOOSE YOU!
ZING
THERE'S KIMIDORI-SAN'S CATCHPHRASE!
YAAAY!
LET'S SEE, THIS LETTER IS FROM PUYO-SAN.
I REALLY LOVE MORI-SAN. PLEASE PUT HER IN COMICS MORE.
PUYO
FLIP
THAT'S ALL HE WROTE.
HE EVEN DREW A PICTURE. HOW FLATTERING!
MUTTER
IT'S NOT VERY GOOD.
PFFT.
SO, ASAKURA-SAN, DO YOU HAVE A RESPONSE FOR THIS LETTER?
I SURE DO.
SCRIBBLE
ALL DONE!
KEEP YOUR PERSONAL FEELINGS OUT OF THIS.
ASAKURA
THIS MESSAGE IS A PRESENT FOR PUYO-SAN! SEE YOU NEXT TIME!
END
LABEL: SHIKISHI

THE MELANCHOLY

HARUHI-CHAN

⑤

Original Story: Nagaru Tanigawa
Manga: PUYO
Character Design: Noizi Ito

Translation: Paul Starr
Lettering: Keiran O'Leary

The Melancholy of Suzumiya Haruhi-chan Volume 5
© Nagaru TANIGAWA • Noizi ITO 2010 © PUYO 2010. First published in Japan in 2010 by KADOKAWA SHOTEN Co., Ltd., Tokyo. English translation rights arranged with KADOKAWA SHOTEN Co., Ltd., Tokyo through TUTTLE-MORI AGENCY, INC., Tokyo.

English translation © 2012 by Hachette Book Group, Inc.

Yen Press
Hachette Book Group
237 Park Avenue, New York, NY 10017

www.HachetteBookGroup.com
www.YenPress.com

Yen Press is an imprint of Hachette Book Group, Inc.
The Yen Press name and logo are trademarks of Hachette Book Group, Inc.

First Yen Press Edition: March 2012

ISBN: 978-0-316-20945-8

10 9 8 7 6 5 4 3 2 1

BVG

Printed in the United States of America